PRESIDENTIAL POLICYMAKING

PRESIDENTIAL POLICYMAKING

AN END-OF-CENTURY ASSESSMENT

EDITED BY
STEVEN A. SHULL

With a Foreword by Norman C. Thomas

M.E.Sharpe
Armonk, New York
London, England

Library of Congress Cataloging-in-Publication Data

Presidential policymaking : an end-of-century assessment /
edited by Steven A. Shull.
p.   cm.
Includes bibliographical references and index.
ISBN 0-7656-0259-8 (alk. paper).   ISBN 0-7656-0260-1 (pbk. : alk. paper)
1. Presidents—United States. 2. Poitical planning—United States. I. Shull, Steven A.
JK501.P74 1998 1999
352.23′0973—dc21   98-8233
CIP

Printed in the United States of America

The paper used in this publication meets the minimum requirements of
American National Standard for Information Sciences—
Permanence of Paper for Printed Library Materials,
ANSI Z 39.48-1984.

BM (c)   10   9   8   7   6   5   4   3   2   1
BM (p)   10   9   8   7   6   5   4   3   2   1

Dedicated to Norman C. Thomas, Teacher and Scholar

Contents

About the Editor and Contributors

Steven A. Shull received his Ph.D. from Ohio State and is University Research Professor at the University of New Orleans. He has written or edited fifteen books, including *Presidential-Congressional Relations, The President and Congress,* and dozens of articles in scholarly journals.

James E. Anderson is professor of political science at Texas A&M University. He received his Ph.D. at the University of Texas and is widely published in the areas of public policy and the presidency. His volumes include *Public Policymaking* and *Managing Macroeconomic Policy.*

Colin Campbell is University Martin Chair of Political Science at Georgetown University. He is the author or editor of several important volumes on the presidency, including *The Clinton Presidency* and *Managing the Presidency.* He received his Ph.D. from Duke University.

Jeffrey E. Cohen is professor of political science at Fordham University in the Bronx, New York. He received his Ph.D. from the University of Michigan and has written extensively on the presidency, including *The President's Cabinet* and *Presidential Responsiveness to Public Policymaking.*

Ken Collier is assistant professor at the University of Kansas and received his Ph.D. from the University of Texas. He is the author of the recently published *Between the Branches: The White House Office of Legislative Affairs.*

George C. Edwards III is Distinguished Professor and director of the Center for Presidential Studies at Texas A&M University. He is well known for his work on presidential-congressional relations, including *At the Margins* and *Presidential Influence in Congress.*

Louis Fisher is associated with the Congressional Research Service. He received his Ph.D. from the New School for Social Research and has written many books including *Presidential Spending Power, Politics of Shared Power,* and *Presidential War Power.*

Robert M. Howard is a doctoral candidate in political science at the State University of New York at Stony Brook and concentrates on studying American political institutions.

Lance T. LeLoup is professor and chair of Political Science at Washington State University. He received his Ph.D. from Ohio State University and has written widely on the presidency and budgeting. His volumes include *The President and Congress* and *Budgetary Politics.*

Sidney M. Milkis is associate professor of political science at Brandeis University. He received his Ph.D. from the University of Pennsylvania and is the author of several volumes about the presidency and/or policymaking, including *The President and the Parties* and *Politics of Regulatory Change.*

Bruce Nesmith is associate professor of political science at Coe College in Cedar Rapids, Iowa. He received his Ph.D. from the University of Illinois–Urbana and his research interests are American institutions and public policy.

James P. Pfiffner is professor of political science at George Mason University. He received his Ph.D. from the University of Wisconsin and has written extensively on the presidency, including *The Strategic Presidency* and *The Modern Presidency.*

Joseph A. Pika is professor of political science at the University of Delaware. He received his Ph.D. from the University of Wisconsin and is coauthor of *Politics of the Presidency* and *The Presidential Contest.*

Paul J. Quirk is professor of political science at the University of Illinois. He received his Ph.D. from Harvard and has written widely on the presidency and domestic policy. Professor Quirk is well known for his book, *Industry Influence on the Federal Regulatory Process.*

Lyn Ragsdale received her Ph.D. from the University of Wisconsin and is professor of political science at the University of Arizona. She is the author of the important reference work, *Vital Statistics on the Presidency* and coeditor of *Political Research Quarterly.*

Bert A. Rockman is Research Professor at the University of Pittsburgh. He received his Ph.D. from the University of Michigan and has written widely on the presidency and comparative executives. He is well known for his book, *The Leadership Question.*

Jerrold G. Rusk is professor of political science at the University of Arizona. He is known for his research on presidential elections including articles in the *American Political Science Review.*

Jeffrey A. Segal received his Ph.D. from Michigan State University and is professor of political science at State University of New York at Stony Brook. His many works on the presidency and the courts have appeared in *Western Political Quarterly* and the *Journal of Politics.*

Mary E. Stuckey is associate professor at the University of Mississippi. She received her Ph.D. from the University of Notre Dame and writes extensively on presidential rhetoric. Her most recent volumes are *Getting into the Game* and *Playing the Game* on the Reagan presidency.

Shirley Anne Warshaw is associate professor of political science at Gettysburg College. She received her Ph.D. from Johns Hopkins University. Her most recent books including *The Domestic Presidency* and *Powersharing.*

Richard W. Waterman is associate professor at the University of New Mexico. He received his Ph.D. from the University of Houston and has written extensively on the presidency and bureaucratic politics, including *Presidential Influence and the Administrative State.*

List of Tables and Figures

Tables

Figures

Foreword

My interest in the presidency as a subject for serious study dates from the fall of 1951 when, as a junior political science major at the University of Michigan, I took the late Joseph E. Kallenbach's course on The American Chief Executive. The text for the course was Edward S. Corwin's *The President: Office and Powers,* 3d ed. (1948). Joe Kallenbach's approach, like Corwin's, was the historical development of the office and its formal powers. The principal actors were individual presidents and the precedents they set, Congress and the statutes through which they delegated authority to the president, and the Supreme Court and its decisions interpreting the dimensions of presidential power. The powers of the presidency were more than adequate for the president to discharge his responsibilities, and the problem that the presidency presented to American politics was the potential for abuse of those powers.

Ten years later, in 1961, I read for the first time Richard E. Neustadt's *Presidential Power* (1960). It was an eye-opener. Contrary to the views of Corwin, Kallenbach, and other traditional institutional analysts, the presidency was an inherently weak office as a result of the limitations imposed by the separation of powers. The president was little more than a glorified constitutional clerk performing services for others. By 1960, however, the functional responsibilities of the federal government had become so extensive that it was beyond the capacity of Congress, the courts, and political parties to manage them. The political system could not function effectively without active, purposive presidential leadership. The basis for this, Neustadt argued, lay not in the formal but in the informal powers of the presidency. Those powers, *real* presidential power, was personal—the power to persuade. What the political system required in the presidency was a power-sensitive, power-maximizing professional politician, skilled in the arts of persuasion and bargaining. Neustadt's focus was behavioral, and it was compatible with the behavioral revolution that was transforming political science. It made sense to most of us who embraced the behavioral approach, and it served as the dominant paradigm for a generation of presidential scholars.

But both Corwin and Neustadt were primarily concerned with power and its uses by individual presidents. The power approach was not fully satisfactory as a unifying construct for presidential studies. It neglected or, at the least, was not a satisfactory basis for examining many of the important factors that subsequent scholars identified as important determinants of presidential performance. These included the political, economic, social, and international contexts within which the president must function; his intragovernmental relations with Congress, the judiciary, the bureaucracy, and the federal system; and political relations with parties, interest groups, and the public. Nor did the power approach suffice for analysis of presidential involvement in and impact on the major areas of public policy.

As presidential scholars searched for theoretical cohesion, they missed the significance in this regard of what should have been apparent. Public policy can serve as an overarching framework for the study of the presidency. In the twentieth century the presidency has become the institution with primary responsibility for policy leadership in American political life. And policy cuts across and intersects with virtually every presidency that has been studied seriously. The contributions to this volume clearly illustrate this point. I am most grateful to my colleagues for their efforts and to Steve Shull for organizing and directing the project.

Norman C. Thomas
Cincinnati, Ohio

Acknowledgments

This book came about due to the pending retirement of Norman C. Thomas, long-time teacher and scholar of the presidency and public policy. I was not looking for yet another research project when the idea for an edited volume dedicated to Norm was first broached by his colleague at the University of Cincinnati, Stephen Bennett. I already had three projects under way and doubted that I could get the kind of scholars I wanted to prepare original essays for a collection. The contents lists the distinguished authors who have contributed a chapter to this volume on presidential policymaking. I can only attribute this willingness to Norm's legacy, not to any persuasive influence I might have had.

Each of the sixteen contributions focuses on the contemporary presidency in a comparative context. The volume argues the utility of a public policy approach to studying the most important but least understood institution in American politics. The book is designed to be very current but also brief and accessible in understanding the presidency as we approach the millennium. *Presidential Policymaking* is modeled only somewhat on a 1985 book edited by George Edwards, Norman Thomas, and myself and published in both hard cover and paperback editions by the University of Pittsburgh Press. That volume did quite well, and I think this book has even greater potential to receive attention in the academic community. Although the selections in the volume are scholarly treatments, they are accessible, certainly to graduate students and even to advanced undergraduates. Again, I would not have taken on this project had I been unable to secure top-flight presidency scholars, and the contributors clearly are among the best in the discipline on this topic. I am grateful for their participation.

In addition, I very much appreciate the encouragement of my wife, Janice, and my children, Amanda and Ted. Patricia Kolb, senior editor at M.E. Sharpe, thought this volume had considerable potential for classroom use, and I think she is right. She did not bat an eye when I said a paperback edition was essential so that the book could be used as a supplemental text. I greatly appreciate Pat's continuing support for my efforts. All the staff at M.E. Sharpe performed their usual competent roles, and I am very proud to have another volume with this solid press.

Part I

The Nature of
Presidential Policymaking

1

Presidential Policymaking:
An Introduction

Steven A. Shull

Presidential Policymaking honors the retirement of Norman C. Thomas, a long-time scholar of the presidency and policymaking and mentor to many contributors to this volume. Each of the prolific scholars writing chapters herein know how to write, and all have contributed important books and articles on this topic. The sixteen contributions focus on the contemporary presidency in a comparative and policy context, an approach that I have long tried to incorporate in studying American national institutions.[1] The rather traditional organization evident in the contents shows that all of the major topics of the presidency are covered. In the foreword Thomas lays out the argument that national political institutions, including the presidency, are best studied using a public policy approach. This theme is picked up in the two chapters in Part I, *The Nature of Presidential Policymaking.* As Edwards, Thomas, and I did in an earlier volume,[2] this book argues the utility of a public policy approach to studying the most important but least understood institution in American politics as we approach the millennium.

Nature of Presidential Policymaking

In this first chapter, I take the prerogative as editor to introduce the remaining carefully chosen fifteen selections. I follow up on Norm's ideas about why a public policy approach offers advantages toward more analytical understanding of the most crucial institution in American politics. A policy approach reminds us of the necessary interactions among institutions, processes, and policies. This volume's organization emphasizes these interactions between presidents and actors inside and outside government. Such an approach emphasizes comparison, generalization, and concern for relevance, themes that appear throughout the selections in the volume. A policy approach may seem all encompassing, which contributes to complexity, but it also forces scholars to consider the complex structure and environment within which presidents must operate. It is an approach that virtually all of the fine scholars in this volume have found useful regardless of their particular emphases in presidential studies. A policy approach encompasses power, but also much more and, thus, enhances our understanding of the American presidency. Subsumed within a policy approach are the notions of leadership and accountability that relate to the "so what" question about presidential power.[3]

Is presidential power always desirable, or is it better to have divided government as the American public seems to have preferred in recent years? A power approach to the presidency also focuses far too much on characteristics of the individual versus the institutional presidency. However, a policy approach emphasizes not only the internal structure but also the external environment. It also argues for considering a dynamic process of policymaking as well as the importance of issue content.[4] All these components of policymaking help move research from discrete case-study analysis toward more cumulative knowledge, which is vitally important toward arriving at a fuller understanding of the American presidency.[5]

Accordingly, if there is one constant in presidential policymaking, it is change. Changes obviously occur when different individuals hold the office, but also within the institutionalized presidency and in the broader political environment. Changes in policy itself usually are more gradual.[6] Indeed, major change in public policy at any given time is rare, and, even when accomplished, change may not always be significant or intended. As a conservative entity, government often resists change. Because policymakers other than presidents tend to hold office for longer periods of time, they may be less willing to countenance policy change. They often defer hard decisions in the firm knowledge that the general public also prefers stability and continuity to change and innovation. Considerable debate exists over whether presidents can really accomplish much policy change. The remaining chapters in *Presidential Policymaking* address the degree to which presidents are able to influence public policy.

In the second chapter in this section, James P. Pfiffner continues his important work on presidential transitions.[7] In this effort, he shows how important it is for presidents to "hit the ground running," thereby giving life to the notion of political time within particular administrations. Pfiffner cites other authors who have argued that the first (honeymoon) year provides significant opportunities but also constraints for a new administration. Indeed, chapter 2 shows that first years may differ from last or reelection years within a single presidential four-year term of office.[8]

Pfiffner emphasizes three areas where a new president has considerable leeway to make certain choices without incurring substantial costs: organizing a new administration, selecting political appointees, and pursuing a policy agenda. In all these activities, he argues that careful attention must be paid to the lessons of past presidential transitions. Chapter 2 shows that personal preferences are important but that presidents are greatly limited by organizational and environmental factors. For example, in organizing a new administration, presidents have some discretion over structures and processes but now must embrace a chief of staff for organizational reasons and cannot adopt "cabinet government" due to environmental factors. A new president can exert many of his preferences in selecting officials for government positions but cannot centralize too much in the White House without serious costs in organization. The changing political environment requires a serious personnel operation for such recruitment. Portions of a new policy agenda are subject to presidential preferences, but a president cannot expect to achieve significant agenda items without substantial planning, prioritizing, and carefully expending political capital. Thus, organization and environment constrain all presidential activities, even in the honeymoon year.

Presidential Relations with Those Outside Government

After these two introductory chapters, Part II of *Presidential Policymaking* concentrates on *Presidential Relations with Those Outside Government*. In the first selection, Jeffrey E. Cohen and Ken Collier follow up on Pfiffner's notion of agenda in "Reconceptualizing 'Going Public.'" Chapter 3 extends Cohen's recent book about the roles of public opinion and the media,[9] finding that both actors can influence presidents' policy agendas. The focus here is to examine Kernell's idea that presidential going public[10] is used to pressure Congress on legislation. They begin by drawing a distinction between the president's agenda-setting ability and his efforts to persuade members of Congress on legislation before them. Cohen and Collier then examine different presidential strategies to influence members of Congress through the use of public opinion. The authors suggest that going public also includes three other agenda-building activities: promoting issues through persuasive activities (which they call "merchandising"), building influence in Congress by seeking public support (which they call "presidential prestige"), and by appealing to more select constituencies (which they call "special publics").

Cohen and Collier find that going public through both direct and indirect means allows opportunities but is also fraught with potential dangers. Presidents have vast resources to steer the agenda, such as the relatively unified nature of the executive, staff resources, and the use of the veto. Perhaps most important, the president is the center of public attention. At the same time, important limitations exist in presidential influence over the agenda. Much of the agenda is ongoing and presidential impact over public opinion, except in the realm of foreign policy, seems to evaporate quickly. The authors conclude that, despite its many different versions, going public is problematic for presidents and does not guarantee the effects sought; at times it may be a very costly presidential activity.

Joseph A. Pika, coauthor with Norm Thomas of the best-selling text on the presidency,[11] discusses the emerging role of interest groups in the institutionalized presidency and factors affecting this access to the president. Pika shows how interest groups have only recently been recognized as playing an important role in presidential policymaking, in addition to more traditional interactions with Congress and the bureaucracy. In the modern era, presidents must decide how to manage such relations, which became more formalized beginning in the Gerald Ford administration. After reviewing existing frameworks, Pika provides a useful, more encompassing analytical device that helps address developments in the relationship over time. This comprehensive framework considers presidency–interest-group relations from three levels of analysis: systemic, interest group, and presidency perspectives. He considers the organizational features of these three elements and argues that both structural and environmental elements account for the relationships that emerge.[12]

Chapter 4 concludes that while some important research on the interest-group–presidency nexus has occurred, we need a more comprehensive understanding of how these relationships have changed over the course of American history. The Office of Public Liaison, created in the 1970s, symbolizes these changes, but does not operate in isolation.[13] Many other elements of the Executive Office of the President maintain their own, often separate ties with the interest-group community. By all accounts, interest groups play a much more important role in presidential decision making than commonly recognized, but commonalities also appear and can be studied more systematically. Pika points out that while institutional arrangements are understudied, we should not abandon efforts to assess individual presidential preferences in such relationships.[14] The White House exerts influence with groups through both passive and active activities, but groups themselves are hardly without influence. In that sense, Pika calls the relationship "doubly dynamic."

The role of political parties is amply covered by Sidney M. Milkis. Like Pika, he compares the roles of these organizations across contemporary presidents. Chapter 5 traces the presidential-party role to the founders of the Constitution "who sought to establish a nonpartisan executive who would stand above, and thus moderate, party conflict." This desire was unrealistic, since parties quickly formed, and presidents needed to become supreme politicians. Thus, presidential authority also depended on the ability of presidents to transcend party politics. In the end, Milkis points out how highly regarded presidents (e.g., Jefferson, Lincoln, Franklin Roosevelt) became strong party leaders after realigning elections helped build strong governing coalitions.

But chapter 5 laments the lessening potential for party leadership since Roosevelt. Contemporary presidents have been freer from party constraints but also must govern without a strong partisan core. This situation leads to a "volatile political environment that can rapidly undercut popular support." Milkis considers whether the phenomenon of divided government, so prevalent since the 1960s, has restrained the extreme tendencies of both parties by providing some protection against the abuses of centralized administration. Although policy gridlock did not occur, divided government "tends to obscure political responsibility and mire government in petty, virulent clashes that undermine respect for American political institutions."

Milkis goes beyond his previous research[15] by providing here a case study of Bill Clinton's party role in claiming to be a "New Democrat." He examines several Clinton policies, including NAFTA, health care, welfare reform, and a balanced budget. Chapter 5 concludes that "Clinton's success in forging a 'third way' between Republican conservatism and Democratic liberalism will determine his legacy for the presidency and political parties." He credits Clinton with great gifts for compromise but worries that his lame-duck status and accusations of personal and campaign improprieties may dampen his place in history. Milkis concludes that presidential party leadership is unlikely to determine the contours of political action.

To round out this section on nongovernment actors, Lyn Ragsdale and Jerrold Rusk discuss the importance of elections and their policy implications for studying the presidency. They point out that since the beginning of the nineteenth century, presidents have claimed powers resulting from their electoral victories. Elections provide the ultimate opportunity for the general public to evaluate presidential performance and, if the results are decisive, may provide candidates with at least a symbolic mandate to further their policy preferences. Ragsdale and Rusk argue that electoral aspects have often been ignored by policy-oriented scholars of the presidency and then they provide an empirical test of the policy implications of presidential elections. Much of these statistics are drawn from Ragsdale's invaluable book of data on the presidency.[16]

Chapter 6 assesses the influence of election outcomes on three measures of presidential policy activity and observes some influence on each. Ragsdale and Rusk find that presidents are more assertive in taking positions on legislative votes if they have experienced a large electoral victory. In addition, presidents are more successful in such positions when they had substantial election margins and if large proportions of their partisans in Congress have also been elected. The presidential vote negatively affects executive order issuance and, thus, presidents may use this device for independent policymaking. Ragsdale and Rusk conclude that presidents do seek to be responsive to voters in their policymaking choices. Because they find relatively few differences among individual presidents, the authors conclude that institutional factors of the office are more important than individual characteristics in explaining the linkage between presidential election results and their policy activities.

Presidential Relations with Those Inside Government

In the companion Part III, the volume shifts focus from external actors to examine *Presidential Relations with Those Inside Government.* George C. Edwards III continues his important research on presidential influence in Congress.[17] He considers both the resources and constraints under which presidents operate in legislative policy formulation and adoption, with special attention to Bill Clinton's early years in office. Chapter 7 seeks to apply new, neutral criteria to evaluate presidential performance in Congress, which include understanding strategic position and fashioning an appropriate strategy. Clinton is an illustration of such strategy, which appeared to change dramatically near the end of his first term and into his second. Edwards believes that evaluation of presidents is inevitable but should be more systematic, encompassing goals, possibilities, and strategies. In considering these features, Edwards argues that the president's environment must be taken into account. This element, of course, is one that policy-oriented scholars are likely to encompass in studying American political institutions.

Edwards argues that during Clinton's first two years, he "accentuated a problem inherent in our separation of powers system by overreaching, overestimating the extent of change that a president elected with a minority of the vote could make." Chapter 7 shows how, despite unified government and some accomplishments, the odds were stacked against presidential success on other complicated issues such as health care. He reveals the Clinton efforts in rhetoric, structuring choice, and obtaining public support. During the second two years of Clinton's first term, his strategic position changed dramatically. The primary goal was defensive, to block the most ambitious elements of the Republicans' Contract with America. Clinton's strategy was relatively successful, in part by enlisting the more moderate Senate and coopting some of the Republican agenda (e.g., taking the lead on both welfare reform and the balanced budget). Ironically, Edwards believes that the White House actually did better in the more complex environment of the last two years (1995–96) than the first two years (1993–94).

Ultimately, Edwards concludes that Clinton "found it difficult to fashion and implement a governing strategy appropriate to his goals and circumstances." Clinton's large and diverse agenda precluded a clear strategy, and he also "experienced self-inflicted wounds." Edwards faults Clinton for having no clear positions and questions whether he will be able to leave much of an imprint on public policy. In this regard, he echoes concerns expressed by other contributors about the likely Clinton legacy. The analysis in chapter 7 continues the debate over the relative influence of Congress and the president in the formulation and adoption of public policy.[18]

Then, Shirley Anne Warshaw compares "Staffing Patterns in the Modern White House." Her particular focus is on whether structural differences matter much in presidential policymaking from the Franklin Roosevelt through the Bill Clinton administrations. Chapter 8 argues that staffing patterns for both the formulation and dissemination of policy have changed dramatically over this period. Warshaw sees four stages in White House development: (1) the early growth stage, characterized by the Roosevelt and Truman administrations; (2) the shift toward larger staffs with functional responsibilities in the Eisenhower, Kennedy, and Johnson administrations; (3) the institutionalization of domestic and economic policy staffs in the Nixon and Ford administrations, and the expansion of that staff under Carter, Reagan, and Bush; and finally, (4) the increased use of political staff in the Clinton administration.

Warshaw's interesting analysis, which also form the basis for her two recent books,[19] shows how changing staff arrangements are due to both structural and environmental circumstances that required greater presidential participation in policymaking. She shows that staff size is only one, but an important element in the staffing patterns that emerged under modern presidents. Chapter 8 concludes that no one staffing style is ideal, but it must reflect presidential management style to be effective. She argues that a strong but adaptable advisory structure has become essential for modern presidents.

In studying presidential relations with the bureaucracy, Richard W. Waterman continues his administrative presidency focus[20] to examine how federal and state bureaucrats view presidential influence in environmental policymaking. His original research finds that, despite arguments by some authors of presidential control, bureaucrats do not perceive presidents as wielding great influence. In fact, in comparison to other actors who interact with the bureaucracy, presidents are viewed as being quite limited. Indeed, both federal and state bureaucrats view Congress and federal courts as more influential on their decisions than the president. Nevertheless, presidential appointees are perceived by these same bureaucrats as being very influential.

Waterman calls this phenomenon the presidential-appointee dichotomy, which seems to suggest that presidential influence over the bureaucracy works only indirectly through their appointees. Yet, such may not be a great disadvantage to presidents, since they can take credit for favorable policy successes by their employees and, at the same time, may avoid being blamed directly for policy failures. This administrative presidency strategy provides the president with the best of both worlds: being able to hide behind policy disasters but still take responsibility for policy achievements. Chapter 9 thus explores the bureaucratic as well as the presidential dimension to this crucial intrabranch relationship.

In the final selection dealing with presidential relations with actors inside government, Jeffrey A. Segal and Robert M. Howard discuss the relationship between the Supreme Court and the presidency. In this regard, they focus on presidential nominees to the Supreme Court and also the role of the solicitor general, who is often regarded as an intermediary between presidents and the Court. This approach is in line with Segal's previous research.[21] Chapter 10 discusses both the nomination and confirmation processes, showing the considerable variation in presidential preferences and the political environment. Presidents must concern themselves with many aspects when making such nominations if they hope to see their policy preferences followed in the judiciary.

The authors focus their empirical analysis on the issue area of civil liberties, showing that the Supreme Court clearly has become more conservative on the topic. Some presidents (e.g., Lyndon Johnson) show greater congruence with their preferences than others (e.g., Dwight Eisenhower), but Segal and Howard reveal a trend in Court voting toward the preferences of the sitting president. This finding shows that individual president's preferences matter and can help shape Court decision making but, of course, are not always followed, either by justices or solicitor's general they appoint. Like most of the selections herein, chapter 10 shows that all such relationships are reciprocal. Presidents exert influence but are also influenced by their appointees. Numerous historical examples of this reciprocity are offered in this book showing how public policy approaches help us to understand these interbranch relationships more comprehensively.

Policy Areas and the Presidency

Part IV focuses on major substantive *Policy Areas* with which presidents deal. Obviously, the other selections in this book also deal with both process and content issues, but this section provides a good opportunity to compare presidential resources and constraints more directly. We begin with Paul J. Quirk and Bruce Nesmith, who cite the dominant theme in the literature that policy outcomes reflect a struggle between Congress and the president. The former's interests and behavior are more special-interest based than the latter, due largely to constituency differences. They present a fascinating comparison of domestic policymaking in three issue areas over a thirty-five year period: tax preferences, agricultural subsidies, and environmental regulation.[22] In their assessment of legislation, chapter 11 finds only partial support for a general-interest presidency and a special-interest Congress. Presidents do seem more willing to push general-interest policies in the first two issue areas but not in environmental regulation. They explain the discrepancy by asserting that tax preferences and agricultural subsidies are of low salience to the general public, thereby giving presidents greater latitude to champion broader rather than more local interests. In environmental regulation, however, Congress is more assertive in policy initiation because of greater interests to the public, while costs are relatively invisible.

Chapter 11 concludes that the president is more nationally oriented than Congress but only on issues of modest salience. In this regard, they confirm the need to examine policy areas, which reveal substantial differences in influence by these political institutions. The supposedly more national-oriented legislative bodies in other countries serve broader policy interests no better than our own Congress. In the United States, divided government appears to make no difference in the interest orientations of Congress and presidents. Also, institutional reforms, like the item veto, have not elevated policymaking from local to broader interests in the states and thus did not do so at the national level, prior to being declared unconstitutional. Like many political scientists, Quirk and Nesmith see no reason to believe that any proposed reforms to strengthen the presidency vis-à-vis Congress will further general as opposed to more specific interests or public policies.

Then, Lance T. LeLoup discusses the changing presidential role in budget policy based on his current research on the impact of budget reforms on presidential-congressional relations.[23] He argues that presidential budgeting has been transformed during the twentieth century. From the adoption of the Budget and Accounting Act of 1921 under President Warren Harding to the balanced budget agreement reached between President Clinton and Congress in 1997, both the presidency and the budget have changed profoundly. Chapter 12 identifies and examines a number of critical changes, focusing in particular on the post–World War II era. By the end of the twentieth century, the president's budget has evolved from a closed process dominated by insiders to an open, permeable process influenced strongly by external audiences. Now, presidents face a much more coequal budgeting partner in Congress than they did before the 1970s.

Presidential budgeting has shifted from a definitive policy statement based on accepted assumptions and information to bargaining with Congress where virtually everything may be challenged. The president's budget used to arise from a more distinct, autonomous process within the executive branch, but has become a more comprehensive, central governing process that encompasses the entire political system. The growth of entitlements and mandatory programs as well as concern about deficits have increased constraints on presidential budgeting. Once a fiscal tool to stabilize the economy, the budget has become unstable, highly sensitive to other actors. Despite all these changes and difficulties, budgeting has become more important than ever for presidents, forcing them to adapt, improvise, and innovate, both substantively and procedurally, to achieve important presidential policy objectives.

In chapter 13, James E. Anderson discusses economic policy, which overlaps greatly with all the other broad policy areas, such as domestic and foreign policymaking. To carry out his responsibility for stabilizing the economy satisfactorily, the president needs help in appraising the state of the economy, in developing appropriate policies to control inflation, reduce unemployment, stimulate economic growth, and to secure the adoption and implementation of his preferred policies. Anderson shows the myriad agencies and officials in the executive branch, as well as players in the private sector, who assist the president in his role as manager of the economy.[24] Chapter 13 compares presidential advisory arrangements mostly from the 1946–80 period by which presidents secure needed information, advice, and policy proposals. Then Anderson examines the administrative arrangements or structures used by various presidents to coordinate macroeconomic policymaking.

Anderson finds that while presidents have not drawn heavily upon White House personnel for assistance other than coordination, the economic advisory process has evolved into a number of phases. The earlier period (1946–60) was characterized by a lack of structural arrangements, whereas in the post-1960 period the economic advisory process was more structured, even though many such arrangements survived only a single administration. In the more recent period it became more difficult to distinguish between macro and microeconomic policy and between domestic and international economic policies. As these developments intensified, pressures for expanded capabilities and participation by economic organizations intensified. More inclusive and more formal economic advisory arrangements emerged, which increased the range and perspectives of economic advice available to presidents. The disadvantage, however, is that expanded participation made consensus on economic policy more difficult to achieve.

Finally, Louis Fisher rounds out the discussion of policy areas in his coverage of foreign and defense policy by pointing out the dangers of individual presidents acting unilaterally. To be effective, he contends, such policies need to be developed with the full participation of Congress. Fisher argues that "the decade-long struggle in this country over executive dominance in foreign affairs is over. The recognition that the Congress is a coequal branch of government is the dominant fact of national politics today." Fisher recognizes that Congress must insist on this role because legislative passivity encouraged such damaging unilateral actions by presidents as Korea, Vietnam, and Iran-Contra. He has a long list of publications regarding policymaking in American national institutions.[25]

Chapter 14 takes a position of coequality of the branches even in foreign as well as defense policy, a view that it is not widely shared in the literature.[26] He discounts the view that congressional involvement places undue constraints on the president as chief diplomat and commander in chief. In fact, Fisher argues that independent executive actions lead to isolation and weaknesses, whereas presidential strength lies in fuller cooperation. Fisher's essay serves to remind us of the crucial nexus among actors resulting from historical separation of powers and checks and balances. Chapter 14 also emphasizes the need for even greater cooperation in modern times among these crucial political actors and policy areas.

Conclusion

Part V of *Presidential Policymaking* is labeled *Conclusion* and focuses on two particular themes in policy research on the presidency. Both selections relate important concepts to the scholarship of Norman Thomas and other authors. Mary E. Stuckey performs "yeoman's duty" in attempting to relate the chapters in this volume to one another. She also focuses on the role of accountability in presidential policymaking. In deviating from her earlier research,[27] Stuckey observes that Thomas's work emphasizes opportunities for presidential power but also constraints on presidents' freedom of action.

Chapter 15 also relates the two notions of the conclusion, accountability and leadership, back to Richard Neustadt's influence, which has been pervasive in presidency research since 1960.[28] Stuckey argues that level of power is not as important as accountability or control, the concept of primary concern in her chapter. Regardless of the amount of power available to presidents, the potential for abuse is ever-present. Chapter 15 argues that accountability invariably concerns links with the mass public, but such links, even through the electoral process, provide insufficient guarantees.

Stuckey considers whether either political or institutional mechanisms can attain accountability. In this regard, she reflects the cynicism shared with many political scientists about the viability of reform efforts: the public frequently is inattentive and may be manipulated by a cynical media.[29] Chapter 15 then examines whether legal curbs would have prevented scandals and controversies in the last three presidential administrations, arguing that such strictures may lead presidents to break the law in achieving their own definition of the "public interest." She concludes that "the tension between the perceived need for strong leadership and the fear of what a strong leader may do has never been adequately resolved, either in theory or in practice." In short, structural tinkering does not substitute for personal presidential responsibility.

In the final selection Colin Campbell and Bert A. Rockman discuss presidents and policy leadership in a comparative context. In this regard, they follow up on their own highly regarded research on presidential leadership and its relationship to power.[30] They argue that policy leadership requires representational or democratic efforts in the short run, but greater detachment and rationality in the long run. Rockman and Campbell tie this seeming polarity between rationality and accountability to both the earlier and later work of Norman Thomas. They reveal how Thomas recognized that while government had to be efficient, it was not itself the problem but rather the potential solution if government was also legitimate. Chapter 16 reviews the various executive branch reform efforts in the United States and elsewhere and assesses their implications for government policymaking and accountability.

Campbell and Rockman offer New Zealand as a case study of administrative reforms to attain both representativeness and government responsibility. They find that "the New Zealand governmental reforms were very far reaching and have been commented upon widely as a beacon for those seeking to create a highly flexible, adaptive government forever on its toes." The authors point out how these efforts have been lauded by officials in the United States as having relevance for their own country. The authors show how scholars see advantages and disadvantages to adopting that faraway nation's administrative system here. Campbell and Rockman recognize the difficulty of importing reforms but also they argue for comparative, cross-national analysis of American executive institutions and policies. They also conclude, as did Thomas, that governments must "reconcile representation and legitimacy in policymaking with the desire to find the authority to integrate choices so as to achieve policy rationality."

Although presidents occupy the center of the policymaking arena, we have seen in this book that they must interact effectively with significant others, both inside and outside government, to see their preferred policies prevail. When they do so, presidents can often obtain their preferred policy results. So the question becomes can and how do presidents influence policymaking? Presidential influence is related to many phenomena, including the internal structure and external environmental conditions that served as organizing devices for this volume. Yes, the personalities and preferences of individual presidents matter, but perhaps not as much as the institutional nature of the office itself.[31] Policy area differences are also substantial. Some of these elements of presidential influence have been observed in this volume, but others require further analysis before more definitive judgments can be drawn.

All the chapters in this book seek to explain presidential policymaking as we reach the millennium. We have seen that there is no simple way to study such policymaking because its very nature makes studying the presidency even more complex and encompassing. As we observed earlier in this introductory chapter, a policy approach encompasses processes, actors, and results.[32] It must cover the processes of making government decisions but also differences in policy content.[33] Much of the best policy literature is not by presidency scholars, some of whom continue to incorporate non-systematic approaches in their analysis. However, the policy perspective has been incorporated much more widely today than when I first wrote a book with this very same title in 1979.[34] The policy approach by definition is anti-case study.[35] But too much presidency research is of this type: descriptive and not theoretically based, as some have observed.[36] Only recently have presidency scholars become more concerned with broader notions as systems theory and Lasswell's famous characterization of policymaking as "who gets what, when, and how."[37] *Presidential Policymaking* strives to point to some important theoretical and empirical directions in this search.

Notes

1. Steven A. Shull, *Presidential Policy-Making: An Analysis* (Brunswick, OH: King's Court, 1979); *Domestic Policy Formation: Presidential-Congressional Partnership?* (Westport, CT: Greenwood Press, 1983); *The Two Presidencies: A Quarter Cen-

tury Assessment (Chicago: Nelson-Hall, 1991), edited; *A Kinder, Gentler Racism? The Reagan–Bush Civil Rights Legacy* (Armonk, NY: M.E. Sharpe, 1993); *Presidential-Congressional Relations: Policy and Time Approaches* (Ann Arbor: University of Michigan Press, 1997); *The President and Congress: Collaboration and Controversy in National Policymaking* (Boston: Allyn and Bacon, forthcoming, with Lance T. LeLoup); *Explaining Congressional-Presidential Relations* (Albany, NY: State University of New York Press, forthcoming, with Thomas C. Shaw).

2. George C. Edwards III, Steven A. Shull, and Norman C. Thomas, eds., *The Presidency and Public Policy Making* (Pittsburgh: University of Pittsburgh Press, 1985).

3. The best-known study using a power approach to studying the presidency is by Richard E. Neustadt, *Presidential Power* (New York: Wiley, 1960). Some of the many interpretations of this approach include Matthew R. Kerbel, *Beyond Persuasion* (Albany, NY: SUNY Press, 1991); Bert A. Rockman, *The Leadership Question* (New York: Praeger, 1984); Dennis W. Gleiber and Steven A. Shull, "Presidential Influence in the Policy Making Process," *Western Political Quarterly* 41 (1992): 441–67.

4. Studies that consider the relationship between policy process and content include Charles O. Jones, *Introduction to the Study of Public Policy*, 3rd ed. (Monterey, CA: Brooks/Cole, 1984; originally published in 1968); James E. Anderson, *Public Policy Making*, 2nd ed. (Boston: Houghton Mifflin, 1995); Austin Ranney, ed., *Political Science and Public Policy* (Chicago: Markham, 1968); Shull, *A Kinder, Gentler Racism?*; J.V. May and Aaron B. Wildavsky, eds., *Policy Cycle* (Beverly Hills: Sage, 1977); Paul Sabatier and Hank Jenkins-Smith, *Policy Change and Learning* (Boulder, CO: Westview Press, 1993); Steven A. Shull and Dennis W. Gleiber, "Testing a Dynamic Process of Policy Making in Civil Rights," *Social Science Journal* 31 (1994): 53–67.

5. See Gary King, "The Methodology of Presidential Research" in George C. Edwards III, John H. Kessel, and Bert A. Rockman, eds. *Researching the Presidency* (Pittsburgh: University of Pittsburgh Press, 1993): 387–414; George C. Edwards III, "Quantitative Study of the Presidency," *Presidential Studies Quarterly* 11 (1981): 146–47; Norman C. Thomas, "Studying the Presidency: Where Do We Go from Here?" *Presidential Studies Quarterly* 7 (1977): 169–75.

6. Many authors have written about incrementalism in policymaking and include Aaron B. Wildavsky, *Speaking Truth to Power* (Boston: Little, Brown, 1987); Wildavsky, *The New Politics of the Budgetary Process*, 2nd ed. (New York: Harper-Collins, 1992); Charles E. Lindblom and E.J. Woodhouse, *Policy Making Process*, 3rd ed. (Englewood Cliffs, NJ: Prentice Hall, 1993); Eugene Bardach, *Implementation Game* (Cambridge, MA: MIT Press, 1977).

7. James P. Pfiffner, *The Strategic Presidency*, 2nd ed. (Lawrence: University Press of Kansas, 1996).

8. Neustadt, *Presidential Power*; Paul A. Light, *The President's Agenda* (Baltimore: Johns Hopkins University Press, 1982); John H. Kessel, *Presidential Parties* (Homewood, IL: Dorsey Press, 1984); Shull, *Presidential-Congressional Relations*; Steven A. Shull and Dennis W. Gleiber, "Presidential Cycles in Civil Rights Policy Making," *Presidential Studies Quarterly* 25 (1995): 429–46.

9. Jeffrey E. Cohen, *Presidential Responsiveness to Public Policymaking* (Ann Arbor: University of Michigan Press, 1997).

10. Samuel Kernell, *Going Public*, 3rd ed. (Washington, DC: CQ Press, 1997).

11. Norman C. Thomas and Joseph A. Pika, *Politics of the Presidency*, 4th ed. (Washington, DC: CQ Press, 1998).

12. Two broad concepts in studying public policy are structure and environment. For interpretations of these concepts, see Stella Z. Theodoulou and Michael A. Cain, eds., *Public Policy* (Englewood Cliffs, NJ: Prentice Hall, 1995); Ira Sharkansky, ed., *Policy Analysis*

in Political Science (Chicago: Markham Publishing Co., 1970); Randall B. Ripley and Grace A. Franklin, eds., *Policymaking in the Federal Executive Branch* (New York: Free Press, 1975); Richard I. Hofferbert, "The Relationship Between Public Policy and Structural and Environmental Variables," *American Political Science Review* 60 (1966): 73–82; Michael Lewis-Beck, "The Relative Importance of Social, Economic and Political Variables for Public Policy," *American Political Science Review* 71 (1977): 559–66; Steven A. Shull, *Interrelated Concepts in Policy Research* (Beverly Hills: Sage, 1977).

13. Other studies of the Office for Public Liaison include Martha J. Kumar and Michael B. Grossman, "Political Communication from the White House: Interest Group Connection," *Presidential Studies Quarterly* 16 (1986): 92–101; Mark A. Peterson, "The Presidency and Organized Interests," *American Political Science Review* 86 (1992): 612–25.

14. The individual versus institutional debate in presidential studies has been discussed by Lyn Ragsdale, *Vital Statistics on the Presidency* (Washington, DC: CQ Press, 1996); Joseph A. Pika, "Moving Beyond the Oval Office," *Congress and the Presidency* 9 (1981): 17–36; Gregory L. Hager and Terry Sullivan, "President-Centered and Presidency-Centred Explanations of Presidential Public Activity," *American Journal of Political Science* 38 (1994): 1079–1103; Terry Moe, "Presidents, Institutions and Theory," in Edwards, Kessel, and Rockman, eds., *Researching the Presidency,* 337–86.

15. Sidney M. Miliks, *The President and the Parties* (New York: Oxford University Press, 1993).

16. Ragsdale, *Vital Statistics on the Presidency.*

17. George C. Edwards III, *Presidential Influence in Congress* (San Francisco: W.H. Freeman, 1980); Edwards, "Measuring Presidential Success in Congress," *Journal of Politics* 47 (1985): 667–85; Edwards, *At the Margins* (New Haven, CT: Yale University Press, 1989).

18. Steven A. Shull, *Domestic Policy Formation* (1983); Michael Mezey, *Congress, the President, and Public Policy* (Boulder, CO: Westview Press, 1989); Robert J. Spitzer, *The President and Congress* (New York: McGraw-Hill, 1993); Edwards, *At the Margins*; Jon Bond and Richard Fleisher, *The President in the Legislative Arena* (Chicago: University of Chicago Press, 1990); Lance T. LeLoup and Steven A. Shull, *The President and Congress.*

19. Shirley A. Warshaw, *Powersharing: White House–Cabinet Relations in the Modern Presidency* (Albany, NY: SUNY Press, 1995); *Domestic Presidency* (Needham Heights, MA: Allyn and Bacon, 1997).

20. Richard W. Waterman, *Presidential Influence and the Administrative State* (Knoxville: University of Tennessee Press, 1989).

21. Jeffrey A. Segal et al., "Senate Confirmation of Supreme Court Justices," *Journal of Politics* 49 (1987): 998–1015; Segal, "Supreme Court Support for the Solicitor General: the Effects of Presidential Appointments," *Western Political Quarterly* 43 (1990): 137–52. Also, on the relationship between presidents and solicitors general, see Stephen S. Meinhold and Steven A. Shull, "Policy Congruence Between Presidents and Solicitors General," *Political Research Quarterly* 51 (1998): 527–37.

22. For a fine overview of research on the presidency from a predominantly public policy perspective, see Paul Quirk, "What Do We Know and How Do We Know It?" in William Crotty, ed., *Political Science: Looking the Future* (Evanston, IL: Northwestern University Press, 1992): 37–66.

23. LeLoup bases parts of this discussion on his own work and from Lance T. LeLoup and Steven A. Shull, *The President and Congress.*

24. Anderson has long written on the presidency and economic policymaking, including "Presidential Management of Wage–Price Policies," in Edwards, Shull, and

Thomas, eds., *The Presidency and Public Policy Making:* 173–91, and with Jared E. Hazleton, *Managing Macroeconomic Policy: The Johnson Presidency* (Austin: University of Texas Press, 1986).

25. Louis Fisher, *Presidential Spending Power* (Princeton, NJ: Princeton University Press, 1975); *Politics of Shared Power* (Washington, DC: CQ Press, 1981); Fisher, *Constitutional Conflicts Between Congress and the President* (Princeton, NJ: Princeton University Press, 1985).

26. James L. Sundquist, *Politics and Policy* (Washington, DC: Brookings Institution, 1968): 535; Hugh G. Gallagher, "The President, Congress, and Legislation," in T. Cronin and R. Tugwell, eds., *The Presidency Reappraised*, 2nd ed. (New York: Praeger, 1977); Charles O. Jones, *An Introduction to the Study of Public Policy,* 3rd ed. (Monterey, CA: Brooks/Cole, 1984); Shull, *Presidential-Congressional Relations;* Randall B. Ripley and James M. Lindsay, eds., *Congressional Resurgence in Foreign Policy* (Ann Arbor: University of Michigan Press, 1993); Barbara Hinckley, *Less Than Meets the Eye* (Chicago: University of Chicago Press, 1994); L.H. Chamberlain, "President, Congress, and Legislation," *Political Science Quarterly* 61 (1946): 42–60; Paul E. Peterson, ed., *The President, the Congress, and the Making of Foreign Policy* (Norman: University of Oklahoma Press, 1994); Steven A. Shull, ed., *The Two Presidencies: A Quarter-Century Assessment* (Chicago: Nelson-Hall, 1991).

27. *Getting into the Game: The Pre-Presidential Rhetoric of Ronald Reagan* (New York: Praeger, 1989); *Playing the Game: The Presidential Rhetoric of Ronald Reagan* (Westport, CT: Greenwood Press, 1990).

28. See note 8 about Neustadt's influence.

29. Among the many authors discussing reforms are L.G. Crovitz and J.A. Rabkin, *The Fettered Presidency* (Washington, DC: American Enterprise Institute, 1989); John Orman, *Presidential Accountability* (Westport, CT: Greenwood Press, 1990); Theodore Sorenson, *A Different Kind of Presidency* (New York: Harper & Row, 1984); James L. Sundquist, *Constitutional Reform and Effective Government* (Washington, DC: Brookings Institution, 1992).

30. Rockman, *The Leadership Question*; Colin Campbell, *Managing the Presidency* (Pittsburgh: University of Pittsburgh Press, 1986).

31. Ragsdale, *Vital Statistics on the Presidency*; Ragsdale and John J. Theiss, "The Institutionalization of the American Presidency," *American Journal of Political Science* 41 (1997): 1280–1318.

32. Randall B. Ripley, *Policy Analysis and Political Science* (Chicago: Nelson-Hall, 1985); Daniel Greenberg et al., "Developing Public Policy Theory," *American Political Science Review* 71 (1977): 1532–43.

33. Wildavsky, *Speaking Truth to Power*.

34. Shull, *Presidential Policy Making*.

35. Robert H. Salisbury, "The Analysis of Public Policy," in *Public Policy: The Essential Readings,* ed. Stella Z. Theodoulou and Matthew A. Cain (Englewood Cliffs, NJ: Prentice Hall, 1995): 34–37; Norman C. Thomas, "Case Studies," in *Studying the Presidency,* George C. Edwards and Stephen Wayne eds. (Knoxville: University of Tennessee Press, 1983), 50–78.

36. See various selections in Edwards, Kessel, and Rockman, eds., *Researching the Presidency.*

37. Harold Lasswell, *Politics: Who Gets What, When, and How* (New York: St. Martin's Press, 1998; originally published in 1936).

2

Presidential Constraints and Transitions

James P. Pfiffner

The traditional serenity prayer goes: Lord, give me the courage to change those things that I can change, to accept those things that I cannot change, and the wisdom to know the difference. Upon taking office, newly elected presidents are faced with the dilemmas implied in this formulation. The main challenge for a president-elect before inauguration is to prepare to take office so that the first few months in office are successful. First impressions are important and, if negative, hard to overcome. Ronald Reagan benefited from his early successes, whereas Jimmy Carter and Bill Clinton suffered from their early mistakes, despite significant improvements in each of their administrations.

From among the many things that presidents-elect must do, this chapter examines three areas that are crucial to the success of each new president: organizing the administration, making political appointments, and pursuing a policy agenda. In each of these areas the range of presidential discretion is examined. The paper distinguishes among those areas where a new president has the most leeway to make decisions based on (1) personal preference and contrasts to those areas that are relatively constrained by (2) organizational dynamics or ruled out by (3) environmental determinants.[1]

The presidency in many ways is a personal office and has been shaped in important ways by the personality of those who have held the office. Many people believe the president can do whatever he wants, but as Richard Neustadt pointed out in *Presidential Power,* the president is in a weak position constitutionally.[2] Some things are at the president's discretion, but many are impossible or possible only at a high price. The key to presidential wisdom is choosing those areas where presidential action will have the greatest effect. This chapter takes up the range of presidential choice in three areas crucial to a successful transition into office: organization, political appointments, and policy. In some aspects of each of these areas a new president can do broadly what he or she chooses, and in other dimensions of these areas a new president is constrained in important ways.

For instance, in *organizing a new administration* a new president is free to choose new processes and structures (personal preference), but cannot operate effectively without a chief of staff (organizational constraints), and cannot decide to adopt a "cabinet government" approach to running the executive branch (environmental determinants). For instance, in *selecting political appointees* a new president is able to select individual candidates for many of the White House, cabinet, and subcabinet positions (personal preference), but cannot centralize too much in the White House without serious costs in time (organizational constraints), and cannot begin an administration without a substantial personnel operation to organize political recruitment (environmental determinants). For instance, in pursuing the new administration's *policy agenda,* a new president can choose some pet projects based on personal preference or campaign promises. But he cannot expect to achieve significant agenda items without substantial planning (organizational constraints) and must limit the ambition of the policy agenda to the political capital available (environmental determinants).

Organizing the Administration

On the surface, a new president has complete discretion to organize the White House and administration in accord with personal preference. After all, the executive branch works for the president, and the White House staff was created specifically to help the president perform his duties. But as the size and policy duties of the White House have increased, the range of discretion of the president has decreased. Hugh Heclo has written about the "deep structure" of the White House that is determined by other people's expectations about what the White House staff will do for them.[3] Because of this, "cabinet government" is no longer a viable option for presidents.

Personal Preference: White House Personnel and Advisory Structure

Because of months of intense teamwork and sometimes years of service to the candidate, most presidents bring with them into office members of their campaigns. Once the election has been won, the president-elect will naturally want to keep those who have proven their loyalty and competence in the crucible of the campaign, and there is insufficient time to revamp completely a personal staff.

Often new White Houses are staffed by young people who are ambitious, hard working, competitive, and devoted to the candidate.[4] And often these former campaigners turn into effective White House staffers. But campaigning is not the same as governing, and the failure to distinguish which aides have talent in one but not the other may lead to trouble. For instance, Hamilton Jordan was a brilliant campaign strategist but was much less effective when he was later appointed chief of staff. Care must be taken to ensure that campaigners are also suited for governance. David Livingstone was an effective advance man for candidate Bill Clinton in the 1992 campaign. But when he was put in charge of personnel security in the Clinton White House his talents as an advance person came to be drawbacks when he obtained sensitive FBI background files on former Republican White House staffers.

The White House Office has about 400 staffers, all of whom serve at the pleasure of the president, and the EOP has several hundred others. Here presidents have the leeway to choose whomever they want to serve. There is no requirement for Senate confirmation, and no one can second-guess the president. Here it is especially important for presidents to have staffers they feel comfortable with and who possess the combination of skills that the president feels is most important.

But a new president is not entirely free to choose whomever he or she pleases. Although the White House staff is most often filled with young campaigners, presidents also need experts who were not necessarily in the campaign, for example in the national security area.[5] But just as the cabinet came to be seen as a symbolic representation of the diversity of the nation (ideological, geographical, religious, ethnic, gender), so now the White House staff is being scrutinized for diversity (ideological within the party, gender, race, etc.). The consequence is that presidents are no longer entirely free to choose their own staffs without the second-guessing from outsiders. What used to be almost entirely at the personal discretion of the president is now more constrained by the expectations of others. So despite broad flexibility, *presidents are not free to choose whomever they want for their staffs* without reference to their electoral and governing coalitions.

Organizational Constraints: White House Organization

Presidents are relatively free to set up advisory structures to suit their own preferences. President Truman came to use the National Security Council

(NSC) to advise him weekly during the Korean War. President Eisenhower institutionalized the NSC staff processes, and Kennedy discarded Eisenhower's processes. President Ford used his Economic Policy Board to advise him on his policy priorities. Ronald Reagan set up seven cabinet councils to structure White House staff-cabinet interactions in his first term. Bill Clinton introduced a National Economic Council and added members to the National Security Council.

Thus some organizational issues are subject to the personal preferences of the president, but the broader issue of running the White House without a chief of staff is no longer a viable option for presidents. Eisenhower introduced the office of chief of staff to the White House, and used the office as the center of a very effectively organized administration.[6] During the Kennedy and Johnson presidencies of the 1960s having a chief of staff was still optional, and each ran an effective administration without one. Richard Nixon began his administration with H.R. Haldeman as his chief of staff, and during his administration the White House staff was increased in size to such an extent that operating without a chief of staff was no longer a viable option.

This was proven when President Ford, trying to distinguish his administration from the discredited Nixon, tried to run the White House as the "knights of the round table." Within several months he gave up and asked Donald Rumsfeld to act as his chief of staff. Similarly, Jimmy Carter began his administration with promises not to have a chief of staff. But after two years of trying to run his administration without one, he gave up and appointed Hamilton Jordan and then Jack Watson to be chiefs of staff. Presidents Reagan and Bush both used a chief of staff from the beginning.

This point was reinforced in the 1990s. President Clinton realized intellectually that he would need a chief of staff, and he was the first Democrat to begin his administration with one. But viscerally Clinton did not want anyone in charge but him; he did not want to delegate. Thus his first chief of staff, Mack McLarty, had a tough time; and he did not try to play the role of a traditional chief of staff. His personality was low-key, he spent most of his time as a personal counselor to Clinton and as an emissary to the business community and to conservative Democrats in Congress. These are important functions, but someone needs to be running the White House. It is more than a full-time job.

Clinton finally recognized this and replaced McLarty with Leon Panetta, who took charge and canceled staffers' right to walk into the Oval Office without checking with him first. All paperwork had to flow through him, and he took control of White House staff appointments. He tightened up meetings so that there were fewer people and brought closure to issues.

Basically, he installed more discipline into White House operations. When Erskine Bowles took over from Panetta, he continued the same, orderly approach. Thus Clinton finally admitted that he needed a more traditional chief of staff, though he would never allow a chief of staff the authority that Haldeman had.[7]

But the corollary to the need for a chief of staff is that if the person takes too domineering an approach to the job, the administration is in for trouble. The domineering chiefs of staff tried to control too much, and asserted personal control to the point where it became counterproductive. There have been four domineering chiefs of staff in the presidency—Sherman Adams for Eisenhower, H.R. Haldeman for Nixon, Donald Regan for Reagan, and John Sununu for Bush. Each of these domineering chiefs, in seeking to control all aspects of the White House, alienated members of their administration, members of Congress, and the press; and each of them ended by resigning in disgrace after doing serious harm to their presidents.[8]

So with respect to organizational matters *presidents are no longer free to run the White House without a chief of staff, and if that chief takes too domineering a role, there will be trouble.*

Environmental Determinants: White House Centralization and "Cabinet Government"

Cabinet government American style, that is with the separation of powers structure rather than a parliamentary system, was practiced in the modern era most effectively by President Eisenhower. That is, Eisenhower delegated a reasonable amount of leeway in policy development to his cabinet secretaries, and he used his cabinet as a deliberative body to advise him on the major issues of his administration.

While Kennedy did not think that the cabinet was of much use, aside from the individuals in it, and Johnson was afraid of leaks from his cabinet, subsequent presidents sought to return to the Eisenhower ideal. Presidents Nixon, Ford, Carter, and Reagan each promised cabinet government. But each was forced to admit that their original ideals of delegation to cabinet secretaries along with a relatively weak White House staff was unachievable, and each of them abandoned their early ideals and opted for strong White House staffs.[9]

The reality of the modern presidency is that the White House staff dominates the administration, and cabinet secretaries inevitably play a secondary role. The reasons for this are several. In contrast to cabinet secretaries, White House staffers have no institutional turf to protect and perceive issues from a presidential perspective. If they are to be effective, cabinet members must worry about their programs, people, and turf. White House staffers are chosen more for their loyalty than for the symbolic reasons that affect cabinet selection. Staffers also have the advantage of proximity to the president and can drop all other matters in order to respond immediately to presidential needs.

But the most important reason that a large and dominant White House staff is necessary in the contemporary presidency is that the White House has taken over a number of functions that used to be performed by cabinet departments and political parties. Even if presidents wanted to, it would be difficult to push these functions out of the White House. As the presidency has grown, the size and reach of the White House has extended deeper into the executive branch. Just as executive branch departments and agencies have become more presidentialized (with political appointees and White House control), the presidency has become more bureaucratized (with more specialized units and hierarchical organization).[10]

National security policymaking has become centralized in the assistant to the president for National Security Affairs and the *NSC staff,* which often overshadow the secretaries of the State and Defense Departments. Domestic policy used to be the bailiwick of domestic departments and agencies but is now dominated by the *Office of Policy Development.* Legal advice to the president that used to be provided by the attorney general is now supplied by the *Counsel's Office* in the White House. Trade policy used to be developed in the Departments of State, Commerce, Agriculture, and so on, but now the *Office of U.S. Trade Representative* in the EOP is the president's agent to coordinate trade policy.

Political parties used to be the source of many of the presidential and other political appointees that would lead the administration. Now the *Office of Presidential Personnel* is the president's recruiter of political appointees. Coalitions on the Hill to pass the president's agenda were built with the help of the political parties, but the *Office of Congressional Liaison* does the job now. OCR is often aided by the *Office of Public Liaison,* which mobilizes interest groups to support the president's agenda, a function that parties used to perform. Partisan political strategy and activities used to be centered in the Democratic and Republican national committees. Now the *Office of Political Affairs* in the White House Office dominates political strategy.

Thus *presidents are not free to choose a "cabinet government" approach* to their administrations, as Nixon, Ford, Carter, and Reagan found out. Nor are presidents free to abolish or delegate White House functions without outcries from those who think that the function is being downgraded.[11]

The Recruitment of Political Appointees

Making political appointments to the executive branch is one of the major authorities granted to the president in the Constitution. This is an area where presidents are free to use their own judgment, subject only to Senate confirmation, which though occasionally assertive, is in the vast majority of cases perfunctory. It would seem on the surface that presidents have virtually complete discretion in their choice of people who will make up the administration. But the size of the cohort that must be chosen imposes organizational imperatives if the task is to be accomplished with any dispatch at all. The broader political environment also imposes constraints that make it impossible for presidents to pursue only their own personal preferences in making appointments. This section examines the range of flexibility that presidents have in making political appointments.

The Development of Presidential Control

In the 1930s and 1940s political parties dominated the recruitment of political appointments, which were seen as patronage. As the government grew in size and scope after the New Deal and World War II, the need for policy expertise began to assert itself over the mere needs of patronage.[12] The qualifications of political operatives were no longer up to the demands of the highly technical programs the government now managed. In addition, with the increase in the importance of primary elections, presidents were no longer tied so closely to their political parties, and they began to want to control their appointments by their own political organizations rather than through the parties.

Thus the political recruitment function developed in the White House and became institutionalized. Harry Truman put one staffer in charge of political appointments. John Kennedy had a three person "talent hunt." By the end of his first term Richard Nixon had thirty-five people working on political recruitment; Ronald Reagan had 100 people in the personnel operation at the beginning of his administration, and Bill Clinton had even more.[13]

The centralization of control of political appointments in the White House was possible only because the institutional apparatus was created to handle the volume of appointments that each new administration has to make. The institutional development of a White House personnel recruitment capacity in theory gave the president the ability to make personal choices for appointments. The problem is that the number of candidates seeking a job with a new administration is enormous, and if the president does not deflect the entreaties, he will become inundated with applicants.

Thus while new presidents have the constitutional authority to pick whomever they choose for the administration (subject to Senate confirmation), the practical reality is that *they must set up a sizable personnel operations* to do it for them. And once that organization is set up, there are certain organizational imperatives that must be met if the task is to be accomplished effectively.

Organizational Constraints: Organizing for Political Recruitment

The first problem that becomes obvious to a new administration is the tremendous volume of jobs that must be filled. The total number of executive branch appointments available to a new president totals over 5,500. About 2,000 of these are part-time, and thus less important appointments, but that leaves about 1,000 appointments requiring Senate confirmation in the executive branch (PAS, including executives and commissioners, ambassadors, and United States attorneys and marshals) and more than 400 in the White House who do not need to be confirmed (PA). In addition, there are about 700 noncareer Senior Executive Service appointments available and about 1,700 Schedule C appointments (at the GS-15 and below level).[14] With this volume to handle, a professional personnel operation is a necessity, and such an operation has developed in the White House, though it must be created again for each new president, since there is little institutional memory in the White House, especially for such a sensitive matter as political appointments.

In the 1950s and 1960s presidents tended to delegate the selection of the subcabinet appointments (associate, deputy, and assistant secretaries, etc.) to their cabinet secretaries, and Presidents Nixon and Carter initially delegated broad personnel leeway to their cabinet heads. But after some experience, each of them felt that they had given away too much and tried to pull back the authority into the White House. The Reagan administration decided to avoid these problems by centralizing all political appointments in the White House. The result was the most centralized and tightly controlled personnel operation in the modern presidency.

The price paid for this centralization and thoroughness was time. The Reagan administration was the slowest recruitment effort to that time, with many complaints from departments and agencies that essential leadership was missing until late in the first year of the administration. The Clinton administration decided to use Reagan as a model and centralize appointments, rather than delegate some discretion to cabinet secretaries. The driving criterion, however, changed from ideology to diversity. The White House played the dominant role in recruitment and President Clinton along with the first lady played an active role in personnel selection. Again, the price was paid in time. The Clinton personnel effort was even slower than Reagan's. According to Calvin Mackenzie's calculations, Kennedy averaged 2.4 months, Nixon 3.4, Carter 4.6, Reagan 5.3, Bush 8.1, and Clinton 8.5.[15]

Thus, with the growing number of political appointees and the felt need of presidents to control all appointments in the White House, an elaborate and professional personnel operation is necessary. Presidents can in theory choose whomever they want in their administration, but there is no way that any individual can know the best people for the thousands of positions available, and a high price in time will be extracted if the president tries personally to oversee appointments to any great extent. *The personnel recruitment function must be delegated to a professional operation that has been carefully planned and organized.*

Environmental Determinants: The Politics of Constituency

To put things into perspective, any appointments that are personally important are at the president's discretion (subject to Senate ratification), and most of the very top layers of an administration will be determined by the president personally. The president should also set the tone for the entire personnel recruitment operation by communicating to the directors of the personnel search his own values, the priorities of the administration, and his personal preferences in building the administration team. But a president cannot become too deeply involved in the process of recruitment, or it will become bogged down. The president will be kept from the many other priorities to which he must attend, and the personnel process will become slowed down waiting for presidential decisions.

In any new administration the onslaught of applications for positions is voluminous and sudden. In the 1970s and 1980s in the first weeks of a new administration résumés poured in at 1,500 per day. In 1989 before the inauguration 16,000 résumés had been accumulated by the transition personnel operation. By the end of May 1989 more than 70,000 applications and recommendations had been received, though 25,000 were duplicates. One official likened separating the wheat from the chaff to "trying to take a sip from a fire hydrant." After the Clinton election 3,000 job requests had arrived within one week of the election, and by February 1993 they were receiving 2,000 résumés a day.[16]

In subsequent administrations the pressures for patronage remained as strong, but the source of the pressures began to shift. Political parties continued to exert what pressure they could, but their influence waned as presidential candidates began to organize their campaign organizations independently of the parties. Because of the declining influence of parties, presidents could ignore their demands with impunity. But as the influence of political parties decreased in electoral politics, their pressures were replaced by constituency and interest groups which supported candidates and expected that their support would be rewarded with appointments of their representatives.

In the Reagan administration these were "movement conservatives," those ideologically committed to the Reagan agenda and who had campaigned for his election. The Clinton administration's commitment to diversity reflected the coalition of groups that had campaigned for his election. The personnel operation had special recruitment staffers to act as liaison to its important supporting groups: African Americans, women, Hispanics, gays, and disability groups.[17]

Political appointments are seen as symbols of the direction of the new administration and its commitment to various priorities and constituent groups. Thus *new presidents do not have a free hand to choose whomever they please to serve in their administrations.* The challenge is to satisfy the inevitable (and legitimate in the context of American political history) demands for patronage without jeopardizing loyalty to the president or the competence necessary to run the government.

Pursuing a Policy Agenda

In deciding an initial policy agenda presidents possess a range of options, and understanding the constraints on policy possibilities will enable a new administration to make wise choices about where to place its limited energies. Presidents usually have the option of pushing their own "pet projects" if the policy is not very costly or far reaching. For more extensive programmatic proposals presidents can also be successful, but must be aware of the need for planning the concrete details of programs and the need to limit the range of their initial policy agendas. Finally, the likelihood of achieving broad changes in policy direction, though it can be enhanced by presidential skills, is often determined by broad environmental factors over which the president has little control.

Personal Preference: Campaign Promises and Pet Projects

Presidents often come to office with a psychological commitment to certain projects based on idealism or campaign promises. John Kennedy moved quickly to establish the Peace Corps. Jimmy Carter wanted to eliminate what he considered to be wasteful water projects from the agenda of the Army Corps of Engineers. Richard Nixon wanted to eliminate the Office of Economic

Opportunity created in the Great Society push of Lyndon Johnson, and Ronald Reagan wanted to "zero out" its successor, the Community Services Administration. Bill Clinton hoped to create a National Service Corps and make college loans more accessible to students of varying backgrounds.

It was not until very late in the campaign that Kennedy actually proposed a Peace Corps, but once in office Kennedy decided to act quickly and signaled his seriousness about establishing it by making his brother-in-law, Sargent Shriver, its director. Shriver succeeded in lobbying Congress sufficiently to win congressional backing and sufficient funding. Kennedy later took great pride in the Peace Corps, and it is remembered as one of the programs that symbolized Kennedy's youthful idealism.[18]

At the beginning of his administration, Jimmy Carter wanted to eliminate the pet water projects of many members of Congress by canceling Army Corps of Engineer projects that he considered wasteful and environmentally unsound. Despite warnings from the Office of Management and Budget (OMB) about the importance of these projects to members of Congress, Carter went ahead with his proposal. Legislators became very upset and attached funding for the projects to an economic stimulus bill that Carter felt he had to sign.[19] In his first budget Ronald Reagan wanted to "zero out" the Community Services Administration. CSA was the successor to the Office of Economic Opportunity created in the Johnson administration's War on Poverty. Reagan succeeded where Nixon had failed in a similar effort because he convinced Congress to approve the shutdown in a package with other budget cuts.[20]

In his campaign for the presidency Bill Clinton had emphasized the theme of "putting people first." The day after the election, he held a press conference in which he said that national service would be one of the important initiatives of his administration, in addition to economic recovery, health care, and deficit reduction. His choice of a successful businessman and his friend of many years, Eli Segal, to head the project signaled his commitment to this agenda priority. As his proposal made its way through the administration's deliberations and the legislative process, significant cuts in the initial size of the program were made. But in the end, the symbolic, legislative, and programmatic statement was made. Clinton won approval of a relatively small, though important to him personally and symbolically, part of his initial policy agenda.[21]

The lesson here is that *pet projects can be pursued and won, but they require effort and compromises*; and they are not a sure thing.

Organizational Dynamics: Issues, Alternatives, and Choice

In considering a policy agenda a new president must do two things: translate general issues and campaign proposals into concrete programmatic proposals and decide among competing priorities in the agenda. John Kingdon argues that in the policy process there is an important distinction between agenda items and policy alternatives.[22] Presidents have the ability to set the agenda in the sense of raising issues to a level of visibility, for instance energy policy, welfare reform, tax simplification, deficit reduction, or health-care reform. But taking these general policy issues and generating a small set of concrete alternatives is another matter. The kind of broad societal problems that these policies are intended to deal with are so complex and the implications so far-reaching that only policy experts can meaningfully lay out concrete alternative approaches to deal with them. If a president wants to undertake major policy change, general issues will need quickly to be translated into specific policy alternatives, and those alternatives will have to be narrowed down to one legislative proposal.

Victory in the election gives a president a narrow window of opportunity for policy change. The longer a president waits to introduce key parts of the agenda, the less likely it is that the proposals will be enacted. Presidents can take advantage of relatively high public approval that will surely decline over the first several months in office. Congress is relatively open to cooperation with the new president. The election is fresh in the minds of Congress and the people, and a mandate can be claimed. Mistakes and policy choices will not yet have been made, and opportunity is at its greatest.

Lyndon Johnson's landslide in 1964 brought into office large Democratic majorities in both houses of Congress. Johnson's Great Society and War on Poverty legislative victories are legendary, but much of the specific planning for the policy initiatives had been circulating in Democratic policy circles for years, and transforming them into specific legislative proposals was not a major problem.[23] Johnson pushed his domestic agenda relentlessly, believing that his window of opportunity would soon close.

Richard Nixon did not have Johnson's luxury of a large legislative victory or partisan majorities in Congress; instead, he faced an opposition-controlled Congress and had a narrow margin of victory over Hubert Humphrey in 1968. Nixon proposed his Family Assistance Plan to replace the welfare system's several programs with a negative income tax early in his administration. But his White House staff did not have a fully formulated proposal until August 1969.[24] The problems in timing were that welfare was a contentious area, and it took time for the administration itself to agree on one reform proposal. The plan was eventually defeated; the proposal may have been doomed in any case because of the deep value disagreements between Democrats and Republicans, liberals and conservatives. But it may have had a better chance if it had been ready to go earlier in Nixon's first term.

Jimmy Carter decided to pursue a national energy policy that would make the United States more independent of foreign oil. He put James Schlesinger in charge of the policy and charged him with coming up with a plan within ninety days of the inauguration. This was a tight time frame, given the technical complexity of the issues, and Schlesinger compounded other difficulties by working in secret without vetting his plans with Democrats on the Hill or even members of the Carter administration. The deadline for the proposal was met, but over the next year it was significantly changed in Congress due to the political failure to work with members but also because of disagreements over the substance of the policy. It eventually passed, but not in the form Carter had originally proposed. Carter's original proposal may have been doomed in any event, but there is little doubt that the chances would have been better had it been ready to go shortly after inauguration.

Ronald Reagan's major budget priorities were passed, virtually intact, within six months of his taking office. It helped that Reagan had a perceived mandate, but the victories were also due to careful planning on the part of his team. The priorities of domestic budget cuts, tax cuts, and increased military spending were clear during the campaign. And the work of translating these general policy directions into concrete proposals was begun well before the election by David Stockman, a member of Congress who became Reagan's OMB director. This advance planning and early decision on the part of the Reagan administration enabled them to achieve unprecedented budget changes within months of taking office. If the proposals had been delayed significantly, it is doubtful that they would have been successful.[25]

One of Bill Clinton's top policy priorities in 1993 was health-care reform. In addition to his decision to attack the budget deficit, he wanted to move quickly on reforming the health-care system to provide universal coverage for health insurance. Clinton understood that this was a complex issue and that there was not a problem of lack of preparing specific alternatives. A health-care planning group had been set up in the fall of 1991 in Washington to lay out alternatives. Once in office, President Clinton decided that the planning group's efforts were not acceptable and created a task force headed by Hillary Clinton and Ira Magaziner to come up with the administration's proposal, but the actual proposal did not get to Congress until late fall of 1993. The delay turned out to be one of the reasons for the failure to enact health-care reform.

The problem with the timing of the Clinton health-care plan was not lack of preparation but the president's refusal to make an early choice of which alternative to select. There were a number of elements that Clinton could back, but he wanted a comprehensive proposal that would achieve universal coverage and cost neutrality. Perhaps any proposal that could achieve both of those virtually incompatible goals would have been unacceptable to the public, but whatever proposal they had would have had a better chance if it had been ready to go earlier in the administration.[26]

A similar problem faced Clinton on his deficit-reduction package. Even though he made his budget speech on February 17, a day before Reagan had in 1981, the final decisions on how to deal with the budget were not made until mid-February. Again, it was not due to lack of planning; Clinton had held an economic "summit" in Little Rock in December in which all alternatives had been explored, and his OMB director, Leon Panetta, was intimately familiar with the budget details from his years as chair of the House Budget Committee. Whereas Reagan's budget direction was clear from the time of the election, Clinton's was not clear until mid-February. The delay was not due to lack of planning but to Clinton's delay in deciding. The economy was changing and it was not clear to Clinton whether the economy was still in recession and thus needing stimulus or coming out of the recession and thus able to take the restraint of deficit reduction. Delay meant a better policy, but a tougher time getting it through Congress.[27]

Thus, *if presidents want early policy success, it helps to have concrete proposals ready to go* early in their administrations. This necessarily entails early planning and a decision on specific alternatives during the transition. This may not provide the necessary time for deliberation and time for wise policy choice, but it will maximize the chance of passage.

Environmental Determinants: The Limits of Political Capital

President's have most control over small pet projects that they personally identify with and push early in their administrations. Presidents have some control over planning their major policy proposals, choosing specific alternatives, and deciding on how broad their initial policy agendas should be. But the overall success of the policy agenda is often determined by factors in the political environment beyond presidential control. These factors include most importantly the partisan margins in each house of Congress, the president's electoral margin of victory, and the "mood of the times."[28]

In considering presidential policy success with Congress much of the popular press dwells on the force of personality and the tactical details of winning votes, but the consensus of scholars is that presidential success with Congress depends on factors over which presidents have little control. For instance, George Edwards argues that presidential skills—that is, the ability to effectively lobby members of Congress, do favors, and make threats—are effective only "at the margins."[29] Paul Light argues that political capital—partisan seats in Congress, electoral margin, and public approval—is most likely to determine success with Congress, not presidential personality, skills, or energy.[30]

Charles O. Jones in *The Presidency in a Separated System* argues that the U.S. Constitution did not set up a presidential system and takes issue with those who judge our system by whether or not presidents can get their way with Congress.[31] Jones argues that we should change our criteria of evaluating presidents from implicit comparisons with FDR, LBJ, and Ronald Reagan. We should, instead, judge presidential accomplishment in relative terms. "What can a president reasonably be expected to accomplish?"[32]

In his warning he echoes Richard Neustadt, who warns about the high expectations implied in the "100 days syndrome" and urges caution to new presidents lest they make mistakes due to the ignorance, arrogance, or hubris engendered by election victory. In contrast, Roger Porter, veteran White House staffer, argues that despite these legitimate cautions, optimism ought to prevail. Transitions are a time of opportunity, and much can be accomplished in transforming "a limited electoral mandate into a capacity to govern."[33]

From this perspective we should not be surprised that Bill Clinton did not achieve all that he had hoped to early in his administration, but we should be surprised that he did as well as he did. Despite unified government with Democrats in control of Congress, Clinton suffered from the narrowness of his 43 percent electoral victory and his relatively low approval ratings in the spring of 1993.[34] With the Democrats divided, he had no natural coalition of support in Congress, and the Republicans were able to use filibusters effectively in the Senate. Clinton's high presidential support scores and high party unity scores in his first year were misleading, indicating more support in Congress than he had in reality. Emblematic of Clinton's optimism was his health-care initiative, which proposed a much larger change than Americans were willing to accept (there were also, of course, many other factors that contributed to the defeat of the health-care initiative).

Given this analysis, what should new presidents do? They are caught in a dilemma: either take the time to develop a carefully thought out policy or move quickly with a less-well-formed option. The main point is to *be aware of the likely range of opportunities for a new administration and choose carefully*. Jones, Neustadt, and others rightly argue for caution and care not to overreach. But I, along with Porter, would argue for optimism and urge new administrations to hit the ground running with well-thought-out policy initiatives. If a new president does have a policy agenda, regardless of size, the best chance to achieve that agenda is at the beginning of an administration. And the better prepared a new administration is to go after its policy goals, the better chance they have of achieving them.

Conclusion

What stands out in the above analysis is the wide range of challenges facing a new president. This chapter has chosen only several of the top priorities each new administration must face: organizing the executive branch, selecting presidential personnel, and choosing a policy agenda. Other priorities and demands must also be faced: formulating a foreign policy, dealing with the press, symbolic and rhetorical appeals to the nation, and so on. And what is worse, all of these things must be done at the same time immediately after the election.

No wonder that presidential staffs feel that there is never enough time between election and inauguration. Yet the early weeks and months of a new administration can be crucial to its overall success. Early mistakes hurt, as Carter and Clinton found out, even if the lessons are learned and performance improves. Early victories also set a tone out of proportion to the overall performance of the administration. Most of the major policy changes of the Reagan administration were accomplished in a very successful first year.

While not addressing the wisdom of the policies, the model for hitting the ground running remains the Reagan administration. Through careful and conscious planning and focus of energy, the administration was able to accomplish much of what it wanted to in the first year. The White House was effectively organized, political appointments were used effectively, and the policy agenda was closely focused and pursued systematically. Admittedly, Reagan had a politically plausible mandate. Neither Presidents Bush nor Clinton had the same opportunity that Reagan had in 1981, but neither was as organized or as strategically oriented as was the Reagan administration in 1981. Political accomplishment depends upon both opportunity and the ability to take advantage of that opportunity.

The lessons of recent presidential transitions are these:

1. With respect to *organization,* the general rules of transition are fairly evident. A strong White House staff is necessary, and a nondomineering chief of staff must be in charge.
2. With respect to *political appointments,* there is no way to do the job well. The inherent difficulty of pleasing all factions is now aggravated by the huge volume of appointments to be made. Regardless of how well a personnel operation is organized, it will take well into the first year to get a majority of political appointments in place. But planning can mitigate the extent of the inevitable problems.
3. With respect to the *policy agenda,* much will depend on the historical

circumstances of the election and the margin of victory. Is there enough public consensus that major issues are ripe for action? Can a president bent upon bold policy changes hold strong enough public support throughout the policy process?

But regardless of the constraints and opportunities faced by each new president, the range of possibilities will be enhanced by careful planning, coherent organization, and a focused agenda. And careful attention to the lessons of past transitions.

Notes

1. In their fine book Walcott and Hult distinguish three factors that affect presidential control over White House organization: personal preference, organizational dynamics, and environmental factors. See Charles Walcott and Karen Hult, *Governing the White House* (Lawrence: University Press of Kansas, 1995).

2. Richard Neustadt, *Presidential Power* (New York: Wiley, 1980).

3. See Hugh Heclo, "The Presidential Office," in James P. Pfiffner, ed., *The Managerial Presidency* (Pacific Grove, CA: Brooks/Cole, 1991).

4. See Patrick Anderson, *The President's Men* (Garden City, NY: Doubleday Anchor Books, 1969); Jeffrey H. Birnbaum, *Madhouse* (New York: Times Books, 1996).

5. For an analysis of the types of aides a president needs, see Matthew Holden Jr., "Why Entourage Politics is Volatile," in Pfiffner, ed., *The Managerial Presidency.*

6. On Eisenhower's approach to organization, see Fred I. Greenstein, *The Hidden-Hand Presidency* (New York: Basic Books, 1982); and Phillip G. Henderson, *Managing the Presidency* (Boulder, CO: Westview Press, 1988).

7. For an analysis of Clinton's White House organization, see James P. Pfiffner, *The Strategic Presidency: Hitting the Ground Running,* 2nd ed. (Lawrence: University Press of Kansas, 1996), 151–62.

8. For a detailed elaboration of this argument, see James P. Pfiffner, "The President's Chief of Staff: Lessons Learned," *Presidential Studies Quarterly,* Winter 1993, 88–102.

9. See Pfiffner, *The Strategic Presidency,* ch. 2, "The Holy Grail of 'True' Cabinet Government." See also Shirley Anne Warshaw, *Powersharing: White House-Cabinet Relations in the Modern Presidency* (Albany, NY: SUNY Press, 1996).

10. See Francis Rourke, "Presidentializing the Bureaucracy: From Kennedy to Reagan," in Pfiffner, *The Managerial Presidency,* 123–34.

11. Both Presidents Carter and Clinton tried to remove the Council on Environmental Quality from the EOP, but each was defeated by those who insisted that this would symbolize the downgrading of environmental priorities. The concentration of these functions in the White House is also why presidents have a hard time fulfilling campaign promises to cut the White House staff. Both Clinton and Carter had to resort to creative accounting and box shuffling in order to claim to have accomplished their goals. For analyses of Clinton's White House staff cuts, see Pfiffner, *The Strategic Presidency,* 154–55; and "Cutting Staff No Easy Task for Clinton," *Maine Sunday Telegram,* December 12, 1993. See also John Hart, "The Politics of Symbolism: President Clinton's White House Staff Reductions," paper presented at the American Political Science Convention, New York City, September 1, 1994.

12. See Calvin Mackenzie, "Partisan Presidential Leadership: The President's Appointees," in L. Sandy Maisel, ed., *The Parties Respond* (Boulder CO: Westview Press, 1990).

13. For the development of the political recruitment capacity in the White House, see Thomas Weko, *The Politicizing Presidency* (Lawrence: University Press of Kansas, 1995).

14. PAS data provided to the author in 1992 by the executive clerk to the president. For details, see James P. Pfiffner, *The Modern Presidency* (New York: St. Martin's Press, 1994), 123; and Pfiffner, *The Strategic Presidency*, 194.

15. Data compiled by Calvin Mackenzie; see Paul Light, *Thickening Government* (Washington, DC: Brookings Institution, 1995), 68. See also Pfiffner, *The Strategic Presidency*, 168–72, 190–99.

16. See Pfiffner, *The Strategic Presidency*, 56–58, 137–41, 163–72; see also Weko, *The Politicizing Presidency*, 100. Even President Eisenhower, who did not want patronage issues in the White House, ended up with many patronage issues run by Sherman Adams. The pressures from the Republican Party after twenty years of Democratic rule were too strong for even the president to resist. For a detailed analysis and documentation of the Eisenhower patronage operation, see Charles Walcott and Karen Hult, *Governing the White House* (Lawrence: University Press of Kansas, 1995), 83–84. See also Weko, *The Politicizing Presidency*, 35–39.

17. Weko, *The Politicizing Presidency*, 100–101.

18. See the analysis by James N. Giglio, *The Presidency of John F. Kennedy* (Lawrence: University Press of Kansas, 1991), 152–58.

19. See Pfiffner, *The Strategic Presidency*, 120–22.

20. For the Nixon actions, see James P. Pfiffner, *The President, the Budget, and Congress: Impoundment and the 1974 Budget Act* (Boulder, CO: Westview Press, 1979), 30, 116; for the Reagan action, see Pfiffner, *The Strategic Presidency*, 84.

21. For an account of the development and passage of the legislation, see Steven Waldman, *The Bill: How the Adventures of Clinton's National Service Bill Reveal What Is Corrupt, Comic, Cynical—and Noble—About Washington* (New York: Viking, 1995).

22. John Kingdon, *Agendas, Alternatives, and Public Policies* (New York: Little, Brown, 1984).

23. See Paul C. Light, *The President's Agenda: Domestic Policy Choice from Kennedy to Carter* (Baltimore: Johns Hopkins University Press, 1982), 50.

24. See Joan Hoff, *Nixon Reconsidered* (New York: Basic Books, 1994), 115–37.

25. For a detailed analysis, see James P. Pfiffner, "The Reagan Budget Juggernaut," in Pfiffner, ed., *The President and Economic Policy* (Philadelphia: ISHI Press, 1986), 108–34.

26. Haynes Johnson and David Broder, *The System: The American Way of Politics at the Breaking Point* (Boston: Little, Brown, 1996), 70–109.

27. For an analysis of Clinton's first year agenda, see James P. Pfiffner, "President Clinton and the 103rd Congress: Winning Battles and Losing Wars," in James Thurber, ed., *Rivals for Power* (Washington, DC: CQ Press, 1996).

28. For the importance of the mood of the times in major legislative eras, see David Mayhew, *Divided We Govern* (New Haven: Yale University Press, 1991).

29. George C. Edwards, *At the Margins* (New Haven: Yale University Press, 1989). See also Jon Bond and Richard Fleisher, *The President in the Legislative Arena* (Chicago: University of Chicago Press, 1990); Mark A. Peterson, *Legislating Together: The White House and Capitol Hill* (Cambridge: Harvard University Press, 1990); and Lance T. LeLoup and Steven A. Shull, *The President and Congress* (Needham Heights, MA: Allyn & Bacon, 1999).

30. Paul Light, *The President's Agenda* (Baltimore: Johns Hopkins University Press, 1982), 26.

31. Charles O. Jones, *The Presidency in a Separated System* (Washington, DC: Brookings Institution, 1994).

32. Ibid., 50.

33. Richard Neustadt, *Presidential Power* (New York: Wiley, 1980), 220–25. See also Roger Porter, "Of Hazards and Opportunities: Transitions and the Modern Presidency," paper prepared for the Conference on Presidential Power revisited, Woodrow Wilson International Center for Scholars, Washington, DC, June 13, 1996. Forthcoming a festschrift for Richard Neustadt, edited by Roger Porter.

34. For an elaboration of this point, see Pfiffner, "President Clinton and the 103rd Congress," in Thurber, *Rivals for Power*.

Part II

Presidential Relations with Those Outside Government

3

Public Opinion: Reconceptualizing Going Public

Jeffrey E. Cohen and Ken Collier

The legislative impact of the alliance between the president and citizens has been debated since Andrew Jackson claimed the public as a presidential ally in his struggles with Congress. The most widely read book on the working relationship between the president and the public is Samuel Kernell's *Going Public.*[1] Kernell describes going public as a strategy for promoting presidential popularity and policy through public appeals. This chapter suggests that several distinct presidential strategies for using public support have an impact on legislation and the presidency directly or indirectly.

Going public is most often discussed in terms of presidential persuasion of members of Congress on matters before them. As part of this persuasive task, presidents speak to national audiences and the president's aim is narrow: to rally public support behind his policies and apply public opinion pressure on Congress so that Congress will accept his policy proposal. In this conceptualization, public opinion is viewed as a direct influence on Congress, while presidential influence on Congress is indirect, routed through this public pressure avenue.

We assert that going public includes a wider array of presidential activities than using public support to affect the outcomes of bills on the floors of the congressional chambers. Using the public, as Kernell suggests, to place pressure on Congress to pass legislation that the president supports is clearly one aspect of going public. But using the public to influence the congressional agenda and nonlegislative presidential-congressional relations of Congress may also be aspects of the "going public presidency."

Kernell defines going public as "a strategy whereby a president promotes himself and his policies in Washington by appealing to the American public for support."[2] We begin by drawing a distinction between the president's agenda-setting ability and his ability to persuade members of Congress on legislation before them. We then examine different presidential strategies to influence members of Congress through the use of public opinion.

Going Public and Presidential Agenda Setting

In this section, we detail going public activities as they relate to presidential attempts to set the congressional agenda. Presidential setting of the congressional agenda and presidential influence over Congress's policy outputs are linked. Influencing the structure of the congressional agenda may result in presidential attainment of policy goals, but without having to "go public" in the narrow sense of rallying public pressure for specific policies up for consideration.

Presidents and Agendas

One of the president's most important sources of political influence may be his ability to structure the agenda. While the literature on presidential agenda setting is not highly developed,[3] there are suggestions that this type of presidential influence may exceed his often restricted ability to affect congressional decision making.

In his study of the agenda-setting process, Kingdon finds that respondents cite the president and his administration as perhaps the most important actor with agenda influence. As Kingdon states, "there is little doubt that the president remains a powerful force in agenda setting, particularly compared to other actors."[4] Moreover, the views of department heads and others associated with the administration are usually thought of as the president's or as having the president's stamp of approval. When they speak, it is for the administration and the president. Thus, the president has many "voices."

The president has several important agenda-setting resources.[5] Combined, they give him many advantages over others in the agenda-setting process. These include institutional resources, such as those that emanate from his constitutional powers and position, like the veto. Other institutional resources include his ability to hire and fire staff and advisers, for instance, his cabinet secretaries and EOP personnel. Moreover, the unitary nature of the presidency brings policy and other conflicts to the president for resolution. This critical "decision point" of the presidency affords the president a major say over the direction of policy and the agenda. The president also is at the center of public attention. No other political figure can compete with the president in this regard, and the presidential presence in the public space may be over-powering. Miroff uses a phrase that captures this public dominance of the president—his "monopolization" of the public space.[6]

Given this broad array of resources, it is easy to see the president as being able to steer the agenda. But there are important limits on presidential influence over the agenda. For instance, Charles Jones argues that much of the agenda is ongoing, that presidents inherit problems and issues that they must address.[7] Thus, while the president may be a more forceful actor on the agenda than anyone else, there are limits to his impact.

Still, within these structural boundaries, presidents have wide latitude in affecting the agenda. Presidents may affect how much emphasis an item coming from the set of inherited issues receives. Further, presidents may try to expand the agenda to accept other issues not included in that inheritance. Perhaps as important, presidents may affect the terms of debate on issues, they may frame the issue in a way that will enhance the likelihood that it will get onto the congressional agenda. Proper framing of an issue may increase the likelihood that Congress will enact a policy to the president's liking.

While Jones is correct that many elements of the agenda are continuous, he views presidents, to use Kingdon's notion, as problem advocates or entrepreneurs. It may be more accurate, however, to view the president as a "solution entrepreneur" than a "problem entrepreneur." For example, the issues that Ronald Reagan talked about, such as the state of the economy and U. S. relations with the Soviet Union, were on the agenda long before Reagan came to office. His contribution was to change the nature of debate on the solutions to these problems, Reaganomics in the case of economic policy, and a military buildup with regard to Soviet relations. This may be the most important aspect of presidential ability to affect the agenda; not so much in its problems, but in its solutions.

Presidential agenda influence, then, comes from the possibility that the president can affect two of Kingdon's agenda streams—the solution stream and the political stream, in effect coupling these two streams, and attaching them to a problem stream that is already in existence. From this perspective, it is harder for presidents to influence the agenda when a problem stream is not already in place. In a crowd of problem streams, it may be difficult for the president to focus attention on a new one. But presidents may be able to link a new solution stream to an already existing problem stream with relative ease.

Presidential Routes to the Congressional Agenda: Direct Access

Presidential ability to affect the congressional agenda can come about through two routes, directly or indirectly through public opinion. Presidents have many direct access points to the congressional agenda. First, there is an expectation that the president will aid Congress in structuring its agenda. The most important element of this expectation is that the president will submit a program to Congress for consideration. While no formal program document exists, the essence of a program is transmitted to Congress through important and institutionalized presidential activities and reports, most notably the annual State of the Union Address and the President's Economic Report.

Beyond this expectation, the president has access to the congressional agenda through the budget process. This is a structural path that has become increasingly important in recent decades, as the budget and the budget deficit have become overriding concerns, consuming more and more congressional time and effort. It may be the most important direct-access route for the president to the congressional agenda.

Another direct route exists when the president's party controls Congress. Party leaders may become the president's agents in Congress, serving his agenda through their control over majority party resources, such a scheduling.[8] Divided-party control and periods when party is a less potent force in structuring Congress limit presidential use of this avenue to influence the congressional agenda. Also, the process of submitting names of appointees to Congress for confirmation provides the president with another direct access avenue to Congress. These opportunities may also be used to help structure the congressional agenda.

Successful use of these direct-access routes to the congressional agenda is a function of presidential influence on Capitol Hill. Thus, while Reagan was required to submit a budget to Congress for consideration, during the last term of his tenure, his budget was pronounced "dead on arrival." His position was so weakened in the face of opposition control of Congress and his lame-duck status, that his influence was too weakened to affect the agenda very much. The limitation of direct access to affect the congressional agenda comes down to the fact that often direct-access activities, like the budget, are forced on the president. This compulsion limits strategic manipulation of presidential resources, such as timing of initiatives. Presidents must go with what they have at the deadline for action.

One important implication is that the direct path may be more effective with a restrictive agenda than an expansive one. As a case in point, Reagan may have had more success initially in affecting the congressional agenda through this path because he focused on a few items of high priority, like his economic program and the redirection of military spending. Other issues that arose were discarded if they could not fit under the rubric of these themes. For instance, reform of social security posed a problem for the administration, but administration efforts were quickly abandoned, and dealing with social security fell in priority.[9]

In contrast, Carter is reputed to have overloaded Congress and the public with issues. Congress may be able to attend to many issues at one time,[10] as the congressional division of labor in committees allows, but Carter constantly eroded the priority of issues already sent to Congress by suggesting that new proposals held the highest presidential priority. Confusion about administration goals set in, derailing presidential efforts.

With little progress being made on any presidential policy initiative, more effort must be expended by presidents on behalf of favored items just to get them through the policy making process and toward the legislative floors for a vote. Such a troubled path may undermine support for a policy initiative at the floor stages if the policy even makes it that far. In contrast, a policy initiative that gets on to the agenda easily and makes progress across the policymaking process creates a sense of movement or momentum that may carry the policy through to floor adoption, with little action on the part of the president being required. Thus, successful agenda setting by the president may improve probabilities that Congress will adopt the policy.

Presidential Routes to the Congressional Agenda: Indirect Access

Presidents may also gain access to the congressional agenda indirectly, through their ability to influence public opinion. Inasmuch as Congress responds to the public agenda, the ability of the president to structure the public or systemic agenda may enable him to structure, or at least affect, Congress's agenda.

Evidence exists that presidents can affect the public agenda. Cohen finds that presidential attention to issue areas in his State of the Union Address affects public concern with those issue areas.[11] Other studies find that presidential speeches dedicated to specific policy problems and topics affect levels of public attention to those issues, as well as the way that the public thinks about those issues. Presidents, then, may affect the issues of concern to the public and the way those issues are framed in the public consciousness.

Furthermore, unlike direct access, which is so dependent upon presidential resources, presidents seem able to affect the public's agenda irrespective of resources, like popularity. Cohen's study found that popular presidents were not better able at influencing the public agenda than less popular ones.[12] Other studies indicate that presidents may boost their popularity, at least in the short run, when they speak to the public.[13] Presidential resources may accrue when they speak to the public; these may be opportune times to affect the public agenda with eyes on indirectly influencing the congressional agenda.

The question then becomes, does the Congress respond to public opinion in structuring its own agenda? To our knowledge, no such study exists, but other research indicates that Congress is responsive to public opinion, as well as other forces, in making public policies.[14] It might then follow that public opinion affects the structure of the congressional agenda.

Lastly, direct and indirect access to Congress may be linked. For example, the State of the Union Address provides the president with direct access, but inasmuch as the address affects public opinion, it may indirectly affect Congress through its impact on public opinion. This indirect route may reinforce the direct route that the address offers, strengthening the effect of the address on Congress. This basic process of combined access paths may exist for all major speeches and presidential activities that garner widespread public attention.

Going public to set the congressional agenda is an indirect path of influence, though it may be linked to the direct route through such multipurpose activities as the State of the Union Address, which combine direct and indirect paths to Congress. Presidents aim to influence the congressional agenda to affect congressional public policy output. The policymaking progress of some issues may be smoothed because they hold high agenda priority. Other issues might be stalled because of their inability to attain such high priority.

Presidential influence over the congressional agenda aims not only to open the gates for some issues but to block other issues from progressing through the policymaking process. Presidents may try to block some issues by not addressing them, by being inattentive. Often presidential involvement is required for a policy to get onto the agenda. Lack of presidential attention may signal that the problem is not as important as others. Policy advocates seek to prove that their issue is worthy of national attention; getting the presidential "stamp of approval," may be a necessary step in making an issue "national."

Also a president may block one set of issues from reaching the agenda by focusing his attention on a different set of issues. This helps divert attention in one direction versus another, helping to reduce immediate public concern with the diverted issue, though latent concern with that issue may still exist. Thus, presidential influence over the agenda is not only measured in the success that he has in getting Congress to attend to favored issues but also in keeping Congress from attending to less favored issues. Impact over the agenda, is thus, highly strategic, and may have important implications for a broad array of presidential concerns.

The major limitation of the indirect-access route to affecting the congressional agenda is that much may be lost in the translation process. The public's understanding of issues may not perfectly reflect the president's under-standing. This lack of information, attention, and interest may undermine the ability of the president to inject his more complex understanding of issues into the body politic. More important, the public may present Congress with vague or ambiguous cues about their own policy concerns. This may weaken the presidential element in that public message to Congress.

As a hypothetical example, the president may focus on a single economic problem, such as inflation. The public response may be not so much to increase concern with inflation as to increase its concern with the economy overall, including inflation. This overall concern with the economy may be transmitted to Congress. While inflation may be an element of that concern, other economic problems may also be included, and inflation may not be the highest-ranked problem to Congress, though it was for the president. Through this route, the president got inflation onto the congressional agenda, but not with the priority that he sought.

The Limits of Going Public for Agenda Setting

Unlike the conventional view of going public, which hints that presidential influence attempts are likely to be successful, we view going public as more problematic. As noted earlier, the indirect path, or going public method, of influencing the congressional agenda, may lose much in the translation process from the presidential agenda, to the public's agenda, to Congress's agenda. Other pitfalls may also befall a president when using the indirect path.

For one, the president's attempts at steering the public's agenda might fail. As Cohen's study indicates, presidential impact over public opinion seems to evaporate quite quickly, except perhaps for foreign relations issues.[15] Public attention is short lived; there are many other factors competing for the public's attention. Successful use of the indirect path to influencing Congress requires that either the effects of presidential steerage of the public's agenda be felt quickly on Congress or that presidents engage in a longer-term campaign to keep the public's attention focused on an issue.

The first intended result, quick impact on Congress, depends on timing. While Congress may naturally become aware of a change in the public mood, there is often a time gap between congressional awareness and congressional action. To use the indirect path for this type of effect, Congress must be able to absorb this new public concern into already existing institutions or into a policy stream that is already flowing in Congress. This type of intended effect, therefore, is best suited when the president can strategically time his appeal to the public to give Congress that extra push on an issue that may already be gaining some credence within the legislature's halls.

Many indirect routes that use the public to get to Congress do not allow such strategic timing because their timing is preset. Discretionary speeches and occasions for presidential influence, when the timing and subject of the presidential activity are left to the president, are better at effecting these quick effects, when so sought, but only when Congress is ripe to act quickly on an issue.

Another important consideration in using the indirect path to influence the congressional agenda is that presidential impact on the public evaporates very quickly. If public pressure on Congress is essential to congressional attention and action on a policy, presidents may have to engage in long-term campaigns that will continually stoke public attention and insulate the public from diversions that may dissipate concern with that issue.

Such campaigns may be risky, as presidents become closely identified with the issue. This heightened presidential leadership activity may begin to resemble direct presidential attempts to influence Congress. One of the virtues of the indirect path to Congress's agenda is that Congress may look upon the issue as emanating from public wellsprings of concern. Congress may not be able to resist such public "pressure." Once Congress begins to notice that public concern is presidentially orchestrated, however, Congress may try to counter presidential leadership with its own attempts at steering public opinion. The virtue of the indirect path is that it is in part stealthy. When presidential leadership becomes so overt that this stealthiness is lost, the indirect path loses its advantages and redounds to a matter of presidential influence over Congress, something the indirect path has tried to go around.

Another cost of the indirect path is that failure to effect a desired result may erode the president's leadership reputation. This is doubly significant if the president is engaging in a campaign to steer public attention to an issue. Public support may not be crucial to the president's ability to set the agenda, especially if employing the indirect path, as relevant agenda-setting activities tend to have the impact of boosting public support for the president. Thus, when presidents are unable to move the public in agenda-setting exercises, presidents are not able to explain that failure by pointing to a lack of public support or low popularity levels. Instead, other presidential resources much closer to the president himself, such as his reputation, may suffer.

All presidents enter office being able to draw upon the natural resource reserves that the office bestows on them. But as the administration ages, more and more judgment about the president is based upon the incumbent's experiences, not the office's attributes. When presidents lose the reputation as effective leaders, especially in agenda-setting activities, they may become quite vulnerable. They may look presidentially "incompetent"; consequently, they may be less able to influence the public's agenda. Jimmy Carter may have suffered from such a reputational deficit, and as such he may have been unable to sway the public to his way of thinking about public issues. The failure of the famous "malaise" speech may be one example.

A president who loses such a reputation may be irrelevant to political debate. To ensure his agenda leadership reputation, presidents must be strategic about trying to set the agenda. The president's ability to set the agenda is not foreordained nor is it a constant; it is variable and problematic, as we have been arguing. Moreover, presidential attempts at influencing the public's agenda may meet countermobilization by opponents who either favor other issues or ways of defining the issue that differ from the president's. Thus, there is always a risk when presidents try to set the agenda that opponents will challenge him. They may successfully block his agenda-setting attempts, they may be able to reconfigure the agenda after his attempt at setting the agenda, and/or they may redefine the issue that the president was promoting. Each action that a president takes to alter the agenda poses the risk of successful challenges; presidential mobilization may ironically stir countermobilization. Again, the point is that presidents must be strategic about their attempts to set the agenda.

The costs and potential benefits of going public for agenda setting suggests that such activity on the part of the president is strategic and thus purposive. Presidents have many choices to make in setting the agenda, and choice is not only a matter of substance. Presidents must calculate which pathway to Congress is best: direct, indirect, or some combination. "Going public," the indirect path, is not always the best option. There are costs involved, as detailed above.

The Persuasive Task

The most commonly discussed strategy for presidential influence over the legislative process is the president's ability to influence the voting of members on legislation before Congress. In this section three distinct components of "going public" are described in how the president goes about influencing members of Congress. While these strategies are designed to demonstrate distinct elements of "going public," the labels applied to them are drawn from Richard Neustadt, reflecting that the differences between the approaches are not new, they have simply been overlooked.[16] One distinction within the persuasive task is whether the president turns to the public to promote himself or his policies. Kernell describes going public as "a strategy whereby a president promotes *himself and his policies* in Washington by appealing to the American public for support" (emphasis added).[17] The strategy of promoting presidential policy is distinct from promoting the president himself, however. The strategy by which the president attempts to promote issues we term "merchandising" while attempts to build influence in Congress by building support among the public we term "public prestige." We also propose a second distinction of whether the president attempts to influence the legislative process through appeals to the public as a whole or through more select constituencies. This "special publics" strategy, while less visible, is often used by the White House and represents another approach to going public.

Public Prestige

Richard Neustadt describes the link between the public standing or "prestige" of the president and his success or influence in Congress.[18] The strategy of building public prestige emphasizes enhancing the public's opinion of the president and using presidential popularity to prod reluctant members of Congress.

Nixon's dramatic decline in popularity associated with the Watergate scandal provides some evidence on the limited impact of public opinion on congressional support and influence. During his second term, Nixon's approval rating, as reported by Gallup polls, dropped from 67 percent in January 1973 to 23 percent at the time of his resignation in August 1974.[19] The Nixon White House publicly discounted the impact of Nixon's lack of popularity on their legislative package. Bill Timmons, a Nixon aide, argued that Watergate "may have affected some individual votes, but members' votes reflect their state, their constituency, their party and institutions more than they reflect scandals and things like that."[20]

The impact of a fall like Nixon's is limited by the nature of a personal or political scandal. Much of Nixon's lack of popularity in 1973 and 1974 resulted from reservations about his character, rather from concerns about the legislative proposals of his administration; decline in the polls implicated his character more than his policies. This is not to say that a tarnished character is not irrelevant but that it creates a different dynamic in the legislative process than policy-related disapproval. Nixon's character-based popularity problems undermined his personal credibility and his general bargaining position with Congress, but Watergate had little to do with most votes that members cast.

Public prestige is the linkage most often tested in political science, with mixed results. Some researchers have uncovered evidence of a public prestige effect. Ostrom and Simon use a structural equation to demonstrate a dynamic or reciprocal linkage between presidential success in Congress and popular support. They estimate this effect at a three-point decline in roll-call victories for each ten-point decline in presidential popularity. Rivers and

Rose use a simultaneous equations model to suggest a slightly more complex, dynamic relationship in which a 1 percent change in approval generates a 1 point increase in legislative success. More recently, Brace and Hinckley have uncovered a similar effect in which presidents gained 7.5 percent in victories for each 10 percentage points they get in the polls. In contrast, research by Bond and Fleisher suggests that as presidential prestige increases, support increases only among the president's partisans and that partisan opponents actually responded negatively to increased presidential prestige. Edwards and Collier and Sullivan also failed to find any empirical linkage.[21]

One of the reasons for the uncertain empirical evidence behind the public prestige linkage is that there is no solid theoretical linkage. Members of Congress have little reason to believe that any popularity the president might enjoy reflects on most of the legislation that comes before them. George Bush's success in the Gulf War and the following surge in popularity had little connection to domestic legislative issues such as cable regulation, and personal scandals like Watergate may damage a president's personal popularity but not tarnish legislative concerns. Success in Congress can build presidential popularity, but the two are often independent enough to make a strong relationship unlikely. Further, the existence of divided government suggests that citizens may not always see a link between the presidents and members of Congress when they vote. Members of Congress in the 1980s watched as Reagan's popularity failed to produce a Republican majority in the House or protect a Republican majority in the Senate.

The political reality of district concerns suggests that most votes will be independent of a president's popularity. Members of Congress, however, may use votes of little or no interest to their district to distance themselves from a president, especially an unpopular one. Clearly, the political reach of a popular president is neither absolute or automatic.

Merchandising

The primary focus of the research that has followed Kernell has focused on White House attempts to build popular support for particular issues. Much of this literature seems to have been motivated more by the presidency of Ronald Reagan than by the specifics of Kernell's book. Reagan came to Washington expecting little support from the forces inside Washington, planning instead to turn to the people for support on issues. Thus, the Reagan team considered public appeals an integral part of its legislative strategy.

This kind of support differs from building public prestige because it is more selective than a general prestige effect. Presidents who engage in the strategy of advancing particular issues do not focus on building a reserve of public approval that can be drawn out when needed. Instead, support is specific to a policy and may appear and disappear quickly around critical legislative votes. One White House veteran described to us presidential popularity as being capital that is not always "drawn out":

> Popularity can be important, but it's overrated. There are caveats that run both ways. . . . The more popular a president is the more they want to be with him on important issues. Obviously, in order to make that work the president must be willing to go to the public and draw out that political capital because their support is basically what influences members.

Too often in the existing political science literature presidential popularity is taken as a force in Washington politics. Hovering over the dome of the Capitol, presidential popularity protects presidential allies and sends potential enemies scurrying for cover. When presidential disapproval is high, it gives strength to the president's opponents and casts doubts on the work of the president's friends. But in a representative system, the president's standing in the polls is only one indicator of voters' sentiments. Just as pilots may check a windsock before flying, members of Congress may check presidential standing before taking sides on an issue. The windsock itself is not important; the broader conditions that it reflects are. Members of Congress are not reluctant to disturb a popular president; they are reluctant to challenge the public sentiments behind that popularity.

Therefore, when the president goes to the public with an issue, he is attempting to connect more directly with the constituency pressures that influence members. By going public the president puts the weight of the office behind a piece of legislation, but more important, the president can also put the weight of the public behind the legislation.

The president's attempt to mobilize the public behind legislation might be labeled *merchandising*. Merchandising represents a theoretically distinct form of influence from prestige. A general prestige effect involves a dynamic created by the link between citizens and the president, while a policy-specific appeal such as merchandising relies more on a dynamic between citizens and issues. Kernell has suggested that going public undermines the legitimacy of others in the system as the president attempts to usurp the representative role of members of Congress.[22] This need not always be true. If the president uses his popularity to intimidate other representatives of the people, then he is supplanting their representative role. If, on the other hand, the president is advocating policies in a manner that makes it difficult for members of Congress to oppose popular proposals, he is presenting a different challenge to others.

The White House's use of an issue-based public opinion strategy may help explain why presidential popularity has not consistently produced statistically significant links to success in Congress. While presidential popularity or prestige is a constant force that operates continually in the background, specific appeals for support on policies are sporadic, even for enthusiastic practitioners like Reagan. While there may be a general prestige effect, the skilled use of public persuasion can be a powerful tool in selected cases and further, serve as a deterrent to future political resistance.

Leading the public on an issue can be either a way of persuading members to change their vote or a way of making casting a difficult vote easier. Kernell has argued that "going public fails to extend benefits for compliance, but freely imposes costs for noncompliance."[23] Nevertheless, as one member of the Reagan congressional liaison staff pointed out to us, Reagan was able to offer members political cover by making issues popular.

Reagan's heavy use of using going public may have numbed presidential opponents to some of the fallout of going public that Kernell describes.[24] One Democratic congressional leader explained that coalition building can continue in the charged atmosphere created by going public because there is an understanding that there is a "theater of politics" and members of Congress understand the need of their opponents to draw lines between the parties. Underneath the contentiousness there is an understanding of the process.

Reagan's ability to appeal to the public was seen by some as creating a dramatic shift in power. Jeffrey Tulis warned that the Reagan presidency had completed a transformation of the presidency that was now empowered by rhetoric.[25] The impact of merchandising is often overstated. Congressional Democrats were ready to point out that Reagan spoke to the nation on Latin American policy several times but that he lost in Congress. One Democratic congressional leader described Reagan's success in Congress by saying, "He had a window when he was great, beyond that. . . ."

Reagan went public in part because it made use of his skills as an actor. However, the reasons for the rise of going public has more to do with the changes in Washington, and the rise of going public is a reflection of presidential weakness rather than strength. As Kernell described the presidency's needs, "As Washington comes to depend on looser, more individualistic political relations, presidents searching for strategies that work will increasingly go public."[26]

Barefoot Sanders, who headed congressional relations for President Johnson, suggested that more intense media coverage has made it more difficult for the president and Congress to communicate privately and that it is tempting for them to communicate through these public channels. "That practice clearly imperils the maintenance of the close relations which are basic to effective executive-congressional relations."[27] Kernell raises a similar point when he describes how bargaining becomes more difficult because, having stated their position publicly, it is more difficult for both sides to accept a compromise.[28] Thus, the intense coverage given to the White House and Capitol Hill has reduced the flexibility that both sides need to bargain.

Special Publics

Presidents need not turn to the entire citizenry to apply pressure on Congress. The general public may not support the president's legislation or, while supportive, may remain too disinterested to be motivated enough to become a factor. In this case the White House may attempt to mobilize what might be called "special publics."[29] With the rise of interest groups and the personalization of politics in Washington, working with special publics has become a more important strategy for presidents. Moreover, it offers an alternative way of reaching Congress for a president not overly effective with appeals to the broad mass public.

A clear example of this can be found in the Carter White House, which sought to bring in a large portion of the interest-group universe and to bring grassroots pressure to bear on Congress. The Carter public liaison operation exclusively focused on legislative priorities. As one Carter staffer told us: "All of our work was building support for issues." These operations were run by the Office of Public Liaison, with Anne Wexler as its head.

Her office created an outreach program designed to contact key constituents and activate potential allies, convert opponents to the administration's point of view, or neutralize those who could not be converted. Thus, the Carter administration would bring in people from "out of town" (their phrase for constituents) for White House briefings by the president, senior White House staff, and cabinet members. A reception in the State Dining Room would follow each meeting. Wexler described the purpose of their outreach programs: "Our job is to create lobbyists." While not formally lobbyists, these "out of towners" would often go directly to Congress or to an organized interest, which would then bring the president's message "indirectly" to Congress.

At other times, the outreach efforts were designed to "activate" individuals who shared the Administration's policy views. While this was usually done by staff or the president speaking to large groups in the White House, occasionally the president talked one-on-one with important individuals. On occasion, the White House attempted to convert opponents into allies, sometimes successfully. One member of the staff reported that "In many,

many cases people would come in, especially on the international issues but also on energy or urban policy issues, people came with a preconceived notion, and changed their minds. And they'd go out to the press and say afterward, 'I talked to the president. I've decided I'm going to support him.'" Just as important as converting opponents was to neutralize their potential opposition and, in the process, provide political cover for members of Congress to, if not vote with the president, not oppose him either.

Legislators benefited from this strategy because it provided an opportunity to diffuse potential problems. Members of the president's party are usually willing to help him if the electoral risks are low. By having key contributors or constituents brought into the White House, members of Congress could gain political cover if the White House succeeded in converting or at least neutralizing opposition in the district, thereby reducing the electoral risks of supporting the president on controversial issues.

The Office of Public Liaison was often successful because it built support for presidential legislation in a way that did not interfere with the electoral security of members of Congress. Rather than leave members of Congress to explain their decision to support the president's policies, by going to constituents first, such outreach programs lowered the risk of supporting the president.

Discussion

Neustadt describes the relationship between the president, the public, and Congress by discussing how the president and Congress share their publics:

> Most members of the Washington community depend upon outsiders to support them. The dependence may be as direct as votes, or it may be as indirect as passive tolerance. The Dependent men must take account of popular reactions to their actions. What their publics may think of them becomes a factor, therefore, in deciding how to deal with desires of a President. His prestige enters into that decision; their publics are part of his.[30]

In this chapter, we have suggested that their are several distinct ways in which members of Congress share their public with the presidents and tried to open up the idea of "going public" first introduced by Kernell. In doing this, we suggested that there are many different versions of going public, with different objectives or goals. Also, as our presentation indicates, the success or impact of going public varies. It is not always a successful strategy of influence. Its success depends upon context, presidential resources, and strategic sensitivity. In this sense, the maxims that Neustadt offered in his ground-breaking work of three decades ago still ring loudly, and we may thus link going public to the behavioral model that Neustadt advanced. Going public is thus a behavioral strategy of influence.

Kernell's model of going public suggests several things. First, going public arose as a method of influencing Congress because the structure of politics in Washington atomized, from what Kernell terms institutional pluralism to individual pluralism. Going public became an adaptation to that new environment, a way of pressuring many members of Congress simultaneously. One consequence of going public, according to Kernell, is that the give-and-take of bargaining under the older institutional regime suffered, and going public has come to look like presidential coercion of Congress through public pressure. This has stiffened the relationship between the president and Congress, making it more brittle and less open to negotiated compromise, where both can come out looking like winners.

Another consequence is that many have come to view Kernell as suggesting that going public, being the most effective strategy open to presidents, is an effective strategy. This is compounded by the fact that so many in academia and Washington look to presidential popularity as a mark of his potential political influence. Going public is linked to presidential popularity. So it goes, presidents may build popularity through going-public activities, and this popular pressure will move Congress. We take a more probabilistic view of going public. The success of going public depends on the objectives or goals of the activity, presidential resources or context, and the strategic environment.

We identify three goals to going public: agenda setting, mechanizing of policies before Congress, and enhancing personal presidential prestige. Kernell's discussion focuses on the middle category, that of merchandising. Presidents, however, who successfully set the agenda may not need to merchandize policies for Congress to enact them.

Second, presidential resources may affect the likely impact of going-public activities. Two resources may be especially important: majority control of Congress and presidential popular support, expressed either as majority electoral support and/or popularity. Here we find an important irony. Presidents with resources such as these may not have to engage in going-public activities, but when they do, they are likely to be successful. Moreover, resource-holding presidents may be able to affect Congress through the agenda-setting mode, and not need to merchandise.

Similarly, minority presidents may be less successful in both agenda setting and merchandizing, and thus are forced to go public to build up their prestige, the resource that might enable them to set the agenda and merchandize policies. But little research has uncovered presidents being able to enhance their prestige structurally. Going public to build prestige has impacts, but those effects are short-lived. Moreover, the more that an unpopular or less popular president goes to the public well to enhance his own popularity, the less effective such calls for support will be.

Third, the strategic environment of going public is an important element in its potential for impact. Two factors seem crucial: the ability of presidents to manipulate the timing of going public and the institutional ability of Congress to digest those messages. Many activities with going-public implications have forced deadlines. These may be less effective forums than those in which the president can time his going public. The public may not be ripe for his call, its agenda may be too full, its mood may be antagonistic. When a president can determine the timing of his going public, such activity may be more successful.

Moreover, Congress must be institutionally able to "hear" the public and the president and then possess the resources to take action. A Congress unprepared may be willing but unable to act. For example, Carter's troubles with his energy package, despite going public, may have faltered because Congress was not organized to deal with the issue. A new committee structure had to be created. In an environment of many issues competing for attention, a committee system structured to accept issues on the terms that presidents define them is an important element in the success of going public, or any presidential influence attempt, for that matter.

Thus, going public is not a strategy of influence with a certainty of success. To judge its success, presidents must define their objectives, correctly mobilize their resources, and correctly read the strategic environment. Put into this framework, going public is an even richer concept than Kernell first offered. Our effort at building and expanding on the concept is but a first attempt. More work in the direction of specifying and elaborating on going public still needs to be done.

Notes

1. Samuel Kernell, *Going Public: New Strategies of Presidential Leadership,* 2nd ed. (Washington, DC: CQ Press, 1993).

2. Ibid., 12.

3. But see Charles O. Jones, *The Presidency in a Separated System* (Washington, DC: Brookings Institution, 1995); and Paul C. Light, *The President's Agenda* (Baltimore: Johns Hopkins University Press, 1982).

4. John W. Kingdon, *Agendas, Alternatives and Public Policies* (Boston: Little, Brown 1984), 25.

5. Ibid., 26–28; also see Mark A. Peterson, *Legislating Together: The White House and Capitol Hill from Eisenhower to Reagan* (Cambridge: Harvard University Press, 1990).

6. Bruce Miroff, "Monopolizing the Public Space: The President as a Problem for Democratic Politics" in T. Cronin, ed., *Rethinking the Presidency* (Boston: Little, Brown, 1982), 218–32.

7. Jones, *The Presidency in a Separated System,* ch. 5.

8. Kingdon, *Agendas, Alternatives, and Public Policies,* 28.

9. Paul C. Light, *Artful Work: The Politics of Social Security Reform* (New York: Random House, 1985).

10. Frank R. Baumgartner and Bryan D. Jones, *Agendas and Instability in American Politics* (Chicago: University of Chicago Press, 1993).

11. Jeffrey E. Cohen, "Presidential Rhetoric and the Public Agenda," *American Journal of Political Science* 39 (1995): 87–107.

12. Ibid.

13. Paul Brace and Barbara Hinckley, *Follow the Leader* (New York: Basic Books, 1992); Lyn Ragsdale, "The Politics of Presidential Speechwriting," *American Political Science Review* 78 (1984): 971–84.

14. James A. Stimson, Michael B. MacKuen, and Robert S. Erikson, "Dynamic Representation," *American Political Science Review* 89 (1995): 543–65.

15. Cohen, "Presidential Rhetoric."

16. Richard Neustadt, *Presidential Power and the Modern Presidents* (New York: Free Press, 1990).

17. Kernell, *Going Public,* 2.

18. Neustadt, *Presidential Power,* ch. 2.

19. Gary King and Lyn Ragsdale, *The Elusive Executive: Discovering Statistical Patterns in the Presidency* (Washington, DC: CQ Press, 1988), 302.

20. Congressional Quarterly, "The White House Persuaders: Timmons and his Team," *Congressional Quarterly Weekly Report,* December 1, 1973, 3122.

21. Charles W. Ostrom Jr. and Dennis M. Simon, "Promise and Performance: A Dynamic Model of Presidential Popularity," *American Political Science Review* 79 (1985): 334–58; Douglas Rivers and Nancy L. Rose, "Passing the President's Program: Public Opinion and Presidential Influence in Congress," *American Journal of Political Science* 29 (1985): 183–96; Brace and Hinckley, *Follow the Leader;* Jon Bond and Richard Fleisher, "The Limits of Presidential Popularity as a Source of Influence in the US House," *Legislative Studies Quarterly* 5 (1980): 69–78; Bond and Fleisher, *The President in the Legislative Arena* (Chicago: University of Chicago Press, 1990); Ken Collier and Terry Sullivan, "New Evidence Undercutting the Linkage of Approval with Presidential Support and Influence," *Journal of Politics* 57 (1995): 197–209; George Edwards, *At the Margins: Presidential Leadership in Congress* (New Haven: Yale University Press, 1989).

22. Kernell, *Going Public,* 4.

23. Ibid., 3.

24. Ibid.

25. Jeffrey K. Tulis, *The Rhetorical Presidency* (Princeton, NJ: Princeton University Press, 1987), 189.

26. Kernell, *Going Public,* 31.

27. Barefoot Sanders, "Congressional-Executive Relations during the 1960s," in W. Livingston, L. Dodd, and R. Schott, eds., *The Presidency and the Congress: A Shifting Balance of Power?* (Austin, TX: Lyndon B. Johnson School of Public Affairs, 1979), 299.

28. Kernell, *Going Public,* ch. 2.

29. Neustadt, *Presidential Power,* 77.

30. Ibid., 73.

4

Interest Groups:
A Doubly Dynamic Relationship

Joseph A. Pika

Interest groups have long been viewed as an integral part of the congressional and bureaucratic policymaking processes but have only recently been recognized as significant actors in presidential stages of the policy process as well. Since the presidency of Franklin D. Roosevelt, the conduct of relations between presidents and interest groups has been transformed. Once the province of party leaders and agency officials, interest-group liaison has now been brought into the presidency with responsibility given to members of the White House and Executive Office staffs. In this way, presidents have ensured that they can be more attentive to the programmatic needs and demands of organized interests and can also enlist groups as members of their electoral and governing coalitions. Starting with FDR, staff assistants developed increasingly well-defined responsibilities for *interest-group liaison* until a separate staff unit for *public liaison* (Office of Public Liaison) emerged during the Ford administration to take its position next to the congressional relations and the press offices as specialized links to outside constituencies.[1] Since Ford, each administration has maintained such an "outreach" capability for interest groups, although the status of the unit has varied.[2]

The courtship has not been totally one-sided. Some groups, especially those who represent historically unorganized interests, turned to presidents because they had no place else to go with their problems. More established groups found that as policymaking increasingly came to be centralized in the Executive Office of the President, the inability to influence presidential initiatives or to know the details of their gestation placed them at a disadvantage. It was advantageous, if not essential, to include the presidency on their list of targets to influence while continuing to pursue their traditional connections in Congress and the bureaucracy. Interest-group opportunities to exercise leverage over presidents also grew during the past four decades: social movements took advantage of national media coverage to dramatize their concerns, and important changes in the campaign finance laws enabled established interests to influence elections in new ways.[3]

Just because the conduct of these relations has been changed, however, does not mean the relationships themselves have been transformed. As in the past, most analysts use an exchange framework to illustrate and analyze relations with interest groups, the same framework used to study interactions between presidents and other centers of power in the American political system.[4] Nonetheless, some scholars have argued that there has been a qualitative change in the president's connections with interest groups. As Stephen Skowronek suggests, the "political universe" faced by twentieth-century presidents "is in every way more fully organized and more densely inhabited" than it was previously.[5] As a result, presidents needed to negotiate more actively with congressional committees and bureaucrats while "directly soliciting support from major client groups in the society at large."[6] This macroperspective takes one beyond the day-to-day political exchanges that constitute the activity of interest-group relations to emphasize more fundamental implications for the larger political system.

To understand the full array of relations between presidents and interest groups, one needs an analytic framework that can address changes in both the presidency and the interest-group community over time. In short, it needs to be *doubly dynamic*. Such a framework cannot be time bound and it must seek to explain as well as describe contemporary patterns. Suggesting the outlines of such a framework is the purpose of this chapter.

Existing Frameworks

Based on an extensive review of the literature, one can identify four frameworks that have guided academic accounts of presidential relations with interest groups: exchange, modal patterns, organizational evolution, and state theory. Each is briefly described below.

Exchange

Because bargaining for mutual support is the quintessential feature of group contacts with presidents, it should not be surprising to find this as the explicit or implicit framework used in virtually all accounts. As Bradley

Patterson, a long-time participant observer of the Washington community, explains in his discussion of public liaison, "To the lobbyists, the White House is a target. To the White House, interest-group power is presidential opportunity."[7] Many accounts offer a detailed analysis of how presidents seek to enlist interest-group assistance in pursuing their goals. For example, Michael Grossman and Martha Kumar's account of public liaison in the Carter and Reagan administrations centers on the roles filled by White House aides responsible for managing the ongoing relationships between the two sides to a series of bargains. From the White House perspective, essential tasks are performed by four types of aides:

> *Markers* deal with the accumulated credits held by groups that supported the president's nomination and election. *Communicants* establish a basis of shared interest with groups that the president needs in his ongoing governmental and political efforts. *Constructors* seek group support for policy campaigns, particularly those that involve congressional lobbying. *Brokers* make agreements with groups for the president and intercede with him on behalf of interest groups [emphasis added].[8]

Although the Office of Public Liaison (OPL) is central to these relationships, some of the roles are either shared or largely fulfilled by aides located in other White House units.

Other work has identified functions performed by the group liaison staff members—congressional lobbying, policymaking, campaigning, and casework—but recognizes that liaison is maintained for two types of exchanges:

> Wooing group support for the administration's governing coalition is no less important than maintaining the support of groups who were part of its electoral coalition, and the White House is usually interested in finding ways to attract those groups whose allegiance to the opposition is marginal. To build these coalitions, an administration must be willing to embrace the group's legislative or policy goals. . . .[9]

It should not be surprising to learn that most of the accounts that emphasize exchange are based on elite interviews and/or use of administration documents at presidential libraries. Both data sources are likely to emphasize the exchange perspective of presidents and their aides.

Modal Patterns

By far, the most ambitious effort to create a conceptual and analytic framework for analyzing group interaction with the presidency was undertaken by Mark Peterson. Unlike virtually all other studies of these interactions, Peterson provides data from both sides of the relationship; elite interviews are supplemented with results from an extensive survey of interest groups centered in Washington, D.C. that reveals patterns of "selective interaction" between groups and the presidency, that is, groups interact with different parts of the EOP staff and at varying levels of frequency. "Regular, ongoing interactions" were maintained by the Reagan White House with only a "limited number of groups."[10] A third of the groups included in the survey had no White House relationship at all, while half had at least occasional contact.

Peterson suggests four ideal-typical patterns of interaction between presidents and interest groups based on the breadth and substance of White House ties: contacts can be more or less inclusive (breadth) and have a programmatic or representational focus (substantive focus). The resulting four-cell table is intended to capture the range of general approaches to interest-group interactions and is also used to characterize the nature of interactions during some administrations (see chart).

		Breadth of Group Interactions	
		Exclusive	Inclusive
Substantive Focus of Group Interactions	Programmatic	Governing party	Consensus building
	Representational	Outreach	Legitimization

"These approaches derive from the context of a particular president's tenure in office and reflect the political and organizational biases of the individual chief executive." *Legitimization* is an effort to use group relations as a way "to solidify the president's image and prestige among the general public"[11] in conjunction with the kind of media strategy that was prominent during the Ford administration. *Consensus building*, exemplified by the Johnson administration, seeks to build "broad political consensus" resting on an equally broad array of programmatic initiatives designed to satisfy as many group demands as possible. *Outreach* provides "representation to segments of the president's political coalition that otherwise lack close ties to the government establishment," as found particularly prominent in the Carter administration. *Governing party* is focused on "partisan coalition building for the purpose of achieving programmatic goals,"[12] as was found in the efforts of OPL during both the Carter and Reagan administrations when groups were enlisted in cooperative lobbying efforts.

Peterson acknowledges that most administrations in the modern era will simultaneously pursue multiple forms of interest-group liaison. For example, Reagan's aides initially demonstrated a governing-party focus but also engaged in legitimization and outreach. Nonetheless, Peterson seems to suggest that administrations reveal a dominant pattern or characterization. An administration's emphasis may also change over time as circumstances alter, for example, conservative outreach became the dominant mode during the latter part of Reagan's term as governing party and legitimization diminished in importance.

Ultimately, Peterson suggests that as party leader and "facilitator of group coalition building," presidents now serve as the common link between parties and interest groups.

> Modern interest-group liaison also has much to do with how we should interpret the dynamic relationship between interest groups and the party system and between the interrelated group and party systems and the society they together reflect.[13]

Organizational Evolution

Charles Walcott and Karen Hult have examined the emergence and persistence of constituency outreach as a staff assignment in the White House with particular attention to "three clusters of explanatory factors": environmental, presidential choice, and organizational.[14] Although recognizing the significance of environmental changes—the proliferation of groups, the decline of political parties, the centralization of policymaking in the White House and decentralization of power in Congress—Walcott and Hult are convinced that "the targets of staff outreach generally reflected presidential strategies and interests as well as environmental changes."[15] Their detailed study of how presidents from Roosevelt through Johnson established and maintained ties to civil rights groups, business, and labor illustrates their general framework.

"Staff outreach to civil rights groups extended beyond seeking fairer treatment of blacks; it sought to provide direct links to presidents, secure electoral support from blacks and, in many cases, contain black protest."[16] The explicit attention provided to such groups by members of the Roosevelt and Truman staffs markedly declined under Eisenhower as political conditions changed: civil rights advocates had turned their attention to the courts as a means to address their demands; the role of black voters in the Republican coalition had become ambiguous; and southern congressmen were strongly opposed to civil rights initiatives. Moreover, the president was reluctant to pursue a civil rights agenda. In contrast, numerous members of the Kennedy staff dealt with civil rights during a period when "incremental change" was sought "through low-visibility alternatives in executive branch

practices."[17] Under Johnson, however, the White House staff's involvement
in civil rights matters shrank dramatically when "more sweeping legislative
actions" and efforts "to quell racial violence" came to the forefront.[18]

In contrast to civil rights groups, "both business and labor had other
places in the executive branch and the political parties to turn to with their
demands, and most administrations had officials with longer-term ties to
such interests."[19] As a result, successive White House staffs were intermit-
tently attentive, occasionally mounting cooperative lobbying ventures with
their "natural" allies: business groups for the Republican and labor for the
Democratic presidents.

Because this first volume in what is likely to become a series of White
House staff studies ends at the Johnson presidency, the impact of organizational factors is less significant than it is likely to become during the period
following official organization of OPL in 1974–75. The work of both Pika
and Peterson has suggested the importance of "institutional structure and
traditions."[20] By conceptualizing liaison as an organizational phenomenon
shaped by multiple influences, Walcott and Hult introduce an important
perspective to help understand the evolution of a White House staff activity.
Their comparison of staff relations to two interest-group sectors also
illustrates some of the variety one is likely to find arising from differences
in the group universe.

State Theory

Taken together, the work of Stephen Skowronek and Benjamin Ginsberg, Walter Mebane and Martin Shefter presents yet another perspective on presidency-
group relations. Anticipating Skowronek's focus on how presidents can remake
the political order in which they serve, Ginsberg and Shefter closely examined
the reconstruction of Reagan's political environment wrought by his administration. "Rather than shape his policies to meet the demands of society, Reagan
undertook to reconstitute society to fit his policies."[21]

> ... the groups and forces with which U.S. chief executives contend ulti-
> mately are a product not simply of autonomous social processes but also of
> struggles between presidents and their opponents. In the United States it is
> through conflicts between the presidency and other political institutions that
> society is shaped by politics.[22]

For Skowronek, Reagan was a president of "reconstruction" who, like Jefferson, Jackson, Lincoln, and the second Roosevelt, repudiated the "commitments of ideology and interest" inherited from the previous political regime.[23]

Ginsberg and Shefter elaborate on how Reagan was able to transform the political identities of several established groups (white southerners, urban ethnics, and middle-class voters), create new social and political forces by dividing elements of the New Deal coalition, and construct new interests by uniting previously disparate elements—religious conservatives, the bourgeoisie, Main Street, and Wall Street. What emerges is a sophisticated portrait, later updated for the Bush and Clinton eras, of how presidents relate to societal forces more generally.[24] Ultimately, these authors see Republicans and Democrats substituting "competitive entrenchment" in the federal bureaucracy for "mass electoral mobilization as a means of securing power in the United States."[25] The Democrats have become entrenched in agencies overseeing social and regulatory programs and the Republicans in the military and national security apparatus. "Entrenchment in governmental institutions provides modern political parties and interest groups with access to public resources without requiring them to engage in full-scale electoral mobilization."[26]

This perspective recognizes that presidents are not merely subject to their political environment but also have the capacity to reshape those conditions in fundamental ways. At a minimum, this framework enables us to see how presidents and groups can have reciprocal effects on each other and how they relate to the larger constellation of political forces in the U.S. system.

Seeking a Comprehensive Framework

Is it possible to construct a comprehensive framework for studying interest-group relations with presidents over time? As the preceding discussion demonstrates, analysts approach the problem with distinctive concerns—to illustrate the contemporary political process, to identify major patterns of interaction, to trace the evolution of a staff activity, and to reveal the more fundamental structure of state-societal relations. What will be presented here is a conceptual framework that emphasizes characteristics and potential sources of change at three levels of analysis: the political system, the interest-group community, and the presidency. Each level is discussed separately.[27]

Systemic Level

Analysts have identified several critical factors at the systemic level. Three are highlighted here: the relationship between organized interests and political parties; the centralization of decision making; and the policy agenda. These factors should be viewed as permissive rather than determinative causes; that is, they establish the context within which presidential and group choices will be exercised. In this sense, they are necessary but not sufficient for understanding the nature of these relationships.[28]

Alternative Intermediation Structures

Perhaps the most important systemic factor is the relationship of groups to other intermediation structures in the political system, particularly political parties. To what extent do parties, during a political era, function as the principal structure for linking groups to elections and political elites?[29] Clearly this relationship has varied over time, reflecting changes in the potential for communication and travel, the capacity for organizational development, and the resulting extensiveness or "density" of organized group efforts. To use one grand historical account of these changes, Skowronek sees the transition from a "partisan" to a "pluralist" period of politics hinging on the emergence of a powerful national state and the simultaneous organization of national interests.[30] Parties vary in their effectiveness as a means to articulate group demands and channel their political activities, a point demonstrated in the vast literature on reforms of the presidential nomination process since 1968. In this regard, it is not surprising to discover that all administrations in the postreform era have heightened direct presidential attention to mediating group interests. Although an explicit *public liaison* office was first organized under Ford, it was originally advanced as a proposal under Nixon, whose administration was the first to operate in the postreform context.[31]

Reforms adopted over the past three decades altered the connection between political parties and interest groups in two respects. In the wake of presidential selection reforms, candidate-based coalitions came to eclipse party-based coalitions, making it clear to interest groups where their electoral efforts should be directed. In addition, campaign finance reforms adopted during the 1970s enhanced interest-group independence and their ability to compete directly with parties in the electoral process. Groups became more influential as a source of funding for both congressional and presidential candidates, a shift that was quickly recognized for congressional elections. Although groups explored the presidential possibilities more slowly, it is now apparent that they have the capacity to mount independent efforts on behalf of presidential candidates and to contribute "soft money" for nominal "party-building" activities that have become thinly veiled efforts in behalf of the presidential ticket. In the wake of 1996 campaign finance scandals, scholars are likely to devote more attention to how groups use their growing financial importance to influence presidential elections.[32]

Location of Decision Making

Influence over decision making is not fixed in American politics. During some periods of our history it has resided mainly in the states, rather than at the national level. At other times it seems to have resided primarily in Congress or the permanent bureaucracy, rather than in the presidency. Although such grand characterizations of the policymaking process are dangerously imprecise, they may be especially important for understanding interest-group relations with government. A traditional observation holds that "interest groups tend to gravitate toward the effective centers of power in a given political system."[33] There is widespread agreement that, starting with Kennedy and Johnson, presidents have centralized federal policymaking in the White House,[34] although congressional assertiveness and divided government have imposed limits on such efforts. In some respects, Congress may even have encouraged the White House focus by delegating broad policy responsibilities to the president and establishing specialized policy units within the Executive Office. Thus, interest groups will find it advantageous to cultivate contacts in the presidency, and presidents will exhibit the same needs for information and support evidenced by officials in other institutions.

One would therefore expect group interactions with the presidency to vary according to the office's importance in national policymaking. In particular, one should find significant differences between the periods before and after 1921, when presidents were given a critical role in creating the national budget.

Policy Agenda

A factor closely related to the role of institutions in policymaking is the shifting nature of the policy agenda. Some issues are more likely to receive presidential attention than others. In particular, "the president is likely to play a more important role in issues of moderately high visibility, which are often characterized by conflict among contending interests."[35] In the contemporary period, these are likely to include redistributive and regulatory policies, where consequences are viewed in zero-sum terms as well as in policy areas where presidential discretion is relatively high, for example, international trade. During other historical periods, the policy agenda and associated presidential significance are likely to have differed. Thus, rather than rely on broad generalizations regarding the relative prominence of Congress, the president, or the bureaucracy in policymaking, the consequences for group relationships may vary by policy area.

Interest-Group Community

Students of presidential liaison have devoted remarkably little attention to the activities, perceptions, and structure of the interest-group community. The one major exception is Peterson, whose work presented important findings about group contacts with the White House and other Executive Office units. But even Peterson did not venture very far into this terrain. This section offers preliminary observations on relevant differences among groups, structural features of the interest-group community, and reciprocal effects that the presidency and groups can have on one another.

Group Variation

In light of the enormous differences among interest groups, the challenge is to identify those factors most relevant for studying relations with the president. Peterson identifies several group factors that shape interaction, including Washington representation, a shared partisan association, and resources enabling the group to play a significant role in legislative outcomes. However, both Polsby and Walcott and Hult suggest the importance of a broader distinction between groups organized on traditional grounds—"economic or status needs of their clientele" and geographic compactness—versus the new groups based on militant advocacy of rights (women, blacks, youth, Hispanics, seniors, gays, etc.) and "the mobilization of rectitude," so-called public interest groups such as Common Cause and those associated with Ralph Nader.[36]

The 1960s and 1970s were decades particularly marked by the emergence and political mobilization of such groups, and the White House received a considerable share of their attention. It is clear that much of the group representation that developed in the White House staff over the past half-century centered on including "representatives" of the newly mobilized demographic interests. Groups that perceived themselves as having been previously disadvantaged not only sought appointments in the administration but also a White House contact person. These actions serve to "confer legitimacy on groups and on their political claims—and to withdraw it."[37] As a position with unusual symbolic power in American political life, the presidency became the preeminent source of legitimization in the political system.

Some attention has been devoted to the interaction between presidents and social movements. Bruce Miroff used relations between the Johnson White House and the civil rights movement to illustrate how presidents might relate to social movements more generally.

The White House thus may try to modify the character of a social movement; it may seek to influence its leadership, to delimit its objectives, or to slow the tempo of its actions. It may attempt to forestall movement projects that conflict with its own projects, thereby averting the explosion into public notice of embarrassing clashes. It may hope, ultimately, to transform social movements from political liabilities into political advantages.[38]

In general, Miroff suggests that presidents prefer the "quiet coalition-building" of relations with established interest groups to the public controversy preferred by movements, at least in part because presidents hope to control the "content and tempo of domestic issues."[39] My own research on the Roosevelt and Truman administrations' files labeled "Marches on Washington" suggests that Miroff's generalizations are accurate; the Johnson administration was not alone in trying to redirect the activities and deflect the demands of social movements. A close look at the Reagan and Bush administrations' relations with the evangelical and fundamentalist religious movement of the 1980s will provide further perspective on these relationships.[40]

Communitywide Characteristics

Not only are there variations among groups, but there are also likely to be broader characteristics of the interest-group universe that influence relations with the presidency. Skowronek, for example, uses the term "density" to characterize the breadth of group organization and political mobilization, arguing that contemporary presidents confront a broader array of groups pursing their goals more actively than ever before. Developing indicators for this dimension and linking it to White House operations remains a future challenge.

The level of inter- and intragroup conflict may also have an impact on the relationship. Over the past half-century, presidents have often intervened in conflicts that affected especially significant interests. Thus, in the period following World War II and during the Korean War, Truman was heavily involved in labor negotiations, an activity that later presidents have also found necessary. Other types of intergroup conflict have also been troublesome, for example, bad feelings between Jews and African Americans have sometimes erupted into public disputes. Prior to the consolidation of the AFL and CIO, conflict within the labor movement was an especially difficult problem for Democratic administrations, sometimes occasioning their careful intervention into squabbles that are all the more intense because they are so narrowly focused. Similar problems have afflicted other interest-group sectors, including business, agriculture, seniors, and civil rights. Keeping peace within the body politic can become a thankless job for presidents that goes well beyond the "consensus-building" activities discussed by Peterson.

Reciprocal Impacts

Presidents and interest groups are likely to have both intentional and unintentional impacts on each other. Like Lyndon Johnson, presidents may choose to throw their support behind the moderate voices in a movement to the disadvantage of firebrands and to encourage certain leaders by providing them with tangible successes that demonstrate effectiveness to their members. Less obviously, however, the presidency may have encouraged the creation of umbrella organizations or "peak associations" as a way to articulate group views and demands more effectively. There is evidence to suggest that William Howard Taft was instrumental in creating the U.S. Chamber of Commerce, and one can find comparable evidence for the emergence of similar structures to coordinate the efforts of consumers, seniors, and Jewish Americans, among others. Such patterns of group representation are more commonplace in other political systems with stronger tendencies toward "corporatism" but may not be wholly absent in the United States.

Flowing in the other direction, group demands for representation may have contributed substantially to White House staff growth in the early 1970s though the impact seems to have diminished subsequently.[41] Less obviously, injecting a cadre of staff members perceived by others as "special pleaders" may have disrupted presidential decision making as staff with policy responsibilities may have increased their resistance to "political" considerations.[42] This is one of several presidency-related factors that may influence the relationship.

The Presidency

As the literature makes manifestly clear, presidents vary in how they conduct relations with interest groups. If analysis were to include presidents from earlier historical periods, one would expect this presidential variation to reflect some of the broad systemic changes reviewed above. But, there is considerable variation across administrations even during the last half of the twentieth century, a period of relatively comparable conditions. We review several factors associated with "the presidency" that might help to explain these interactions: management strategy, political strategy, and organizational development.

Management Strategy

Presidents vary in the extent to which they delegate or centralize responsibility for interest-group relations. Although the general trend toward centralization has created a need for interest-group liaison in the presidency over the past twenty-five years, bureaucrats and party officials remain important group contact points, a role they played to an even greater degree in the past. Although there may be long-term institutional trends at work, presidents have made explicit choices over where to lodge liaison responsibilities, and even in the modern era some chose not to bring group ties into the White House. To some degree, this variation may rest on different *attitudes of individual presidents* about liaison. Eisenhower, for example, explicitly rejected mounting as extensive a White House liaison effort as his predecessor, and even Lyndon Johnson explicitly avoided bringing some kinds of liaison into the White House.[43] It is less clear whether any administration since Johnson has demonstrated comparable restraint. Clearly, presidents may choose to avoid some relations because of partisan differences or conflicts over goals, but explicit avoidance of contact seems to have been rare in recent years.[44]

Political Strategy

Peterson emphasizes that the pattern of a president's interactions with interest groups depends on the "contextual and strategic situation" that greets a president and "the character of the goals he wished to advance."[45] "Crippling opponents and organizing the sympathetic" were dual features of Reagan's partisan program while "securing the assistance of groups whose goals were compatible with those of the administration"[46] and who possessed significant resources critical to securing the legislative agenda. Ginsberg and Shefter paint a no less stark picture of an administration intent on creating a dominant political coalition.

Both of these accounts emphasize how Reagan sought to establish a new era of Republican control.[47] Stephen Skowronek suggests, however, that Reagan's political task was not unique; other presidents had also sought to refashion their relationship with the nation's social forces. Reagan's effort at remaking his political context was merely one of several possible "projects" that presidents have undertaken in relation to the political and policy commitments established by their predecessors. Thus, Skowronek presents an opportunity to examine the political strategies of presidents across time.

Skowronek offers a four-cell typology of how presidents relate to the constellation of social forces encountered during their terms in office.[48]

According to this framework, one would expect to find that Reagan's strategies were quite comparable to those of Jefferson, Jackson, Lincoln, and FDR. All were practitioners of the *politics of reconstruction*, in Skowronek's terms; they were presidents intent on creating a new, dominant political coalition of support.

Presidents engaged in the *politics of preemption* resemble the reconstructors by pursuing offensive strategies in their probes for new coalition possibilities. Tyler, A. Johnson, Wilson, Eisenhower, and Nixon lacked support from a stable coalition—they were mavericks within their own party and stood in opposition to the dominant political regime. Such presidents might hope to create a more stable coalition of their own by aggravating differences in the dominant coalition and thereby creating opportunities through shifting loyalties. This pattern is readily apparent in the activities of Charles Colson, director of the White House staff office that was a precursor to OPL. Colson sought to help Nixon create a new Republican majority by disrupting the Democratic coalition with a series of "wedge issues" that appealed to Southern whites, blue-collar workers, and members of the suburban middle class. Eisenhower, however, who faced a comparable strategic situation, mounted no such effort.

For other "affiliated" presidents (e.g., Monroe, Polk, T. Roosevelt, Truman, LBJ, and Bush), the challenge was to maintain ties with the disparate elements of the coalition that brought them to power but whose vitality was waning—the *politics of articulation* where repairing ruptures in the coalition seems a never-ending job. Presidents mired in the *politics of disjunction* have an even more difficult job; they are caught in a set of contradictions inherent in the political order and beset by demands from groups disappointed with the unresponsiveness of the administration and from those who are not yet part of a newly created, well-articulated coalition. Skowronek sees this as the situation confronted by both Adamses, Pierce, Buchanan, Hoover, and Carter.

Thus, Skowronek provides analysts with a means to examine not merely the strategic calculations of single administrations as emphasized in Peterson's framework, but also with a way to analyze comparable strategic problems across time. Interest-group liaison also emerges as a means to test Skowronek's controversial framework.

Organizational Development

The presidency is not merely the reflection of strategic choices made by presidents regarding management and politics, but it is also an organization where staff members' specialized knowledge and skills can contribute to collective endeavors. In this regard, the emergence of *public liaison* as a staff unit represents a conscious effort to provide the White House with intelligence about key centers of external power and autonomy and with the capacity to influence the conduct of the leaders of significant organized interests.[49] The range of staff activities is captured in the discussion of staff roles reviewed earlier.

Most research has focused on ways in which presidents *actively* pursue relations with interest groups. Such efforts are undertaken in conjunction with the president's "prime ministerial" role, that is, as a political leader requiring public and elite support to advance an agenda. But presidents have also developed more *passive* patterns of interaction. Over time, a range of largely ceremonial White House activities developed that are consistent with the president's role as "head of state." As described by Frederic Fox, a congregational minister who joined Eisenhower's staff in 1956 as correspondence secretary and liaison with religious groups, the president performs a variety of *pastoral duties:* "He endorses worthy pursuits, promotes charity, encourages the fitness of American youth. He rejoices in various individual and collective victories and, on occasion, sympathizes in sorrow."[50]

Fox was responsible for providing roughly 4,500 presidential messages per year to a wide range of individual citizens and groups celebrating special occasions: 90th birthdays; 50th wedding anniversaries; retirements of particularly noteworthy citizens; centennial anniversaries of corporations, cities, counties, states; eagle scout ceremonies. Like a pastor relating to his flock, presidents help these citizens observe significant events in their lives by offering encouragement, sympathy, and congratulations.

More significantly from the perspective of group relations, national groups petition for "a message of greetings from the president on the occasion of their annual conventions," a practice that can be traced back to FDR and probably earlier. As Fox noted in the same memo, "some have grown so accustomed to these annual messages that they have become a kind of 'invocation' to their meetings which cannot be left out." Presidential messages of great import were sometimes delivered by administration spokespersons, but the effort was not well coordinated in the Eisenhower administration, which missed an opportunity to multiply the president's influence. Later presidents found ways to make these messages more personal by taping remarks that were played for the gathering and more recently speaking live via satellite feed, but the idea was largely the same—demonstrate the president's personal interest, concern, and recognition of the group's importance in American life.

Fox's activities were both a reflection of past White House practice and a guide for the future. On the memo summarizing his duties was a handwritten note indicating that Bill Hopkins, the White House chief usher who served successive administrations for nearly four decades, make this summary available to Fox's successors in the Kennedy, Johnson, and Nixon administrations to help guide their issuance of greetings.[51] Here we see that the presidency's organizational character can have an independent influence on the conduct of group relations through provision of a functional equivalent to the "organizational memory" found in structures that adhere more closely to classic features of a bureaucracy. There are multiple ways that such cross-administration continuity can emerge. In addition to the chief usher's advice, Walcott and Hult point to a process they term "partisan learning" whereby Republicans and Democrats copy the practices of the most recent predecessor from their own party.[52] Richard Neustadt's work has also suggested the importance of "Washington lore" and the expectations held by others of how the presidency should be conducted.[53] In each case, organizational factors may have an independent influence on the conduct of interest-group liaison, and presidential decisions will become less important to the extent that White House liaison becomes "institutionalized."

Conclusions

Developing a full appreciation for the role that interest groups play in presidential policymaking requires a comprehensive understanding of how these relationships have developed throughout American history in light of complex changes in the larger political system, the universe of organized groups, and the presidency itself. Ample evidence suggests that groups today play a larger role in presidential calculations than they did in the past, but as studies from the state theory perspective suggest, there may be greater comparability across political eras than most analysts have assumed.

Although there is a clear role for expanded historical research, the contemporary era also seems to evidence several distinctive characteristics. Changes made in the organization and operation of the presidency make it possible for presidents and their aides to accommodate the demands of a wider array of groups than in the past and actively to seek their support. Emergence of a specialized Office of Public Liaison in the mid-1970s symbolizes this expanded effort that gradually developed over the five preceding administrations. Despite the emergence of this staff unit, however, many other parts of the Executive Office of the President maintain ties to the interest-group community. Mapping these interactions remains a major scholarly task since it is clear that not all groups receive the same friendly welcome at the White House door.

Group relations have always been important for presidents but their significance has probably been enhanced in the modern era by changes in other modes of group intermediation. Not only has the effectiveness of parties declined, but groups have also found ways to exert influence in elections independent of political parties. The ways in which these possibilities—for example, independent expenditures and soft money contributions—impinge on the presidency are fertile areas for future research.

In addition to the *active* efforts intended to shape politics and programs, the White House exerts enormous symbolic power through *passive* activities. At first blush, these ceremonial actions may appear to have little relevance to policymaking, but they establish an institutional presence in the system that other centers of government power—Congress and the bureaucracy—are hard-pressed to match. Legitimization of group claims is an important part of the policy process, and presidents enjoy a preeminent role in this domain. This preeminence may be even greater during the contemporary era thanks to the emergence of a national communications system.

If coalition-building—both electoral and governing—stands as the prototypical activity of *active interest-group liaison*, symbolic gestures such as representative appointments and public acknowledgments are classic expressions of *passive interest-group liaison*. Both forms of liaison remain significant in the modern era although most attention has concentrated on *active* presidential efforts. Depending on their standing in the larger political system, both groups and presidents will vary in the value attached to different types of liaison and pursue different strategies in advancing their interests. The relationship, in short, is *doubly dynamic*.

Notes

1. Mark Peterson distinguishes between "interest-group liaison" and "public liaison" as a way to demonstrate that groups have multiple points of contact within the presidency and are not exclusively limited to the Office of Public Liaison ("The Presidency and Organized Interests," *American Political Science Review* 86(3) 1992: 613). The distinction also allows one to recognize that relationships have been differently organized during different historical periods, that is, interest-group liaison encompasses a wider range of possible relationships.

2. Joseph A. Pika, "Interest Groups and the Executive: Presidential Intervention," in Allan J. Cigler and Burdett A. Loomis, eds., *Interest Group Politics* (Washington, DC: CQ Press, 1983), 298–323; Pika, "Interest Groups and the White House under Roosevelt and Truman," *Political Science Quarterly* 102:4 (Winter 1987): 647–68; Pika, "Opening Doors for Kindred Souls: The White House Office of Public Liaison," in Allan J. Cigler and Burdett A. Loomis, eds., *Interest Group Politics*, 3rd ed. (Washington, DC: CQ Press, 1991), 277–98. Martha Joynt Kumar and Michael Grossman, "The Presidency and Interest Groups," in Michael Nelson, ed., *The Presidency and the Political System* (Washington, DC: CQ Press, 1984), 282–312. Mark A. Peterson, "The Presidency and Organized Interests. Charles E. Walcott and Karen M. Hult, *Governing the White*

House: From Hoover Through LBJ (Lawrence: University Press of Kansas, 1995). Bradley H. Patterson, Jr., *The Ring of Power: The White House Staff and Its Expanding Role in Government* (New York: Basic Books, 1988).

3. Nelson W. Polsby. "Interest Groups and the Presidency: Trends in Political Intermediation in America," in Walter Dean Burnham and Martha Wagner, eds., *American Politics and Public Policy* (Cambridge: MIT Press, 1978), 41–52.

4. Michael Grossman and Francis Rourke, "The Media and the Presidency: An Exchange Analysis," *Political Science Quarterly* 91 (1976): 455–70. Richard E. Neustadt, *Presidential Power: The Politics of Leadership* (New York: Wiley, 1960).

5. Stephen Skowronek, *The Politics Presidents Make: Leadership from John Adams to George Bush* (Cambridge: Harvard University Press, 1993), 30–31.

6. Ibid., 54.

7. Patterson, *The Ring of Power,* 200.

8. Kumar and Grossman, "The Presidency and Interest Groups," 290.

9. Pika, "Opening Doors for Kindred Souls," 278.

10. Peterson, "The Presidency and Organized Interests," 617.

11. Ibid., 614 for both quotations.

12. Ibid., 615 for both quotations.

13. Ibid., 624.

14. Walcott and Hult, *Governing the White House,* 16, 118–34.

15. Ibid., 120. For more discussion of these environmental changes see Pika, "Interest Groups and the Executive," and Kumar and Grossman, "The Presidency and Interest Groups."

16. Walcott and Hult, *Governing the White House,* 121.

17. Ibid., 128.

18. Ibid., 129.

19. Ibid.

20. Pika, "Opening Doors"; Peterson, "The Presidency and Organized Interests," 619.

21. Benjamin Ginsberg and Martin Shefter, "The Presidency and the Organization of Interests," in Michael Nelson, ed., *The Presidency and the Political System,* 2nd ed. (Washington, DC: CQ Press, 1988), 328. Also see Skowronek, *The Politics Presidents Make,* chapters 1–3.

22. Ginsberg and Shefter, in ibid., 329.

23. Skowronek, *The Politics Presidents Make,* 9–10, 34–39.

24. Ginsberg and Shefter, "The Presidency, Interest Groups, and Social Forces: Creating a Republican Coalition," in Michael Nelson, ed., *The Presidency and the Political System,* 3rd ed. (Washington, DC: CQ Press, 1990), 335–52. Benjamin Ginsberg, Walter R. Mebane, Jr., and Martin Shefter, "The Presidency and Interest Groups: Why Presidents Cannot Govern," in Michael Nelson, ed., *The Presidency and the Political System,* 4th ed. (Washington, DC: CQ Press, 1995), 331–47. Ginsberg, Mebane, and Shefter, "The Presidency, Social Forces, and Interest Groups: Why Presidents Can No Longer Govern," in Michael Nelson, ed., *The Presidency and the Political System,* 5th ed. (Washington, DC: CQ Press, 1998), 358–73.

25. Ginsberg, Mebane, and Shefter, "The Presidency and Interest Groups: Why Presidents Cannot Govern," 336.

26. Ginsberg, Mebane, and Shefter, "The Presidency, Social Forces, and Interest Groups," 368.

27. Like Walcott and Hult, *Governing the White House,* I believe that a framework based on levels of analysis is especially appropriate for studying the presidency. Not only does it enable the analyst to be conceptually comprehensive, but it also facilitates

explicit attention to classes of variables including the potential impact of presidential preferences, strategic calculations, and personal needs. See Joseph A. Pika, "Moving Beyond the Oval Office: Problems in Studying the Presidency," *Congress and the Presidency* 9:1 (Winter 1981–82): 17–36. While such an approach is especially valuable for descriptive purposes, it has been criticized as inhibiting theory building which would be best achieved through a much more parsimonious framework as set forth by Terry Moe, "Presidents, Institutions and Theory," in George C. Edwards III, John H. Kessel, and Bert A. Rockman, eds., *Researching the Presidency: Vital Questions, New Approaches* (Pittsburgh: University of Pittsburgh Press, 1993). A reasonable position is to recognize the value of both approaches, as argued by Norman C. Thomas and Joseph A. Pika, "Institutions and Personality in Presidency Research," paper presented at the Annual Meeting of the American Political Science Association, San Francisco, August 30, 1996.

28. The role of environmental factors has become a major issue in presidential studies with the emergence of two important new frameworks. Both the "rational-choice institutionalism" of Terry Moe and the "new institutionalism" of Stephen Skowronek place such heavy emphasis on the impact of environmental conditions on presidential decision making that the significance of presidential choice becomes problematic. In terms of group relations, both Peterson and Walcott and Hult stress the strategic choices made by presidents as do Ginsberg and Shefter.

29. Focusing on presidents' relationships with interest groups might be viewed as excessively narrow. Interest groups are but one of several "political intermediation" structures in American politics. Twenty years ago, Nelson Polsby explicitly cast the presidency–interest-group connection in relation to two alternative structures to achieve electoral and governing goals—the media and political parties. By placing increased reliance on media strategies, Polsby suggested that presidents were contributing to a change in the character of American politics, a movement toward "direct "or "plebiscitary" democracy in contrast to "pluralist" or "polyarchical" democracy. In some respects, then, an effort to focus exclusively on presidents' relations with interest groups ignores important features of a much larger landscape. But the argument here and in virtually all the work cited in this chapter considers the interest-group connection a major analytic problem that warrants separate treatment.

30. Skowronek, *The Politics Presidents Make,* 52–55. Also see Stephen Skowronek, *Building a New American State: The Expansion of National Administrative Capacities, 1877–1920* (New York: Cambridge University Press, 1982).

31. Pika, "Opening Doors."

32. Charles Lewis, *The Buying of the President* (New York: Avon Books, 1996).

33. Robert H. Salisbury, "Interest Groups" in Nelson Polsby and Fred I. Greenstein, eds., *The Handbook of Political Science* (Reading, MA: Addison-Wesley, 1975).

34. Terry Moe, "The Politicized Presidency," in John E. Chubb and Paul E. Peterson, eds., *The New Directions in American Politics* (Washington, DC: Brookings Institution, 1985).

35. Pika, "Interest Groups and the Executive," 303.

36. Polsby, "Interest Groups and the Presidency," 45. Walcott and Hult also implicitly recognize the importance of this distinction between established and "new" groups in their comparison of administration liaison with civil rights groups versus labor and business.

37. Polsby, ibid., 47.

38. Bruce Miroff, "Presidential Leverage over Social Movements: The Johnson White House and Civil Rights," *The Journal of Politics* 43:1 (1981): 2.

39. Ibid., 7.

40. Allen D. Hertzke, "Faith and Access: Religious Constituencies and the Washington Elites," paper delivered at the Annual Meeting of the American Political Science Association, September 3–6, 1987.

41. Stephen Hess, *Organizing the Presidency* (Washington, DC: Brookings Institution, 1976).

42. See Pika, "Opening Doors," 289–90; and Patterson, *The Ring of Power,* 202.

43. Pika, in ibid., 283, 286.

44. Patterson notes the possible exception of gay rights organizations, who were unwelcome in the Reagan and Bush White Houses. Midge Costanza's open interaction with gay rights groups in the Carter administration had received embarrassing media coverage. Under Clinton, access for gay rights groups became even stronger.

45. Peterson, *The Ring of Power,* 616–17.

46. Ibid., 617.

47. Also see Harold Wolman and Fred Teitelbaum, "Interest Groups and the Reagan Presidency," in Lester Salamon and Michael Lund, eds., *The Reagan Presidency and the Governing of America* (Washington, DC: Urban Institute, 1984), 297–336.

48. Skowronek, *The Politics Presidents Make,* 36ff.

49. Although some might argue that analysts ascribe such goals to White House actors who never consciously think about extending staff capabilities, the papers of William Baroody, Jr., director of the first OPL staff, make it clear that conscious thought was given to how this staff specialization would extend collective capabilities. See the Baroody and OPL staff files at the Gerald R. Ford Library.

50. For the Record Memo "Re: Greetings from the President," July 21, 1959, Dwight D. Eisenhower Library, Papers of Frederic E. Fox, Box 34.

51. Fox was unusually aware of the tradition that surrounded his position. In a reflective essay completed sometime after he left the White House, Fox wrote the following: "On January 20, 1961, I left the White House with President Eisenhower—actually, I left a few minutes after he did—and that morning I took all his papers from my file cabinets and stuffed them in a cardboard box addressed to Abilene, Kansas. But I couldn't wrap up the White House tradition for handling birthday cards and greetings. That tradition stayed behind to govern my successor—as it has governed every Corresponding Secretary from the Administration of George Washington to the present day." Dwight D. Eisenhower Library, Frederic E. Fox Papers, Box 34, "Official White House Guide for Messages—Fox 1959."

52. Walcott and Hult, *Governing the White House,* 18.

53. Richard E. Neustadt, "Presidency and Legislation: The Growth of Central Clearance," *American Political Science Review* 57:3 (September 1954): 641–71.

5

Political Parties and Divided Democracy

Sidney M. Milkis

The relationship between the presidency and the American party system has always been difficult. The architects of the Constitution sought to establish a nonpartisan executive who would stand above, and thus moderate, party conflict. Their hope was that the president, with the support of the judiciary, would play the principal part in controlling the "violence of faction" that the framers feared would destroy popular government. Even though this plan proved chimerical and the executive quickly became immersed in partisan maneuvers, its authority continued to depend on an ability to transcend party politics. The president is nominated by a party but, unlike the British prime minister, is not elected by it. Moreover, the Constitution makes possible a situation of divided government, in which the executive and Congress are held by different parties, thus further testing the fragile alliance between the president and his party.

The inherent tension between the presidency and the party system reached a critical point during the 1930s. The institutionalization of the modern presidency, arguably the most significant constitutional legacy of Franklin D. Roosevelt's New Deal, ruptured severely the limited, albeit significant, bond that linked presidents to their parties. In fact, the modern presidency was crafted with the intention of reducing the influence of the party system on American politics. In this sense Roosevelt's extraordinary party leadership contributed to the decline of the American party system.[1]

To be sure, political parties did not whither away. Indeed, under Ronald

Reagan, the party system showed at least some signs of transformation and renewal. Reagan and his successor, George Bush, supported efforts by Republicans in the national committee and congressional campaign organizations to restore some of the importance of political parties by refashioning them into highly untraditional but politically potent national organizations. These parties can muster a significant polarizing of politics within the Washington beltway, but recent developments have raised serious doubts about the capacity of these emergent national parties to build popular support for political principles and programs. Thus, contemporary executive-legislative relations are characterized by a basic disconnection between the parties weak relationship with the public and their increasingly important role in government.[2]

Programmatic Liberalism and Party Politics

The public philosophy of the New Deal provides the key to understanding its legacy for the presidency and party politics in the United States. Above all, the New Deal represented a redefinition of the social contract, a doctrinal change that presupposed an increase in administrative authority and efficiency and, concomitantly, the decline of the traditional two-party system. Roosevelt first spoke about the need to modernize elements of the old faith in his Commonwealth Club address. His theme was that the time had come—indeed, had come three decades earlier—to recognize the "new terms of the old social contract." It was necessary to rewrite the social contract to take account of the national economy remade by national industrial capitalism and the concentration of economic power and to establish a countervailing power—a stronger national state—lest the United States steer "a steady course toward economic oligarchy." "The day of enlightened administration," Roosevelt insisted, "has come."[3]

As FDR would later detail in his 1944 State of the Union Address, constructing a foundation of economic security meant that the inalienable rights secured by the Constitution (speech, press, assembly, worship, due process, and so on) had to be supplemented by a "second bill of rights," so to speak, "under which a new basis of security and prosperity can be established for all—regardless of station, race, or creed." Among these new rights were the right to a useful and remunerative job; the right to a decent home; the right to a good education; the right to adequate protection from the economic fears of old age, sickness, accident, and unemployment; the right to earn enough to provide adequate food, clothing, and recreation; and the right to adequate medical care.[4]

Roosevelt's reappraisal of values is important in understanding the New

Deal, but it is also important in understanding FDR's influence on political parties and the separation of powers. The new understanding of the Declaration of Independence required an assault on the established party system, which had long been allied with constitutional forms that favored a decentralization of power. This effort to weaken traditional party organizations began during the Progressive era, but it fell to FDR and the architects of the New Deal to make progressive democracy an enduring part of American politics.[5] The origins and organizing principles of the American party system established it as a force against the creation of the modern state. The New Deal commitment to building such a state—that is, a national political power with expansive programmatic responsibilities—meant that the party system had to be either transformed or weakened. Paradoxically, the New Deal both strengthened the national resolve of political parties and attenuated partisan loyalties in the electorate.

Party Responsibility and the Creation of the Modern Presidency

In part, Roosevelt undertook an assault on the party system to make it more national and principled in character. He wanted to overcome the state and local orientation of the party system, which was suited to congressional primacy and poorly organized for progressive action by the national government, and to establish a national, executive-oriented party, which would be more suitably organized for the expression of national purposes. With such a task in mind, the Roosevelt administration modified traditional partisan practices in an effort to make the Democratic party, as FDR put it, one of "militant liberalism." This, in turn, would bring about a structural transformation of the party system, pitting a reformed Democratic party against a conservative Republican party. As Roosevelt wrote in the introduction to the seventh volume of his presidential papers, "Generally speaking in a representative form of government there are generally two schools of political belief—liberal and conservative. The system of party responsibility in American politics requires one of his parties to become the liberal party and the other the conservative party."[6]

The most dramatic moment in Roosevelt's challenge to traditional party practices was the so-called purge campaign of 1938. This involved FDR directly in one gubernatorial and several congressional primary campaigns (twelve contests in all) in a bold effort to replace conservative Democrats with candidates who were "100 percent New Dealers."[7] The special concern of this campaign was the South (Southern Democracy), a Democratic stronghold since the Civil War but, given the commitment to states' rights in that region, one that also represented, as prominent journalist of the time

Thomas Stokes put it, "the ball and chain which hobbled the party's forward march."[8]

As the press noted frequently after the 1938 purge campaign, no president had ever gone as far as Roosevelt in striving to stamp his policies upon his party. In the context of American politics, where presidential dominance over the decentralized party system was a cardinal vice, this was an extraordinary effort. With the purge and other initiatives, such as the elimination of the "two-thirds" rule, the Roosevelt administration initiated a process whereby, increasingly, the party system evolved from predominantly local to national and programmatic party organizations.[9]

Yet at the same time, the New Deal made partisanship less important. Roosevelt's partisan leadership, though it effected important changes in the Democratic party, envisioned a personal link with the public that would enable the president to govern from his position as leader of the nation rather than just leader of the party.[10] For example, in all but one of the 1938 primary campaigns in which he personally participated, Roosevelt chose to make a direct appeal to public opinion rather than attempt to work through or reform the regular party apparatus.

The spread of the direct primary, which Roosevelt supported,[11] gave the president the opportunity to make a direct appeal to the people and provided an attractive vehicle for Roosevelt to put his own stamp upon the party. Of course, this was bound to be especially tempting to an extremely popular president with as fine a radio presence as Roosevelt.

In the final analysis, the "benign dictatorship" Roosevelt sought to impose on the Democratic party was conducive to corroding to the American party system. Indeed, the emphasis Roosevelt placed upon forging a direct link between himself and the public reflected a lack of faith in party politics and a conscious attempt to supplant collective responsibility (based upon give-and-take between the president and Congress) with executive responsibility. For practical and principled reasons, the Roosevelt administration did not seek to remake American party politics; rather, they championed the executive as the guarantor of a "second bill of rights," as the steward of an administrative constitution. This explains why the most significant institutional reforms of the New Deal did not promote party government but fostered instead a program that would enable the president to govern in the absence of party government.

For example, the enactment of FDR's proposed executive reorganization bill would mean that party politics would be displaced by executive administration, by an executive-centered administrative state generated by the activities of a dominant and dominating president. A reconstituted party system would strengthen ties between the executive and legislature; but in the administrative design of the New Deal, the president and executive agencies would be delegated authority to govern, making unnecessary the constant cooperation of party members in Congress and the states. Ironically, a policy aimed at making party politics less important became a major focus of party responsibility. FDR lost this vote of confidence on administrative reform in April 1938, as the House of Representatives, with massive Democratic defections, voted down the legislation. It was a devastating defeat for Roosevelt, which together with that of the court-"packing" plan, also closely linked to strengthening administrative power, led FDR to undertake the purge campaign.[12]

The purge failed at the polls, but it scared recalcitrant Democrats, who became more conciliatory toward their president on a few matters after the 1938 election. Administrative reform was one of these, and in 1939 an executive-reorganization bill passed the Congress. This legislation (the Executive Reorganization Act of 1939) was, in effect, the organic statute of the "modern" presidency. Roosevelt's extraordinary leadership was, so to speak, institutionalized by the administrative reform bill, for this statute ratified a process whereby public expectations and institutional arrangements established the president as the center of government activity. It not only provided authority to create the Executive Office of the President, which included the newly formed White House Office and a strengthened and refurbished Bureau of the Budget, but also enhanced the president's control over the expanding activities of the executive branch. As such, this legislation represents the genesis of the "administrative presidency," which was better equipped to govern independently of the constraints imposed by the separation of powers.

The battle for the destiny of the Democratic party during Roosevelt's second term, therefore, was directly tied to strengthening the presidency and the executive branch as the vital center of government action. FDR's success transformed the Democrats into a party of administration, dedicated to enacting an institutional program that would make parties less important. Traditional localized parties had provided presidents with a stable basis of popular support and episodically during critical partisan realignments with the opportunity to achieve national reform. What was once episodic must now become routine. As the Brownlow report put it: "Our national will must be expressed not merely in a brief, exultant moment of electoral decision, but in a persistent, determined, competent day-by-day administration of what the nation has decided to do."[13]

For a time, the modern presidency was at the center of this new political universe. With the strengthening of executive administration, the presidency became distanced from party politics, undermining the latter's importance. In effect, personnel in the Executive Office of the President transformed the presidency into an alternative political organization that gradually preempted party leaders in many of their limited but significant tasks: linking the president to interest groups, staffing the executive department, policy development, and, most important, campaign support. Presidents no longer won election and governed as heads of a party; instead, they won and governed as heads of a personal organization they created in their own image.

Still, the purpose of New Deal reforms was not to strengthen presidential government per se. Rather, the presidency was strengthened under the assumption that as the national office, it would be an ally of progressive reform. Consequently, executive power was refurbished in a way compatible with the objectives of programmatic liberalism, and administrative reform was intended to insulate reformers and reforms from the presidential election cycle. Whereas the original objective of administrative reformers, who first became prominent after the Civil War, was to separate politics and administration—to further "neutral competence"—the New Deal transformed the character of administrative politics. Previously, the choice was posed as one between party politics and spoils, on the one hand, and nonpolitical administration, on the other. The New Deal celebrated an administrative politics that denied nourishment to the regular party apparatus but fed instead an executive department oriented toward expanding liberal programs. As the administrative historian Paul Van Riper has noted, the new practice created another kind of patronage, "a sort of intellectual and ideological patronage rather than the more partisan type."[14]

The future of the American political system, then, was predicated on the emergence of a policymaking state; party politics and debate were subordinated to a "second bill of rights" and the delivery of services associated with those rights. Indeed, the New Deal was placed beyond partisan politics to such a degree that Republican presidents, even an ardently conservative one such as Ronald Reagan, oftentimes felt as though they were relegated to managing the liberal state.

The Modern Presidency and Divided Government

Of course, these Republican presidents faced not only a recalcitrant bureaucracy and a public philosophy that celebrated an expansive understanding of rights, but a Congress, as well as a majority of state and local governments, that were controlled by the Democratic party. The institutional and policy disputes between Republicans in the White House and Democrats in Congress and the states testify to the partial resurgence of partisanship in the 1970s and 1980s.

As a party of administration, the Democrats established the conditions for the end of parties unless, or until, a party sprang up that was anti-administration. No such party has arisen in American politics, although the Republicans have slouched toward that role. As programmatic liberalism began to lose support, the Republicans under Richard Nixon and especially Ronald Reagan embraced programs, such as new federalism and regulatory relief, that challenged the institutional legacy of the New Deal. This bolder conservative posture coincided with the construction of a formidable national Republican organization with strength at the federal level that is unprecedented in American politics. After 1976, the Republican National Committee and the two other Republican campaign bodies, the National Republican Senatorial Committee and the National Republican Congressional (House) Committee, greatly expanded their efforts to raise funds and provide services at the national level for state and local candidates. The Democrats lagged behind in party-building efforts, but the losses they suffered in the 1980 election encouraged them to modernize the national political machinery, openly imitating some of the devices employed by the Republicans. Arguably, a party system had finally evolved that was compatible with the national polity forged on the anvil of the New Deal.[15]

Nevertheless, the importance of presidential politics and unilateral executive action suggest that Nixon and Reagan essentially continued the institutional legacy of the New Deal. Thus, Republican presidents, intent upon transforming the liberal political order, have conceived of the presidency as a two-edged sword that could cut in a conservative as well as a liberal direction. Indeed, given that the New Deal was based on a party strategy to replace traditional party politics with administration, it is not surprising that the Republican challenge to liberal policies produced a conservative administrative presidency, which also retarded the revival of partisan politics.

The administrative ambition of Republican presidents was encouraged by, and, in turn, helped perpetuate, the condition of divided government that prevailed virtually without interruption between 1968 and 1992. Prior to 1994, the challenge to programmatic liberalism never extended beyond the presidency, leaving Congress, as well as most states and localities, under Democratic control. Republican presidents, facing hostility not only in the bureaucracy, but also in the Congress and the States, were, even more than Democrats, encouraged to pursue policy goals by seeking to concentrate executive power in the White House. The Reagan administration frequently expressed common cause with a modern conservative movement, whose advocates prefer not to limit the national state forged on the New Deal realignment, but to put it to new uses. Consequently, the Reagan administration, while promising to bring about "new federalism" and "regulatory relief," was stalled in these tasks by the conviction that a strong national state was necessary to foster economic growth, oppose communism, and "nurture" family values. The Iran-Contra scandal, for example, was not simply a matter of the president's being asleep on his watch. Rather, it revealed the Reagan administration's determination to assume a more forceful anticommunist posture in Central America in the face of a recalcitrant Congress and bureaucracy.

The Reagan administration's assertion of the "administrative presidency" was hardly an aberration. As a matter of course, when the president and his advisers confronted legislative resistance on an issue, they charted administrative avenues to advance their goals. Indeed, often they did not even try to modify the statutory basis of a liberal program, relying instead on administrative discretion as a first resort. Even in the area of regulatory relief, a project ostensibly designed to "get government off the backs of the people," the Reagan administration's efforts came not through legislative change but through administrative action, delay, and repeal. President Reagan's executive orders 12291 and 12498 mandated a comprehensive review of proposed agency regulations by the Office of Management and Budget.[16] Reagan also appointed a Task Force on Regulatory Relief, headed by Vice President Bush, to apply cost–benefit analysis to existing rules. This pursuit of conservative policy options through the administrative presidency continued with the accession of George Bush to the White House. The burden of curbing environmental, consumer, and civil rights regulations fell on the Competitiveness Council, chaired by Vice President Quayle, which, like its predecessor, the Task Force of Regulatory Relief, required administrative agencies to justify the costs of existing and proposed regulations.

The conservative administrative presidency did not go unchallenged. As designed by the Democrats, the modern presidency was conceived as an ally of programmatic rights. When this supposition was seemingly violated by Vietnam and its aftermath, reformers set out to protect liberal programs from unfriendly executives. By the time Lyndon Johnson left the White House, support for unilateral executive action had begun to erode, occasioned by the controversial use of presidential power in Vietnam, and it virtually disappeared under the strain of divided government. The result was a "reformation" of New Deal administrative politics, which brought Congress and the courts into the details of administration. The institutional reforms in the Congress during the 1970s that devolved policy responsibility to subcommittees and increased the number of congressional support staff members were compatible with the attention being paid by legislators to policy specialization, which increased congressional oversight of the administrative state while making Congress more administrative in its structure and activities.

Similarly, the judiciary's decreasing reliance on constitutional decisions in its rulings affecting the political economy and its emphasis on interpreting statutes to determine the responsibilities of executive agencies were symptomatic of its post–New Deal role as "managing partner of the administrative state." Consequently, the efforts of Republicans to compensate for their inability to control Congress by seeking to circumvent legislative restrictions on presidential conduct were matched by Democratic initiatives to burden the executive with smothering legislative and judicial oversight.[17]

The opposition to programmatic liberalism, then, did not result in a challenge to national administrative power, but in a virulent, enervating battle for the administrative state's services. The political toll of this battle appears to be a badly frayed connection between American government and its citizenry, a serious deterioration of American civil society.[18] Political parties, which once provided a connection between the governing institutions and the public, are certainly not absent from the administrative politics spawned by the New Deal and the opposition it aroused. But, in the wake of the New Deal, parties have been weakened as electoral institutions—both parties have shifted much of their attention from the building of constituencies (the building of a vital link with the public) to an "inside the beltway" administrative politics.[19] Moreover, this administrative politics has been associated with expansion of new rights that has further shifted partisan disputes away from parties as associations that organize public sentiments as an electoral majority. Even conservatives in the abortion debate talk of the rights of the unborn in a way that requires centralized administration— consider the so-called "gag rule" of the Reagan and Bush administrations. When rights dominate policy discourse, majority sentiments are commonly viewed as a problem and not the solution.

Thus, during the Reagan and Bush presidencies, divided government tended to belittle efforts by Democrats and Republicans alike to define a collective purpose with a past and a future, and yielded instead a partisanship joined to a form of administrative politics that relegated electoral conflict to the intractable demands of policy advocates. Indeed, both parties were hobbled in their efforts to form vital links with the public. The emergence of parties of administration strengthened the national party organization and created more discipline among party members in Congress, but at the cost of weakening party loyalties among the electorate. The tendency for growing numbers of voters to split their tickets, or to stay at home on election day, represented their estrangement from these parties of administration—a plague on both your houses.

To be sure, the checks that divided government imposed on the parties did not always lead to "policy gridlock"; during the Nixon, Reagan, and Bush presidencies, a number of important laws were passed, in spite of, and in some cases, because of, the persistence of separate partisan realms. Indeed, to a point, divided government has restrained the extreme tendencies of the Democrats and Republicans, thus providing some protection against the abuses of centralized administration. But this security did not come without its costs. As the extraordinary budgetary evasions and the jarring nomination fights during the 1980s and early 1990s revealed, the dark side of divided government is that it tends to obscure political responsibility and to mire government in petty, virulent clashes that undermine respect for American political institutions.

Bill Clinton and the "New" Politics of Divided Democracy

Bill Clinton dedicated his 1992 campaign to principles and policies that "transcended," he claimed, the exhausted left–right debate that had afflicted the nation for two decades. During the mid-1980s, Clinton was a leader of the Democratic Leadership Council, a moderate group in the Democratic party that developed many of the ideas that became the central themes of his run for the presidency. As Clinton declared frequently during the campaign, these ideas represented a new philosophy of government that would "honor middle class values, restore public trust, create a new sense of community and make America work again." He heralded "a new social contract," a "new covenant," one that would seek to constrain, in the name of responsibility and community, the demands for rights summoned by the Roosevelt Revolution. Clinton declared that the liberal commitment had gone too far. The objective of the "New Covenant" was to correct the tendency of Americans to celebrate individual rights and government entitlement programs without any sense of the mutual obligation they had to each other and their country.[20]

Clinton's campaign, thereby, promised to correct and renew the progressive tradition as shaped by the New Deal. Vital parties require some compromise between a deep and abiding commitment to rights and due attention to common deliberation and choice—some decisions must be left to a party majority. Roosevelt's party politics, however, rested on a new understanding of rights, one associated with the expansion of national administrative power, that is not congenial to such partisan responsibility. In challenging the explosion of rights and hidebound bureaucracy that arose from the New Deal and the opposition it spawned, Clinton pledged to dedicate his party to a new public philosophy that might redress many of the troubling aspects of the New Deal legacy—the decline of parties as civic associations, the rise of virulent administrative politics, and the deterioration of public trust in American political institutions.

Although Clinton pledged to dedicate his party to the new concept of justice he espoused, his words and actions during the early days of his presidency seemed to betray this commitment. No sooner had he been inaugurated then Clinton announced his intention to lift the long-standing ban on homosexuals in the military. The president soon learned, however, that there was no prospect that such a divisive issue could be resolved through the "stroke of a pen." To be sure, the development of the adminis- trative presidency gave presidents more power to exercise domestic policy autonomously. Yet with the expansion of national administration to such issues that shaped the direction and character of American public life, this power proved to be illusory.

Most damaging for the new president was that the issue became a glaring benchmark of his inability to revitalize progressive politics as an instrument to redress the economic insecurity and political alienation of the middle class. The bitter partisan fight in the spring and summer of 1993 over the administration's budgetary program served only to reinforce doubts about Clinton's ability to lead the nation in a new, more harmonious direction. Even though Clinton's budget plan promised to reduce the deficit, it in- volved new taxes and an array of social programs that Republicans and moderate Democrats perceived as tax-and-spend liberalism. The Republi- cans marched in lockstep opposition to Clinton's economic program, espe- cially to his $16 billion stimulus package, which he offered as a partial antidote to the economic contraction that he feared deficit reduction would cause. In April 1993, Senate Republicans unanimously supported a filibus- ter that killed the stimulus package. Congress did enact a modified version of the president's budgetary plan a few months later, albeit by razor thin margins and without any support from Republicans, who voted unani- mously against it in the House and Senate. Clinton won this narrow victory only after promising moderate Democrats that he would put together an- other package of spending cuts in the fall.[21] But this uneasy compromise failed to dispel the charge of his political opponents that Clinton was a conventional liberal whose commitment to reform had expired at the end of the presidential campaign.[22]

The apologetic stance that Clinton displayed in the face of traditional liberal causes was, to a point, understandable; it was a logical response to the modern institutional separation between the presidency and the party. The moderate wing of the Democratic party that he represented—including the members of the Democratic Leadership Council—was a minority wing. The majority of liberal-interest group activists and Democratic members of Congress still preferred entitlements to obligations and regulations to re- sponsibilities. Only the unpopularity of liberal groups and the emphasis on candidate-centered campaigns in presidential politics made Clinton's nomination and election possible. The media-driven caucuses and primaries that dominate the presidential-nomination process gave him an opportunity to seize the Democratic label as an outsider candidate but offered no means to effect a transformation of his party when he took office. Clinton's Democratic predecessor, Jimmy Carter, who intended to be fiercely independent and a scourge to traditional liberal approaches, faced a situation of nearly complete political isolation during his unhappy term in office.

To bring about the new mission of progressivism that he advocated during the election, Clinton would have to risk a brutal confrontation with the major powers in the Democratic party, a battle that might have left him even more vulnerable politically than Carter had been.[23] In truth, no president had risked such a confrontation with his party since Roosevelt's failed purge campaign. It is not surprising, therefore, that Clinton's allies in the Democratic Leadership Council urged him to renew his "credentials as an outsider" by going over the heads of the party leadership in Congress and taking his message directly to the people. The new president could "break deadlock," they argued, only by appealing to the large number of independents in the electorate who voted for H. Ross Perot, whose 19 percent of the vote was the most significant challenge to the two-party system since Theodore Roosevelt's Progressive party campaign of 1912. Clinton's presidency could be rescued, the DLC insisted, only by forging "new and sometimes bipartisan coalitions around an agenda that mov[ed] beyond the polarized left-right debate."[24]

In the fall of 1993, Clinton took a page from his former political associates in his successful campaign to secure congressional approval of the North American Free Trade Agreement (NAFTA) with Canada and Mexico. The fight for NAFTA caused Clinton to defend free enterprise ardently and to oppose the protectionism of labor unions, which still represented one of the most important constituencies in the national Democratic party. Clinton's victory owed partly to the active support of the Republican congressional leadership; in fact, a majority of Republicans in the House and Senate supported the free trade agreement, while a majority of Democrats, including the House majority leader and majority whip, opposed it. No less important, however, was the Clinton administration's mobilization of popular support. The turning point in the struggle came when the administration challenged Perot, the leading opponent of NAFTA, to debate Vice President Gore on "Larry King Live." Gore's optimistic defense of open markets was well received by the large television audience, rousing enough support for the treaty to persuade a bare majority of legislatures in both houses of Congress to approve it.[25]

With the successful fight over NAFTA, moderate Democrats began to hope that Clinton had finally begun the task of dedicating his party to principles and policies he had espoused during the campaign. But the next major legislative battle was for the administration's health-care program, which promised to "guarantee all Americans a comprehensive package of benefits over the course of an entire lifetime." The formulation of this program appeared to mark the apotheosis of New Deal administrative politics; it was designed "behind closed doors" by a Health Care Task Force, which was headed by First Lady Hillary Rodham Clinton and the president's long-time friend Ira Magaziner. Moreover, it would create a new government entitlement program and an administrative apparatus that would signal the revitalization rather than the reform of the traditional welfare state. Although the administration made conciliatory overtures to the plan's opponents, the possibilities for comprehensive reform hinged on settling differences over the appropriate role of government that had divided the parties and country for the past two decades.

By proposing such an ambitious health-care reform bill, Clinton enraged conservatives. By failing to deliver on his promise to provide a major overhaul of the health-care system, he dismayed the ardent liberals of his party. Most significant, the defeat of the president's health-care program created the overwhelming impression that he had not lived up to his campaign promise to transcend the bitter philosophical and partisan battles of the Reagan and Bush years.

The dramatic Republican triumph in the 1994 mid-term election led scholars and pundits to suggest that the nation might be on the threshold of a critical partisan realignment. But the American people had become alienated from the Republican and Democratic parties by the 1990s, so much so that the renewal of partisan loyalties in the electorate, let alone a full-scale partisan transformation, seemed unlikely. The events that followed in the wake of the election did nothing to ameliorate the voters' estrangement from political parties. Indeed, the first session of the 104th Congress quickly degenerated into the same sort of administrative politics that had corroded the legitimacy of political institutions since the presidency of Nixon. This time, however, the struggle between the branches assumed a novel form: institutional confrontation between a Democratic White House and a Republican Congress.

The battle between Clinton and Congress became especially fierce in a contest over legislation to balance the budget. More than any other idea celebrated in the GOP's Contract with America, Republicans believed that a balanced budget bill would give them their best opportunity to control Congress for years to come.

The Republicans proposed to scale back the growth of Medicare, a federal health insurance program for the elderly and disabled, by encouraging beneficiaries to enroll in health maintenance organizations and other private, managed health-care systems. Rallied by their militant partisan brethren in the House, Republicans sought to pressure Clinton to accept their priorities on the budget by twice shutting down government offices and even threatening to force the U.S. Treasury into default. These confrontation tactics backfired and roused popular support for the administration. In attacking Medicare and social policy, such as environmental programs, the Republicans' militant assault on programmatic liberalism went beyond what was promised by the Contract with America, thus giving Clinton the opportunity to take a political stand that was supported by most of the country.

When Congress returned for the second session of the 104th Congress in January 1996, it was not to Speaker Gingrich's agenda of reducing the role of Washington in the society and economy, but to the measured tones of Clinton's third State of the Union message. On the one hand, the president addressed many of the themes of his Republican opponents, boldly declaring, "the era of big government is over."[26] This was not merely rhetoric; withstanding furious criticism from liberal members of Congress and interest-group activists, Clinton signed welfare reform legislation in August that ended the sixty-one-year-old federal entitlement to cash payments for low-income mothers and their dependent children. Clinton conceded that the act was flawed, cutting too deeply into nutritional support for low-income working people and denying support unfairly to legal immigrants. Nevertheless, by encouraging welfare recipients to take jobs, it served the fundamental principle Clinton championed in the 1992 campaign of "recreating the Nation's social bargain with the poor."[27]

On the other hand, warning that "we cannot go back to the time when our citizens were left to fend for themselves," Clinton called for a halt to Republican assaults on basic liberal programs dedicated to providing economic security, educational opportunity, and environmental protection.[28] Employing Democratic National Committee funds, the White House had orchestrated a national media blitz toward the end of 1995 that excoriated the Republican's program to reform Medicare and presented the president as a figure of national reconciliation who favored welfare reform and a balanced budget but also would protect middle-class entitlements, education, and the environment.[29] Clinton's carefully modulated State of the Union message underscored this media campaign, revealing the president as a would-be healer anxious to bring all sides together.[30]

Clinton held firmly to the centrist ground he had staked out after the 1994 election, campaigning in 1996 on the same "New" Democratic themes of "opportunity, responsibility, and community" that had served him well during his first run for the White House. In a decisive victory, he became the first Democratic president to be elected to a second term since FDR. But his candidate-centered campaign, abetted by a strong economy, did little to help his party. The Democrats lost two seats in the Senate, and gained but a modest nine seats in the House, thus failing to regain control of either legislative body. In truth, Clinton's campaign testified to the fragility of the nationalized party system that arose during the 1980s. Clinton scarcely endorsed the election of a Democratic Congress; moreover, his fundraising efforts for the party supported congressional candidates only late in the campaign. Adding insult to injury, the administration's questionable fundraising methods led to revelations during the final days of the election that might have reduced Clinton's margin of victory and, thereby, undermined the Democrats' effort to retake the House.[31]

In the final analysis, Clinton's success in forging "a third way" between Republican conservatism and Democratic liberalism will determine his legacy for the presidency and political parties. The disjuncture between the bitter partisanship within the capitol and the weakening of partisan affiliation outside of it has given Clinton, and his skill in combining doctrines, a certain appeal in the country.[32] This gift for forging compromise was displayed in May 1997 as the White House and Republican leadership reached a compromise on a tentative plan to balance the budget by 2002. To be sure, this uneasy agreement was made possible by a revenue windfall caused by the robust economy, thus enabling Clinton and GOP leaders to avoid the sorts of hard choices over program cuts and taxes that animated the bitter struggles of the 104th Congress.[33] Even so, this rapprochement, which promises to bring about the first balanced budget in three decades, testifies to the potential of modern presidents to advance principles and pursue policies that defy the sharp cleavages characteristic of the nationalized party system.

Discussion

The "extraordinary isolation" of the modern presidency has its limits.[34] Since FDR, the president has been freed from the constraints of party, only to be enslaved by a volatile political environment that can rapidly undercut popular support. Thus, Clinton's command eventually might be jeopardized not only by his lame-duck status, but also by accusations of improper campaign fundraising for the 1996 election. Not surprisingly, Democratic members of Congress, still smarting from the president's seeming indifference to their programmatic commitments and election prospects, maintained a deafening silence as the Republicans sought to exploit the White House's campaign peccadillos.[35] Moreover, toward the end of 1997, the great majority of House Democrats refused to support legislation that would give Clinton fast track trade-negotiating authority, the very same power that Democratic Congresses gave Republican presidents Ford, Reagan, and Bush. The House Democrats' revolt against free trade underscored the continuing split between Clinton and his party; just as significant, it suggested that leading Democratic opponents of the bill, such as Minority Leader Richard Gephardt, would pose hard challenges to Clinton-style centrism for the remainder of the president's term. This estrangement, of course, is also likely to affect the course of the presidential campaign in 2000, when Gephardt is expected to run against Clinton's heir apparent, Vice President Al Gore. Thus, even after his triumphant reelection, Clinton still faced the profound challenge of establishing the boundaries in which his party and domestic policy could be reformed.

Yet it might be unreasonable, indeed, dangerous, to rely so heavily on presidents to determine the contours of political action. The modern presidency operates in a political arena that is seldom congenial to meaningful political debate and all too often guilty of deflecting attention from the painful struggles about the appropriate meaning of liberalism or the relative merits of contemporary liberalism and conservatism. With the liberation of the executive from many of the constraints of party leadership and the rise of the mass media, presidents have resorted to rhetoric and administration, tools with which they have sought to forge new, more personal ties with the public. But, as the nation has witnessed all too clearly during the past thirty years, this form of "populist" presidential politics can all too readily degenerate into rank opportunism. Moreover, it risks exposing the people to the kind of public figures who will exploit citizens' impatience with the difficult tasks involved in sustaining a healthy constitutional democracy.

Presidents who enjoy prominent places in history have justified their reform programs in constitutional terms, claiming to restore the proper understanding of first principles, even as they have attempted to transfuse the Declaration and Constitution with new meaning. But they have done so as great party leaders, in the midst of major partisan realignments. Critical partisan elections have enabled each generation to claim its right to redefine the Constitution's principles and reorganize its institutions. The New Deal continued this unending task to ensure that each generation could affirm its attachment to constitutional government. It remains to be seen, however, whether the legacy of the New Deal for the presidency and party politics has left room for still another rendezvous with America's political destiny.

Notes

1. For a more detailed treatment of the issues discussed in this chapter, see Sidney M. Milkis, *The President and the Parties: The Transformation of the American Party System Since the New Deal* (New York: Oxford University Press, 1993).
2. Michael J. Malbin, "Was Divided Government Really Such a Big Problem?" in Bradford P. Wilson and Peter W. Schramm, eds., *Seperation of Powers and Good Government* (Lanham, MD: Rowman and Littlefield, 1994), 233.
3. Franklin D. Roosevelt, "Address at the Commonwealth Club in San Francisco," September 23, 1932, *Public Papers and Addresses,* ed. Samuel J. Rosenman, 14 volumes (New York: Random House, 1938–1950), I: 751–52.
4. Franklin D. Roosevelt, "State of the Union Address," January 11, 1944, *Public Papers,* ed. Rosenman, 13: 40.
5. On the tension between party politics and government centralization, see James Piereson, "Party Government," *Political Science Reviewer* 12 (Fall 1982): 51–52; and Stephen Skowronek, *Building a New American State: The Expansion of National Administrative Capacities, 1877–1920* (Cambridge: Cambridge University Press, 1982). I discuss the alliance between the two-party system and local self-government in Milkis, "Localism, Political Parties, and Civic Virtue," in Martha Derthick, ed. *Dilemmas of American Federalism* (Cambridge: Cambridge University Press, forthcoming).
6. Franklin D. Roosevelt, Introduction to *Public Papers,* ed. Rosenman, 7: xxix.
7. Arthur Krock, "New Deal Victory Laid to Federal Money Lure, *New York Times,* May 28, 1938, section 4, 2.
8. Thomas Stokes, *Chip off My Shoulder* (Princeton: Princeton University Press, 1940), 503.
9. The two-thirds rule of the Democratic party required support from two-thirds of the delegates for the nomination of the president and vice president. This rule had been defended in the past because it guarded the most loyal Democratic region—the South—against the imposition of an unwanted ticket by the less habitually Democratic North, East, and West. The Roosevelt administration's push to abolish the two-thirds rule, therefore, weakened the influence of Southern Democrats and facilitated the adoption of a national reform program.
10. Morton J. Frisch, *Franklin D. Roosevelt: The Contribution of the New Deal to American Political Thought and Practice* (Boston: St. Wayne, 1975), 79.
11. Franklin D. Roosevelt, radio address, June 24, 1938, *Public Papers and Addresses,* ed., Rosenman, 9: 28.
12. Significantly, the two Supreme Court cases that triggered the dispute between Roosevelt and the Judiciary were *Humphrey's Executor v. U.S.,* 295 U.S. 602 (1935); and *A.L.A. Schecter Poultry Corp. et al. v. United States,* 295 U.S. 553 (1935); both of which imposed constraints on the executive authority of the president.
13. *Report of the President's Committee on Administrative Management,* (Washington DC: Government Printing Office, 1937), 53.
14. Paul Van Riper, *History of the United States Civil Service* (Evanston, IL: Row, Peterson, 1958), 327.
15. See A. James Reichley, "The Rise of National Parties" in "John E. Chubb and Paul E. Perterson, eds., *The New Direction in American Politics* (Washington, DC: The Brookings Institution, 1985). By the end of the 1980s, however, Reichley was much less hopeful that the emergent national parties were well suited to perform the parties' historic function of mobilizing public support for political values and substantive gov-

ernment approaches and policies. See *Life of the Parties: A History of American Political Parties* (New York: Free Press, 1992), especially chapters 18–21.

16. Nixon transformed the Bureau of the Budget into the Office of Management and Budget (OMB) by executive order in 1970, adding a cadre of presidentially appointed assistant directors for policy to stand between the OMB director and the bureau's civil servants. Consequently, the budget office both attained additional policy responsibility and became more responsive to the president. In the Reagan administration, the OMB was given a central role in remaking regulatory policy.

17. Richard B. Stewart, "The Reformation of American Administrative Law," *Harvard Law Review*, vol. 88, no. 8 (June 1975): 1712; Allen Schick, "Congress and the 'Details of Administration,' " *Public Administration Review*, vol. 36 (September/October, 1976): 516–28; Jeremy Rabkin, "The Judiciary in the Administrative State," *The Public Interest*, no. 71 (Spring 1983): 662–84; and R. Shep Melnick, "The Courts, Congress, and Programmatic Rights," in Richard A. Harris and Sidney M. Milkis, eds., *Remaking American Politics* (Boulder, CO: Westview Press, 1989).

18. Robert Putnam, "Tuning In, Tuning Out: The Strange Disappearance of Social Capital in America," *PS*, vol. 28, no. 4 (December 1995): 664–83.

19. W. Carey McWilliams, "Two-Tier Politics and the Problems of Public Policy," in Marc K. Landy and Martin A. Levin, eds., *The New Politics of Public Policy* (Baltimore and London: Johns Hopkins University Press, 1995).

20. William Clinton, "The New Covenant: Responsibility and Rebuilding the American Community," Washington, DC, October 23, 1991. This speech marked the first pronouncement of these "sacred principles." From then on, Clinton repeated them at every defining moment of his journey to the White House: the announcement of Senator Albert Gore, who shared his ideas, as his running mate; the party platform; his acceptance speech at the Democratic convention in New York; and his victory remarks in Little Rock on election night.

21. The willingness of Senate Republicans to resort to the filibuster as a tool of party opposition on key Clinton proposals such as the economic stimulus package and health-care reform testified to the fundamental conflicts that divided the parties in Congress and prevented harmonious relations between the executive and legislature. Such a course was virtually unprecedented; historically, the filibuster had only been employed by mavericks or regional minorities to obstruct party leaders. That its use was orchestrated by the Republican party to ensnare President Clinton was a mark of the bitter partisanship that lingered from the Reagan–Bush era, as well as of Clinton's failure to move the country beyond the institutional conflicts spawned by partisan estrangement. See Alan Brinkley, "The 43 Percent President," *New York Times Magazine*, July 4, 1993, 2. Finding themselves in the minority after the 1994 election, Democrats in the Senate resorted to similar obstructionist tactics to keep the Republican majority at bay. See Eliza Newlin Carney, "Running Interference," *National Journal*, November 22, 1997, 2360–63.

22. Sidney Blumenthal, "Bob Dole's First Strike," *New Yorker*, May 3, 1993, 40–46; Douglas Jehl, "Rejoicing Is Muted for the President in Budget Victory," *New York Times*, August 8, 1993, 1, 23; David Shribman, "Budget Battle: A Hollow One for President," *Boston Globe*, August 8, 1993, 1, 24.

23. Indeed, during the early days of his presidency, Clinton sought to identify with his party's leadership in Congress and the national committee—partly, one suspects, to avoid the political isolation from which Carter suffered. Whereas Carter kept party leaders in Congress and the national committee at arms' length, Clinton sought both to embrace and empower the national organization. The White House lobbying efforts on Capitol Hill focused almost exclusively on the Democratic caucus; and the administra-

tion relied heavily on the Democratic National Committee to marshal public support for its domestic programs. Interviews with White House staffer, November 3, 1994, not for attribution; David Wilhelm, chairman, Democratic National Committee, October 18, 1993; and Craig Smith, political director, Democratic National Committee, October 19, 1993. Also see Rhodes Cook, "DNC Under Wilhelm Seeking a New Role," *Congressional Quarterly Weekly Report,* March 13, 1993, 634.

24. Al From and Will Marshall, *The Road to Realignment: Democrats and the Perot Voters,* Democratic Leadership Council, July 1, 1993, 1-3–1-5.

25. David Shribman, "A New Brand of D.C. Politics," *The Boston Globe,* November 18, 1993, 15; Gwen Ifill, "56 Long Days of Coordinated Persuasion," *New York Times,* November 19, 1993, A27.

26. William Clinton, "Address Before a Joint Session of Congress on the State of the Union," January 23, 1996, printed in *Congressional Quarterly Weekly Report,* January 27, 1996, 258–62.

27. William Clinton, "Remarks on Signing the Personal Responsibility and Opportunity Reconciliation Act," August 22, 1996, *Weekly Compilation of Presidential Documents,* no. 1484.

28. Clinton, State of the Union Address, January 23, 1996.

29. Bob Woodward, *The Choice* (New York: Simon and Schuster, 1996), 344.

30. Not surprisingly, Clinton's speech received praise from the Democratic Leadership Council's president, Al From, who celebrated it as an attempt "to speak to the main concerns of the millions of disaffected voters in the political center" who were estranged from the ideological and institutional combat between liberal and conservatives and "were likely to be the margin of difference in the 1996 election." From, "More than a Good Speech: The State of the Union Address Could Have Marked a Turning Point in History," *New Democrat,* March–April 1996, 35–36.

31. Michael Nelson, "The Election: Turbulence and Tranquility in Contemporary American Politics," in Michael Nelson, ed., *The Elections of 1996* (Washington, DC: Congressional Quarterly Press, 1997), 52; and Gary Jacobson, "The 105th Congress: Unprecedented and Unsurprising," in *The Elections of 1996,* 161.

32. Clinton's "third way" politics is placed in historical perspective and carefully analyzed in Stephen Skowronek, *The Politics Presidents Make: Leadership from John Adams to Bill Clinton* (Cambridge: Harvard University Press, 1997), 447–64.

33. Richard Stevenson, "After Year of Wrangling, Accord Is Reached on Plan to Balance the Budget by 2002," *New York Times,* May 3, 1997, 1.

34. The term "extraordinary isolation" is Woodrow Wilson's. See *Constitutional Government in the United States* (New York: Columbia University Press, 1908), 69.

35. Adam Clymer, "Under Attack, Clinton Gets No Cover from His Party," *New York Times,* March 16, 1997, 1.

6

Elections and Presidential Policymaking

Lyn Ragsdale and Jerrold G. Rusk

Writing in *Federalist #70* about the constitutional outline of the American presidency, Alexander Hamilton characterized two central elements of the office: energy and safety in a single executive. He commented, "The ingredients which constitute energy in the executive are unity; duration; an adequate provision for its support; and competent powers. The ingredients which constitute safety in the republican sense are a due dependence on the people and a due responsibility."[1] Through the development of the office, Hamilton's words regarding energy have encompassed a policy role for presidents. Since Washington, presidents have proposed legislation, taken positions on bills they have not directly sponsored, independently promulgated executive orders, commanded troop movements, and negotiated treaties and other international agreements. The framers' concern for a republican office has led to an American fixation on presidential elections in which candidates present themselves as voices of the people courting voters' attention and favor. Winning the election is an uncommon prize that makes presidential candidates and presidents a unique focus of national politics.

The framers' interest in the policy power of the office and the public responsiveness of its occupants presents a nexus between policy decisions and electoral choices. An intuitive sense of politics suggests that elections matter to the policy course of the nation. James K. Polk promises and delivers expansionism, on which Henry Clay hesitates. Abraham Lincoln's support of emancipation wins out against Stephen Douglas's calls for popular sovereignty. Franklin Roosevelt's victory offers a New Deal rather than Herbert Hoover's opposition to the "dole." Even those elections in which the choices are less boldly defined seemingly have consequences for national policy decisions. The very lack of sharp contrast between candidates' positions during the election may create or continue equivocal policy choices after the election. The choices may perpetuate the status quo or leave major problems unsatisfactorily addressed. In 1968, voters heard Hubert Humphrey's outline of possible negotiations to end the war in Vietnam and Richard Nixon's secret plan to do the same. Faced with this ambiguous choice, voters were closely divided. After the election, the ambiguous policy ideas became discrepant policy roads taken by Nixon, whose plan included removing American troops from Vietnam, while at the same time invading the neighboring countries of Cambodia and Laos.

Presidents have bolstered this intuition by announcing that their election victories grant them mandates to govern. The larger the winning margin, the louder presidents proclaim that they have received this directive from the people to exercise power on their behalf. Presidents attempt to create the impression that voters not only approve of the winner's positions and programs, but, in fact, the electorate voted for the president because of these policies. With often lopsided, even landslide, victories found in the electoral college results, presidents can point with assurance to the unity of the nation behind their causes. Even though this math makes little real sense, especially when calculated from the aggregation of winner-take-all state results in the electoral college, it makes powerful political sense. Since Jefferson, presidents have interpreted their election victories as a keen source of power rather than the restriction on power—the safety—the framers sought. Jefferson observed, "In a government like ours, it is the duty of the Chief Magistrate, in order to enable himself to do all the good which his station requires, . . . to unite in himself the confidence of the whole people. This alone, in any case, where the energy of the nation is required, can produce a union of the powers of the whole, and point them in a single direction, as if all constituted by one body and one mind."[2] Presidents can then use the perception of an electoral mandate to encourage members of Congress to support the White House, since it is the people, not just the president, who have spoken. Thus, mandates are powerful political symbols for presidents which add to their credibility as policymakers.

Analysts, however, openly discount mandates, in Raymond Wolfinger's words, "as inherently implausible."[3] Presidential elections are set to a constitutional four-year clock that is not necessarily in time with a policy crisis or a particular set of pressing issues. In addition, candidates often downplay the importance of issues and stress their images as potential presidents. As

Charles Jones concludes, "an election should not ordinarily be treated as a national policy test."[4] These investigators point to the 1980 election as a classic case in point. Exhaustive public opinion data strongly indicated that there was no Reagan mandate. Instead the electorate voted against Jimmy Carter's lack of mastery of his job, not for Ronald Reagan's conservative, anti-government platform.

Yet presidents may well have the last laugh. Political scientists categorically stating that there is no mandate on election day do not prevent presidents from convincing the public and Washington politicians that indeed such a mandate exists by inauguration day. As much as the 1980 election is a clear-cut example of the absence of a real mandate, at the same time, it is a notable instance of the presence of a created mandate. Reagan, with the help of many post-election media commentators and members of Congress, claimed a new era of conservative dominance had dawned, and his administration proceeded to act as though it had. Because the precise intentions of voters and their reasons for voting for one candidate and not another are never fully clear, creating a mandate even where one does not exist remains a temptation that few presidents can resist.

Presidents are not the only ones discussing mandates on election night. A *Washington Post* editorial commented in 1980: "Governor Reagan surely has both a strong public mandate and a strong personal inclination to do something."[5] Mandates are convenient framing devices around which the news media, particular television news in the modern era, can tell the election night story. Mandates say in simple, direct terms what the election results mean—what voters were really doing in the voting booth just hours before. If the president's party also wins large numbers of congressional seats or captures one or both houses of Congress from the other party, then the mandate story can be told in especially vivid ways. Members of Congress also find mandates to be useful tools to prioritize the endless flow of legislation on Capitol Hill. Suggesting that there is a policy mandate for the newly elected president means that the positions the president takes and the specific policy proposals he issues become the agenda for Congress. While this is nothing more than a starting point, not an ending point, for the policy process, it nonetheless offers the members of the president's party an easy set of goals for legislative action and gives the opposition party an easy target for counterclaims.

There are of course limits to the symbolism of mandates and their practical political advantages. Some presidents win in very close races and may well pick up only a few seats in Congress, as Richard Nixon did in 1968 and Jimmy Carter did in 1976. Under these circumstances, it is undoubtedly politically wiser for such presidents to downplay mandates and thereby dampen the expectations the nation has of what they can accomplish as policymakers.

Beyond mandates, there are other possible electoral effects on presidential policy. Mandates, by their very nature, capture only the biggest issue picture—the most pressing issues identified during the campaign and what presidents are able to do about them after the inauguration. Yet there are countless policy stands presidents take and numerous policy issues that arise in the daily work between presidents and Congress during the four years of the president's term, that may or may not be caught up in mandate symbolism. Still, on these numerous issues, the election may have a telling effect. The president's victory margin may dictate how active he is, how large an agenda he offers, and how frequently he pursues policy initiatives independently of Congress.

Despite these possible connections of elections to policy, little is actually known about the extent to which election results affect presidents' policy efforts. Beyond interpretative accounts of individual elections and the mandates they may or may not offer presidents, there has been no systematic test of the influence of election results on presidential policymaking.[6] So whether elections affect presidential policymaking is an open question worthy of exploration.

The purpose of this chapter is to uncover the degree to which presidents' policy actions are responsive to voters' electoral choices. To accomplish this, the chapter briefly considers the prevailing approaches in the literatures on presidential policymaking and presidential elections. It then outlines a theory of embedded institutions—presidential elections and the presidency—in which elections are nested into policymaking decisions in the White House in such a way that they cannot be separated from them. An empirical test of this theory of embedded institutions is then presented for two types of presidents' policy activities: policy positions taken on roll call votes in Congress from Dwight Eisenhower to Bill Clinton and policy-specific executive orders signed by presidents from Franklin Roosevelt to Clinton. The effect of elections on a third measure, that of presidential success on roll call positions, is also considered from Eisenhower to Clinton.

Approaches to Policymaking and Elections

Scholars who study presidential policymaking are usually not those who study presidential elections. The topics employ different theoretical orientations and address distinct empirical questions. So electoral-policy links are often not made amidst these differences.

Currently, three perspectives prevail in the study of presidential policymaking. The most traditional and well developed of these approaches treats policymaking as an exercise of presidential power. Beginning with Richard Neustadt's pivotal work, research has focused on the policy success of presidents attempting to secure bargains with other political decision makers through their constitutional vantage points, professional reputations, and public prestige. Louis Fisher considers the constitutional power presidents have in their relations with Congress. Paul Light examines the political capital presidents acquire from their election margins, public support, and congressional strength in setting their policy agendas. George Edwards and Jon Bond and Richard Fleisher examine how presidents' political resources, in particular the status of their party in Congress and their standing with the public, affect their success in winning votes on Capitol Hill. Thus, these authors and others are interested in presidential strategy and leadership. Election victories, to the extent they are considered, are a resource presidents can use to play out the strategies and exercise leadership.[7]

A second approach considers presidential policymaking from a process perspective. Steven Shull asserts that "the roles, emphases, and behaviors of actors vary across stages of the policy process."[8] Scholars investigate the several stages of the policy process and identify how presidential influence shifts across agenda setting, formulation, adoption, implementation, and evaluation. These researchers recognize that elections are an initial phase of the policy process but do not directly examine how elections may have ongoing effects on policy across presidents' terms.

A third approach addresses presidential policymaking as the management of different types of policies.[9] Authors examine the offices and staffs involved in domestic, economic, military, and foreign policymaking. They are especially interested in how this policymaking differs across administrations. Each type of policy offers distinct challenges for presidents from the prevailing political and economic environments, various governmental and nongovernmental actors, and shifting public opinion. In turn, these external factors create pressure on the internal organizations of key White House units—the National Security Council staff, the Office of Management and Budget, and the Office of Policy Development.[10] Since researchers who employ this approach are primarily interested in organizational development across different policy types, there is little mention of elections.

Each of these approaches offers insights into presidential policymaking. There is only limited overlap among the topics pursued in the three approaches as each tackles a different part of the elephant in a different way. The first and the third approaches are often interested in the differences among individual presidents, while the second is more concerned with how the policy process often drives presidents to behave similarly. In addition, none of the approaches is expressly interested in the connections between presidential elections and policymaking.

To make matters worse, electoral studies are far more diverse in their approaches and subjects than is research on presidential policymaking.[11] Perhaps the sharpest focus in election research is on understanding the electoral *process* and how the images and issues presented by candidates develop throughout the campaign, how the media captures these campaign elements, and how voter support ebbs and flows for specific candidates. Students of elections are interested in electoral *outcomes* to the extent that they reveal what and how voters decide as part of the process. But once election day has come and gone, election scholars have little interest in the consequences of the elections for government and politics.

Embedded Institutions

What is lacking, then, is a theoretical understanding of the connection between voters' electoral choices and presidents' policy actions and an empirical test of that connection. To make that link, we begin by reorienting research on the American presidency away from the study of presidential power, and toward the study of the presidential institution. As noted above, presidential power is the dominant approach to the study of presidential policymaking. But it is also *the* approach to the study of the presidency generally. While several studies have examined the presidency as an institution, they have not explicitly examined presidential policymaking within an institutional framework.[12] We consciously drop the central assumption made in the study of presidential power—that individual presidents matter. This is indeed an assumption, not an incontrovertible empirical fact of the presidency. Imagine, instead, that American presidents are faceless bureaucrats whose behavior is largely directed by the office in which they work. Rather than having ample flexibility to get what they want done, they work within structures and are bound by rules that govern their daily decisions. They follow standard operating procedures that require certain actions and discourage others. Continuity more than change marks the transition from one president to the next. While this depiction is deliberately extreme, it is necessary to recognize that presidents have "power" only within the constraints of the presidency as an institution.

As March and Olsen observe, "modern political science has, for the most part, described political events as the consequence of calculated decisions" of individual political actors. As an alternative, the institutional approach stresses that "political behavior [is] embedded in an institutional structure of rules, norms, expectations, and traditions that severely limit the free play of individual will and calculations."[13] Institutions have stability and value as ends in themselves. They lack expendability. Rather than being dispensable tools doing an assortment of jobs, institutions are indispensable social entities with unique histories, permanence, and predictability, and particular ways of conducting business that people take for granted regardless of whether these ways are the best ways of doing business and regardless of who is conducting the business at any point in time. Stability denotes that an organization, rule, or practice is not a mechanistic operation that can be easily altered or eliminated. The institution survives various challenges and achieves self-maintenance—it exists in the future because it has existed in the past.

As a mechanistic entity, a presidential election merely provides a way to choose between alternate candidates with an easy plurality decision rule determining the winner. As an institution, the election creates a cycle of government power during which it is known when those in office may relinquish power. As a mechanistic entity, the presidency exists to perform the technical tasks of executing the laws passed by Congress. As an institution, the presidency has longevity, independence, and symbolic import which allows it to proceed in many policy directions not authorized by Congress. Value denotes "the prizing of the [entity] for its own sake."[14] The institution has a distinct identity and a unique way of conducting business. Elections are valued as rituals of the democratic process. The presidency is seen as the single most powerful office in the world, offering innovative policies and leadership to bring the innovations to fruition.

The responsiveness of presidents' policy choices to voters' electoral choices then hinges on the interconnection between two institutions: the presidency as a policy apparatus and elections as venues for public responsiveness. Elections as the ritual of democracy are thus embedded in the presidency as the most powerful office in the land. Part of the power the presidency draws is from the democratic ritual and, indeed, from the very mandates that presidents claim to have received. The elections serve to legitimize and expand presidents' policy roles which are present in only the briefest sketch in the Constitution. The modern conception of the presidency as an active policy institution, developed by Theodore Roosevelt and Woodrow Wilson, rests on presidents' dominating foreign policy, pursuing a domestic policy agenda, and running the executive branch *because* they are representatives of the people. Presidential policy activism runs on claims of public support that is obtained in the first instance at election time.

Elections also create policy expectations for the administration. With the numerous promises made during the campaign, Washington politicians and others around the country expect a certain level of policy activity from the

White House, even if the word "mandate" is never uttered by the incoming president. As one Office of Management and Budget staff member explained it, it is a matter of quantity not quality: "There is not enough time or reward in thinking carefully about effectiveness and implementation. The emphasis is really on quantity, not quality. The president could never be reelected on the effectiveness theme. 'We didn't do much, but it is all working very well.' Do you think the president could win on that?"[15] This fits with the modern conception of the presidency as an active policy institution. Presidents' election margins may provide them the opportunity to address specific policy issues more effectively than they could otherwise. Policy expectations drawn from the presidential election are then readjusted after the midterm congressional elections. Invariably the single word signaled to the presidential administration about policy at the midterm is not mandate but "caution." The presidential institution adapts to the new numbers on Capitol Hill as priorities and other policy stances are reshaped.

Much of the policy activism of the presidency is pegged to work in Congress. But as an institution, the presidency has gained autonomy to act unilaterally on key policy matters.[16] Presidents can unilaterally commit American troops to situations around the globe, sign executive agreements without Senate advice or consent, and issue executive orders without securing their passage in Congress. What effect do elections have on these independent policy actions? A theory of embedded institutions would suggest that elections have as much to say about these actions as they do about presidential policymaking in Congress, but with a crucial difference. Large election victories invite presidential policymaking in Congress. Presidents can claim Theodore Roosevelt's mantel of "steward of the people" and rally congressional attention and support. But what about those presidents who barely squeak out a victory? In these situations, the electoral-policy connection is likely to move presidents away from the congressional arena and toward more independent efforts that do not require the substantial outlay of political capital that presidents with small election wins may not have. Using independent policy actions, they may still claim they are working, in Roosevelt's words, "in the best interest of the people," but they do not need to do so in the halls of Congress. As an example, having won a modest election victory in 1992, Bill Clinton issued an executive order upon taking office to end discrimination against gays in the military. He did this rather than sending legislation to Congress. The White House was correct in assuming that they did not have the political capital necessary to win a fight on Capitol Hill over the issue; they were incorrect in assuming that there would be no fight if they issued an executive order. Congress and military officials forced Clinton to rescind, revise, and reissue the order. Thus, elections embedded in the presidency direct presidents as policymakers in different ways depending on how big their election night victory is.

Finally, elections create and maintain the political time on which the office runs. This political time has two important properties. First, the election time clock ticks much faster than a normal clock. Presidents know that they have a short four-year time period in which they can act and this period is interrupted by congressional elections at the midterm that invariably worsen the president's party's strength in Congress. As one White House aide described it, "You should subtract one year for the reelection campaign, another six months for the midterms, six months for start-up, six months for closing, and another month or two for an occasional vacation. That leaves you with a two-year presidential term."[17] Second, the election time clock ticks much louder than a normal clock at the start of the president's term than it does later on. Elections define a honeymoon for presidents who have now won the mantel of democratic leader. The honeymoon opens a policy window for presidential administrations that will not be open for long. In the words of a Kennedy adviser, "If you don't get going early, you'll be out of office before you get the program set."[18] Lyndon Johnson put it more bluntly: "You've got to give it all you can that first year. Doesn't matter what kind of majority you come in with. You've got just one year when they treat you right and before they start worrying about themselves."[19] Elections thus embed symbolism, policy expectations, and political timing into the presidency.

Models, Measures, and Methods

We now present an empirical analysis of the influence of election outcomes on three measures of presidential policy activity: presidents' positions taken on roll call votes in Congress, the degree of success presidents have on those positions, and the promulgation of policy-specific executive orders. Elections are multifaceted institutions that encompass separate presidential and congressional elections with distinct results. We therefore examine two measures of national election results as the independent variables of principal interest: the president's own winning popular vote percentage and the total number of congressional seats won by the president's party in both the House and Senate in a given presidential or midterm election year.[20] A third measure of the presidential election cycle is also included. Presidents act according to how much or how little time they have until the next presidential election.[21]

The three dependent variables are among the most important ways that presidents can influence or enact policy in the United States. They reflect the ongoing nature of White House policy activity regardless of who is president. Since Jefferson, presidents have been expected, with greater or lesser degrees of regularity, to take positions on legislation before Congress. Presidents are usually selective in taking stands on legislation. While lawmakers introduce thousands of pieces of legislation and take hundreds of roll call votes every year, presidents take positions on only a small portion of these votes. When the White House takes a position on a piece of legislation, it does not necessarily mean that it is one of the crucial items desired by the White House (although it may be), but it does mean that it is an item of some visibility and controversy. We expect that the larger presidents' election victories, the more actively they will take positions on legislation. Election results not only direct presidents to be policymakers for the people but they indicate how active those policymakers will be. The presidential positions are measured by the number of times the president takes a clear public position on roll call votes in either the House or the Senate as determined by Congressional Quarterly Inc.[22]

Presidential success in Congress denotes how frequently Congress agrees with the positions the president takes. We would expect presidents with larger election victory margins to be more successful in their position-taking in Congress. Electoral strength, as a feature embedded in the presidential institution, may help presidents convince members of Congress of their legislative positions. This success is measured by the percentage of times a majority of the House or Senate supports the president's position on a roll call vote.[23]

One of the most seemingly invisible, yet ubiquitous, policy activities of American presidents is their issuance of executive orders. Distinct from positions on legislation, executive orders give presidents a freer hand. They make the decisions without congressional authorization. Beginning with Monroe, but with much greater frequency in the twentieth century, presidents have signed executive orders that have specific policy content on such matters as war, civil rights, banking, abortion, and environmental standards. These executive orders reflect the autonomy of the presidency as a policy institution to conduct business and make binding decisions independently of other parts of the government, especially Congress. All executive orders were coded for policy content affecting a segment of the population, region of the country, or foreign nation. The remaining orders were administrative in nature, providing largely pro forma internal guidelines for the surveying of public lands, civil service rules, the retirement of government employees, and federal holidays.[24] We hypothesize that presidents with smaller victory margins are more likely to actively issue policy executive orders. This becomes a way for them to act outside the legislative arena and seek policy solutions that do not require congressional approval.[25] With bigger victories, presidents can more comfortably act on Capitol Hill.

In addition to the two electoral measures as independent variables, we consider several control measures. We choose those factors that both can be expected to influence the dependent variables and are correlated with the election variables. If a control variable is either uncorrelated with the electoral variables or has no influence on the dependent variable (but not necessarily both), then that variable can be safely left out of the equation, as estimates of the effects of the electoral measures will not be biased. Based on these criteria, we have selected three categories of control variables. First, presidents' policy activities are likely to be influenced by key exogenous political and economic factors: their public approval ratings, inflation, and unemployment. The president's approval ratings are likely to inversely affect presidents' position-taking on legislation and their policy executive orders. The lower the president's popularity, the more likely they will attempt to compensate for this with high levels of policy activity, perhaps in an attempt to improve their standing with the public. However, we would expect presidential approval to be positively related to presidential success in Congress. Although research typically shows the effect of approval on success to be small, presidents' popularity ratings may well convince wavering members of Congress to side with the White House.[26] Inflation and unemployment are likely to increase presidential policy efforts. Presidents respond to the pressures of a weakened economy with various proposals and positions on legislation that may alleviate the situation. As these economic conditions worsen, however, presidential policy success is likely to decline.[27]

Second, seasons of presidential politics may influence presidents' policy activities. Presidents are typically less ambitious and less successful in their second terms than they are in their first terms.[28] So we would expect fewer positions on matters before Congress and less success in the second term.

Finally, we include a measure of individual presidents to capture variations across them. We would expect little variation among presidents in their positions on legislation or their policy executive orders. Both are well developed patterns of activity in the White House that do not depend on the current incumbent. We would expect, however, some variation across presidents in their success on legislation because this may well depend on the president's individual style with members of Congress, and his degree of political experience, skill, and knowledge in handling Capitol Hill.[29]

We estimate models of presidential position-taking on legislation and presidential success on legislation for Eisenhower to Clinton during the period 1953 to 1996. We estimate the model of policy executive orders for Roosevelt to Clinton during the period 1941 to 1996.[30]

Table 6.1

Electoral Effects on Presidents' Positions on Roll Call Votes, 1953-1996
(OLS estimates)

Variable	Coefficient	Standard error	T-ratio
Presidential vote	4.755	1.428	3.330
Congressional seats	.411	.149	2.760
Election cycle	−7.055	6.095	−1.157
Presidential approval	−2.233	.701	−3.184
Consumer prices	1.428	1.483	.962
Unemployment	−.151	−.004	−.030
Second term	−23.534	21.435	−1.098
Individual presidents	2.407	4.257	.565
Intercept	−62.811	—	—

Notes: R^2 = .629.
Standard error of equation = 39.923.
Number of cases = 42.

The Electoral-Policy Connection

Table 6.1 presents estimates from an ordinary least squares regression equation testing the effects of electoral factors, relative to the controls, on presidents' public positions on roll call votes. The results indicate that the presidential vote has a strong positive effect on the number of legislative positions presidents take. The larger the presidential victory, the more active presidents are likely to be. With a 1 percent increase in the popular vote, presidents take nearly five more positions on legislation. In addition, the congressional election results also affect presidential policy action. A gain of two congressional seats prompts presidents to take at least one more legislative position. Of course, the presidential party typically wins and loses far more than a single seat in presidential and midterm election years. For instance, the Republicans won twenty-three total congressional seats in 1952 prompting nearly twelve more policy positions by Eisenhower in 1953, all other things being equal. The election cycle does not affect position-taking. The negative sign of the coefficient indicates that presidents take fewer positions later in their terms than they do upon taking office, but relative to the effects of the other factors, this is not a statistically significant effect.

Among the control variables, only presidential approval has a statistically significant influence on presidents' legislative position-taking. As anticipated, the lower the president's approval ratings, the more likely he will take additional legislative positions. With a percentage point decline in

Table 6.2

Electoral Effects on Presidents' Success on Roll Call Votes, 1953–1996
(OLS estimates)

Variable	Coefficient	Standard error	T-ratio
Presidential vote	−.610	.250	−2.435
Congressional seats	.121	.026	4.646
Election cycle	−2.334	1.069	−2.183
Presidential approval	−.083	.123	−.671
Consumer prices	−.110	.260	−.421
Unemployment	1.190	.887	1.342
Second term	−7.248	3.760	−1.928
Individual presidents	−2.317	.747	−3.103
Intercept	97.180	—	—

Notes: $R^2 = .785$.
Standard error of equation = 7.002.
Number of cases = 42.

approval, presidents take an additional two legislative positions. Notably, the other control measures have no influence on presidential position-taking. The economic factors do not affect presidents' legislative efforts. In addition, the estimate for the individual president variable reveals that there are few differences among the nine presidents from Eisenhower to Clinton on their levels of legislative position-taking.

Table 6.2 reports the results of an equation testing the effects of the electoral factors on presidents' success in Congress. The results again reveal the strong effects of the presidential and congressional election results on presidents' success in Congress. Congressional seats obtained by a president's party improve the president's chances at success. Ten additional congressional seats improve presidents' success by one percentage point. Contrary to expectations, however, the presidential vote adversely affects presidential success. The larger the presidential election victory, the lower the success achieved. A 1 percent increase in the popular vote result prompts nearly an equal decline in success. So while major electoral victories increase presidents' legislative activity, they do not translate into legislative success. The bigger the victory, the more likely presidents will take policy positions. At the same time, however, these victories are no assurance of success on behalf of those positions. Unlike the results for presidents' position-taking, the election cycle variable is a statistically significant determinant of presidents' success on roll call votes. Not unexpectedly, the longer the president has been in office, the lower his success rate. For every year of the term, presidential success drops by over 2 percentage points.

Table 6.3

Presidents' Victories, Policy Positions, and Congressional Success

President	Popular vote (%)	Positions[a]	Success[b]
Eisenhower, I	55.1	98	79.1
Eisenhower, II	57.4	142	65.5
Kennedy	49.7	187	84.7
Johnson	61.1	265	81.3
Nixon, I	43.4	124	73.2
Nixon, II	60.7	284	54.8
Ford	—	143	57.4
Carter	50.1	242	76.4
Reagan, I	50.7	199	71.9
Reagan, II	58.8	179	51.8
Bush	53.4	187	51.7
Clinton	43.0	191	66.0

Notes:
[a]Entries are the annual mean number of positions taken for the term.
[b]Entries are the annual mean percentage success for the term.

The control variables have greater influence on presidential success than they do presidential position-taking. Consistent with the election cycle effect, presidents in their second terms are less successful than presidents in their first terms. On average, success falls seven percentage points in the second term relative to the first. The results also show variations across individual presidents, the negatively signed coefficient revealing that later presidents have been less successful than earlier presidents. Economic conditions and presidential approval do not affect presidential success. Past research has indicated an effect of presidents' public approval ratings on their ability to see legislation they approve of passed in Congress. The results here suggest that the approval ratings do not have such an effect relative to the other indicators in the equation.

The divergent effects of presidents' election victories on their level of activity in Congress distinct from their success in Congress deserves more careful scrutiny. Table 6.3 presents a comparison of the presidential vote, presidential positions (annual mean number for the term), and presidential success (annual mean percentage for the term) for presidents from Eisenhower to Clinton. The table reveals the dilemma that second-term presidents face in their policy actions. Eisenhower won by 57 percent of the vote in 1956, a 2 percent gain from his winning total in 1952. He took an additional fifty positions on matters before Congress, but watched his success rate drop by almost 14 percentage points. Nixon's problem, intensified by Watergate, was far more dramatic. Winning by almost 61 percent of the vote, Nixon more than doubled the positions his administration took on legislation in 1973 and 1974 over the first term. The Nixon success rate, however, plummeted 18 percentage points. Reagan handily won his second term by 59 percent of the vote and although the number of the positions the administration took in the second term actually declined slightly, the overall success on those positions dropped 20 percentage points. Bush faced a predicament similar to that of the second-term presidents. While winning his election comfortably and actively taking policy positions, he did poorly in Congress with a 51.7 percent success rate for his term, the lowest of any president studied.

Table 6.4 presents findings on the effects of electoral factors on the number of policy executive orders presidents sign annually. The election factors again influence these independent policy actions. The presidential vote negatively influences the number of orders. As expected, when presidents win in close races, they are more likely to engage in independent policy actions. For every 2 percentage points gained in their victory at the polls, presidents are inclined to issue one less executive order. The number of congressional seats held by the president's party positively influences executive order activity. Ten congressional seats held by the president's party translate into one more policy executive order. The effect of national elections on presidents' policy executive orders does not extend to the election cycle. Presidents issue just as many policy executive orders at the end of the term as they do at the beginning. So policy executive orders are not timed with elections in mind even though election results affect the number of orders issued.

Among the control variables, deteriorating economic conditions increase the number of policy orders. Most notably, a percentage increase in the unemployment rate prompts presidents to issue two more executive orders, ceteris paribus. Presumably some of these orders are designed to address the prevailing economic situation. Presidential approval has a strong negative influence on presidents issuing policy executive orders. For every 1 percentage point drop in presidential approval, presidents issue three more executive orders. They may use this form of policy activity to shore up public support with independent policy actions that make them appear to be in charge. The individual presidents variable does not affect policy executive orders.

What Difference Do Elections Make?

What difference do elections make to the presidency? What is their impact on presidents' policy activity and on support for the victorious president's

Table 6.4

Electoral Effects on Presidents' Policy Executive Orders, 1941–1996
(OLS estimates)

Variable	Coefficient	Standard error	T-ratio
Presidential vote	−.422	.279	−1.716
Congressional seats	.115	.030	3.818
Presidential approval	−.369	.119	−3.113
Consumer prices	.516	.306	1.685
Unemployment	2.018	1.004	2.010
Term cycle	.470	1.316	.357
Second yerm	3.221	3.449	.934
Individual presidents	−.618	.823	−.751
Intercept	35.841		

Notes: $R^2 = .537$.
Standard error of equation = 9.494.
Number of cases = 53.

positions in Congress? Presidential elections are the most prominent and striking expression of public opinion that quadrennially punctuate American national politics. The results of this analysis suggest a direct presidential policy responsiveness to voters' electoral choices. Big victories prompt presidents to make numerous policy positions in Congress; smaller victories prompt less ambitious activities. Presidents respond to the degree of popular support they receive on election day and adjust the extent of their policy activity accordingly. Presidents not only calibrate the level of policy activity, but they also alter the type of activity in which they engage. Presidents with small victories shy away from the legislative arena in favor of making independent policy efforts. This connection between elections and presidential policymaking is an institutional feature of the office that all presidents encounter.

At the same time, this presidential responsiveness is complicated by the negative effect of elections on presidents' policy success in Congress. This negative result provides a central insight into the mandates that presidents claim on election day. While presidents can indeed proclaim their duty to act as policy activists with a strong electoral showing and take numerous positions on legislation before Congress, there is no necessary reason that this will translate into success. Presidents claiming mandates and taking positions on numerous controversial pieces of legislation should not be surprised to find out that they are roughed up in the legislative process. Second-term presidents, in particular, are likely to enjoy large election victories with no accompanying benefit in their efforts to win votes on Capitol

Hill. So election mandates permit greater policy action, but the more stands presidents take the more their chances for defeat increase. Members of Congress are bound by their own links to the people, which do not coincide with that of the presidents.

Presidents' policy responsiveness to the public is revealed in a different way through the negative effect of presidential approval on presidents' legislative position-taking and executive orders. Mandates, real or created, can only take presidents so far; the shifts in public opinion throughout their terms also affect presidents' policy moves. When presidents are "in trouble" with the public, they increase their levels of policy activity, presumably to shore up declining public confidence. This provides added evidence of presidential responsiveness, which occurs not just through the election results but continues as public opinion polls map the ebb and flow of public support for the president's job performance.

These connections between elections and presidential policymaking permit a generalization about the presidency as a policy institution and individual presidents as policymakers. Individual presidents have little to do with setting the levels of policy activity they undertake, at least in legislative position-taking and executive orders. They do have something to say about the success they achieve with those positions. While those who study policymaking from the perspective of presidential power would suggest that there is a good deal of variation across presidents, these findings indicate the limits to the impact of that variation. This study does not address whether election outcomes may influence those proposals that presidents consider to be the most important issues advanced by their administrations on Capitol Hill. This remains for future work, which may well discover other individual president effects. Yet how busy presidents are on policy matters does not reflect the tastes and preferences of individual presidents for action or reticence. Instead, the level of policy activity is a feature of the presidential institution.

In *Federalist #72,* Alexander Hamilton wrote of the interval between presidential elections that "there would be time enough. . . [for the president] to make the community sensible of the propriety of the measures he might be incline to pursue ... and [he] would derive support from the opportunities which his previous continuance in the station had afforded him, of establishing himself in the esteem and good-will of his constituents."[31] Presidents' ability to look forward to the next election rests on their past election and its sway on policy. Who is elected and by how much has a direct bearing on presidential policy action and success. The institutional mechanisms that connect elections to presidential policy prompt presidents' behavior to rest on a "due dependence on the people."

Notes

1. *The Federalist Papers* New York: New American Library, 1960, 424.

2. Paul Ford, ed. *The Writings of Thomas Jefferson* (Lawrence: University of Kansas Press, 1976), 41.

3. Raymond Wolfinger, "Dealignment, Realignment, and Mandates in the 1984 Election," in A. Ranney, ed., *The American Elections of 1984* (Washington, DC: American Enterprise Institute, 1985), 293.

4. Charles Jones, *The Presidency in a Separated System* (Washington, DC: Brookings Institution, 1994), 148.

5. *Washington Post,* November 6, 1980, A-18.

6. For an excellent discussion of individual elections and types of mandates see Jones, *The Presidency,* 1994, 149–64.

7. Richard Neustadt, *Presidential Power* (New York: John Wiley, 1960); Louis Fisher, *The Politics of Shared Power,* 3rd ed. (Washington, DC: Congressional Quarterly, 1993); Louis Fisher, *Presidential War Making* (Lawrence: University of Kansas Press, 1995); Paul Light, *The President's Agenda,* rev. ed. (Baltimore: Johns Hopkins University Press, 1991); George Edwards III, *At the Margins: Presidential Leadership of Congress* (New Haven: Yale University Press, 1989); Jon Bond and Richard Fleisher, *The President in the Legislative Arena* (Chicago: University of Chicago Press, 1990).

8. Steven A. Shull, *A Kinder, Gentler Racism?* (Armonk, NY: M.E. Sharpe, 1993), 15; Steven A. Shull, *Domestic Policy Formation* (Westport, CT: Greenwood Press, 1983).

9. Steven A. Shull, *Presidential-Congressional Relations* (Ann Arbor: University of Michigan Press, 1997).

10. For examples of this approach, see chapters in George C. Edwards III, Steven A. Shull, and Norman C. Thomas, eds., *The Presidency and Public Policy Making* (Pittsburgh: University of Pittsburgh Press, 1985).

11. As an example see Richard Niemi and Herbert Weisberg, eds. *Controversies in Voting Behavior* (Washington, DC: Congressional Quarterly, 1984).

12. Cf., John Burke, *Institutional Presidency* (Baltimore: Johns Hopkins University Press, 1992); Terry Moe, "The Politicized Presidency" in John Chubb and Paul Peterson, eds., *New Directions in American Politics* (Washington, DC: Brookings Institution, 1985); Lyn Ragsdale and John Theis III, "The Institutionalization of the American Presidency," *American Journal of Political Science,* 41 (October 1997): 1280–1318.

13. James March and Johan Olsen, "The New Institutionalism: Organizational Factors in Political Life," *American Political Science Review* 78 (September 1984): 736.

14. Philip Selznick, *Leadership in Administration* (Evanston, IL: Row, Peterson, 1957), 17.

15. Quoted in Light, *The President's Agenda,* 145.

16. Ragsdale and Theis, "The Institutionalization of the American Presidency."

17. Quoted in Paul Light, *The President's Agenda,* 17.

18. Ibid., 43.

19. As told by Harry McPherson, *A Political Education* (Boston: Little, Brown, 1972), 268.

20. The president's popular vote is calculated as a percentage of the total vote for all candidates, including significant third-party candidates. The measure is found in Lyn Ragsdale, *Vital Statistics on the Presidency* (Washington, DC: Congressional Quarterly, 1996), 103–4. The congressional seats measure is found in Ragsdale, 369–72. We investigated the effect of two other electoral measures: the presence of divided govern-

ment and the percentage of electoral college votes won by the president. Neither are presented in the final models estimated because of problems of multicollinearity. Divided government was highly collinear with congressional seats of the president's party; the electoral college vote percentage was collinear with the popular vote percentage. We also substituted a measure of the presidents' victory margin (the difference between the presidents' popular vote percentage and that of the leading opponent) for the popular vote percentage, but this measure obtained less robust results.

21. The cycle variable is coded 1 for the first year of the term and 2 for the second year, and so on. It starts again at 1 for the first year of the second term.

22. The positions are taken from Ragsdale, *Vital Statistics,* 378–79.

23. Ibid., 383–84.

24. The orders are found in Ragsdale and Theis, "The Institutionalization of the American Presidency." An inter-coder reliability test performed on a random sample of 200 orders revealed strong agreement between the coders on distinguishing policy orders from administrative orders (r = .91).

25. This position is countered in Shull, *Presidential-Congressional Relations,* 1997, ch. 7, where executive order issuance is positively related to legislative support of the president.

26. Edwards, *At the Margins;* Bond and Fleisher, *The President in the Legislative Arena;* Mark Peterson, *Legislating Together* (Cambridge: Harvard University Press, 1990); Steven A. Shull and Thomas C. Shaw, *Explaining Congressional-Presidential Relations: A Multiple Perspective Approach* (Albany: State University of New York Press, forthcoming).

27. Presidential approval is measured as annual average approval as taken from polls of the Gallup organization found in Ragsdale, *Vital Statistics,* 193. The consumer price variable is the annual change in consumer prices. The unemployment indicator is average annual unemployment. The economic indicators are taken from the U.S. Department of Commerce, *Survey of Current Business.*

28. The second term variable is coded 1 for those years of presidents' second terms and 0 otherwise.

29. Stephen Wayne, *The Legislative Presidency* (New York: Harper and Row, 1978). The individual president variable is coded sequentially for each president: 1 for Roosevelt, 2 for Truman, etc.

30. Position-taking and success data are available reliably only since 1953. While executive order data are available since George Washington, public approval data are available only since 1938. We start at the beginning of Roosevelt's fourth term rather than in the middle of his third, since the focus of the analysis is elections.

31. *The Federalist Papers,* 1960, 434–35.

Part III

Presidential Relations with Those Inside Government

7

Evaluating Clinton's Performance in Congress

George C. Edwards III

Evaluating presidents is a favorite American pastime among pundits and the public alike. Most evaluations of presidents reflect the ideological proclivities of the evaluator. Liberals are sympathetic to more liberal presidents and fault conservative presidents for not sending up enough—or any—liberal legislation. In other words, liberals tend to evaluate conservative presidents rather poorly because these presidents were, well, conservative. Conservative analysts, of course, are just as likely to evince their ideology in their own evaluations of presidents.

Ideological overtones are probably inevitable in anything as inherently "soft" as evaluations. Yet if we express only our ideologies in our evaluations, we are unlikely to be satisfied. The process will be rather simple, of course. If we are conservative, we like conservative presidents and dislike liberals. End of story.

Few of us would be content with such an analysis, however. We also want to know whether the president was an effective leader on behalf of his views, whatever they may have been. How did the president fare in facing the common challenges of leadership in the White House? We can make progress in escaping at least some of our ideological baggage and enriching our evaluations of presidents (and our understanding of American politics) if we add to our list of criteria for evaluation some more neutral standards that are typically overlooked when evaluating leadership.

It is reasonable to evaluate a presidency at least in part on the basis of what the president sets out to accomplish and how he has tried to govern to accomplish these goals. By examining the president's goals, we, in effect, control for ideology. Liberal presidents will have some different goals than conservative presidents.

The focus on governing to accomplish goals requires us to answer two central questions. First, has the president accurately identified the possibilities in his environment for accomplishing his goals? Second, has the president adopted an effective strategy to actually accomplish his goals? These questions tap the essential aspects of the leadership challenges faced by all presidents, independent of their ideologies.

Implicit in the first question is an appreciation for the importance of the context in which the president operates. It makes little sense to fault presidents for not passing a great deal of legislation if their parties had only a modest number of seats in Congress, for example. Similarly, it is much easier to win support for bold initiatives when budgetary resources are available (as in the mid-1960s) than when they are scarce (as in the 1990s).

The first question is also premised on the view that presidents will not be able to change their environments very much. I have discussed this at length elsewhere.[1] For present purposes, I will simply summarize the argument by maintaining that there is little evidence that presidents can restructure the political landscape to pave the way for change. Although not prisoners of their environment, they are likely to be highly constrained by it.

A critical aspect of presidential leadership, then, is understanding the constraints and possibilities in the environment so as to exploit them most effectively. Having once evaluated the environment, effective presidents must fashion a strategy to work within them to accomplish their goals.

To illustrate the relevance and possibilities of this approach to evaluating presidents, I will examine Bill Clinton's relations with Congress in his first term. Because the first and second halves of this term were so different, I will discuss them separately.

Clinton's First Two Years

Understanding His Strategic Position

At the core of successful political leadership in America is the ability to understand the political system in general and one's strategic position in it at any point in time so as to assess accurately the potential for policy change. Success in this endeavor may also help presidents manage the lavish expectations under which they labor in our system.

In his first two years in office, President Clinton accentuated a problem inherent in our separation of powers system by overreaching—overestimating the extent of change that a president elected with a minority of the vote could make.[2] Any president elected with only 43 percent of the vote should not expect to pass far-reaching social legislation without involving the other party, especially when the public is dubious and well-organized interest groups are fervently opposed. So, a partisan, unitarian approach was unlikely to succeed; yet this is exactly the strategy the president adopted. For example, the "us against them" approach to policymaking encouraged the president to develop his health-care plan in Democrats-only secrecy and pursue a left-in coalition-building strategy instead of a center-out one. Failure was inevitable.

Moreover, the greater the breadth and complexity of the policy change a president proposes, the more opposition it is likely to engender. In an era when a few opponents can effectively tie up bills, the odds are clearly against the White House. Yet when it came to health-care reform, the president proposed perhaps the most sweeping, complex prescriptions for controlling the conduct of state governments, employers, drug manufacturers, doctors, hospitals, and individuals in American history.

A third important element in President Clinton's political environment was the lack of resources for policy initiatives. When resources are scarce, those proposing expensive new programs have to regulate the private sector to get things done, which inevitably unleashes a backlash. So the costs of action are more expensive politically.

In health care, the complex and coercive mechanisms created to require employers to pay for health insurance and for controlling costs (managed competition) were designed to avoid government responsibility for paying—but it should have come as no surprise that those who bear greater costs, face higher risks, or have their discretion constrained are likely to oppose change.

The president's first major proposal was a fiscal stimulus bill. Clinton thought he would be able to arouse the country behind this traditional liberal policy. Few were persuaded, however, and the bill was filibustered by the Republicans in the Senate and died without a vote. Once again the president misread the possibilities in his environment.

In the end, the president was not able to cut taxes for the middle class or substantially increase spending on education, job training, public works, and health care. Nor was he able to obtain welfare reform on his terms. He could not devise strategies for moving in the context in which he found himself, partly because he misread his political environment.

Many of his most notable successes, including the North American Free Trade Agreement (NAFTA), family leave, and motor vehicle voter registration had substantial support in Congress before he arrived in Washington. In the former case, he was able to rely on Republican support for George Bush's policy initiative. He understood that he needed to engage in a bipartisan strategy that had the additional advantage of entailing no direct budgetary implications. In the latter two cases, the bills had passed before (and been vetoed by Bush) and little leadership was required.

Fashioning a Strategy

Barber has argued that all presidents must perform three political roles: rhetoric, personal relations, and homework. The habitual way of performing these roles is what he terms presidential style.[3] We can assess a president's performance in the accomplishment of goals by examining a president's style. The relative emphases in a president's style reflect not only the president's strengths but also his perceptions about the requirements of effective leadership.

Since space is limited, it is not possible to do justice to the entire Clinton style. Thus, I will focus on the most important element of Clinton's presidential style: rhetoric.

The Clinton presidency is the ultimate example of the Public Presidency—a presidency based on a perpetual campaign to obtain the public's support[4] and fed by public opinion polls, focus groups, and public relations memos. This is an administration that spent $18 million on ads in 1995, a nonelection year![5] And this is an administration that repeatedly interpreted its setbacks, whether in elections or health-care reform, in terms of its failure to communicate[6] rather than in terms of the quality of its initiatives or the strategy for governing. As Bill Clinton put it, "the role of the President of the United States is message."[7]

To evaluate the success of this governing style, we can ask whether the president was able to

- set the country's policy agenda;
- set the terms of debate over the issues on the agenda;
- increase public support for himself or his proposals.

Setting the Agenda

An important element of a president's legislative strategy is to set the agenda of Congress. In the public presidency, this means setting the agenda of the public first. An important component of agenda setting is establishing priorities among legislative proposals. If the president is not able to focus attention on his priority programs, they may become lost in the complex and overloaded political environment. Setting priorities is also important because the White House can lobby effectively for only a few bills at a time. Moreover, the president's political capital is inevitably limited, and it is sensible to focus it on the issues he cares about most.

Setting the agenda requires first limiting it and then keeping a focus on priority items. From its very first week in office, the Clinton administration did a poor job at both. The president promised to have legislation ready for improving the economy at the very beginning of his term and to propose a comprehensive health-care package within his first 100 days in office. Neither program was ready on time, creating a vacuum that was filled with controversies over issues of lower priority such as gays in the military, the bungled nominations of Zoe Baird and Kimba Wood, and public funding for abortion. These issues left an impression of ineptitude and alienated many in the public whose support the president would need for his priority legislation.

The defining issue of the Clinton presidency was to have been health-care reform. The administration set and then badly overshot its deadline for delivery of a health reform plan, first arousing and then dissipating public interest. It was more than eight months after taking office before the president made a national address on health-care reform, his highest priority legislation. Even then, the pace of rhetoric was out of sync with the pace of lawmaking. The president's speech had the effect of peaking attention in a legislative battle two months prior to the introduction of the bill.

In the meantime, there were important distractions from the president's bill. Eighteen American soldiers were killed on a peace-keeping mission in Somalia, and the *U.S.S. Harlan County*, carrying U.S. troops as part of a United Nations plan to restore democracy in Haiti, was forced to turn around and leave in the face of pro-military gunmen. In addition, the president had to devote his full attention and all the White House's resources to obtaining passage of NAFTA.

Yet part of the problem was also the president himself. Clinton and his advisers understood the virtue of a clear, simple agenda, and the president knew that his defining issues had been overwhelmed as he has engaged in issue proliferation. He was not able to contain himself, however. He rarely focused on any bill for more than a few days at a time.

The president has an undisciplined personal style, tremendous energy, a desire to please many sides, a mind stuffed with policy ideas, and a party of interest groups clamoring for policy. He came into office with a large agenda, and Democrats had a laundry list of initiatives that had been blocked by George Bush, ranging from family and medical leave to motor vehicle voter registration and health-care reform.

He and his fellow partisans believe in activist government and are predisposed toward doing "good" and against husbanding leadership resources. But no good deed goes unpunished. The president's major proposals certainly obtained space on the congressional agenda in the first two years. But the more the White House tried to do, the more difficult it was to focus the country's attention on priority issues. And it was equally difficult for Clinton to receive credit for his achievements when there were so many issues that lay ahead.

Structuring Choice

Presidents not only want the country and the Congress to be focused on their priority issues, they also want the debate to be on their terms. Framing issues in ways that favor the president's programs may set the terms of the debate on his proposals and thus the premises on which the public evaluates them and on which members of Congress vote on them.

One of the most serious limitations of the Clinton administration in its first two years was its lack of rhetorical definition. The administration's failure to effectively structure choice for the public and for Congress was not the result of an administration that was unaware either of the importance of projecting a strong, clear vision of its policies or of its failure to do so. Nevertheless, it did not clearly define what it was about. The failure to do so left the Clinton administration vulnerable to the vicissitudes of events and to the definitions of its opponents.

The White House allowed the Republicans to define the president's fiscal stimulus program in terms of pork barrel. On his FY 1994 budget, the president's political consultants complained that the Republicans had succeeded in focusing public debate on tax increases rather than economic growth or deficit reduction.

Regarding health-care reform, the White House was unable to keep the public's attention focused on the inadequacies of the health-care system and the broad goals of reform, partially due to the bill's complexity and partially due to competing plans in Congress, and a myriad of health-care industry voices with a deluge of direct mail, radio spots, and advertising, picking out pieces of the plan to oppose. Instead of revolving around a central theme, then, public debate focused on the Clinton plan's pitfalls.

During the first two years of the Clinton administration, Republicans dominated the symbols of political discourse and set the terms of the debate over policy. In the 1994 congressional elections, the Republicans framed the vote choice in national terms—making taxes, social discipline, big government, and the Clinton presidency the dominant issues. They tied congressional Democrats to Clinton, a discredited government, and a deplorable status quo. They set the terms of the debate—and won.

Obtaining Public Support

A basic problem for Bill Clinton was his overestimation of the extent to which the public was susceptible to his appeals for support. When the president's first major economic proposal, the fiscal stimulus plan, was introduced, it ran into strong Republican opposition. During the April 1993 congressional recess, Clinton stepped up his rhetoric on his bill, counting on a groundswell of public opinion to pressure moderate Republicans into ending the filibuster on the bill. (Republicans, meanwhile, kept up a steady flow of sound bites linking the president's package with wasteful spending and Clinton's proposed tax increase.) The groundswell never materialized, and the Republicans found little support for any new spending in their home states. Instead, they found their constituents railing against new taxes and spending. The bill never came to a vote in the Senate.[8]

The president's next major legislative battle was over the budget. On August 3, 1993, he spoke on national television on behalf of his budget proposal, and Senate Republican leader Robert Dole spoke against the plan. A CNN overnight poll following the president's speech found that support for his budget plan dropped.[9] Several million calls were made to Congress in response to Clinton and Dole, and the callers overwhelmingly opposed the president's plan.[10]

When the crucial rule regarding debate on the 1994 crime bill was voted down in the House, the president immediately went public. Speaking to police officers with flags in the background, he blamed special interests (the National Rifle Association) and Republicans for a "procedural trick," but his appeal did not catch fire. Meanwhile, Republicans were talking about pork barrel spending tapping public resentment. Clinton's public push yielded only the votes of three members of the Black Caucus, so he had to go to moderate Republicans and cut private deals.

Most painful of all to President Clinton was his inability to sustain the support of the public for health-care reform despite substantial efforts. Nevertheless, the White House held out against compromise with the Republicans and conservative Democrats, hoping for a groundswell of public support for reform. It never came.[11] Indeed, by mid-August 1994, only 39 percent of the public favored the Democratic health-care reform proposals while 48 percent opposed them.[12] Clinton's tendency to carry the campaign mode to governance by demonizing opponents such as the medical establishment and the drug and insurance industries activated Republican counterattacks, and negative advertisements only exacerbated his problem.

Despite energetic efforts, then, the White House was not able to produce groundswells of support for the economic stimulus plan, nor for the budget deal, the crime bill, or for health-care reform, and it only did a little better on NAFTA. The president's own approval levels averaged less than 50 percent for each of his first two years in office. In 1994, an association with Clinton decreased votes for Democratic candidates for Congress, and the midterm election was widely seen as a repudiation of the president. It is difficult to conclude that the president had a successful governance style.

Clinton's Third and Fourth Years

Understanding His Strategic Position

The dramatic Republican congressional victory in the 1994 elections forced Bill Clinton to reevaluate his strategic position. The election was a repudiation of his leadership. It was clear that his program was dead. He would not be able to build coalitions and succeed in advocating new, controversial policies in the new political environment. Yet by freeing him from the possibility, and thus the responsibility, for enacting policies, the election also provided the president a new opportunity to define his presidency.

Fortunately for the president, the new Republican majorities overplayed their hands and refused to budge on their proposals to reverse the course of public policy, leading to government shutdowns and public perception of the culpability of the Republican Congress. Clinton (and Dick Morris) recognized and exploited the opportunity the Republicans gave him. The president could characterize them as "radicals" and present himself as a "reasonable" alternative in opposition to change.

At the same time, Clinton read his new strategic position as providing for a scaled-down presidency. In this model the president employs executive orders to promote his policy views and the veto to defend moderation. As the president said, "One of the things I have learned in the last two years is that the President can do an awful lot of things by executive action."[13] He viewed government as a conciliator and catalyst of private actions. This more modest conception of the presidency disappointed Democrats desiring a more activist executive, but Clinton now saw the potential of the presidency in a new light. For example, having lost the opportunity to define the argument in 1994, Clinton did not even reintroduce his welfare bill in 1995. He could not find the funds to pay for his version, his name had become a liability, and he had more flexibility to negotiate if he did not have his own plan to defend. This was a far cry from health-care reform in 1993, but it reflected the environment in which the president was operating.

Fashioning a Strategy

Understanding his new strategic position, Clinton's primary goal became to block the Republicans' most ambitious plans to reshape government. To accomplish this goal, he fashioned a new strategy, switching from offense to defense. By opposing the Republican majority in Congress, he was able to unify his party, which was scared of staying in the minority for two years following its devastating defeat in 1994. His defensive strategy met with substantial success; divided government matters.[14]

It is ironic that following twelve years of conservative Republican presidents, the Clinton presidency's greatest success was in the realm of opposition to change. Nevertheless, Bill Clinton was more successful in defending the status quo against cuts in Medicare, Medicaid, environment protection, and education spending than he had been in advocating policy change. In other words, he was much more effective as an obstacle to change than he was as an agent for it.

The biggest payoff for the president was reelection. The 1994 congressional elections set the terms of the debate over public policy in America so that the election of 1996 was about the excesses of the GOP as much as high taxes, big government, social decay, and intrusive public authority. This, along with a classic backdrop of peace and prosperity, enabled Clinton to win easily a second term.

There are costs to the defensive strategy, however. Structuring the choice for voters and seeking public support as a more moderate version of the Republicans was apparently quite good for campaigning, and it lifted the president in the public opinion polls. Yet, campaigning, with its posturing and pronouncing, although it may have been Clinton's strength, is not governance—certainly not in the usual sense precipitating great national debates on important questions of public policy or of driving legislation through Congress.

Although the president benefited from standing in counterpoint to the Republicans, he was forced to embrace some of their more appealing imagery in his rhetoric. He changed his rhetoric from programs and dollars to inspiration and values. He defused a host of promising Republican cultural and values issues with his symbolic stands to attract anxious parents: V-chips in television sets, school uniforms, teenage curfews, restrictions on teenage smoking, limits on Internet pornography, school competency tests, a Hollywood ratings system, and increased educational funding.

But Clinton did more than simply expropriate the language of values from Republicans. He also coopted many of their issues. As a result, he had much of his agenda determined by the opposition party. He declared the era of big government to be over and signed the Republican welfare reform bill. Most important, the Republicans forced the president to deal with the budget on their terms. The issue became, first, not whether to balance the budget but when and how—and, later, just how. After submitting a budget in early 1995 that envisioned $200 billion deficits for years to come, a few months later he embraced the Republican orthodoxy of a balanced budget. Shortly thereafter he agreed to New Gingrich's timetable of balancing it within seven years.

Conclusion

Understanding the constraints and possibilities in the environment and fashioning strategies to govern most effectively within this environment are at the core of successful presidential leadership. As the example of the first Clinton term illustrates, evaluating presidential performance on these two dimensions reveals much about the success or failure of an administration. Our evaluations also provide the basis for comparison among presidents.

It is always useful—and fair—to remember that evaluating strategic position and fashioning a strategy appropriate for governing in it can be a difficult and complex task. Moreover, the political environments of some presidents are more difficult to assess than those of other presidents. (Interestingly, the Clinton White House seemed to do better in the more complex environment of 1995–96 than in the more typical years of 1993–94.) In addition, some administrations lend themselves to agenda setting and structuring choice better than do others. It is especially difficult to develop a clear focus and convey a consistent theme when the president has a large, diverse agenda, as Bill Clinton has, and when the president's views are a complex blend of populism and traditional values, as Clinton's are. This has made it difficult to establish a central organizing theme for the Clinton presidency.

Yet the Clinton presidency has also experienced self-inflicted wounds. In 1992, Clinton campaigned as a populist, economically liberal and socially conservative, and as a "New Democrat" who was cautious in domestic policy. Yet he governed in the first two years as an economic conservative, a social liberal, and an activist in domestic policy. As his pollster Stan Greenberg put it, "The mandate he ran on was not necessarily the one he executed. He was the first Democrat to talk about welfare reform and the death penalty. The cultural conservative side of Bill Clinton disappeared in the first two years."[15]

Instead, gays in the military, gun control, and abortion came to represent the administration in the minds of many in the public. His major accomplishments, and the ones where he made the crucial difference, were economically conservative policies, including deficit reduction and two free trade agreements. As Clinton himself declared sarcastically to aides, "We're Eisenhower Republicans here, and we are fighting with Reagan Republicans. We stand for lower deficits and free trade and the bond market. Isn't that great?"[16] To confuse matters further, he also had an ambitious activist domestic agenda in his first two years, signaling that he was more left leaning than his claims of being a centrist New Democrat.

It is not surprising, then, that the president found it difficult to fashion and implement a governing strategy appropriate to his goals and circumstances. His governing style undercut his campaign style. He undermined his supportive coalition and thus his ability to govern or even to receive credit for his accomplishments. In the second half of his first term, he better understood his strategic position and rediscovered his roots as a Democratic centrist, supporting a balanced budget but fending off extreme cuts and emphasizing social conservatism and family values.

By then, however, the president's strategic position was greatly weakened by the Republican victories in the congressional elections. In addition, because Clinton's new campaign style reflected a reactive agenda, it undermined his ability to govern. Although he could gain public support in opposition to the Republicans, he was not able to obtain public support for his own policy initiatives. The two most notable Democratic successes in the 104th Congress, health insurance portability and the increase in the minimum wage, were congressional, not White House, initiatives. Moreover, Clinton's newfound moderation led some to once again charge that he was afflicted with serial sincerity, a man without a gyroscope. This made it more difficult to create a new supportive coalition. Would anyone take political risks for Bill Clinton?

In his second term, when he became the first Democratic president since Franklin D. Roosevelt to win reelection, the question remained whether he could align his campaigning and governing styles to leave his imprint on public policy.

Notes

1. See, for example, George C. Edwards III, *At the Margins* (New Haven: Yale University Press, 1989); and George C. Edwards III and Stephen J. Wayne, *Presidential Leadership*, 4th ed. (New York: St. Martin's, 1997).

2. "Interview with Clinton: Political Landscape," *New York Times*, July 28, 1996, 11.

3. See James David Barber, *The Presidential Character*, 4th ed. (Englewood Cliffs, NJ: Prentice Hall, 1992).

4. See Samuel Kernell, *Going Public*, 3rd ed. (Washington, DC: Congressional Quarterly Press, 1997).

5. Bob Woodward, *The Choice* (New York: Simon and Schuster, 1996), 344.

6. Ibid., 54, 126.

7. Elizabeth Drew, *Showdown: The Struggle Between the Gingrich Congress and the Clinton Congress White House* (New York: Simon and Schuster, 1996), 19.

8. "Democrats Look to Salvage Part of Stimulus Plan," *Congressional Quarterly Weekly Report,* April 24, 1993, 1002–3.

9. Bob Woodward, *The Agenda: Inside the Clinton White House* (New York: Simon and Schuster, 1994), 285. A CBS News/*New York Times* poll with before and after samples on August 2 and 3 found that support for the president's budget remained unchanged even in the immediate aftermath of the speech, but that opposition weakened.

10. "Switchboards Swamped with Calls over Tax Plan," *New York Times,* August 5, 1993, A18.

11. "Health Care Reform: The Lost Chance," *Newsweek,* September 19, 1994, 32.

12. Gallup poll of August 15–16, 1994.

13. Quoted in Alison Mitchell, "Despite His Reversals, Clinton Stays Centered," *New York Times,* July 28, 1996, 10.

14. George C. Edwards III, Andrew Barrett, and Jeffrey Peake, "The Legislative Impact of Divided Government," *American Journal of Political Science* 41 (April 1997): 545–63.

15. Quoted in Mitchell, "Despite His Reversals, Clinton Stays Centered," 10.

16. Woodward, *The Agenda,* 165.

8

Staffing Patterns in the Modern White House

Shirley Anne Warshaw

The staffing patterns of the modern White House have changed dramatically since 1939 when Congress first provided the president a formal staff. Franklin Delano Roosevelt, with the first formal White House staff in the American presidency, used a relatively small group of staff to assist him in oversight and policy issues. All of the top staff had direct access to the president and none had specific or regularized jobs. Their job assignments varied as circumstances changed.[1]

In contrast, more recent presidents have built White House staffs numbering 400–600, each member having a specific job assignment, and most serving within a specific staffing unit. Even the chief of staff today is considered a staffing unit, since numerous people work in the chief of staff's office with titles such as "deputy chief of staff" and "executive assistant to the chief of staff." The White House staff today is characterized by its size, its functional division of labor, and its hierarchal structure. Everyone knew each other in the Roosevelt White House and knew each other quite well, a description not easily made of the modern White House.

As we try to gain greater insight into the changing staffing structures within the White House over the last fifty years, and why we have this rather large and functionally specific organization, a brief discussion of the evolution of the White House staff seems pertinent. As a means of perhaps enhancing this discussion, the following few paragraphs provide some background on the emergence of the formalized White House staff structure.

Creation of the White House Staff

Following Franklin Delano Roosevelt's call for help in managing presidential charges, Congress approved the Reorganization Act of 1939,[2] which created a small staff of six "anonymous" aides to assist the president. Since 1939, the White House staff has grown dramatically, from the first six aides to a personal staff numbering in the hundreds and an institutional staff numbering nearly 2,000.

Prior to 1939, presidents relied on a small cadre of volunteers and clerical staff to assist them in their official duties. Some presidents borrowed staff from the departments, known as detailees, to bolster their own staff. Staff from the State and War Departments were at times detailed to the White House to assist the president in foreign policy deliberations. Most policy advisers, however, were either personal associates, often referred to as the "kitchen cabinets," or were cabinet officers recommending policy ideas. The policy development process was complicated by the president's lack of staff to oversee the cabinet members and their departments. Frederick Mosher described this problem, stating that "the President had no immediate machinery for directing and controlling the conduct of executive agencies."[3]

George Washington ran the country with only an aide de camp, who had served him throughout the revolutionary war. Finally, frustrated with the growing workload, Washington hired his nephew in 1792 to assist him and paid him $300 per year using his own savings.[4] Thomas Jefferson served with only one messenger and one secretary. During this early period, presidents often hired family members and other relatives to serve as their secretaries. John Quincy Adams, Andrew Jackson, and John Tyler all hired their relatives as their private secretaries.

Not until 1857 did Congress specifically appropriate funds for a small White House staff when it authorized $2,500 for a presidential secretary. By 1900 the White House staff had grown to a personal secretary to the president, two assistant secretaries, two executive clerks, a stenographer, three clerks, and four general office personnel. Under Warren Harding the office grew even larger. Harding had a staff of twenty-one clerks, two stenographers, a records clerk, an appointments clerk, a chief clerk, an executive clerk, and a secretary to the president.[5] Herbert Hoover further increased the staff by adding two more secretaries and additional typists and messengers. The White House staff, although growing, remained populated by clerical rather than advisory staff. This began to change in the 1930s during Franklin Roosevelt's second term with the creation of a White House staff that would have a role in substantive policy decisions.

Franklin Delano Roosevelt's drive to establish a policy-oriented White House structure emanated from his own presidential activism, particularly as he strove to deal with the economic crises of the depression. The White House deliberations on the New Deal programs with his "kitchen cabinet" convinced Roosevelt that the president needed a formal staff to provide systematic advice on national issues. In 1936 Roosevelt created the Committee on Administrative Management, to design a plan for enhancing the president's oversight of the executive branch. Roosevelt selected Columbia University professor Louis Brownlow to chair the three-member committee, which became known more popularly as the Brownlow Committee.

The committee's deliberations took but one year, and in 1937 the committee issued its recommendation that "the president needs help." Their solution was to create a formal White House staff with six assistants with a "passion for anonymity." They argued that the president needed staffing help in the White House in the oversight of the executive branch, particularly in carrying out its legislative mandates, and in the creation of new policy initiatives. Congress supported the recommendations of the Brownlow Committee and in 1939 passed the Reorganization Act of 1939, providing the president authority to reorganize the executive branch. As John Hart noted, "The Brownlow Committee's report constituted the boldest and most comprehensive set of proposals for strengthening the presidency since the adoption of the Constitution."[6] The reorganization resulted in creation of the Executive Office of the President, primarily consisting of a White House staff. In 1939 the president's office consisted of three secretaries to the president, four administrative assistants, a personal secretary, and an executive clerk. By 1945 that number had increased to a White House Office of fifty-one, including both policy and clerical staff.

Since the creation of the Executive Office of the President, presidents have grown increasingly reliant on their White House staff. The staff has grown from 51 in 1945 to nearly 450 today, a number that does not include staff in the larger staffing units such as the Office of Management and Budget, National Security Council, or Council of Economic Advisers. During the Nixon/Ford years, the White House staff grew to an even larger size of 600, which every subsequent president has endeavored to reduce. The cost for this growing White House staff has increased from $407,000 at the end of the last Roosevelt administration to the 1994 budget allocation of $39,812,000.[7] The White House staff has grown so large that it is now housed not only within the White House, but within the Old Executive Office building next door to the White House and the new Executive Office building on the north side of Pennsylvania Avenue.

The Growth of Modern Staffing Patterns

The growth in the White House staff is directly related to the growth in the size of the federal government. As executive departments have grown in response to increased legislative mandates, the White House staff has grown to ensure that the departments implement those mandates without duplication or overlapping programs and within budgetary constraints. But just as important as their oversight role is the role of the White House staff as policy innovators. As Congress has become increasingly bogged down in partisan and jurisdictional conflicts, the task of framing the national agenda and developing policies for that agenda has fallen to the president. The majority of the president's staff today are involved with developing policy proposals, ensuring that those policy proposals have the requisite political support, and shepherding those proposals through Congress. The staff of the modern president is a policy staff rather than an administrative or clerical staff, as it was prior to the mid-1940s.

Although the president maintains a large administrative and clerical staff, including such positions as staff secretary, scheduling, advance, management and administration, and personnel, the majority of staff are policy oriented. This discussion of policy staff, however, should be referenced within a broader context. The term policy staff refers to those members of the White House staff involved in both the formulation of policy and the dissemination of policy. Those staff involved in the direct formulation of policy include the chief of staff, the domestic policy adviser, the economic policy adviser (when separate from the domestic policy staff), and the national security adviser. Indirectly impacting policy decisions within the White House are the counselor(s) to the president, special adviser to the president, political affairs, intergovernmental affairs, public liaison, special projects, intergovernmental affairs, cabinet affairs, and legislative affairs. Even the president's counsel has become involved in policy issues, recommending whether the president should veto certain pieces of legislation. The titles of some staff and staffing units may vary from administration to administration, but most have remained stable since the Nixon administration.

The growth of the White House staff has evolved through four distinct stages: (1) the early growth stage, characterized by the Roosevelt and Truman administrations, (2) the shift toward larger staffs with functional responsibilities in the Eisenhower, Kennedy, and Johnson administrations, (3) the institutionalization of domestic and economic policy staffs in the Nixon and Ford administrations, and the expansion of that staff in the Carter, Reagan, and Bush administrations, and finally, (4) the increased use of political staff in the Clinton administration. Each of these four stages has led to added layers of staff and has increased the number of players in the advisory structure.

Stage One: The Early Growth of the White House Staff

The first stage in the evolution of the White House staff is characterized by the relatively small size of the senior staff during the Roosevelt administration following passage of the Reorganization Act of 1939. This group consisted of eight staff in 1939, of which six were professional staff and two were clerical staff:

*Secretary to the President	Stephen Early
*Secretary to the President	Brigadier General Edwin M. Watson
*Secretary to the President	Marvin H. McIntyre
*Administrative Assistant	William H. McReynolds
*Administrative Assistant	James H. Rowe
*Administrative Assistant	Lauchlin Currie
*Personal Secretary	Maguerite LeHand
*Executive Clerk	Rudolph Forster[8]

The six professional members of the White House staff had few specific functions. Most worked on presidential speeches, bill-drafting, and general coordination activities with the departments. There were no formal staff meetings, and each member of the staff had direct access to the president. Roosevelt was the first president to employ the "spokes of the wheel" process of staffing, in which the president served as the hub of the wheel with each of the staff serving as a spoke. Each staff member was equal in importance and in relationship to the president. The White House staff structure had little definition and bore no similarity to the well-defined staff structures of later administrations. Roosevelt met frequently with each staff member and often encouraged competing advice and analysis from the staff.[9]

One of the key functions of the six professional staffers was to serve as radar for the president, picking up pieces of information and transmitting that information to the president. Bradley Patterson, writing in *Ring of Power,* describes a conversation between Roosevelt and James Rowe, Jr., in which the president says simply, "Your job is to be a bird dog. . . . Just run around town and find out what's happening."[10] Unlike the White House staff of the 1990s, the White House staff of the 1940s had ever-changing roles and responsibilities and had no subordinate staff. Senior staff in the White House of the 1990s all have their own staffs, including both clerical and professional staff.

The Roosevelt staff began to grow in both size and functional responsibility during the mid-1940s, as Roosevelt's health began to fail and as the war dominated his attention. White House staff played an increasing role in domestic and economic policy issues. Roosevelt added three new advisers: Harry Hopkins, who served as an intermediary with the State Department and often met with representatives of foreign governments; Admiral William Leahy, who kept Roosevelt abreast of military affairs; and Samuel Rosenmann, who oversaw the span of domestic issues. Particularly after the American troops entered the European theater in 1944, Roosevelt assigned Rosenmann greater responsibility for domestic policy, requiring additional aides assigned to Rosenmann. Although a White House staffing unit was not officially created until 1970 for managing domestic affairs, the foundation for such management was laid by Rosenmann, who built the first in-house domestic policy system.

Roosevelt's major contribution to the organizational development of the White House advisory structure was the creation of in-house policy advisers. The president no longer needed to rely on the cabinet, the "kitchen cabinet," or a host of outside networks to devise policy options for the administration. The in-house policy advisers provided the president both in-house policy options and recommendations for action prepared by the departments.

Once the ball was set in motion, it never stopped. Every succeeding president has continued to build on Roosevelt's plan for an in-house advisory structure. Harry Truman, who succeeded Roosevelt in the Oval Office, initially sought to continue Roosevelt's original plan for generalists in the White House. Truman saw little need for the functionally oriented roles that Hopkins, Leahy, and Rosenmann had played during the latter Roosevelt years.[11] But as the war continued and the agonizing decisions of atomic warfare overshadowed other domestic and international issues, Truman again turned to White House staff to handle specific assignments. Added to the initial White House staff of generalists were John Steelman as assistant to the president, responsible primarily for labor-management issues; Clark Clifford as special counsel, responsible for broad domestic policy formulation; Charles Murphy as administrative assistant to the president responsible for congressional relations; Donald Dawson as administrative assistant to the president responsible for personnel and patronage; and David Niles as administrative assistant to the president responsible for liaison with minority groups.[12]

Truman had during his tenure in office significantly expanded the size of the White House staff. He continued the generalists' positions started under Roosevelt, continued a number of the policy positions started under Roosevelt, and created more policy positions (such as Niles's responsibility for minority groups) and a host of functional positions. Among the functional positions initiated were staff dealing with press relations, correspondence, and appointments. The Truman White House staff was significantly larger (with a staff of thirty-two) and more specialized than the staff had been under Roosevelt.

Stage Two: Creation of a Larger, More Specialized White House Staff

General Dwight David Eisenhower, elected president on the heels of his victories over Germany and the Nazi army, brought further enlargement and functional assignment to the White House staff. One of the most significant changes, however, to the White House staff was the change from the spokes of the wheel structure, in which every member of the senior staff had direct access to the president, to a pyramidal or hierarchal structure. In Eisenhower's hierarchal structure, staff cleared appointments and issues with Sherman Adams, the president's new chief of staff. The term chief of staff, new to the advisory structure lexicon, was taken directly from the military lexicon. Every general had a chief of staff, who served as the gatekeeper to the general's door.[13] Anyone who saw the general first had that meeting cleared through the chief of staff. This protected the general's time and ensured that only significant issues were addressed by the general. Eisenhower used this format, a format in which he had routinely operated during his professional career, as a pattern for the White House. In addition to the chief of staff, Eisenhower added positions for a press secretary, congressional liaison, staff secretary, and cabinet affairs secretary. Again, this was in line with Eisenhower's experience in the military where each member of the staff had a single, focused assignment.[14] Eisenhower preferred the structured, less chaotic staff structure imposed by the hierarchal model than the often free-wheeling structure of the Roosevelt and Truman administrations.

Most of the positions created under the Eisenhower advisory structure tended to be managerial, rather than policy oriented. The press secretary, James Hagerty, helped Eisenhower deal with a national electorate through the new medium called television. Bryce Harlow, the congressional liaison, actively pushed presidential objectives in legislative initiatives, always ensuring that members of Congress knew where the president stood on pieces of legislation. The cabinet secretariat under Max Raab ensured that all cabinet members were consulted on policy issues, and that cabinet-level decisions were always cognizant of the presidential perspective. The staff secretary dutifully ensured that all relevant memos from the cabinet officers to the president were circulated throughout the White House staff and that comments were solicited where appropriate. The Eisenhower staff greatly routinized the management of policy issues that the White House dealt with.

Issues brought to the White House by the departments were "staffed out" by a variety of White House staff, a management structure that had only been haphazardly used in the Truman and to some degree Roosevelt years.

With the White House staff continuing to grow in size and functional assignments during the Eisenhower years, it was perhaps quite predictable that the next phase of White House staff development would be a movement toward increased policy roles for the staff. And this was exactly the case. John F. Kennedy sought to increase the use of White House staff in the development of policy initiatives. Eisenhower had used the staff primarily to review and refine departmental policy initiatives rather than to frame policy initiatives. Eisenhower relied heavily on his cabinet and used the cabinet secretariat in the White House to coordinate the cabinet's policy recommendations. The expansion of the White House staff was not intended by Eisenhower to rival the advisory role of the cabinet, but rather to provide consistent direction to the cabinet and a more orderly discussion of cabinet-originated proposals.

Nevertheless, the expansion of the White House staff under Eisenhower had been quite significant. In a formal recommendation to John F. Kennedy immediately after his election in 1960, the Brookings Institution advised that the president consider reducing the size of the White House staff because it duplicated "the machinery" of the departments.[15] But the call by the Brookings Institution fell on deaf ears, for the White House continued to expand under Kennedy, as it had during Eisenhower's tenure. Kennedy saw the White House staff as an advisory mechanism to provide oversight of departmental proposals and to foster discussions on new initiatives. Although members of Kennedy's staff did not create new proposals, they saw their role as encouraging departmental staff to move in certain policy directions. As Patrick Anderson noted, "not since Roosevelt had there been a President so distrustful of the bureaucracy and so willing to let his personal aides prod, double-check and bypass it."[16]

Members of the Kennedy White House staff not only performed more oversight of the departments than had previous White House staffs, they also began to initiate policy discussions. Rather than reacting, Kennedy White House staff became proactive in policy matters. McGeorge Bundy began direct supervision of foreign policy and Theodore Sorensen similarly began direct supervision of domestic policy. Bundy and Sorensen began leading the departments toward policy proposals initiated in their offices.[17]

One of the key strategies used by Kennedy to gain greater control over departmental policymaking was the use of sub-cabinet personnel. In past administrations, cabinet officers were given authority by the president to appoint their own sub-cabinet personnel. Kennedy reversed this trend to some degree, although not totally, and began to directly appoint sub-cabinet personnel from the White House. Among those appointed directly by Kennedy were Undersecretary of State Chester Bowles and assistant Secretary of State G. Mennen Williams. Both were appointed before Dean Rusk was offered the position of secretary of State. Kennedy also endeavored to increase the number of African Americans in senior federal positions, and appointed George Weaver as assistant secretary of Labor, Carl Rowan as deputy assistant secretary of State, and Robert C. Weaver as Housing administrator.[18]

The move toward greater White House control over the policymaking process during the Kennedy administration included another critical feature: creation of in-house advisory units for policy. Although Eisenhower had created a number of functional units within the White House such as the press secretary, congressional liaison, and office of cabinet affairs, these units were primarily administrative in nature. Kennedy became the first president to create in-house policy units: the Office of Science and Technology and the President's Science Advisory Committee.

Lyndon Johnson continued the trend toward White House staff activism in policymaking. White House staff emerged as activists in both oversight of departmental policymaking and in developing policy recommendations within the White House.[19] Joseph Califano, for example, became Johnson's point person in domestic policy. Califano worked directly with the cabinet officers to ensure that departmental programs were in line with presidential objectives. As the White House increased its staff throughout the Johnson years, in-house coordination of departmental policies became more prevalent. In-house coordination of civil rights issues became a major thrust of White House concern, with Califano working closely with Lee White, the White House civil rights coordinator, on solutions. Both Califano and White worked particularly closely with Robert Weaver, the first African American cabinet officer and secretary of Housing and Urban Development. Califano characterized the personnel activism by the White House staff as follows, "His [Johnson's] staff system was frenetic, seeking a cure for every ill; his appearance one of indefatigable perpetual motion, in constant conversation and consultation."[20] By the end of the Johnson administration in 1969, the White House staff had emerged as the president's primary advisory structure as a variety of policy advisers began to populate the senior White House staff. The tide of change had carried in a new wave of activism in the White House.

The Johnson White House staff, in a trend that had started two and a half decades earlier, was now large enough and specialized enough to craft presidential initiatives and to have some degree of oversight of departmental programs. The White House staff, which had grown in size from 51 in

1944 to 273 in 1968,[21] and had fluctuated to even higher levels, had become the president's principal policy advisory structure.

Stage Three: White House Staff as Policymakers

Richard Nixon, who took the reins of office in 1969, constructed yet another major layer of structure in the staffing organization. Each of Nixon's predecessors from Roosevelt to Johnson had added a significant part of the organizational structure in the growing White House staff. Nixon continued the trend by further enlarging the size of the staff and by formalizing the role of the staff in domestic policymaking.

Nixon entered office in a period of enormous social upheaval. The war in Vietnam had roused national passions to a point where marches against the war had become routine occurrences. Civil rights leaders continued to mount public pressure against racial segregation, voting irregularities, and job inequality. And changes in social welfare legislation through Lyndon Johnson's Great Society programs had rearmed the safety network for economic security of the nation's poor, elderly, and disabled.

The result of this pressure on presidential leadership was a continued movement by Richard Nixon to build in-house structures for policy advice. He heavily relied on the National Security Council (NSC), created by the National Security Act of 1947, for international policy. Deliberations on military tactics were heavily debated in the NSC throughout the war and its recommendations given to Nixon for assessment. Nixon relied on Henry Kissinger, his national security adviser and the staff director of the NSC, for both information and evaluations of military strategy in Vietnam.

Kissinger provided Nixon an in-house advisory structure for foreign policy. For domestic policy advice, Nixon relied on Arthur Burns, who had broad domestic policy responsibilities, and on Daniel Patrick Moynihan, named to head the Urban Affairs Council. Nixon created the Urban Affairs Council (UAC) by executive order[22] to address mounting racial problems in the cities and to develop strategies for improving the growing housing blight and job abandonment in the inner cities. Creation of the Urban Affairs Council was the first step toward creating an institutional in-house advisory structure for domestic policy. Previous administrations had used senior staff, such as Rosenmann, Raab, and Califano, to manage domestic policy. According to Nixon, the UAC would be "the domestic policy equivalent of the National Security Council in foreign affairs."[23] However, not until the creation of the Urban Affairs Council was there a formal organizational unit assigned to domestic issues.

Within a year, however, Nixon realized that personal and professional conflicts between Burns and Moynihan were causing unnecessary tension within his domestic advisory structure.[24] Burns and Moynihan clashed over their relationships with the departments and in particular over the validity of Moynihan's proposals for welfare reform.[25] Burns and Moynihan were both relieved of their domestic policy roles in 1970, and the next phase in the development of the White House policy structure emerged. The Urban Affairs Council was superseded by another in-house domestic policy unit, the Domestic Council, under the auspices of John Ehrlichman. Ehrlichman described a 1969 conversation between Nixon and Roy Ash in which the decision to create the Domestic Council was formulated:

> Nixon asked Roy Ash, "Why do I have to put up with this on the domestic side. There's got to be a more orderly way of going about the development of domestic policy than this. Henry [Kissinger] never bothers me like this. Henry always brings me nice, neat papers on national security problems and I can check the box. Nobody badgers me and picks on me. But these two wild men on the domestic side are beating me up all the time." So they went off and devised the Domestic Council.[26]

Ehrlichman's Domestic Council was formally created through Reorganization Plan No. 2, submitted to Congress on March 12, 1970. The Reorganization Plan called for creation of the Domestic Council as a parallel to the National Security Council and for the creation of the Office of Management and Budget (OMB) to replace the Bureau of the Budget. The Domestic Council would have the domestic cabinet officers and the postmaster general as members plus the president and vice-president and the director of the Office of Economic Opportunity. John Ehrlichman would serve as the assistant to the president for Domestic Affairs and as staff director of the Domestic Council. In essence, the Domestic Council would be used to gather cabinet members on a regular basis to ensure that they understood the president's domestic goals and objectives. Ehrlichman's White House staff would be used to frame domestic policy initiatives and to oversee departmental programs. Nixon's creation of a formal White House structure for domestic policy was the first step in institutionalizing a process for domestic policymaking in the White House. Every successive administration continued to have an in-house unit for domestic policymaking.

When Gerald Ford entered office in mid-1974, he faced mounting public pressure to deal with a growing economic crisis: rising interest rates and unemployment. As the military machine that had brought nearly full employment was cut while the Vietnam War wound down, the economy began to heat up with rising unemployment and interest rates at record levels. Ford's advisers recommended that the White House prioritize managing the mounting economic crisis. To do so, the advisers recommended creation of a new advisory structure called the Economic Policy Board (EPB). Ford envisioned the Economic Policy Board as an equal partner in the advisory process with the Domestic Council and the National Security Council. The Domestic Council would focus on domestic issues, the National Security Council would focus on foreign policy issues, and the Economic Policy Board would focus on economic issues.[27] Thus the Ford administration continued the trend instituted by the Nixon administration of creating a formal policy unit within the White House to manage policy issues.[28] Issues were being managed in the White House by entire units by the mid-1970s with staffs regularly increasing in size.

When Jimmy Carter entered the White House in 1977, the White House staff had grown to nearly 500. Jimmy Carter continued to use the large policy staffs of the domestic and economic units (although Carter merged the domestic and economic policy staffs into the Domestic Policy Staff) and the National Security Council for policy development and departmental oversight. And as had each of his predecessors, Carter expanded the role of the White House staff.[29] He added more policy units, including individual units for managing the drug crisis, dealing with women's issues, interacting with state and local governments, and handling special interest groups. The legacy of the Carter years is its expansion of the White House staff into single-issue units, rather than the broad policy units encompassed under domestic and foreign affairs.

Carter's expansion of the White House staff into this variety of individual units was done for two reasons. First, as a means of providing direct political access to groups that Carter felt had supported him during the 1996 campaign. Since Carter had essentially run against the establishment of the Democratic party, and had publicly reproached the Democratic party, he used the White House to nurture special interest groups for the 1980 election. Second, Carter had campaigned against the federal bureaucracy in the 1976 presidential campaign. He had pledged to deliver services in a more efficient and effective manner to the public, thereby cutting the cost of doing business in the federal government. By expanding the number of White House staff responsible for policy matters, Carter expanded the access points for policy input from special interests. Policy input was no longer limited to the traditional access points of the departments, which could skew the information in their behalf or fail to forward the message to the White House. The expansion of the White House staff was primarily a tool to protect Carter's political base.

The effort by Jimmy Carter to expand the White House staff to protect his political base proved less than successful, for in 1980 former Governor Ronald

Reagan of California captured the Oval Office. The march toward expansion of the White House staff began to moderate under Reagan, who campaigned on a pledge to reduce the federal budget and cut the bureaucracy. Reagan felt it prudent to keep the White House staff at existing levels rather than increase its numbers in light of his efforts to broadly cut departmental staff.

Although Reagan did not dramatically change the size of the White House staff, he continued to centralize policymaking in the White House (which Richard Nixon and Gerald Ford had formalized) and to work with special interest groups (which Jimmy Carter had formalized). Perhaps the most significant contribution of Ronald Reagan to the development of the White House staff was refinement of the domestic policy process under Martin Anderson, director of the Office of Policy Development, which had oversight of domestic and economic policy.[30] Anderson used the White House to oversee the administration's domestic and economic policy agenda, ensuring that departments clearly understood Reagan's priorities and that all departmental policies met those priorities. This entailed frequent and regular interaction with the department secretaries and their policy staff to ensure that departmental programs met presidential objectives. According to Edwin Meese, there would be "an orderly process [within the White House] for reviewing departmental issues requiring a decision by the President."[31] Departments were constantly supervised by the White House. All departmental initiatives flowed through the White House to ensure consistency with presidential objectives. The role of the White House staff was to frame broad policy goals for the administration, craft a few specific policy goals and legislative initiatives, and to provide constant programmatic guidance to the departments.

The White House staff of George Bush was less involved in either programmatic oversight or policy development than the staff of Ronald Reagan. Nevertheless, the staffing size and number of staffing units remained approximately the same. The Bush White House was less controlling than the Reagan White House with regard to policy oversight of the departments. Two reasons explain this pullback. First, the Bush administration was driven by the Reagan Revolution's promise to cut the federal budget. Office of Management and Budget director Richard Darman and chief of staff John Sununu became the point persons of the administration.[32] Their goal, with Bush's approval, was to reduce the mounting deficit and cut the federal budget. This meant no new program initiatives and a series of programmatic cuts. The White House domestic and economic policy office under Roger Porter had relatively little reason to work with the departments.[33] Darman's staff at OMB had replaced the White House staff as the overseers of departmental policy. And just as significant in the policy process, Porter seemed to prefer to focus on micromanagement rather than on the macro issues that his predecessor Martin Anderson had focused on.[34] Porter shied away from broad management issues with the departments and cloaked himself around two pieces of legislation: the Clean Air Act and the Civil Rights Act. Both were reauthorizations of existing legislation that the Republican White House wanted to shape, particularly in light of the Democratically controlled House and Senate. However, Porter continued to have a large staff to handle domestic and economic policy issues. The Bush White House used its staff somewhat differently than did the Reagan White House, but the number and roles remained essentially the same.

The trend that began in 1939 with Roosevelt's small, generalized staff had produced by 1992 a centralized policy structure capable of both short-term and long-term policymaking and of fighting the small fires that emerge daily for the president.

Stage Four: Policy and Politics in the White House

The final stage of the transformation of the White House staff from the small, generalized staff of 1939 to the current centralized policy structure began in 1993 with Bill Clinton's presidency. The Clinton White House is characterized by its large senior staff, with 40 percent more senior staff than George Bush, and by the singularly large number of political positions on the senior staff.

The focus of the development of the White House staff in the Nixon through Bush administrations had been on the increase in policymaking responsibilities and in staff within policymaking units. Jimmy Carter had followed in this process of centralizing policymaking in the White House, but had also increased the number of senior staff involved in political rather than policy responsibilities. The hallmark of the Clinton White House has been its increase in the number of positions on the senior staff assigned to political oversight of policymaking. Clinton created a complex advisory structure with intertwined policy and political staffs that gauged every policy proposal for political acceptability.

In the Nixon through Bush administrations, a period in which the White House became the center of policymaking, policies had been primarily developed during the campaign. Once the campaign staff became the White House staff, their task was to implement the policies generated during the campaign and to ensure that departmental policies met the presidential agenda. The Clinton White House operated somewhat differently. Policies were constantly refined by the White House staff to ensure that they had the broadest possible support within the public. Policies that normally would be

Table 8.1

1993 Senior White House Staff

1.	Chief of Staff	Thomas McLarty III
2.	Senior Policy Adviser	George Stephanopoulos
3.	Counselor to the President	David Gergen
4.	Assistant to the President/Deputy Chief of Staff	Roy Neel
5.	Assistant to the President/Deputy Chief of Staff	Ricki Seidman
6.	Intergovernmental Affairs	Regina Montoya
7.	Legislative Affairs	Howard Paster
8.	Communications	Mark Gearen
9.	Assistant to the Pres./Dep. Dir. of Communications	Rahm Emanuel
10.	Assistant to the President/Senior Adviser	Bruce Lindsey
11.	Public Liaison	Alexis Herman
12.	Scheduling and Advance	Marcia Hale
13.	Office of National Service	Eli Segal
14.	Staff Secretary	John Podesta
15.	Management and Administration	David Watkins
16.	Chief of Staff to First Lady	Margaret Williams
17.	Assistant to the President/Dep. Dir. of Political Affairs	Joan Baggett
18.	Domestic Policy	Carol Rasco
19.	Economic Policy	Robert Rubin
20.	National Security Affairs	Anthony Lake
21.	Science and Technology	John Gibbons
22.	Counsel	Bernard Nussbaum

Source: U.S. Government Manual 1993.

developed by the domestic and economic policy staff and then moved into the departments were subjected to an added layer of political staff in the Clinton White House. Of the twenty-two senior staff (defined as those with the title of "assistant to the President" or its equivalent), only three senior staff were directly involved with policymaking (the domestic adviser, the economic adviser, and the national security adviser; see Table 8.1). The senior staff was dominated by political staff such as the senior policy adviser (George Stephanopoulos), senior adviser (Bruce Lindsey), counselor to the president (David Gergen), political affairs director (Rahm Emanuel), and the deputy chief of staff for political affairs (Harold Ickes). In addition to the blatantly political staff were the covert political staff such as intergovernmental affairs, public liaison, personnel, communications, and press secretary. On the staffing chart issued by the White House of the twenty-two senior staff, the three policy offices were ranked numbers 18, 19, and 20. This illustrates the importance that the president placed on political decision making in the White House. In comparison, the policy staff of every president from Nixon through Bush had ranked within the top ten staff members, and usually within the top five (see Table 8.2).

Table 8.2

Staffing Patterns for Domestic and Economic Policy Positions

President	Position	Name	Staff rank
Nixon	Domestic Affairs	Arthur Burns	1
Ford	Economic Affairs	Kenneth Rush	5
Ford	Domestic Affairs	Kenneth Cole	7
Carter	Domestic/Econ.	Stuart Eizenstat	6
Reagan	Domestic Affairs	Martin Anderson	5
Bush	Domestic/Econ.	Roger Porter	11
Clinton	Domestic Policy	Carol Rasco	18
Clinton	Economic Policy	Robert Rubin	19

Source: U.S. Government Manual, 1969–93.

The Clinton White House expanded the number of players in the president's advisory network and expanded in particular the number of political players in the president's advisory network. The White House staff was by 1997 expanding not only its policy structure but was expanding the framework for making policy decisions.

Conclusion

The White House staff has undergone a variety of changes since George Washington served as the nation's first president. Serving with only a single aide de camp, Washington worked with his department heads to lead the nation. But as the nation grew and the demands on presidential leadership grew, the president began to expand his own staff to help in the decision process. The presidential staff began with a few assistants in the 1800s, often paid out of personal funds by each president, to a small staff of secretaries and clerks authorized by Congress. Not until 1939, however, did the president gain congressional approval to create a White House office with professional and clerical staff funded by the public treasury.

Roosevelt's 1944 staff of fifty-one grew dramatically during the next five decades, both in size and scope of responsibilities. By the time the Clinton administration had taken office, over 400 were counted within the White House Office. The fifty years between Roosevelt and Clinton saw the White House staff evolve slowly, from a few generalists under Roosevelt who provided broad advice to the president to a large staff of specialists in functionally specific staffing units.

The most significant change in White House staffing patterns emerged during the Nixon administration when the White House staff became the center of administration policymaking, with both broad oversight of departmental policymaking and a limited degree of policy development. Some presidents, such as Ronald Reagan, sought to impose presidential doctrine on the departments through the White House staff. Other presidents, such as Bill Clinton, sought to develop and refine policy proposals through the White House staff. The Clinton White House staff spent considerably more time refining and reframing ideas among the large, often disparate members of the staff than working with the departments. This meant fewer programs moving toward fruition.

There is no ideal model for the White House staff. Presidents need to create a staff that reflects their management style. But presidents today have the ability to mold their policy structure in various ways given the institutionalized structures for domestic, economic, and national security policy. How they choose to use those structures will vary from president to president. Ronald Reagan used the structure quite differently than did Bill Clinton. The structure is in place, however, as a result of fifty years of evolution.

Will the White House staff continue to change? Absolutely. Will the White House staff continue to grow? Probably. Will the president continue to use the White House staff as his (or her) primary advisory structure? Probably. Because this is a constantly changing system, we can only make educated guesses as to how it will continue to evolve. It is a fairly reasonable assumption for us to make that in light of the centrifugal forces on cabinet officers, growing federal mandates, divided government, and the failure of Congress to exercise significant policy leadership, the president will continue as the nation's policy leader. This necessitates not only a strong advisory structure within the White House, but a White House staff that will continue to change as presidential needs require. Based on the trends of the four stages in the evolution of the White House staff, the White House will most likely continue to add layers of staff and to increase the number of players. The degree of politicization of the process will vary by president, but the use of White House staff rather than outside political consultants to advise the president on the political wisdom of policy initiatives will undoubtedly continue. In summary, the White House staff will continue to grow both in size and in function in the immediate future.

Notes

1. For an overview of advisory structures in a number of modern presidencies, see John P. Burke, *The Institutional Presidency* (Baltimore: Johns Hopkins University Press, 1992).

2. On September 8, 1939, Roosevelt signed Executive Order 8248 creating the Executive Office of the President.

3. Frederick Mosher, ed., *"The President Needs Help"* (Lanham, MD: University Press of America, 1988), ix–x.

4. Michael Nelson, *The Presidency A to Z* (Washington, DC: Congressional Quarterly Press, 1994), 395.

5. Alfred D. Sander, *A Staff for the President: The Executive Office 1921–52* (Westport, CT: Greenwood, 1989), 52.

6. John Hart, *The Presidential Branch, second edition* (Chatham, NJ: Chatham House, 1995), 5.

7. Lyn Ragsdale, *Vital Statistics on the Presidency: Washington to Clinton* (Washington, DC: Congressional Quarterly Press, 1996), 264.

8. *United States Government Manual, 1939* (Washington, DC: U.S. Government Printing Office, 1939).

9. Stephen Hess, *Organizing the Presidency,* 2nd ed. (Washington, DC: Brookings Institution, 1988), 25.

10. Bradley H. Patterson, Jr., *Ring of Power: The White House Staff and Its Expanding Role in Government* (New York: Basic Books, 1988), 56.

11. For detailed discussions of the White House staff, see Harry S. Truman, *Memoirs,* vol. 1 (Garden City, NY: Doubleday, 1955); and Margaret Truman, *Harry S. Truman* (New York: Pocket Books, 1974).

12. Hess, *Organizing the Presidency,* 2nd ed., 47.

13. For an excellent discussion of Sherman Adams's early role as chief of staff, see Herbert Brownell and John P. Burke, *Advising Ike* (Lawrence: University of Kansas Press, 1993).

14. Stephen E. Ambrose, *Eisenhower,* vol. 2 (New York: Simon and Schuster, 1984), 25.

15. "Study of the 1960–61 Presidential Transition," November 11, 1960, Brookings Institution, Washington, DC.

16. Patrick Anderson, *The President's Men* (Garden City, NY: Doubleday, 1965), 233.

17. For a detailed discussion of Bundy's role in managing the anti-Diem coup, see Richard Reeves, *President Kennedy: Profile of Power* (New York: Simon and Schuster, 1993), 641.

18. Arthur M. Schlesinger, Jr., *A Thousand Days* (Greenwich, CT: Fawcett Crest Books, 1965), 851.

19. Emmette S. Redford and Richard T. McCulley, *White House Operations: The Johnson Presidency* (Austin: University of Texas Press, 1986), 51.

20. Joseph A. Califano, Jr., *A Presidential Nation* (New York: W.W. Norton, 1975), 242.

21. Ragsdale, *Vital Statistics on the Presidency,* 268–69.

22. Executive Order #11452, July 23, 1969. Created through Executive Order as the Council on Urban Affairs, the popular name became the Urban Affairs Council.

23. Richard Nixon, *RN: Memoirs of Richard Nixon* (New York: Grosset and Dunlap, 1978), 342.

24. For a discussion of the Moynihan–Burns relationship, see exit interview of John Whitaker, May 4, 1975, White House Central Files, pp. 8–9, Nixon Presidential Materials, College Park, Maryland.

25. Shirley Anne Warshaw, *The Domestic Presidency* (Boston: Allyn and Bacon, 1997), 30–34.

26. Interview with John Ehrlichman, *The Nixon Presidency: Twenty-Two Intimate Perspectives* (Lanham, MD: University Press of America, 1987), 124.

27. See Roger Porter, *Presidential Decision Making: The Economic Policy Board* (Cambridge, England: Cambridge University Press, 1980).

28. Shirley Anne Warshaw and John Robert Greene, "Brushfires: The Departments, the Domestic Council, and the Policy Agendas in the Ford White House," *Congress and the Presidency,* vol. 21, no. 2 (Autumn 1994): 84.

29. Griffin Bell, *Taking Care of the Law* (New York: William Morrow, 1983), 46.

30. Martin Anderson, *Revolution: The Reagan Legacy* (Stanford, CA: Hoover Institute, 1988, updated 1990).

31. From a speech made by Edwin Meese on April 23, 1981, to the American Society of Newspaper Editors. Quoted in "White House Decision Making Continuation of California System," *Congressional Quarterly,* May 9, 1981, 827.

32. For a wide-ranging discussion of the Bush White House staff structure and its role in policy development, see Richard Darman, *Who's in Control* (New York: Simon and Schuster, 1996).

33. See James Pinkerton, "Life in Bush Hell," *The New Republic,* December 14, 1992, 22.

34. Michael McQueen, "Presidential Policy Adviser Faces Complaints That His Idea Menu Offers Leftovers and No Punch," *Wall Street Journal,* June 20, 1989, A20.

9

Bureaucratic Views of the President

Richard W. Waterman

For many years, scholars assumed that presidents were neither interested in nor capable of influencing the bureaucracy. For example, Clinton Rossiter asserted that the most difficult task most presidents face is trying to sell their programs, not to Congress, but to the bureaucracy.[1] Louis Koenig also stated, "even more resistant [than Congress] to the President's quest for dominion over the executive branch is the giant bureaucracy, with its layers of specialists, its massive paper work . . . , lumbering pace, [and] addiction to routine."[2] Thomas Cronin wrote, "The federal bureaucracy . . . is one of the most visible checks on a president."[3] And Roger Noll wrote, "although the President could exercise authority . . . there is little evidence that he or his administration makes much of an attempt to do so."[4]

Scholarly perceptions of the president's relationship to the bureaucracy began to change with the Johnson and Nixon administrations. Both presidents played a more active role in attempting to influence the bureaucracy than their predecessors. But it was Richard Nixon, with the creation of the "administrative presidency strategy," who was the first president to systematically attempt to control bureaucratic behavior. Nixon used a variety of techniques such as appointing loyalists to cabinet positions, taking the primary role in appointing sub-cabinet appointments (a job that had previously been handled by the president's cabinet appointees), using the budget (and oftentimes the impoundment authority) to alter agency behavior, constructing a counterbureaucracy in the White House, politicizing the Office of Management and Budget, and actively using his reorganization authority to secure greater control over the bureaucracy.[5]

While other presidents have used a variation of the "administrative presidency strategy," Ronald Reagan applied all of the tools Nixon employed (with the possible exception of the counterbureaucracy—which Nixon himself acknowledged had not succeeded) and then added a few new variations (e.g., the use of cost–benefit analysis, the Civil Service Reform Act, and administrative central clearance) to extend his control over the bureaucracy. In addition, while Nixon's administrative strategy evolved over time, Reagan employed his approach from the very beginning of his presidency.[6] While the Reagan strategy resulted in unanticipated consequences in some agencies, it was clear that presidents could now influence the bureaucracy, though not without some political cost.[7]

A number of quantitative studies have demonstrated that presidents can indeed influence the bureaucracy. Several scholars found that presidents actively sought and achieved political control over the bureaucracy and that presidential control extended across a wide variety of federal agencies.[8] Although much empirical research demonstrates that presidents have indeed been successful in controlling the bureaucracy, there is little corresponding evidence regarding the attitudes of bureaucrats with regard to the presidency itself. Aberbach and Rockman; Aberbach, Putnam, and Rockman; and Cole and Caputo examined the political perceptions of bureaucrats to determine if they were in accord with those of the presidents they served under.[9] Likewise, in separate books, Heclo and Kaufman examined the attitudes of presidential appointees in some detail.[10] But specifically, with regard to bureaucratic perceptions of the presidency itself, there is little evidence.[11] Therefore, I am interested in addressing the following question: How does the bureaucracy view the president?

Surprisingly, I find that despite evidence clearly showing that presidents can control the bureaucracy, bureaucrats do not perceive presidents as exerting a great deal of influence. In fact, in comparison to other actors who interact with the bureaucracy, presidents are perceived as having relatively limited influence. As I note, however, their appointees are perceived by the same bureaucrats as exerting considerable influence. I call this phenomenon the president–appointee dichotomy.

Methodology

To address the question of how bureaucrats view the president, I examine two surveys that were designed and implemented by Amelia Rouse, Robert Wright, and myself for a research project we conducted on the subject of political control of the bureaucracy.[12] When I refer to "we" in this section, it is to the able assistance of Amelia Rouse and Robert Wright that I am referring.

As noted, many studies have examined the president's relationship to the bureaucracy from the president's perspective. What is missing is what bureaucrats themselves think about presidential influence. To address this issue, we employed survey research methods to examine how bureaucratic agents perceive the influence exerted by a variety of political actors. Several studies have employed this method to analyze the bureaucracy, some of which have addressed issues related to how bureaucrats perceive the president's influence. For example, Heclo, Kaufman, Aberbach, and Rockman; Cole and Caputo; and Aberbach, Rockman, and Putman have examined the attitudes of bureaucrats as they relate to presidential appointees.[13] Also, Furlong and Stehr have examined bureaucratic attitudes regarding political control of the bureaucracy.[14] With few exceptions, however, such studies have employed nonrandomly generated samples, often with an unstructured or open-ended survey instrument.[15] In order to improve upon past research, we structured the survey instrument and examined two universes of environmental personnel.

Two Surveys

We conducted two separate surveys. The first was a survey of the employees of the Environmental Protection Agency's National Pollutant Discharge Elimination System (NPDES) program, which deals with the regulation of surface water under the Clean Water Act and its amendments. The second was a survey of employees of the New Mexico Environment Department (NMED). Survey responses for the EPA NPDES survey were collected between May and August 1994. Survey responses for the NMED survey were collected between March and June of 1997. Although the surveys were not conducted at the same time, and thus some caution must be applied to our comparison, our intention was to compare how federal and state-level environmental actors perceive the influence of various political actors, including the president and his appointees.

EPA and NMED Personnel

Our first survey consisted of an analysis of the employees of the EPA's regional offices who are responsible for enforcing the NPDES program. We focused on the perceptions of enforcement personnel because most of the top-down political control literature has examined their actions, such as inspections, notices of violation, and administrative orders, as dependent variables. We decided to examine the EPA because many top-down studies already have provided extensive findings supporting the propensity of EPA bureaucrats to respond to presidential influence.[16] We therefore would expect to find in a bottom-up study that these bureaucrats perceive the president as exerting considerable influence.

The task of identifying EPA NPDES personnel was accomplished by obtaining organizational charts and telephone directories from each of the EPA's ten regional offices. Where possible, we also obtained lists of their NPDES personnel specifically. Two of the regional offices chose not to participate in the survey. Thus, our universe consisted of 189 enforcement personnel from eight of EPA's ten regional offices.

The second survey consisted of an analysis of the employees of the New Mexico Environment Department. We selected the Environment Department because we were interested in examining a policy area similar to the one we examined at the national level. We examined all environmental personnel because the subset of individuals working in surface water programs was quite small. We chose New Mexico because we were interested in comparing the perceptions of state and federal-level bureaucrats. Our universe at the state level consisted of 462 employees. The only employees that were not surveyed were those with strictly clerical responsibilities.

Comparing the Surveys

In both surveys, respondents were asked for their views regarding the influence associated with a number of different political actors (fourteen in the EPA survey and seventeen in the state survey; the differences in numbers reflect some state-level actors we examined in the New Mexico survey that we did not examine in the EPA survey). Both surveys were administered through a mail questionnaire. This method has the advantages of eliminating interviewer bias, guaranteeing that all members of our sample have an equal opportunity to be contacted, and providing the confidentiality necessary for agency personnel to answer questions of a potentially sensitive nature. One threat to validity when using a mail questionnaire is a low response rate. Because of the sensitive nature of our survey (i.e., we anticipated that many potential respondents would feel uncomfortable answering questions about their political superiors, as well as officials within their own agency) this point was judged to be of particular importance. To secure as high a response rate as possible we used the Total Design Method.[17] With regard to the EPA survey we first sent an initial letter to all 189 members of our target group in which we identified ourselves and briefly described the nature of our survey. A week later we mailed a copy of the questionnaire with a cover letter and a self-addressed stamped envelope (SASE). Three weeks after that we mailed a second copy of the survey to those people who had not yet responded, along with another brief introductory letter and a SASE. Seventy-two surveys were collected from May 17 to August 31, 1994. Our response rate was 38 percent. For the second survey we mailed the cover letter along with the survey instrument on March 10, 1997 to 462 employees of the New Mexico Environment Department. Then two weeks later on March 24 we mailed a second survey along with a second cover letter. We received 166 completed surveys. Thus, our response rate for this survey was 36 percent.

It is clear in both cases that a higher response rate would have obviated our concerns about a self-selection bias. We did thoroughly consider other alternatives such as a telephone survey. The principal advantage of this approach would have been a potentially higher response rate. A telephone survey of bureaucratic elites, however, entailed several important threats to validity. First, our samples would have likely been biased toward those people who are most likely to be in the office at any given time. Since many EPA and NMED enforcement personnel are regularly in the field (e.g., for on-site inspections) this presented the possibility, as one state enforcement official told us, that we would end up interviewing "potted plants" rather than more active employees. Second, a telephone survey would have involved considerable institutional bias. We would have been interviewing employees in their offices where their responses could have been overheard by colleagues and supervisors. This was a particular concern since many EPA personnel (up to five in some regions) share the same phone. Since our survey involved some potentially sensitive questions, we were concerned that EPA and NMED personnel would be less willing to answer questions fully if their responses could be overheard. Third, various EPA and NMED officials, including several supervisors, were concerned that our survey would interfere with their office's daily operations. Since each interview would take approximately twenty minutes to complete, the administration of the survey could have been very disruptive. Finally, since we would have had to call back many employees, possibly leaving messages on answering machines or with another colleague or supervisor, we did not know what impact "the telephone tag bias," as we call it, would have introduced. Hence, while a telephone survey initially seemed to be the best means of conducting the survey, we eventually rejected this option on several valid grounds.[18]

Operationalization

For this chapter my objective is to examine the perceptions of bureaucrats regarding presidential influence over the bureaucracy. To provide a comparative basis, I will compare perceptions of the president to perceptions of other actors (in and outside of government) at the state and federal levels. To accomplish these goals in the survey we asked the following question[19]:

> The following questions deal with how much influence different institutions or individuals exert over your office. On a scale of zero to four where 0 is no influence and 4 is a great deal of influence, how much influence do the following [political actors] have over how your office enforces the law?

We specifically did not use the term "political influence" because we did not want to bias the results toward more traditional political actors (e.g., the president and Congress at the expense of the courts). In addition, we asked for perceptions of how much influence principals "have over how your office enforces the law," rather than asking how much influence do principals have over how you (the respondent) enforce the law. We used this wording because many respondents might be reluctant to suggest that any principal actually had exerted direct influence over how they enforce the law. By framing the question in terms of their office, then, we provide a means for agents to more easily identify potential sources of influence. In the second survey of state employees we included some state-specific political actors (which accounts for the difference in the number of political principals we asked agents to rate in the two surveys).

How Much Influence Does the President Exert?

The first question I address is how much influence is the president perceived to exert by federal and state-level bureaucrats? In Table 9.1 I present the results from the influence question (see above) for the fourteen actors we asked EPA NPDES employees to evaluate. Given the vast literature which argues that appointees are the president's most effective political tool for influencing the bureaucracy, it is not surprising that EPA personnel identified their regional administrators and the EPA administrator as the two most influential actors.[20] Their mean scores (4.04 and 3.99, respectively) are half a point higher than for any other actor. What is surprising is the relative ranking of the president. The president ranks seventh overall, with a mean 1.2 points lower than the regional administrators and 1.15 points lower than the EPA administrator; furthermore the difference of means tests between the president and the two types of presidential appointees are both statistically significant, which is clear evidence of a disjuncture in perceptions between the influence of the president and that of his appointees. In other words, EPA NPDES personnel do not perceive a direct connection between the influence of the president and the influence of the

Table 9.1

Perceptions of Environmental Protection Agency Employees Regarding the Influence of Various Actors

"On a scale from 1 to 5 where 1 is no influence and 5 is a great deal of influence, how much influence do the following (actors) have over how your office enforces the law?"

Actors	Rank	Mean	Standard deviation
Regional administrator	1	4.04	0.95
EPA administrator	2	3.99	0.97
Federal courts	3	3.44	1.10
Congress	4	3.36	1.30
Environmental groups	5	3.09	1.10
Public opinion	6	2.97	1.10
President	7	2.84	1.40
Permittees	8	2.83	1.03
Media	9	2.72	1.10
Governors	10	2.71	1.00
Business groups	11	2.59	1.10
State courts	12	2.50	1.10
State legislatures	13	2.31	0.90
Agricultural groups	14	2.21	1.00

president's own appointees. I call this the "president–appointee dichotomy."

This may appear to be an unusual finding given the emphasis in the appointment literature on how presidents should choose loyalists to represent them within the bureaucracy.[21] One would therefore think that by adopting this strategy presidents would tie themselves to the actions (both positive and negative) of their appointees. Yet the results provided here suggest otherwise. There may be an advantage in this dichotomy. If presidents name appointees to represent them in the bureaucracy, and if bureaucrats perceive them as exerting influence (but not the president), then presidents may develop an aura of "plausible deniability" if the actions of their appointees should be perceived in a negative light. In other words, the dichotomy may insulate presidents from negative fallout deriving from their appointees. At the same time, however, presidents still gain the policy advantages from naming loyal appointees. In short, presidents get the best of both worlds.

In addition to the relationship between presidents and their appointees, the results from Table 9.1 also indicate that four other actors (in addition to the appointees) are perceived as having more influence than the president. The federal courts, Congress, environmental interest groups, and public

Table 9.2

**Perceptions of New Mexico Environment Department Employees
Regarding the Influence of Various Actors**

"On a scale from 0 to 4 where 0 is no influence and 4 is a great deal of influence,
   how much influence do the following (actors) have over how your office enforces
   the law?"

Actors	Rank	Mean	Standard deviation
NM governor	1	2.84	1.24
NM state legislature	2	2.62	1.20
EPA administrator	3	2.27	1.39
Congress	4	2.11	1.45
NM legislative finance cmt.	5	2.03	1.43
Regional adm. region VI	6	1.99	1.35
NM Department of Finance	7	1.95	1.42
Public opinion	8	1.90	1.17
Business groups	9	1.82	1.33
NM state courts	10	1.81	1.25
Federal courts	11	1.78	1.29
Environmental groups	12	1.71	1.14
Media	13	1.55	1.08
President	14	1.43	1.45
County commissioners	15	1.20	1.21
Mayors	16	1.14	1.00
Agricultural groups	17	1.09	1.02

opinion are seen as more influential than the president. In fact, the president's influence is comparable to that of the permittees that the EPA regulates. Furthermore, the difference between the mean for the president and the mean for least influential actor, agricultural groups, is only 0.63 points, while the difference between the president and the most influential actor, the regional administrators, is 1.2 points. Thus, the president ranks closer to the bottom than to the top of the scale in relation to the perceived influence of other actors.

In summary, while the president is the chief executive, EPA bureaucrats do not perceive the president as exerting a great deal of influence in comparison to other political actors. This is surprising given the large body of empirical research which indicates that presidents have exerted influence over the bureaucracy.[22]

But what about state-level bureaucrats? How do they perceive the president in relation to other actors? In posing this question it must first be stated that the president is not a hierarchical superordinate to state-level officials. I therefore would expect the president to be ranked even lower by state actors than he was ranked in Table 9.1. In fact, as can be seen in Table 9.2, the president is ranked fourteenth out of seventeen political actors by state-level officials. Only county commissioners, mayors, and agricultural groups are seen as having less influence than the president. What is interesting, however, is that the president's appointees are again perceived as exerting considerable influence. The EPA administrator ranks 3 while the EPA regional administrator for Region VI, which oversees activities in New Mexico, is ranked 6. Other federal actors also rank higher than the president. Congress ranks 4 and the federal courts rank 11.

What is perhaps most interesting is that the actor who is perceived to have the most influence at the state level is the state chief executive, the governor of New Mexico. At the state level, the executive is perceived as being the most influential actor, but not at the federal level. State government is smaller and state officials are more likely to interact with the governor and his office than federal bureaucrats are to interact with the president and his staff. This may partially account for this result. Clearly, however, it is another bit of evidence that suggests that despite the prominent role presidents play in bureaucratic politics, they are not perceived as being active participants in that process (either by federal or state-level bureaucrats). Yet both types of bureaucrats do perceive the considerable influence exerted by the president's appointees. Again, this is further evidence in support of the president–appointee dichotomy.

What "Type" of Influence Does the President Exert?

In the last section I examined "how much" influence the president exerts. In this section I examine the "type" of influence the president is perceived as exerting in comparison to other political actors. In particular, I want to know if the president is perceived as being like other political actors or if the president is perceived by federal and state-level bureaucrats as exerting a distinctive "type" of influence. What do I mean by the difference between how much influence an actor exerts and the type of influence they exert? While bureaucrats from the EPA perceive the federal courts (with a mean influence score of 3.44 on a 5-point scale) as exerting more influence than the state courts (with a mean influence score of 2.5), they may still perceive the two principals as exerting a similar "type" of judicial influence. They may also perceive the president as exerting an entirely different type of influence than the courts and other actors or as being similar to other actors (e.g., other executives such as the state governors). But how can one determine perceptions of the "type" of influence exerted by various political actors?

To address this question I will use two different statistical techniques to

Table 9.3

Results of the Multi-Dimensional Scaling: The EPA Survey

	D#1	D#2	D#3	D#4	D#5
President	−0.72	−0.42	−0.29	0.01	0.20
Congress	−0.58	−0.33	−0.31	0.06	0.28
EPA administrator	−0.39	−0.18	0.57	0.10	−0.31
Regional administrators	−0.27	0.13	0.75	0.04	0.14
Federal courts	−0.28	0.66	−0.01	0.00	−0.05
State courts	−0.06	0.55	−0.19	0.09	−0.03
State legislatures	−0.01	0.38	−0.34	0.13	−0.13
Governors	−0.04	−0.10	−0.08	0.11	−0.26
Agricultural groups	0.08	−0.11	−0.04	−0.65	−0.17
Business groups	0.30	−0.12	−0.09	−0.58	−0.12
Environmental groups	0.41	−0.11	−0.05	0.26	−0.29
Media	0.46	−0.18	−0.23	0.33	−0.04
Public opinion	0.59	−0.39	0.18	0.21	0.12
Permittees	0.50	0.22	0.13	−0.10	0.66

determine how EPA and NMED agents perceive presidential influence in relationship to other political actors; multi-dimensional scaling and factor analysis. The first of these techniques, multi-dimensional scaling (MDS), "is designed to analyze distance-like data called dissimilarity data, or data that indicate the degree of dissimilarity (or similarity) of two things."[23] In my case it indicates the degree of dissimilarity between evaluations of the perceived level of "influence" of the fourteen principals we asked EPA NPDES personnel to rate and the seventeen principals we asked the officials from the New Mexico Environment Department to rate. Once the initial scale (from the survey) has been translated into dissimilarity data, MDS analyzes it "in a way that displays the structure of the distance-like data as a geometrical picture."[24] In so doing, the "purpose of MDS is to construct a map of the locations of objects relative to each other from data that specify how different these objects are. This is similar to the problem faced by a surveyor who, once he has surveyed the distances between a set of places, needs to draw a map showing the relative locations of those places."[25] This distance is calculated by using Euclidian distance to model the dissimilarities between the various principals.

I turn my attention first to an analysis of the 1994 survey of EPA NPDES bureaucrats. A stress statistic of 0.05 (or less) indicates that it is appropriate to model the perceptions of the fourteen principals in five-dimensional space. I present the data for each dimension in Table 9.3. For ease of visual presentation in Figure 9.1 I employ a map or geometric picture of the proximity placements of each principal in two-dimensional space. One can

Figure 9.1 **Map of the Perceptions of the Influence of Fourteen Principals by EPA NPDES Enforcement Personnel**

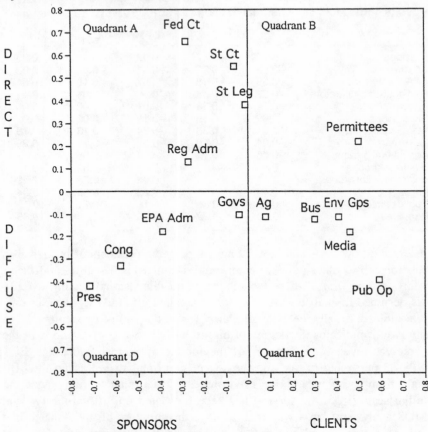

then refer to Table 9.3 to identify any differences that occur as one moves across additional dimensions of space.

The mapping of bureaucratic perceptions in multi-dimensional space is particularly valuable given my purpose. If bureaucrats do not perceive similarities in the influence exerted by various political actors, then I would expect the MDS mapping to reflect these differences with the various actors widely dispersed across multi-dimensional space. On the other hand, if bureaucrats do perceive similarities, then I would expect to see the various actors clustered in relative proximity to each other in multi-dimensional space. Of particular importance will be where the president clusters in comparison to other political actors.

The map in two-dimensional space was created by placing the calculated dissimilarities for Dimension 1 on the x axis and the dissimilarities for Dimension 2 on the y axis and should be interpreted like a map; that is, EPA bureaucrats perceive similarities in the influence exerted by those principals who are located in close proximity to each other in Figure 9.1. The further apart two principals are the more dissimilar their influence is considered to be. The fourteen political actors map into four quadrants of multi-dimensional space which we, for simplicity's sake, identify as quadrants A, B, C, and D.

I am interested in determining how bureaucrats perceive the president in relationship to other actors. The president is located in Quadrant D of Figure 9.1. The political actor closest to the president is Congress. This means that in terms of the perceived "type" of influence employed by each of the fourteen political actors, Congress is seen as most similar to the president. This should not be a surprising finding since the president and the Congress work together at the federal level. What is interesting is that the two types of presidential appointees, the EPA administrator and the EPA regional administrator, are located closer to Congress than to the president. This means that EPA employees see the influence of these presidential appointees as being more similar to that of Congress than to that of the president! This, along with the evidence I provided already in Tables 9.1 and 9.2, is evidence of a disjuncture in bureaucratic perceptions of presidents and their appointees— what I have called the "president–appointee dichotomy." While the two types of appointees are located in relatively close proximity to the president, indicating that their influence is seen as at least somewhat similar to that of the president, we would expect to see these political actors more closely grouped in multi-dimensional space. That they are not suggests that somehow presidents do not get credit from the bureaucracy for the influence of their own appointees, this at a time when presidents are explicitly appointing loyalists to positions in the bureaucracy. This finding might be more understandable if the regional administrators were located closer to the Congress and the EPA administrator closer to the president; since regional administrators are subject to Senatorial Courtesy and members of Congress thus play a greater role in determining who these appointees will be than is the case with the EPA administrator. But even the EPA administrator is located closer to Congress than the president. This finding suggests that scholars need to more closely examine how bureaucrats in other agencies perceive the connection between presidents and their appointees.

Another finding is evident from Figure 9.1. The president's influence is perceived as distinctly different from that of most other political actors. The president is on the opposite end of the figure from the courts and is not located close to the interest groups, public opinion, the media, or the vari-

Table 9.4

Rotated Factor Scores for the EPA Survey

Factor 1	
Congress	.97
President	.96
Factor 2	
Federal courts	.99
State courts	.87
State legislatures	.73
Factor 3	
Media	.90
Public opinion	.87
Environmental groups	.83
Factor 4	
Regional administrators	.94
EPA administrator	.81
Factor 5	
Business groups	.94
Agricultural groups	.93
Factor 6	
Permittees	.87

ous state actors. In short, with the exception of the Congress, and to a lesser extent the president's appointees, the president is perceived as distinctly different from any of the other political actors we examined. In other words, EPA NPDES personnel perceive the president as exerting a distinct type of political influence from all other actors.

In fact, the only other actors that theoretically approach the president in terms of the type of influence exerted are the state governors. Yet, while both are executives, EPA personnel do not perceive them as exerting similar "types" of influence. To a large extent, the influence of the president is perceived as rather unique by EPA bureaucrats.

To provide more evidence on this point, in Table 9.4 I examine the perceptions of EPA NPDES personnel in a yet another manner; through the use of factor analysis to analyze the EPA survey data. The results are strikingly similar to what I found in Figure 9.1 and Table 9.3. The president and Congress load together on one dimension, while the EPA and regional administrators load together on a separate factor. Again, this is clear evidence that bureaucrats do not perceive the similarities between the type of influence exerted by presidents and their own appointees.

Table 9.5

Results of the Multi-Dimensional Scaling for the New Mexico Environment Department Survey

	D#1	D#2	D#3	D#4
President	0.32	0.03	0.29	−0.35
Congress	0.46	0.10	0.23	−0.37
EPA administrator	0.12	0.06	−0.31	0.01
Regional administrators	0.22	0.00	−0.46	−0.19
Federal courts	0.53	−0.02	−0.22	0.19
State courts	0.44	−0.14	−0.30	0.32
State legislatures	−0.13	−0.48	0.14	0.10
Legislative finance cmt.	−0.32	−0.43	0.14	−0.11
Department of Finance	−0.31	−0.38	0.08	−0.17
Governor	−0.01	−0.05	0.11	−0.05
Agricultural groups	−0.06	0.12	0.07	0.45
Business groups	−0.18	0.08	0.14	0.52
Environmental groups	0.31	0.30	0.27	−0.04
Media	−0.25	0.38	0.31	0.08
Public opinion	−0.19	0.43	0.25	−0.06
County commissioners	−0.54	0.19	−0.25	−0.04
Mayors	−0.42	0.24	−0.50	−0.29

Thus far I have examined the perceptions of federal bureaucrats. But what about state-level bureaucrats? In Table 9.5 I present the results of the multi-dimensional scaling model for seventeen principals with whom the officials of the New Mexico Environment Department interact. I also present the model in two-dimensional space in Figure 9.2. As was the case with federal bureaucrats, their state brethren perceive a close relationship between the president and Congress. But what is particularly interesting is that state-level bureaucrats more clearly perceive the connection between presidents and the influence of their appointees. The EPA administrator and the regional administrator for Region VI are located in close proximity to the president. Furthermore, while federal bureaucrats perceived the president's influence as distinctive, that is, different from most other actors, state bureaucrats group the president in with a variety of disparate actors. To state-level bureaucrats, the president is but one of many political actors.

In Table 9.6 I present the results of the factor analysis of the NMED survey. The president and the Congress again load together, but since they are no longer perceived as direct, hierarchical actors, they load on the same factor with other clients that exert diffuse influence (i.e., environmental groups, the media, and the public).[26] The media and the public also load on the same factor with two other diffuse principals (i.e., the local-level actors, the mayors, and county officials). The only puzzling result from Table 9.6

Figure 9.2 **Map of the Perceptions of the Influence of Seventeen Principals by NMED Personnel**

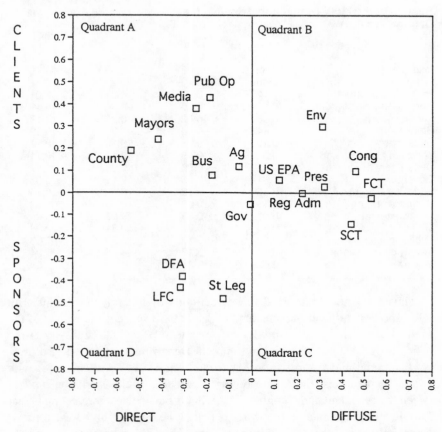

is that the federal and state courts load on the same factor with the two presidential appointees, rather than with the president and Congress. Clearly then, federal and state-level bureaucrats perceive the president's influence in far different terms.

What accounts for these differences in the perceptions of federal and state bureaucrats? I think the answer lies in where each bureaucrat resides. To federal bureaucrats, the president is the "chief executive" who resides atop the executive branch of the federal government. There is no other actor like the president in our federal system. To state-level bureaucrats, the president has no direct hierarchical authority and thus is seen as but one of many possible influences on their policies. In short, to state-level bureaucrats, the president is not particularly special. This does not account, however, for why

Table 9.6

**Rotated Factor Scores for the New Mexico Environment Department
Survey**

Factor 1
Congress	.74
President	.67
Environmental groups	.73
Media	.60
Public opinion	.58

Factor 2
Federal courts	.82
State courts	.75
EPA administrator	.69
Regional administrator	.67

Factor 3
State legislature	.76
Governor	.73
Legislative finance cmt.	.84
Department of Finance	.82

Factor 4
Media	.55
Public opinion	.52
Mayors	.86
County officials	.85

state-level bureaucrats perceive a connection between presidents and their appointees and federal bureaucrats do not. That is a question that certainly deserves more attention.

Conclusions

I find that bureaucrats do not perceive presidents as exerting a great deal of influence over the bureaucracy. Both federal and state-level bureaucrats perceive the Congress and the federal court as exerting more influence than the president. In addition, both perceive the president's appointees as exerting considerable influence over how their offices enforce the law. Over all, presidents are perceived as exerting relatively limited influence.

As I note, however, presidential appointees are perceived by the same bureaucrats as exerting considerable influence. I call this phenomenon the president–appointee dichotomy. What this dichotomy suggests is that presidents may be able to hide behind the active influence exerted by their appointees. In this process, they can take full advantage of the favorable policy changes associated with the active leadership provided by their appointees (i.e., desired changes in an agency's behavior). On the other hand, presidents do not directly get the blame for their appointees' excesses. The president–appointee dichotomy may thus give presidents the best of both worlds. They get the policy change they want without having to step out in front and take responsibility for it. Thus, when things go wrong, presidents have a place to hide.

Notes

1. Clinton Rossiter, *The American Presidency* (New York: Harcourt, Brace and World, 1960), 19–22.

2. Louis W. Koenig, *The Chief Executive* (New York: Harcourt Brace Jovanovich, 1975), 184.

3. Thomas E. Cronin, *The State of the Presidency* (Boston: Little, Brown, 1980), 333.

4. Roger G. Noll, *Reforming Regulation* (Washington, DC: Brookings Institution, 1971), 36.

5. See Richard P. Nathan, *The Administrative Presidency* (New York: John Wiley & Sons, 1983); and Richard P. Nathan, *The Plot That Failed: Nixon and the Administrative Presidency* (New York: John Wiley & Sons, 1975).

6. Judith Michaels, *The President's Call* (Pittsburgh: University of Pittsburgh Press, 1997).

7. See ibid.; and Richard W. Waterman, *Presidential Influence and the Administrative State* (Knoxville: University of Tennessee Press, 1989).

8. See, for example, Terry M. Moe, "Regulatory Performance and Presidential Administration," *American Journal of Political Science* 26 (1982): 197–225; Joseph Stewart, Jr., and Jane S. Cromartie, "Partisan Presidential Change and Regulatory Policy: The Case of the FTC and Deceptive Practices Enforcement, 1938–1974," *Presidential Studies Quarterly* 12 (1982): 568–73; B. Dan Wood and James Anderson, "The Politics of U.S. Antitrust Regulation," *American Journal of Political Science* 37 (1993): 1–39, B. Dan Wood and Richard W. Waterman, *Bureaucratic Dynamics: The Role of Bureaucracy in a Democracy* (Boulder, CO: Westview Press, 1994); Wood and Waterman, "The Dynamics of Political-Bureaucratic Adaptation." *American Journal of Political Science* 37 (1993): 497–528; Wood and Waterman, "The Dynamics of Political Control of the Bureaucracy," *American Political Science Review* 85 (1991): 801–28; Waterman and Wood, "Policy Monitoring and Policy Analysis," *Journal of Policy Analysis and Management* 12 (1993): 685–99; Waterman and Wood, "What Do We Do with Applied Research?" *PS: Political Science & Politics* (September 1992): 559–64; Steven A. Shull and David Garland, "Presidential Influence Versus Agency Characteristics in Explaining Policy Implementation," *Policy Studies Review* 14 (1995): 49–70.

9. Joel D. Aberbach and Bert Rockman, "Administration, Interest Groups and the Changing Political Universe in Washington—Perceptions and Behavior," International Political Science Association Conference on the Structure and Organization of Government (Zurich, Switzerland, 1989); Aberbach and Rockman, "Clashing Beliefs in the Executive Branch: The Nixon Administration Bureaucracy," *American Political Science Review* 70 (1976): 456–68; Joel Aberbach, Robert D. Putman, and Bert Rockman, *Bureaucrats and Politicians in Western Democracies* (Boston: Harvard University

Press, 1981); Richard L. Cole and David A. Caputo, "Presidential Control of the Senior Executive Service: Assessing Strategies for the Nixon Years," *American Political Science Review* 73 (1979): 409–32.

10. Hugh Heclo, *A Government of Strangers: Executive Politics in Washington* (Washington, DC: Brookings Institution, 1977); Herbert Kaufman, *The Administrative Behavior of Federal Bureau Chiefs* (Washington, DC: Brookings Institution, 1981).

11. Though see Steven D. Stehr, "Top Bureaucrats and the Distribution of Influence in Reagan's Executive Branch," *Public Administration Review* 57 (1997): 75–82.

12. Richard Waterman, Amelia Rouse, and Robert Wright, "The Venues of Influence: A New Theory of Political Control of the Bureaucracy," *Journal of Public Administration Research and Theory* 8 (1998): 13–38.

13. Heclo, *A Government of Strangers;* Kaufman, *Administrative Behavior;* Aberbach and Rockman, "Clashing Beliefs in the Executive Branch"; Cole and Caputo, "Presidential Control"; Aberbach, Putman, and Rockman, *Bureaucrats and Politicians in Western Democracies.*

14. Stehr, "Top Bureaucrats"; Scott Furlong, "Political Influence on the Bureaucracy: The Bureaucracy Speaks," *Journal of Public Administration Research and Theory* 8 (1988): 39–65.

15. William T. Gormley, Jr., "Intergovernmental Conflict on Environmental Policy: The Attitudinal Connection," *Western Political Quarterly* 40 (1987): 285–303; Furlong, ibid.; Stehr, ibid.

16. B. Dan Wood, "Principals, Bureaucrats, and Responsiveness in Clean Air Enforcements," *American Political Science Review* 82 (1988): 213–34; Wood and Waterman, "The Dynamics of Political-Bureaucratic Adaptation"; Wood and Waterman, "The Dynamics of Political Control of the Bureaucracy."

17. Don A. Dillman, *Mail and Telephone Surveys: The Total Design Method* (New York: John Wiley & Sons, 1978).

18. One option we considered to increase our response rate was to ask EPA officials in Washington to send a letter to each regional office asking their employees to cooperate with our survey. Given our conversations with EPA officials in Washington, we feel confident that we could have secured such a letter of support. While this almost certainly would have promoted a higher response rate, we were concerned that it would also have introduced considerable bias into the analysis. Since the subject of our survey was political control of the bureaucracy, and since we therefore would be asking EPA employees to answer questions about the very superordinates in Washington who had written the letter of support, we believed a letter could introduce considerable bias into a survey of perceptions of hierarchical political influence.

19. With regard to our EPA survey, we used a scale of 1 to 5 rather than 0 to 4.

20. Nathan, *The Administrative Presidency;* Waterman, *Presidential Influence.*

21. Ibid.

22. Stewart and Cromartie, "Partisan Presidential Change"; Moe, "Regulatory Performances"; Wood and Waterman, *Bureaucratic Dynamics.*

23. SPSS, *SPSS: SPSS Professional Statistics 6.1* (Chicago: Norusis/SPSS Inc., 1993), 155.

24. Ibid.

25. Ibid., 157

26. For a discussion of the client–sponsor and diffuse–direct dichotomies presented in Figures 9.1 and 9.2, see Waterman, Rouse, and Wright, "The Venues of Influence."

10

Justices and Presidents

Jeffrey A. Segal and Robert M. Howard

In June 1968, Chief Justice Earl Warren announced to President Lyndon Johnson his intention to retire from the Supreme Court at "such time as a successor is qualified" to take his place.[1] Thus began a process that resulted in the nomination and rejection of Abe Fortas to take Warren's place as chief justice, and the eventual nomination (by newly elected President Richard Nixon) and confirmation of Warren Burger to take Warren's place. This ascension of Burger signaled the end of a liberal revolution in judicial policymaking[2] that had commenced when Eisenhower nominated Warren to the Court in repayment for Warren's crucial support of Eisenhower at the 1952 Republican convention. Debt or no debt, Eisenhower later considered his Warren nomination to be the biggest mistake he made as president.[3] Indeed, short of the Normandy invasion, it was perhaps the most important decision he ever made.

Unlike Eisenhower, Nixon fully realized the momentousness of Supreme Court nominations. "By far, the most important appointments [a president] makes are those to the Supreme Court of the United States. Presidents come and go, but the Supreme Court through its decisions goes on forever."[4]

In addition to Burger, Nixon was able to name three more conservatives to the Supreme Court: Harry Blackmun, Lewis Powell, and William Rehnquist.[5] As we will show later in the chapter, with these appointments, Nixon was able to move the Court decisively to the right. Indeed, we will use the judicial life-cycle, from Warren's resignation, to the eventual appointment and confirmation of Burger, to Burger's time on the Court, to highlight the relationship between justices and presidents.

168

Presidential Appointments

Article II, Section 2, Paragraph 2 of the United States Constitution states that the president shall nominate, and, by and with the advice and consent of the Senate, shall appoint judges to the Supreme Court. This process starts with either the creation of a new seat, or the death or resignation of a sitting justice. That Earl Warren chose to resign during the Johnson administration should occasion no surprise. Though nominally a Republican, Warren was a liberal in nearly every sense of the word. Facing a potential Republican victory in the 1968 election, Warren was determined to see a liberal replace him on the Court.[6] Warren, though, was not unique in playing the "retirement game."[7] Through 1997, there have been fifty-three resignations from the Court. Thirty-one of them have been during periods in which the president was of the same party of the retiring justice, whereas only twenty-two were during opposite-party presidents. But even here justices can pick their moments. Though liberal Democrats Brennan and Marshall retired during a Republican administration (Bush's), they waited until the far more conservative Ronald Reagan left office before doing so.

Nominations

President Johnson used the constitutional power cited above to nominate associate justice Abe Fortas to Chief Justice Warren's position, and Homer Thornberry to take Fortas's seat as associate justice. Fortas originally served as Johnson's attorney during Johnson's 1948 Senate campaign and thereafter became his close friend and professional confidante. When Johnson became president, he pressured Arthur Goldberg off the Court in order to place Fortas on.[8] Even while on the Court, Fortas continued to serve Johnson. According to one contemporaneous report, "few important presidential problems are settled without an opinion of Mr. Fortas."[9] This type of relationship is not unique. For example, Truman tapped several close friends for seats on the Court. Overall, around 60 percent of Supreme Court nominees personally knew the appointing president.[10]

What else can we say about the presidents' nominees? All told, presidents have nominated 145 men and two women to the Supreme Court. In all cases, the president has nominated an attorney, though this is not required by the Constitution. Most often the president will appoint someone with prior judicial experience (93 out of 147, or 63 percent), who belongs to his political party (87 percent), and who shares the president's political views. This, though, will vary by president as some have far more interest in the process than others. Thus, some presidents have left the selection process to staff, cabinet members, or even current or former Supreme Court justices. For example, former President William Howard Taft was known to have successfully lobbied for his own appointment as well as several others. Justices such as Hughes, Stone, Warren, and Burger have likewise lobbied with varying degrees of success for certain nominees.[11] Ronald Reagan's Attorney's Generals Smith and Meese influenced the selection of Sandra Day O'Connor and Robert Bork, respectively. Ford's attorney general, Edward Levi, played the leading role in the selection of Justice John Paul Stevens.

For presidents who are concerned with the ideology of their nominees, simple partisanship provides some information, but not all. As Senator Henry Cabot Lodge observed, "the nominal politics of the man have nothing to do with his actions on the bench. His real politics are all important."[12] Thus Theodore Roosevelt only nominated Oliver Wendell Holmes when Lodge assured him that Holmes was "in entire sympathy with our views."[13] Eisenhower was disappointed with the Republican, but very liberal Earl Warren, while Democrats often expressed dissatisfaction with the increasing conservatism of Democrat Byron White. On the other hand, Republican Taft nominated three ideologically like-minded Democrats while Democratic presidents Roosevelt and Truman nominated Republicans Stone and Burton.

Beyond ideology, presidents must be concerned with the political context of nominations. It is not a coincidence that the statesman-like Eisenhower, attempting to appear above partisanship, nominated Democrat William Brennan to the Court just one month prior to the 1956 elections. Nixon (unsuccessfully) nominated Clement Haynsworth of South Carolina and G. Harrold Carswell of Florida to the Court in an attempt to attract conservative Southern Democrats to vote for him in 1972. But even without reelection concerns, successful presidents must consider public opinion. Presidents appear to select activities, including appointments, in ways designed to increase their popularity. Reagan's choice of Sandra Day O'Connor for the Court is a clear example of this.

Religion, gender, and ethnicity play roles in the nominating process. Through 1835, when the first Catholic (Roger Taney) was nominated, every nominee was white, male, and Protestant. A second Catholic, Edward White, was not named until 1894. Since then, at least one Catholic has sat on the Court for all but eight years. With Reagan's nomination of Anthony Kennedy in 1987 (he was confirmed in 1988), three Catholics sat on the Court for the first time. Presidents from Wilson through Johnson kept a "Jewish seat" on the Court, going from Brandeis (1916) until Abe Fortas's resignation from his associate justice seat (1969). That the presidents replaced Cardozo with Frankfurter, Frankfurter with Goldberg, and Goldberg with Fortas cannot be coincidence, any more than was Bush's replacement of Thurgood Marshall, the first African-American justice, with Clarence Thomas, the second such justice. In total, while most of the 147 nominees to the Court have been white, male, and Protestant, nine have been Jewish, twelve Roman Catholic, two female, and two African American. It seems a political certainty that at least one African American will always sit on the Court, and that the percentage of females will remain steady if not increase.

Confirmation

The very factors that led Earl Warren to announce his resignation in 1968, the upcoming presidential election and the likelihood of a Nixon presidency, are among the factors that led the Senate to reject Johnson's nomination of Fortas as Chief Justice. First, the timing of the vacancy worked against Fortas. By the summer of 1968, the presidential election was only a few months away. With Johnson's popularity plummeting and Johnson's vice-president heading the Democratic ticket, Republicans and Southern Democrats had every reason to believe that if they defeated Fortas, Richard Nixon would make the new appointment. Indeed, presidential nominees to the High Court have historically fared poorly in the president's final year of his term. In the first three years of a president's term the Senate has confirmed 106 out of 122 nominees (87 percent). In the last year of the president's term the Senate has confirmed only 14 out of 25 nominees (56 percent).

The bad timing of the Fortas nomination was compounded by Johnson's low approval ratings in 1968. Between 1953 and 1990, unpopular presidents, those with approval ratings below 50 percent, lose about twenty additional votes in the Senate in Supreme Court nominations as compared with popular presidents, those with approval ratings above 70 percent.[14] Johnson's approval rating at the time of the nomination was but 40 percent.

The second factor to work against Fortas's nomination was Fortas's liberal ideology. In his four terms on the Court, Fortas supported the liberal position in civil liberties cases (those dealing with civil rights, criminal procedure, First Amendment freedoms, and due process) over 80 percent of the time, aligning himself with the most liberal members of the Court.[15] Members of the Judiciary Committee[16] grilled Fortas about liberal decisions he had rendered, and even some that preceded his tenure.[17] Similar to the effect of presidential popularity, ideologically extreme nominees will lose about twenty votes in the Senate as compared to similarly qualified moderates.[18]

Ideology alone, though, will rarely kill a judicial nominee. It is almost always the case that ideologically extreme nominees can get confirmed if they also have high qualifications. For example, Antonin Scalia, as conser-

vative a nominee as one could imagine, sailed through the Senate unanimously. Alternatively, perceived ideologues against whom plausible
charges against their judgment, character, or qualifications can be made will
face much more difficult times.[19] Such was the case with Fortas, who had
accepted a $15,000 fee for teaching a nine-week seminar at American Uni-
versity. The money was raised from wealthy businessmen involved in litigation that could come before the Supreme Court. Additionally, some
senators questioned the propriety of Fortas's close relationship with Johnson. These considerations allowed conservative senators to oppose Fortas
without appearing partisan.

In fact, this confluence of ideology and qualifications does the best job of
explaining opposition to presidents' Supreme Court nominees in the post-
war era. When senators' constituents are ideologically close to nominees,
senators vote for nominees regardless of their qualifications (about 99 percent of the time). And when nominees are highly qualified, senators vote for
them regardless of the nominee's ideology (about 98 percent of the time).
But when nominees are both ideologically distant and low on qualifications,
the support rate drops to less than 10 percent![20]

Overall, through the history of the Court, the Senate has confirmed 120
out of 147 presidential nominees.[21] Of the twenty-seven rejected candidates, the Senate repudiated twelve, failed to act on five, indefinitely post-
poned four, and pressured the president to withdraw six. The latter category
includes Fortas's nomination for Chief Justice, which was withdrawn by
Johnson after the Senate failed to invoke cloture (i.e., cut off debate).

In addition to the factors affecting confirmation discussed in the Fortas
nomination, a few others deserve mention. Perhaps the most prominent is
whether the president's party controls the Senate. When the partisanship of the
president is the same as the majority in the Senate, the Senate has confirmed 90
percent of nominees (97 out of 108). Conversely, when the Senate majority
partisanship differs from the party of the president, the Senate is less likely to
confirm the nominee. In this situation the confirmation percentage drops to 56
percent (14 out of 25). Recent examples of partisanship differences and rejected nominees include Nixon and Carswell and Reagan and Bork. So, too,
interest-group opposition can hurt nominees, as exemplified by AFL-CIO opposition to Haynsworth and NAACP opposition to Thomas.

Presidential Influence

Following the Senate's rejection of Fortas, Johnson chose not to name a
new justice to take Warren's place. But because Warren's resignation was
contingent on "such time as a successor is qualified" to take his place,

Warren remained in office. "Since they won't confirm Abe, they will have me," he declared.[22]

That fall, Richard Nixon campaigned for the presidency against Hubert Humphrey, against Lyndon Johnson, and against the Warren Court. The Warren Court, he declared, had gone too far in protecting the criminal forces in society, as opposed to the peace forces. He wanted "strict constructionists" who would not read their preferred views of public policy into law. Nixon won. With at least four more years of Republican rule, the seventy-eight-year-old Warren gave in to the inevitable and resigned unconditionally in the spring of 1969, allowing Richard Nixon to name his successor. Nixon swiftly named Warren Burger to take Earl Warren's place.

In the next two and a half years, Nixon named three more conservatives to the Court. The first vacancy occurred when Abe Fortas resigned from the Court following allegations that he accepted $20,000 as part of an annual "consulting" fee from Louis Wolfson, a millionaire businessman later convicted of stock manipulation. Though Nixon failed in his first two attempts to replace Fortas,[23] he eventually appointed Harry Blackmun on the Court. Then, following the resignations of Justices Harlan and Black in September 1971, Nixon nominated and the Senate confirmed Lewis Powell and William Rehnquist to take their places.

In many ways, Nixon reshaped the Supreme Court, not just in personnel, but in policy. Though the Burger Court placed limits on the death penalty, it upheld its constitutionality provided procedural safeguards were followed;[24] it limited the reach of the *Mapp*[25] and *Miranda* decisions;[26] increased the ability of states to ban obscene materials;[27] refused to equalize state spending between school districts;[28] refused to extend the right to privacy to homosexual conduct;[29] and allowed programs within colleges and universities to discriminate without fear of the entire school losing federal funds.[30]

A variety of factors, though, limited the conservative thrust of the Burger Court. First, outside of criminal justice, Nixon was not exceptionally conservative on social issues,[31] and we would not necessarily expect his justices to be universally conservative either. Moreover, we could not have expected him to have paid attention to issues such as privacy and abortion before they became salient issues for the Court. (Similarly, Kennedy nominee Byron White was viewed by most observers as liberal in the area of civil rights, and the important issue of black-white equality. In 1962 breaking down segregation was a highly salient issue area, and one to which President Kennedy was committed. This was prior to the controversial Supreme Court rulings on criminal constitutional law such as *Miranda v. Arizona* [1966] and *Escobedo v. Illinois* [1964], and prior to privacy rulings such as *Griswold v. Connecti-*

cut [1965] and *Roe v. Wade* [1973]. These issues grew in importance and salience over the years and Justice White often took a more restrictive view in this area to the disappointment of liberals.)

Second, like most presidents, Nixon did not get to place a majority of justices on the Court. Still, William Rehnquist's civil liberties score is 20.9, far lower than that of any other justice at the time of his appointment. This alone lowered the overall civil liberties average, but even four nominees did not give President Nixon a guaranteed winning coalition on the Court. In fact, power devolved to the moderate swing justices.

Third, justices who fit ideologically on one end of the spectrum may change over time, a situation exemplified by the career of Nixon appointee Harry Blackmun. Similarly, David Souter's scores jumped from 41.5 under Bush to over 60 under Clinton. Justice Stevens has become increasingly liberal with each administration, while Byron White became increasingly conservative.

Fourth, no justice, however ideologically concordant with his or her appointing president, will support the president on every issue. Warren Burger wrote the majority opinion in support of racial busing,[32] opposing the view of President Nixon. Sandra Day O'Connor wrote the majority opinion upholding the right of a woman to have an abortion despite the opposition of her appointing president, Ronald Reagan.[33] Justice Davis, a personal friend and appointee of President Lincoln's, rejected Lincoln's suspension of the Constitution during wartime in *Ex Parte Milligan* (1866).

Thus, though the Burger Court clearly reversed the trend of increasingly liberal Warren Court decisions, it was the Burger Court that first created abortion rights,[34] protected women under the 14th Amendment,[35] permitted school busing,[36] and accepted race-based affirmative action plans.[37] But, as Nixon supported the ERA and introduced some early affirmative action programs into the executive branch, at least some of these liberal decisions were consistent with Nixon's preferences.

Beyond the case of Nixon, we can more generally examine the influence of presidential regimes on Supreme Court decision making. Figure 10.1 presents the percentage of the Supreme Court's civil liberties decisions that are liberal since 1946.[38]

The dotted line in Figure 10.1 represents the overall trend of the civil liberties scores over time. Clearly there has been a downward trend, meaning that the Court has grown more conservative in civil liberties issues from 1946 to 1994. The trend for each particular president, however, is not as clear. The heavy jagged line depicts the Court's annual civil liberties scores, with the average of those scores given for each president (in initials) as represented by the solid horizontal line between the vertical lines.

As we can see, from the baseline of the Truman era, the Supreme Court

Figure 10.1 **Civil Liberties Scores of Presidential Supreme Court Appointees by Year and President, 1946–1994**

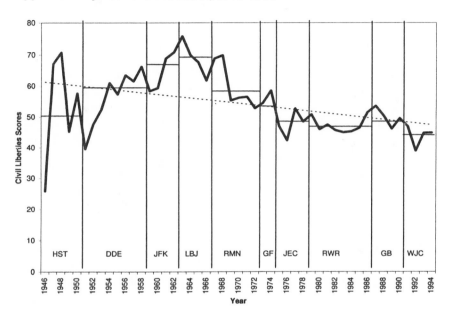

became more liberal during the Eisenhower administration. This was undoubtedly due to the fact that Eisenhower's priority in nominating Supreme Court justices, as noted above, was not ideological concordance. As expected, the average score rose during the presidencies of Kennedy and Johnson and decreased during Nixon's and Ford's tenure. Ronald Reagan, perhaps the most conservative president of the twentieth century, had only a marginally lower average score than Ford and Bush.

Overall, the Court tends to move in the direction of the sitting president. Much of that trend is due to a high degree of concordance between a president's ideology and that of his nominees.[39] Liberal presidents such as Franklin Roosevelt and Lyndon Johnson tend to appoint liberal justices. Thus Roosevelt appointed William Douglas and Hugo Black and Lyndon Johnson appointed Thurgood Marshall and Abe Fortas. And as well, conservative presidents nominate conservative justices. Nixon appointed Warren Burger and William Rehnquist while George Bush appointed David Souter and Clarence Thomas.

Yet, as Reagan's case shows, while the president's ability to shape the Court can be decisive in his appointments,[40] that is not the complete story. Such influence will depend not just on whom the president places on the Court, but

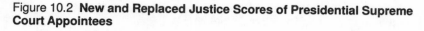

Figure 10.2 **New and Replaced Justice Scores of Presidential Supreme Court Appointees**

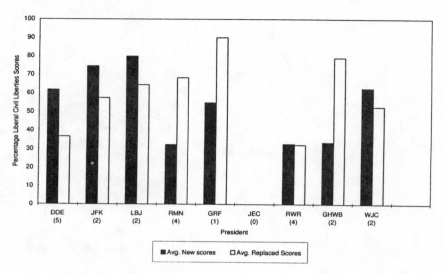

on whom that justice replaces. For example, Reagan placed the extremely conservative Antonin Scalia on the Court, but Scalia took the associate justice seat of William Rehnquist, another extreme conservative. Appointments such as that may have little impact on the Court's decisions.

Thus, answers to why the Court became more liberal during the Eisenhower years, and did not become more conservative during the Reagan years, become clear when we examine Figure 10.2. Figure 10.2 displays the average annual voting scores of each president's appointees and the justices they replaced, with the number of appointees in parentheses.[41] As shown, Eisenhower's five appointees were moderately liberal on average, but they replaced justices who were substantially more conservative.

At the time Richard Nixon took office in 1969, the Supreme Court consisted of Chief Justice Earl Warren, and Associate Justices Black, Harlan II, Brennan, Stewart, Fortas, White, Marshall, and Douglas. The average civil liberties score for these nine justices was 68.9. The four justices that President Nixon replaced (Warren, Black, Fortas, and Harlan II) averaged 69.3, almost exactly the same as the Court average. The four Justices Nixon appointed in their place averaged 35.2, bringing the Court's average down to 52.9, almost directly in the middle of the civil liberties score. But while Reagan's nominees were as conservative as Nixon's, Reagan's appointees replaced other conservatives, leaving his impact on the Court fairly negligible.

The Solicitor General

While the president's most direct path of influence is through the appointment process, the president can additionally wield influence through the solicitor general.[42] The solicitor general represents the government before the Supreme Court. But the power of the office extends beyond that of simple representation.[43] The solicitor general's office not only controls all Justice Department appeals to the Supreme Court, but virtually all appeals by other federal agencies and departments as well.[44]

In addition to representing the government, the solicitor general can file *amicus curiae* (friend of the Court) briefs at the office's own initiative or at the request of the Court when the United States is not a party to the litigation. The solicitor general can file these amicus briefs at the *certiorari* stage, arguing to the Court whether or not it should accept a case for review, or at the decision stage, supporting one or another of the parties on the merits of the case. This entire interaction has led one scholar to refer to the solicitor general as the "tenth justice."[45]

How influential is the solicitor general, and therefore the president he represents? Overall very influential, both in moving the Court to accept or decline cases, and in winning cases before the Supreme Court where the United States is a party. Early research had shown that in cases where the United States favored Supreme Court review, the Court granted certiorari 47 percent of the time as opposed to less than 6 percent when it did not.[46] When the United States was a losing party and appealed, the Supreme Court granted certiorari about 70 percent of the time. Other parties had only an 8 percent success rate.[47]

The office is equally successful when arguing the actual merits of the case. Research on the Supreme Court from the early 1940s through the Burger Court has shown that the solicitor general succeeded at least 65 percent of the time, and during the Kennedy administration won 87.5 percent of the time.[48] Two Court scholars found in a longitudinal study running from 1801 to 1958 that the United States won 62 percent of its cases before the Supreme Court.[49]

In addition to the solicitor general's success on certiorari and on the merits where the United States is a party, the office enjoys considerable success when it files amicus curiae, or friend of the Court, briefs. Many times the United States is not a party to the litigation but has an important interest in the outcome. The equal protection case of *Brown v. Board of Education*[50] is one example. The affirmative action case of the *University of California Regents v. Bakke*[51] is another. In *Brown*, the famous Earl Warren phrase "all deliberate speed" was proposed by the solicitor general in his amicus brief.[52] In *Bakke*, the solicitor general amicus position of approving affirmative action but disapproving strict quotas became the majority holding.[53]

In fact, in amicus cases, the government has an even better record of success than in cases where it is a party.[54] Between 1920 and 1973 the party supported by the solicitor general won 74 percent of the time in all cases, and over 80 percent in political cases.[55] Even higher success rates exist for more recent time periods.[56] While certain solicitors, presidents, and ideological briefs fare better than others do, the solicitor general seems to win regardless of these factors.[57]

The Influence of the Court on Presidents and the Presidency

While we have spent most of the chapter examining the impact of the president on the Court, we would be remiss if we did not examine the impact that the Court can have on presidents and the presidency. For example, between 1933 and 1936 a conservative Supreme Court thwarted Franklin Roosevelt's New Deal policies, striking down a variety of laws and provisions as unconstitutional. It was not until Roosevelt threatened to pack the Court that the Court backed down. Roosevelt, though, was in an unusual situation in that he had no appointments to the Court in his first term in office, an unfortunate (for him at least) happenstance. With an average of nearly two appointments per term, and with some number of justices from the president's party already serving on the Court, few presidents have faced Roosevelt's type of problems. But this is not to say that presidents always get their way. Indeed, in many important cases they have not. Although there are relatively few such cases, the Court, it appears, is not reluctant to assert its authority over the president.

In the first such direct interaction, the treason trial of Aaron Burr, Chief Justice John Marshall granted defense motions to subpoena President Jefferson to produce certain documents. Jefferson refused to personally appear, but sent the documents.[58] In *Ex Parte Milligan,* the Court held some of President Lincoln's wartime actions unconstitutional, but it should be noted that Milligan was decided in 1866, after Lincoln's death and the end of the Civil War.

The Court in *United States v. Curtiss-Wright Export Corp* (1936) upheld the right of the president, under a broad delegation of congressional power, to embargo arms to certain Latin American countries. When President Truman, however, acted unilaterally and without prior congressional authority to seize the steel mills during the Korean War, the Court found the action unconstitutional.[59]

The recent matter involving President Clinton and the sexual harassment claim of Paula Jones continues to demonstrate the authority of the Court over the president. President Clinton had sought a delay in the trial until after his term of office, citing the pressing duties of the president. The Court declined to delay the trial, a decision joined by both of Clinton's appointees, Ginsburg and Breyer.[60] It was, of course, Clinton's deposition in the *Jones* case that led to the Monica Lewinsky scandal.

In perhaps the most important case directly involving a president, *United States v. Nixon*, a unanimous Court, including three of his appointees, declined to back President Nixon's refusal to turn over secret taped Oval Office conversations to special Watergate prosecutor Leon Jaworski. Nixon asserted executive privilege. The unanimous Court ruled that the need for evidence in a criminal proceeding outweighed the claim of executive privilege. Nixon wanted justices who would not create loopholes for accused criminals, and that was exactly what he got. Although presidents may influence the Supreme Court through judicial nominations and the solicitors general, the Court also influence presidents.

Notes

1. "Warren–Johnson Letters," *New York Times,* June 27, 1968, A30.

2. The Warren Court prohibited state-enforced desegregation (*Brown v. Board of Education*, 1954); upheld congressionally passed limits on private discrimination (*Heart of Atlanta Motel v. United States*, 1964); ended malapportioned legislative districts (e.g., *Wesberry v. Sanders*, 1964); prohibited organized school prayers (*Engel v. Vitale*, 1962) and devotional Bible readings (*Abington School District v. Schempp*, 1963); prohibited illegally obtained materials from being used in state trials (*Mapp v. Ohio*, 1961); required that suspects be read their rights (*Miranda v. Arizona*, 1966); guaranteed indigent defendants a right to counsel in felony cases (*Gideon v. Wainright*, 1963); and created the right to privacy (*Griswold v. Connecticut*, 1965) that eventually led to the striking down of laws prohibiting abortion (*Roe v. Wade*, 1973).

3. Earl Warren, *The Memoirs of Earl Warren* (New York: Doubleday, 1977), 5. Truman thought similarly about his nomination of Tom Clark. See Merle Miller, *Plain Speaking: An Oral Biography of Harry S. Truman* (New York: Putnam, 1974), 225–26.

4. Richard Nixon, "Transcript of President's Announcements," *New York Times,* October 22, 1971, 24.

5. Blackmun gradually became more liberal as his career progressed, but at the time of his nomination, he was viewed as a staunch conservative, and indeed voted that way. See Lee Epstein, Jeffrey Segal, Harold Spaeth, and Thomas Walker, *The Supreme Court Compendium* (Washington, DC: Congressional Quarterly, 1994).

6. Edward G. White, *Earl Warren: A Public Life* (New York: Oxford University Press, 1982).

7. For evidence on lower court judges, see James F. Spriggs II and Paul J. Wahlbeck, "Calling it Quits: Strategic Retirement on the Federal Courts of Appeals, 1893–1991," *Political Research Quarterly* 48:573–97.

8. According to a recent book, Secretary of Labor Goldberg hosted a party for Vice-President Johnson that, unknown to Goldberg, had been financed by unsavory char-

acters. When rumors about the funding circulated, Goldberg falsely claimed to have funded the affair himself, which Johnson knew to be a lie. David Stebenne's biography of Goldberg claims that Johnson used this information to force Goldberg off the Court. See David L. Stebenne, *Arthur J. Goldberg: New Deal Liberal* (New York: Oxford, 1996).

9. *Newsweek,* July 8, 1968, 18.

10. Updated from Robert Scigliano, *The Supreme Court and the Presidency* (New York: The Free Press, 1971).

11. Henry Abraham, *Justices and Presidents*, 2nd ed. (New York: Oxford, 1985).

12. Jeffrey A. Segal and Harold J. Spaeth, *The Supreme Court and the Attitudinal Model* (Cambridge and New York: Cambridge University Press, 1993), 127.

13. Ibid., 127.

14. Ibid., 153.

15. Ibid., 135.

16. Following the nomination, and the submission of the nominee to the Senate, the Senate Judiciary Committee holds hearings. The Committee hears testimony from the legal community, interest groups, and the nominee. Generally the nominees refuse to discuss their views on substantive legal issues to avoid at least the appearance of impartiality. In reality such refusal aids the nominee by not offending senators who might hold opposing viewpoints. Clarence Thomas, for example, refused to admit that he had ever discussed the merits of *Roe v. Wade* with anyone ever.

If the Judiciary Committee approves (or fails to disapprove or table the nomination) it goes to the full Senate for a vote. The nomination then gets debated and, unless successfully filibustered, voted on, with confirmation requiring a simple majority.

17. *Mallory v. United States* (1957) overturned the conviction and death sentence of an alleged rapist who confessed after a seven-hour interrogation. Mallory was subsequently convicted of another rape in 1960.

18. These results come from a regression conducted by the authors of the vote in the Senate on the ideology and qualifications of the nominee. Complete analyses will be provided by the authors upon request.

19. The public and the Senate usually have little information on the quality of the nominees. A highly important information source for both is the American Bar Association (ABA). After nomination the ABA is an important player. The ABA influences the confirmation process through its evaluation of the qualifications of Supreme Court nominees. The involvement of the Bar Association has been highly controversial. President Nixon, for example, initially gave the ABA the right to pre-screen nominees. When the ABA used this pre-screening power to vote against two of his potential nominees, Nixon's attorney general, John Mitchell, wrote a scathing letter to the American Bar Association stating that henceforth they would no longer be provided with the names of prospective nominees. Thus, when Nixon nominated Powell and Rehnquist he declined to forward their names to the ABA prior to their nominations. The ABA subsequently unanimously rated Powell highly qualified, while Rehnquist failed to receive such approval. The Senate voted to confirm both of them, but Powell's vote was 89 to 1 in favor, while the vote for Rehnquist was 68 to 26.

20. All data in this paragraph come from Segal and Spaeth, *The Supreme Court and the Attitudinal Models,* 151–52.

21. Not all 120 confirmed nominees served on the Court. Seven declined service. For instance, Robert Harrison declined Washington's appointment to become chancellor of Maryland. John Jay, who left the Court to become governor of New York, declined reappointment due to the Court's low prestige.

22. Abraham, *Justices and Presidents*, 13.

23. As part of his "Southern Strategy" (see above), Nixon first chose Circuit Court

of Appeals Judge Clement Haynsworth, a Democrat from South Carolina, to replace Fortas. Haynsworth appeared certain of confirmation until Judiciary Committee hearings began to focus on cases decided by Haynsworth in which he had a direct, albeit minor, financial interest. Ideological critics alleged that Haynsworth had compiled an anti-union, anti-civil rights record as an appellate judge. The Senate rejected Haynsworth by a vote of 55 to 45.

In angry reaction to Haynsworth's defeat, Nixon nominated G. Harrold Carswell, a little-known federal judge from Florida. So poorly qualified was he that Carswell's Senate floor leader, Roman Hruska (R-NB), declared, "Even if he were mediocre, there are a lot of mediocre judges, and people and lawyers. They are entitled to a little representation, aren't they, and a little chance" (Warren Weaver Jr., "Carswell Nomination Attacked and Defended as Senate Opens Debate on Nomination," *New York Times,* March 17, 1970, A21). But the most damaging blow to Carswell's candidacy occurred when a Florida television station found film of a 1948 speech in which he declared, "I yield to no man as a fellow candidate or as a fellow citizen in the firm vigorous belief in the principles of White Supremacy, and I shall always be so governed" (*New York Times,* "Excerpts from Carswell's Talk," January 22, 1970, A22). Carswell was defeated in a surprisingly close vote, 51 to 45. Nixon eventually replaced Fortas with Harry Blackmun of Minnesota, claiming that the Senate would not confirm a Southerner, an allegation belied by the Senate's near unanimous approval of Lewis Powell of Virginia just two years later.

24. *Gregg v. Georgia* (1976).

25. *Stone v. Powell* (1976) and *United States v. Leon* (1984).

26. *New York v. Quarles* (1984).

27. *Miller v. California* (1973).

28. *San Antonio v. Rodriguez* (1973).

29. *Bowers v. Hardwick* (1986).

30. *Grove City College v. Bell* (1984).

31. Jeffrey A. Segal, Robert M. Howard, and Christopher Hutz, "Presidential Success in Supreme Court Nominations: Testing a Constrained Presidency Model," paper presented at the 1996 Midwest Political Science Association Annual Meeting, Chicago, IL, April 1996.

32. *Swann v. Charlotte-Mecklenburg County Board of Education* (1971).

33. *Planned Parenthood of Southeastern Pennsylvania v. Casey* (1992).

34. *Roe v. Wade* (1973).

35. *Reed v. Reed* (1971).

36. *Swann v. Charlotte-Mecklenburg Board of Education* (1971).

37. *Regents v. Bakke* (1978).

38. We derive the data from Lee Epstein, Jeffrey A. Segal, Harold J. Spaeth, and Thomas G. Walker, *The Supreme Court Compendium,* 2nd ed. (Washington, DC: Congressional Quarterly Press, 1997).

39. Jeffrey A. Segal, Robert M. Howard, and Christopher Hutz, "Presidential Success in Supreme Court Nominations: Testing a Constrained Presidency Model," paper presented at the 1996 Midwest Political Science Association Annual Meeting, Chicago, IL, April 1996.

40. Robert Dahl, "Decision-Making in a Democracy: The Supreme Court as a National Policy-Maker," *Journal of Public Law* 6:179–82.

41. The data are again derived from Epstein et al., *The Supreme Court Compendium,* 1997.

42. Stephen S. Meinhold and Steven A. Shull, "Policy Congruence Between the President and the Solicitor General," *Political Research Quarterly* 51 (1998): 527–47.

43. Jeffrey A. Segal, "Courts, Executives and Legislatures," in John B. Gates and Charles A. Johnson, eds., *The American Courts: A Critical Assessment* (Washington, DC: Congressional Quarterly, 1991).

44. 28 U.S.C. section 2323 (1964).

45. Lincoln Caplan, *The Tenth Justice* (New York: Knopf, 1987).

46. Segal, "Courts, Executives and Legislatures," 377.

47. Doris M. Provine, *Case Selection in the United States Supreme Court* (Chicago: University of Chicago Press, 1980).

48. Jeffrey A. Segal, "Amicus Curiae Briefs by the Solicitor General During the Warren and Burger Courts," *Western Political Quarterly* 41 (1988):135–44.

49. Roger Handberg and Harold F. Hill, Jr., "Court Curbing, Court Reversals and Judicial Review: The Supreme Court Versus Congress," *Law and Society Review* 14 (1980):309–22.

50. 347 U.S. 483 (1954).

51. 438 U.S. 265 (1978).

52. Caplan, *The Tenth Justice,* 31.

53. Ibid., 44.

54. Scigliano, *The Supreme Court and the Presidency,* 179.

55. Steven Puro, "The United States as Amicus Curiae," in S. Sidney Ulmer, ed., *Courts, Law and Judicial Processes* (New York: The Free Press, 1981).

56. Karen O'Connor, "The Amicus Curiae Role of the U.S. Solicitor General in Supreme Court Litigation," *Judicature* 66 (1983):256–64.

57. Segal, "Amicus Curiae Briefs."

58. Scigliano, *The Supreme Court and the Presidency,* 32.

59. *Youngstown Sheet & Tube Co. v. Sawyer* (1952).

60. *Jones v. Clinton* (1997).

Part IV

Policy Areas and the Presidency

11

Domestic Policy:
The General-Interest Presidency?

Paul J. Quirk and Bruce Nesmith

In a good deal of commentary on American national institutions, the president wears a white hat and the members of Congress wear black hats. The president protects the law-abiding citizens, Congress tries to take their property, and the two sides shoot it out. More specifically, the president is the champion of broadly based or "general" interests—those shared by many or all citizens—and Congress is the agent of narrowly based or "special" interests—those of organized groups or specific geographic areas. And policy outcomes, therefore, reflect a struggle between the branches: the greater the president's influence, the better the prospects for general interests; the greater Congress's, the more generous the benefits for special interests.[1]

This image of presidential and congressional roles has obvious implications for institutional reform. The common presumption is that general interests are in most cases more worthy than the special interests that conflict with them, and that the tendency of democratic politics is to give special interests unwarranted deference. At least since the writings of Woodrow Wilson more than a century ago, therefore, reformers have proposed to improve policymaking by strengthening the presidency.[2] They have promoted a variety of measures to enhance presidential leadership—from centralization of budgeting, reorganization authority, and fast-track legislation to unlikely constitutional amendments that would link presidential and congressional elections. In one of the notable episodes of presidency-enhancing reform, the Republican Congress in 1996 set aside both partisan interests and constitutional objections in passing a law giving Democratic president Bill Clinton (short lived as it turned out) a line-item veto over federal spending.

This chapter revisits the premises of pro-presidency reformism, especially with respect to presidential and congressional responses to general interests. Our story, however, is not simple. It resembles the plot of an art-house movie—with surprising twists, an equivocal ending, and meanings that lie beneath the surface. First, we discuss the theoretical issues that underlie the general-interest presidency thesis and an alternative, congressional-parity thesis. In our view, the theoretical case for the general-interest presidency is fairly weak, depending heavily on debatable assumptions.

Second, we assess the competing perspectives empirically by examining the record of presidential and congressional responses in legislative conflicts over a thirty-six-year period in three areas of public policy: tax preferences, agricultural subsidies, and environmental regulation. Except in one area—environmental issues—this evidence belies any theoretical uncertainty and gives the general-interest presidency thesis powerful support. Third, however, we raise two kinds of complications: theoretical issues about interpreting this evidence, and some discrepant comparative observations. Taken together, these considerations suggest that despite the observed differences in institutional responses, presidency-enhancing reforms may have little beneficial effect after all. Finally, we find evidence for this last view in a brief account of the recent experience with the line-item veto. We end with a concise statement of our revised view of the general-interest presidency.

Theoretical Doubts

Political scientists have often treated the general-interest presidency thesis as a self-evident truth.[3] They take it for granted in recommendations for institutional reform and interpretations of institutional politics.[4] In fact, however, the theoretical grounds for this view are less than compelling.

There are several theoretical arguments to support the general-interest presidency thesis; but they are all subject to challenge. One argument, advanced by some scholars[5] and historically by presidents themselves,[6] is easily dismissed. It is that the president is the only elected official who represents the entire nation. Thus he alone serves the whole nation and is consistently responsive to general interests. This arrestingly simple argument encounters an obvious and fatal rejoinder. Congress, collectively, represents exactly the same territory as the president. So if the comparison is to Congress as a decision-making body, in the simple terms of this argument, the two institutions do not differ.

The credible arguments for the general-interest presidency thesis focus on structural differences between the branches. The arguments take several forms, however. The main structural difference is simply that the presidency is a single elected official whereas Congress comprises 535 independently elected members. In what we call the accountability version of the structural argument, Fiorina suggested that these basic features shape the individual elected officials' respective influence over policy outcomes, and thus their accountability and incentives for policymaking.[7]

Fiorina assumes that in evaluating office holders, voters focus on aspects of their performance that substantially affect the voter's interests. On the one hand, the president has vast influence over policy, and he can affect national conditions, like peace and prosperity, significantly. In evaluating his performance, the public has ample reason to consider his positions on national issues, and can hold him accountable for those conditions. The expectation of such evaluations gives the president electoral incentives to choose policies designed to benefit general interests.

In contrast, a single member of Congress (MC) normally has minimal leverage over policy and cannot affect national conditions. In evaluating their MCs, therefore, state and district electorates will ignore their positions on national issues and will not attempt to hold them accountable for national conditions. Rather, they will evaluate MCs on the basis of service to the state or district, where an effective member can produce noticeable results. In contrast with the president, Fiorina concludes, MCs will have little incentive to protect general interests. They will readily defer to organized groups and other narrowly based interests.

As Fiorina points out, a possible solution to this accountability problem is for the political parties to take collective responsibility for governmental performance. In that arrangement, the leaders of a party would direct the party's MCs to support policies that serve general interests; the party would claim credit for the results as a collective entity; and voters would supply the rewards by partisan voting. But such collective responsibility requires a degree of party discipline that does not exist in contemporary American politics.[8]

We can also distinguish another version of the structural argument, concerned with publicity, although it has not been clearly spelled out in the literature. For various reasons, the president receives vastly more attention in the news media than a typical MC—indeed, more than the entire Congress.[9] Presidential campaigns also get more attention than congressional campaigns. As a result, arguably, the president's policy positions are more exposed to public view than an MC's. Because policies oriented toward general interests are generally popular, the president should receive greater electoral rewards than an MC does for supporting such policies, and greater penalties for catering to narrow groups.

To a great extent, these two versions of the structural argument are compatible. The accountability and publicity effects could work together in accounting for a greater presidential response. But taken separately, they also suggest different expectations. The accountability effect predicts a lesser general-interest response by Congress regardless of the issue; individual MCs will lack control, and thus accountability, every time. In contrast, whether the publicity effect predicts such a response may vary with the issue's salience. Some issues may be sufficiently salient to create strong general-interest incentives even for MCs.

Finally, there is a secondary structural argument for presidential general-interest superiority based on the organization of Congress. According to the congressional fragmentation argument, Congress is organized to facilitate the distribution of benefits to members' geographic and interest-group constituencies.[10] In particular, the committee system serves that purpose.[11] In what amounts to an institutionalized log-roll, individual MCs are assigned to committees that affect their particular constituencies. The committees write bills that deliver benefits to those constituencies. Taking one bill at a time, most noncommittee MCs would prefer to reduce the special-interest benefits. But procedural restrictions and norms of reciprocity protect committee bills and keep the log-roll from unraveling. Congress enacts more special-interest policies than the members would approve in separate votes of the whole chamber. For the structure of Congress to have these effects, of course, does not require that it is intended to do so: the committee system could promote special-interest policies even if it is designed mainly to permit the development of expertise.[12]

None of these structural arguments, however, cinches the case for the president's general-interest superiority. There are rebuttals and countervailing considerations that tend to support congressional parity. First, that the president is held accountable for national conditions should not affect his incentives significantly on most issues of special-interest/general-interest conflict. The voters monitor broad conditions, especially the state of the economy.[13] Those conditions, however, are rarely at stake in such conflicts, at least in the short term. Cutting farm subsidies, for example, will not boost economic growth perceptibly within a single election cycle.

Second, as an empirical matter, voters evidently do pay attention to MCs' positions on national issues. They may make judgments either altruistically, with a view to serving the nation's interests, or noninstrumentally, expressing their values and opinions without regard for specific consequences. In any case, issues are often stressed in congressional campaigns.[14] Because claims of "standing up to special interests" and criticisms of "caving in" to them are often effective campaign themes, MCs have incentives to respond to general interests. It is even possible that these themes are more pertinent for congressional campaigns than for presidential campaigns, which may be dominated by larger issues such as macroeconomic management and national security. It is thus not certain that a typical MC has substantially weaker electoral incentives to respond to general interests on a typical issue than the president has.

Third, there are grounds for doubting that the fragmentation of Congress is an independent source of special-interest policymaking. In fact, the giant log-roll theory of the committee system does not imply such a role. It suggests that the committee system helps produce a package of special-interest benefits that the members would adopt in an omnibus bill, if that were possible—even though they would fail to do so in voting separately on each bill. The committee system increases special-interest benefits independently, above the MCs' collectively preferred level, only if the committees' demands somehow get out of hand.

Finally, in addition to these specific rebuttals, the congressional parity thesis gains support from a wild-card argument based on the fluidity of coalitions. Arnold notes that Congress usually can form majority coalitions in various ways.[15] With no change in members' dispositions, it may be able either to combine supporters of numerous interest groups to pass a "Christmas tree bill" or else to form a very different coalition and defeat the same groups in a sweeping reform. Which scenario occurs, and the success or failure of group demands, will depend on the agendas and procedures of legislative action.

By Arnold's account, congressional leaders make the critical choices on agendas and procedures according to their own preferences about the outcomes. The outcomes, in that sense, are up for grabs. And we cannot predict a systematic difference between Congress's responses and the president's.

Stronger Evidence

Although the theoretical case for the president's greater responsiveness to general interests is debatable, the evidence on actual presidential and congressional responses, as we will see next, is more clear. Surprisingly, scholars have made little effort to compare presidential and congressional tendencies in these conflicts systematically. The most relevant literature consists mostly of studies of policymaking in various areas of policy. The research in some areas (trade policy and water resources, for example) stresses presidential general-interest superiority,[16] but that in other areas does not,[17] and none of it strives for precision. Comparing the president and Congress has not been the main focus of this research.

To improve upon the existing evidence, therefore, we have undertaken a study that systematically compares presidential and congressional responses in some of these conflicts.[18] The research is labor intensive and, methodologically speaking, low-tech. Stated simply, we identify appropriate policy areas for the analysis; find and code all of the relevant specific bills; record the positions of the president, Congress, and congressional committees; and count everything up. In this section, we will merely summarize the methods and findings of that study.

For the thirty-six-year period from the beginning of the Kennedy administration through the end of President Clinton's first term, we look at legislation in three areas of public policy: tax preferences, agricultural commodity subsidies, and environmental regulation. In each area, there have been recurring, fairly well defined, and widely recognized conflicts between general or broadly based interests and special or narrowly based ones. Tax preferences (the vast array of credits, deductions, exemptions, and special rates) primarily benefit narrow groups; they are costly for most taxpayers, causing higher rates and reducing the efficiency of the economy.[19] Agricultural subsidies benefit farmers but are notoriously inefficient and costly to taxpayers and consumers.[20] Environmental regulations impose burdens on particular industries to serve broadly based interests in environmental quality.[21] In addition, some opposition to environmental regulation is due to general-interest considerations of conservative ideology, economic efficiency, and consumer costs. We take this complication into account in interpreting the findings.[22]

Taken together, the three areas offer several advantages. They represent a variety of subject matter and largely distinct sets of participants. Each area was active at several points during the period of our study, with both Democratic and Republican presidents. And they exhibit differing and only moderately strong partisan tendencies: Democrats have been more responsive than Republicans to the general interests at stake in environmental policy; but Republicans have been more responsive in agriculture policy; and none of the areas has been consistently partisan.[23]

For each area we sought to examine the entire set of relevant legislative proposals that were actively considered in Congress or prominently proposed by either branch. Altogether, we identified a total of sixty measures. We studied special-interest measures as well as general-interest ones. General-interest bills were those that reduced tax preferences, reduced agricultural subsidies, or expanded the scope of environmental regulation; special-interest bills were those that did the opposite in each area. We also studied measures that were blocked as well as those that became law. This inclusive approach enables us to avoid potential biases—for example, the president could favor general interests in debates on certain highly visible reforms, and yet he could also block other reforms and even collaborate in passing less visible special-interest bills. In that case, studying only the politics of successful reforms would yield a misleading, positive impression of the president's role. Our selection of bills provides a rounded picture of the two institutions' overall tendencies.

For each bill we developed a brief legislative history to answer a few simple questions: Which institution initiated it, the president or Congress? How did each branch then respond, supporting the bill or opposing it? What about each part of Congress that had occasion to act—the House and Senate, the relevant committees, and individual entrepreneurs? We extracted the necessary information from published academic and journalistic accounts.[24] And we analyzed the patterns in each policy area separately.

Although not completely uniform, the findings have a clear pattern: In two areas, tax preferences and agriculture subsidies, the president has been consistently, for our entire period, and by a wide margin, the principal champion of broadly based interests. To that extent, the general-interest presidency thesis is strongly supported. On environmental policy, however, the institutional responses have been more mixed. They tend to support congressional parity. As we will suggest, the congressional response appears to reflect the notable salience of environmental issues.

Tax Expenditures

The development of the tax structure has been a story of many small measures that provide tax breaks for narrow groups, and a few major reforms that sweep away many of these provisions. Without doubt, the president is the most consistent advocate of general-interest tax legislation. For the most part, tax reforms have been executive branch initiatives, and have encountered resistance in Congress. To be sure, even presidents have favorite constituency groups, and they sometimes have pushed special-interest measures to favor them. But presidents were the prime movers in tax reform, and supported every major tax reform proposal regardless of which institution initiated it.

Presidents opposed special-interest tax bills far more often than Congress. This opposition was usually stated in congressional hearings by the Treasury Department; in most cases it resulted in blocking the legislation. For example, the Reagan administration in 1982 publicly opposed two bills that provided new tax breaks for farmers. Treasury Department officials spoke at Energy and Agricultural Taxation Subcommittee hearings on two occasions, defending existing provisions and opposing further tax credits for farmers.[25] In a 1986 case, Representative Guy Vander Jagt (R-MI) rewrote his legislation on real estate investment trusts, removing tax advantages unacceptable to President Reagan.[26]

The position of Congress in contrast is highly variable, sometimes supporting reform but often promoting special-interest tax breaks. Some presidential tax reform initiatives were doomed by congressional resistance; the clearest cases of presidential initiation, in 1963 by Kennedy and in 1978 by Carter, were gutted by the revenue committees.[27] Both presidents coupled reform proposals with tax cuts to make them politically palatable, but by the time the bills were signed into law Congress had removed most of the reform. Moreover, more than 90 percent of special-interest measures had their origins in Congress. The revenue committees face steady pressure from interest groups. Tax economist Joseph Pechman observed that general interest–minded committee members "spend much of their time fighting off new tax advantages and are only moderately successful in eliminating old ones."[28]

On a few occasions, Congress played or at least shared the leadership role in promoting general interest–oriented reforms. But even in such cases, Congress was a fickle partner in the reform effort. The Tax Reform Act of 1969 began as a collaboration between President Richard Nixon's Treasury Department and the House Ways and Means Committee. Lobbying by state and local officials, business lobbies, and the oil and gas industries, however, induced the Senate Finance Committee to restore some tax breaks. And in December the full Senate added more of them, creating a "Christmas tree bill" that Nixon threatened to veto. In the end, the conference committee, after a concerted effort by Assistant Treasury Secretary Charls Walker, removed many revenue-losing provisions and produced a modest reform.[29]

Congress, then, sometimes took the lead on behalf of reform. Moderately successful tax reform efforts in 1976 and 1982 were largely congressionally generated. And the most sweeping reform ever—the Tax Reform Act of 1986—was initiated by individuals in both branches. But even in these cases, reform was a hard sell in Congress. Passing the historic 1986 act required extraordinary efforts by the revenue committee chairs, Representative Dan Rostenkowski (D-IL) and Senator Bob Packwood (R-OR), both of whom suffered critical defeats in committee and had to struggle to resuscitate reform.

Agricultural Commodity Supports

From the Agricultural Adjustment Act in the 1930s until the repeal of that law in 1996, the federal government guaranteed prices of certain agricultural commodities at a congressionally established percentage of "parity," based on prices in 1910–14 and adjusted for inflation. Policymaking during this period took place mainly in periodic, incrementally adjusted reauthorizations of commodity supports. We looked at those reauthorization bills whose initial provisions attempted either to reduce subsidies (general-interest bills) or to increase them (special-interest bills).

As with tax legislation, the president was the most consistent advocate of general interests in this area. Presidents and their administrations produced half of the proposals to scale back or reform the farm programs, and supported all such proposals. Presidential support was central in two important moves toward a more efficient, market-oriented approach in the early 1970s. The Agricultural Act of 1970 replaced voluntary production controls with "set asides," specified cutbacks in farmers' total acreage. The proposal came out of talks between the House Agriculture Committee and Nixon's agriculture secretary, Clifford Hardin. The 1973 reauthorization replaced price supports based on 1910–14 prices with discretionary targets, as Nixon had advocated since 1970.

Although presidents were frequent advocates of market-oriented agricultural legislation, Congress was usually very reluctant, and most presidential initiatives went nowhere. Carter's proposals for the 1977 reauthorization were described as "modest" but ran into opposition from farm advocates in Congress who worried about inducing commodity surpluses.[30] The president's efforts were undermined by Agriculture Secretary Bob Bergland, who testified before the Agriculture Committees that he had recommended higher supports only to be shot down by the president's economic advisers. The Senate Agriculture Committee ignored Carter's veto threats and raised support levels well beyond his proposed limit. When House Agriculture Committee Chair Thomas A. Foley (D-WA) warned that Republicans would capitalize on Carter's stinginess with farm subsidies, Carter relented, allowing a weak bill to become law. Even in successful reform initiatives, the executive branch had to moderate its goals and negotiate terms with the Agriculture Committees.

Congress was the main source of proposals to increase commodity subsidies. Moreover, it was nearly always friendly to such proposals. Both Agriculture Committees and the full Senate approved every such bill they had occasion to vote on; the House defeated only one, the Emergency Assistance Act of 1978. The Senate Agriculture Committee, especially generous toward farm groups, initiated the subsidy enhancements of the Emergency Assistance Act of 1978 and of the tobacco section of the Dairy and Tobacco Adjustment Act of 1983. It added farm benefits to House-passed bills in 1964 and 1975, defeated reform features of the 1970 bill, raised benefits in

1977 and 1981, and rejected Reagan's calls for reform in 1981 and 1985. The full Senate approved special-interest legislation in each case, and it increased target prices and loan rates with floor amendments in 1975 and 1978. The House was less often the driving force behind special-interest farm legislation than the Senate, but still tilted in that direction.

With such contrasting presidential and congressional tendencies, agriculture bills have led to tests of will between the branches. Presidents blocked special-interest proposals in two such cases. In 1975, President Gerald Ford vetoed a bill raising supports for grains, cotton, and dairy products, and his veto was upheld by the House.[31] In 1978, Carter's emphatic opposition to the first Emergency Assistance Act helped defeat it in the House. But the Reagan administration's strong opposition to dairy and tobacco support legislation in 1983 was to no avail. Partly to help Senator Jesse Helms (R-NC) with his reelection campaign, Reagan eventually swallowed his objections and signed the bill.

Environmental Regulation

Most laws establishing federal control over the various forms of environmental pollution were passed in the late 1960s and 1970s, with a few additions in the 1980s and 1990s. Air pollution was first, with motor vehicle emissions standards in 1965 and overall air quality standards in 1967. Laws on water pollution and pesticides were enacted in 1972; hazardous wastes and toxic substances in 1976; abandoned chemical dumps, 1980; and ozone and acid rain, 1990. Three major bills were defeated—one on oil spills (1980), an earlier attempt on acid rain (1986), and one on global warming (1990). There were also five proposals to grant organized groups, such as oil companies or electric utilities, major exceptions to environmental requirements—our special-interest bills in this policy area.

The institutional patterns in environmental policy were quite different from those in the tax and agriculture areas. Presidents were not consistently or even generally in the vanguard of environmentalism. Congress's response was at least comparable; indeed, the Senate usually took the pro-environmental lead. Finally, party differences overshadowed institutional ones, with Democrats more pro-environment than Republicans.

Although environmental interests usually had the upper hand, the interest-group and ideological opposition was politically significant for both branches. Presidents, accordingly, differed in their orientations. All the Democratic presidents (Johnson, Carter, and Clinton) staked out pro-environmental positions; but only two Republicans, Nixon and Bush, did so, while Ford and Reagan mostly opposed such positions. And Congress was internally divided. The Senate Environment and Public Works Committee, led by Senator Edmund Muskie (D-ME), was a hotbed of environmentalism. But the relevant House committees had strong ties to affected industries. In particular, the Commerce Committee, under the chairmanship of Detroit Democrat John Dingell, Jr., through much of this period, frequently opposed regulations affecting the auto industry. It also was more deferential than the Senate to the chemical industry on issues of toxic substances and hazardous wastes.

The president lagged behind Congress in initiating environmental measures. Congress originated eight of the eleven general-interest environmental bills, with most of them originating from the Senate committee. Only three such bills were born in the executive branch. (A fourth bill had mixed origins: in 1972, Congress initiated a clean water bill and Nixon replied by offering a stronger version of his own.)

Moreover, the president was less consistent than Congress in supporting the pro-environmental bills that reached the agenda. With Republican presidents often resisting, presidents supported only 55 percent of such bills. The House passed 89 percent of the bills reaching the floor, and the Senate 80 percent. The president also supported two of the four special-interest bills—fewer than the House (3 of 4), but more than the Senate (none).

Unlike in taxes or agriculture, special-interest bills—cutting back regulation for particular industries—were hard sells no matter where they originated. Rank-and-file MCs sometimes promoted such bills, seeking to favor local economic interests. An effort to deregulate wetlands, sponsored by Representative John Breaux (D-LA) and Senator Lloyd Bentsen (D-TX), reflected such entrepreneurship, and rank-and-file members were instrumental in relaxing auto emissions regulations in the 1970s and proposing to weaken the Clean Air Act in 1981–82. But such measures usually ran into bipartisan opposition in both Senate and House committees. The two chambers repeatedly defeated efforts by various industries to exempt pollution in areas where the air was relatively clean. Even prominent Republicans, such as Senator Pete Domenici (R-NM), objected that such a measure would accommodate polluters instead of making them conform to the law.[32] Committee leaders Representative Henry Waxman (D-CA) and Senator Robert Stafford (R-VT) were central in blocking anti-environmental proposals during the Reagan administration.

Unlike in taxes or agriculture, therefore, conflict between the branches was irregular and primarily partisan and ideological: it occurred when a Democratic Congress pushed to expand regulation and a Republican president resisted. In a few cases, presidents strayed from their parties' mainstream on environmental issues. Nixon tried to top the Democrats on water pollution. Reagan went farther than most Republicans in attacking environmental controls. For the most part, however, presidents took positions broadly consistent with those of their congressional parties.

We believe that these patterns of presidential and congressional response differ from those on tax preferences and agriculture subsidies because of two features of environmental politics. First, the diffuse interest in environmental quality has been highly salient to the public. From the late 1960s to the present, large majorities of the public have consistently supported environmental controls.[33] The intensity of this support has vastly exceeded that for reforming taxes or reducing agriculture subsidies. The case supports the view, mentioned above, that the incentives for members of Congress to serve general interests may match the president's on issues of high salience.

Second, on the other hand, the diffuse costs of environmental control usually have not been highly salient. Environmental regulations tend to raise consumer prices and reduce economic growth. Independent experts criticize certain environmental regulations as inflexible and unduly burdensome.[34] But the costs of environmental requirements, like those of tax preferences or agricultural subsidies, are relatively invisible to the public. Thus the environmental case also reinforces the finding that presidents outperform Congress in representing low-salience diffuse interests.

Dubious Implications

The findings in our three areas, though differing in some respects, appear to tell a coherent story. The president is in fact the main institutional champion of broadly based interests. Congress is considerably less reliable in this respect. It often accepts presidentially sponsored general-interest reforms, and sometimes even provides leadership, as in the joint initiation of the Tax Reform Act of 1986. But only the president provides fairly consistent general-interest leadership, especially on issues of modest salience.

On their face, such findings appear to bolster the case for institutional reforms that would strengthen the presidency in relation to Congress. If the president responds to broadly based interests more than Congress does, it seems reasonable to infer that a stronger presidency would benefit such interests, and do so significantly. Under fire from the bad guys, a helpful citizen should toss the good guy a loaded gun.

In yet another twist, however, this straightforward reasoning turns out to be problematic. To begin with, there are plausible interpretations of the observed responses that do not suggest large, fundamental differences in institutional tendencies. First, the behavior of each branch in these conflicts may reflect strategic adjustment to the anticipated behavior of the other branch.[35] Congress may promote special-interest benefits, for example, because it counts on the president to offer resistance and control the damage. According to Nivola, Congress and the president often do a dance over trade policy—with Congress initially demanding protectionist measures, the president resisting them, and Congress ultimately backing off and mostly endorsing free trade.[36] Both branches know where they will end up when the music stops. By the same token, the president may push general-interest reforms partly because he expects Congress to block them, giving him opportunity for harmless posturing. Such strategic behavior will obscure the policies that each branch is really seeking to effect.

Second, the two institutions' behavior in a series of interactions may give an exaggerated impression of their fundamental differences. As an illustration, consider two people who disagree about the comfortable temperature of a room. One person always turns the thermostat up. The other always turns it down. Yet the difference between their ideal temperatures may be only a few degrees. The finding that the president usually pushes the special-interest thermostat down and Congress usually pushes it up need not indicate a large difference between the outcomes each branch would produce if it somehow gained greater control.

Third, the observed differences in presidential and congressional responses may obscure the effects of institutional conflict itself. That either branch can obstruct the other's efforts and draw wider attention to an issue may induce both branches to prefer general interests more often than they would in a more placid environment. Institutional differences should expand the scope of conflict, bring broader constituencies into play, and work against special-interest policies. If so, increasing the president's power over Congress could shift both branches toward greater support for such policies.

These suggestions could be dismissed as idle quibbles. But some simple comparative observations reinforce the doubts. Advocates of strengthening the presidency should expect more general-interest policymaking when political circumstances give the president greater influence over Congress—in particular, when the president's party controls Congress. But there was no such pattern in our study. Lumping our three policy areas together, we find that unified and divided governments adopted special-interest measures at similar rates: unified governments passed 5 of 12 special-interest bills in fourteen years; divided governments passed 7 of 21 such bills in twenty-two years. Unified governments passed only 3 of 7 general-interest bills; divided governments 16 of 20. If anything, divided government was more responsive to general interests.

Another relevant comparison is international. No other large industrial democracy has a national legislature like Congress—with members elected separately from the executive, representing geographic constituencies, and subject to minimal party discipline.[37] If this structure powerfully promotes special-interest policies, the United States should lead the free world in catering to special interests.

Although systematic comparisons are lacking, American public policy does not appear to have that distinction. On the one hand, the American tax system certainly bestows an unusual abundance of special privileges by world standards.[38] On the other hand, however, the United States has been notable for denying special-interest claims in promoting free trade, deregulating competitive industries, and limiting subsidies for agriculture and other industries. And it has imposed heavy costs on narrow groups through rigorous health, safety, and environmental regulation.[39] Overall, there is no empirical case for an American special-interest exceptionalism.[40]

These considerations suggest an admittedly paradoxical conclusion. In their observable behavior in policy conflict, presidents do respond more consistently to general interests than Congress does, especially to those of low salience; and Congress more often serves special interests. But the differences, for various reasons, are misleading. Giving the president more power over Congress would do little, if anything, to enhance performance in this respect.

A Test Case: The Line-Item Veto

Recent history offers a modest test of this no-effect thesis. As part of the Republicans' Contract with America, Congress in 1996 approved legislation granting the president a line-item veto—the power to strike out specific items in spending bills without vetoing the entire bills.[41] Advocates of this expansion of presidential power have stressed the purpose of making budgeting more responsive to general interests. If the president can veto items in appropriations bills, they suggest, he will block wasteful expenditures intended to benefit special interests, resulting in smaller and more rationally designed budgets.[42] In contrast, for the reasons just outlined, we would expect something closer to business-as-usual.

Even before the federal measure, we should note, experience with gubernatorial line-item vetoes in the states suggested the same expectation. Most studies have found no impact of the line-item veto on overall state spending.[43] Governors evidently use the power to promote their partisan and policy interests rather than to rationalize spending.[44] And legislators anticipate the governor's vetoes by padding their spending proposals or hiding favorite projects within provisions that the governor will want to sign.[45]

In fact, governors use the line-item veto authority only infrequently. Advocates claim annual savings of 1–2.8 percent in states with the strongest measures; but in most states that have the veto, it is used sparingly or not at all.[46] Governors evidently do not want to fight numerous small battles with legislators whose support they need on other matters. "In the states," concludes one analyst, "[the line-item veto] has made little difference in most cases."[47]

At the federal level, President Clinton exercised the line-item veto authority during the 1997 budget cycle. The results were much like the state experience. Under pressure to make some use of the new power, Clinton blocked three items in a budget reconciliation bill in August 1997, and several more in a series of appropriations bills passed by Congress that fall. But the total savings amounted only to $2 billion, one-eighth of 1 percent of the federal budget. Even so, members of Congress whose items were vetoed expressed outrage. They threatened to vote down Clinton's request for fast-track trade authority, to stall confirmation of his appointees, and to overturn his veto of thirty-eight military construction projects.[48] By late fall, Clinton was exercising even more restraint in his use of the authority.

Then, in February 1998 a Federal District Court ruled the line-item veto unconstitutional. The president expressed optimism that the decision would be reversed on an expedited appeal to the Supreme Court. In June 1998, the Court overturned the line-item veto by a 6–3 margin. Reestablishing the line-item veto would require a constitutional amendment.

In the unlikely event that the presidential line-item veto is somehow restored, we would expect that Congress would learn to anticipate some vetoes. Thus it would insert a larger amount of dubious spending with the expectation of losing some of it. The president would adjust to Congress's adjustment. If the congressional padding is extensive, he or she would use the veto more often. Eventually the padding and vetoing would reach an equilibrium, and the associated friction would subside. The use of the line-item veto would reinforce the president's image as the champion of general interests. But despite the loss of this presidential power, the overall results will be much the same as before the veto. And just as before, neither branch will be very far from its preferred outcome.

Conclusion

In the end, our view of presidential and congressional differences in the representation of general interests is subtle but entirely coherent. Fundamentally, the president has stronger incentives than Congress to serve broadly based interests; but the difference, contrary to some accounts, is fairly modest. It exists only with respect to general interests of relatively low salience to the public. And even then, it does not produce vast differences in dispositions toward long-term outcomes.

The actual responses of the two branches give a somewhat different impression. In the low-salience areas, the president far more often takes the side of broad interests while Congress far more often favors narrow ones. But this often striking contrast arises in large part from mutual anticipation and strategic interaction: Congress turns the special-interest thermostat up, the president turns it down, but neither wants to move it far.

Thus, when the president has greater influence over Congress, he does not impose more rigorous barriers to special-interest policies. Political systems that do not even have an institution like Congress do not perform noticeably better in this respect. And institutional reforms that increase the president's power over Congress do not yield substantial gains for the representation of general interests.

Notes

1. James M. Burns, *Presidential Government* (Boston: Houghton Mifflin, 1965); Morris Fiorina, "The Decline of Collective Responsibility in American Politics," *Daedalus* 109:3 (1980), 25–45; Morris Fiorina, "The Presidency and the Contemporary Electoral System," in Michael Nelson, ed., *The Presidency and the Political System* (Washington, DC: Congressional Quarterly, 1984), 204–26; Charles M. Hardin, *Presidential Power and Accountability: Toward a New Constitution* (Chicago: University of Chicago Press, 1974).

2. See, for example, James L. Sundquist, *Constitutional Reform* (Washington, DC: Brookings Institution, 1988); Hardin, *Presidential Power and Accountability*; and Michael L. Mezey, *Congress, the President, and Public Policy* (Boulder, CO: Westview Press, 1989).

3. Gregg, *The Presidential Republic.*

4. Hardin, *Presidential Power and Accountability*; Terry M. Moe, "The Politics of Structural Choice: Toward a Theory of Public Bureaucracy," in Oliver E. Williamson, ed., *Organization Theory: From Chester Barnard to the Present and Beyond* (New York: Oxford University Press, 1990); Terry M. Moe, "The Presidency and the Bureaucracy: The Presidential Advantage," in Michael Nelson, ed., *The Presidency and the Political System,* 4th ed. (Washington, DC: Congressional Quarterly, 1994), 408–39.

5. Richard E. Neustadt, *Presidential Power* (New York: John Wiley and Sons, 1960).

6. Gregg, *The Presidential Republic*; Jeffrey K. Tulis, *The Rhetorical Presidency* (Princeton: Princeton University Press, 1987).

7. Fiorina, "The Decline of Collective Responsibility."

8. See also Fiorina, "The Presidency and the Contemporary Electoral System."

9. Stephen Hess, *The Washington Reporters* (Washington, DC: Brookings Institution, 1981); Richard Davis, *The Press and American Politics: The New Mediator,* 2nd ed. (Upper Saddle River, NJ: Prentice-Hall, 1996).

10. David Mayhew, *Congress: The Electoral Connection* (New Haven: Yale University Press, 1974).

11. Kenneth A. Shepsle and Barry R. Weingast, "The Institutional Foundations of Committee Power," *American Political Science Review* 81:1 (1987): 85–104; Barry R. Weingast and William Marshall, "The Industrial Organization of Congress," *Journal of*

Political Economy 91 (1988): 765–800. For a critique of this literature, see Keith Krehbiel, *Information and Legislative Organization* (Ann Arbor: University of Michigan Press, 1991).

12. See Krehbiel, *Information and Legislative Organization.*

13. Douglas A. Hibbs, Jr., *The American Political Economy: Macroeconomics and Electoral Politics in the United States* (Cambridge: Harvard University Press, 1987); Richard A. Brody, *Assessing the President: The Media, Elite Opinion, and Public Support* (Stanford: Stanford University Press, 1991); Paul Brace and Barbara Hinckley, *Follow the Leader: Opinion Polls and the Modern Presidents* (New York: Basic Books, 1992).

14. Thomas Mann, *Unsafe at any Margin: Interpreting Congressional Elections* (Washington, DC: American Enterprise Institute, 1978); Gary C. Jacobson, *The Politics of Congressional Elections*, 4th ed. (New York: Longman, 1997), ch. 5.

15. Arnold, *The Logic of Congressional Action* (New Haven: Yale University Press, 1990).

16. See Sharyn O'Halloran, *Politics, Process, and American Trade Policy* (Ann Arbor: University of Michigan Press, 1994); Pietro Nivola, in *Regulating Unfair Trade* (Washington, DC: Brookings Institution, 1993), makes many of the same points although he cautions that presidents are not always steadfastly advocates of free trade (113). For taxation, see John F. Witte, *The Politics and Development of the Federal Income Tax* (Madison: University of Wisconsin, 1985). For agriculture, see Willard W. Cochrane and Mary E. Ryan, *American Farm Policy, 1948–1973* (Minneapolis: University of Minnesota Press, 1976); Don Paarlberg, *Farm and Food Policy: Issues of the 1980s* (Lincoln: University of Nebraska Press, 1980); and Steven A. Shull, *Domestic Policy Formation* (Westport, CT: Greenwood Press, 1983).

17. See Mark V. Nadel, *The Politics of Consumer Protection* (New York: Macmillan, 1971); Walter A. Rosenbaum, *Environmental Politics and Policy,* 2nd ed. (Washington: Congressional Quarterly, 1991); Martha Derthick and Paul J. Quirk, *The Politics of Deregulation* (Washington: Brookings Institution, 1985); Jeffrey H. Birnbaum and Alan S. Murray, *Showdown at Gucci Gulch: Lawmakers, Lobbyists, and the Unlikely Triumph of Tax Reform* (New York: Random House, 1987).

18. Paul J. Quirk and Bruce Nesmith, "Who Serves the Public? The President, Congress, and General Interests," manuscripts (1997).

19. Witte, *The Politics and Development of the Federal Income Tax;* Susan B. Hansen, *The Politics of Taxation: Revenue Without Representation* (New York: Prager, 1983).

20. Don Paarlberg, *Farm and Food Policy: Issues of the 1980s* (Lincoln: University of Nebraska Press, 1980); Graham K. Wilson, *Special Interests and Policymaking: Agricultural Policies and Politics in Britain and the United States, 1956–1970* (London: John Wiley, 1977)

21. Michael E. Kraft and Norman J. Vig, "Environmental Policy from the Seventies to the Nineties: Continuity and Change," in Norman J. Vig and Michael E. Kraft, eds., *Environmental Policy in the 1990s: Toward a New Agenda* (Washington, DC: CQ Press, 1990), 3–31; Walter A. Rosenbaum, *The Politics of Environmental Concern* (New York: Praeger, 1973).

22. To simplify our conflicts somewhat, we selected environmental bills that defined the scope of regulation—whether various forms of pollution would be subject to federal control at all. General-interest opposition to environmental policy is mainly about the severity of the standards. In any case, active constituency opposition to environmental control has come mainly from the affected industries.

23. Environmental policy has been more partisan on issues of the nature and costs of regulation, which we generally exclude, than on its scope. We eliminated two potentially relevant areas as possible focuses of the research: trade policy, because the president's

role is affected by his special responsibility for foreign relations; and price and entry regulation, because one of us (Quirk) has written about that area and it had played a role in shaping the questions for this project.

24. Adequate information was generally available—if nowhere else, at least in *Congressional Quarterly Almanac*—with one important exception: many minor special-interest tax proposals are either dropped or merged into larger bills, without publicity, and disappear from the readily available sources without a trace. We include only those tax proposals that we were able to document. We believe that the minor tax proposals that we include are likely to be reasonably representative of those we missed. Where we do not cite other sources, we have relied on the accounts in *Congressional Quarterly Almanac*.

25. *Tax Notes,* May 31, 1982.

26. Ibid., June 16, 1986, 1063, 1185.

27. See Witte, *The Politics and Development of the Federal Income Tax,* 155–60, 159–63, 204–11; James M. Verdier, "The President, Congress, and Tax Reform: Patterns over Three Decades," *Annals of AAPSS* 499 (September 1988), 114–23.

28. Joseph Pechman, *Federal Tax Policy* (Washington, DC: Brookings Institution), 55.

29. Witte, *The Politics and Development of the Federal Income Tax,* 169–71.

30. Paarlberg, *Farm and Food Policy,* 49–50.

31. Hansen, *The Politics of Taxation,* 177.

32. *Congressional Quarterly Almanac,* 1978, 635–45.

33. Benjamin I. Page and Robert Y. Shapiro, *The Rational Public: Fifty Years of Trends in Americans' Policy Preferences* (Chicago: University of Chicago Press, 1992).

34. See, for example, Allen V. Kneese and Charles L. Schultze, *Pollution, Prices and Public Policy* (Washington, DC: Brookings Institution, 1975); Lester B. Lave and Gilbert S. Omenn, *Clearing the Air: Reforming the Clean Air Act* (Washington: Brookings Institution, 1981); Lester B. Lave, "Clean Air Sense" *Brookings Review* 15: 3 (Summer 1977): 41–47; Robert W. Crandall, *Controlling Industrial Pollution: The Economics and Politics of Dirty Air* (Washington, DC: Brookings Institution, 1983).

35. There is debate concerning whether presidential policy proposals are strategic, as our suggestion implies, or strictly sincere. For opposing views see Patrick J. Fett, "Presidential Legislative Priorities and Legislators' Voting Decisions," *Journal of Politics* 56 (1994): 502–12; and Mark A. Peterson, *Legislating Together: The White House and Capitol Hill from Eisenhower to Reagan* (Cambridge: Harvard University Press, 1990). We think there are strong reasons for expecting some strategic positioning on issues with special-interest/general-interest conflict.

36. Pietro Nivola, *Regulating Unfair Trade* (Washington, DC: Brookings Institution, 1993).

37. Arend Lijpart, *Democracies: Patterns of Majoritarian and Consensus Government in Twenty-One Countries* (New Haven: Yale University Press, 1984).

38. Sven Steinmo, *Taxation and Democracy: Swedish, British, and American Approaches to Financing the Modern State* (New Haven: Yale University Press, 1993).

39. Graham K. Wilson, *Business and Politics: A Comparative Introduction,* 2nd ed. (Chatham, NJ: Chatham House, 1990). The American differences from other countries are partly ideological. Because the United States has a stronger commitment than most other countries to free-market liberalism, it makes special-interest exceptions to taxes more easily, but grants protection from competition less easily. This ideological difference does not explain, however, why the United States has strict environmental and consumer protection, roughly comparable to Great Britain's. David Vogel, *National Styles of Regulation: Environmental Policy in Great Britain and the United States* (Ithaca, NY: Cornell University Press, 1986); David Vogel, "Representing Diffuse Inter-

ests in Environmental Policymaking," in R. Kent Weaver and Bert A. Rockman, eds., *Do Institutions Matter? Government Capabilities in the United States and Abroad* (Washington, DC: Brookings Institution, 1993), 237–71.

40. R. Kent Weaver and Bert A. Rockman, "Institutional Reform and Constitutional Design," in Weaver and Rockman, eds., *Do Institutions Matter?* 462–81.

41. Technically, the law did not create a line-item veto power. It enhanced presidential rescission authority (the authority to decline to spend appropriated funds) by making rescissions automatic unless Congress enacts a bill to block them. Since the president could veto the override bill, it would require a two-thirds vote of both houses of Congress to force the president to spend the disputed funds.

42. Russell M. Ross and Fred Schwengel, "An Item Veto for the President?" *Presidential Studies Quarterly* 12:1 (Winter 1982): 66–79.

43. Barton A. Abrams and William R. Dougan, "The Effects of Constitutional Restraints on Government Spending," *Public Choice* 49 (1986): 101–16; David C. Nice, "The Item Veto and Expenditure Restraint," *Journal of Politics* 50 (1988): 487–99.

44. James J. Gosling, "Wisconsin Item-Veto Lessons," *Public Administration Review* 46:4 (July 1986): 292–300; Glenn Abney and Thomas P. Lauth, "The Line-Item Veto in the States: An Instrument for Fiscal Restraint or an Instrument for Partisanship?" *Public Administration Review* 45:3 (May 1985): 372–77.

45. David Hosansky, "Can States Give Washington a Lesson in Veto Politics?" *Congressional Quarterly Weekly Report* 55:32 (August 9, 1997), 1922–23; Alan Rosenthal, *Governors and Legislators: Contending Powers* (Washington, DC: Congressional Quarterly, 1990), 160. Thad L. Beyle and Robert Hueffner, "Quips and Quotes from Old Governors to New," *Public Administration Review* 43:3 (May/June 1983): 268–70, quote an unidentified governor at the 1982 meeting of the National Governors' Association: "Avoid threatening to veto a bill. You just relieve the legislature of responsibility for sound legislation" (268–69).

46. Abney and Lauth, "The Line-Item Veto in the States."

47. Andrew Taylor, "State Vetoes Are a Mixed Blessing," *Congressional Quarterly Weekly Report* 52:50 (December 31, 1994), 3600, quoting Neil Berch. See also Berch, "The Item Veto in the States: An Analysis of the Effects over Time," *Social Science Journal* 29:3 (July 1992): 335–46. Berch did find some impact for line-item veto powers, when they include the ability to reduce the amounts in budget lines, on the rate of change in per capita highway capital spending. Per capita highway capital spending could be seen as an important type of special-interest spending in American states.

48. Andrew Taylor, "Line-Item Boosters Reconsider as Clinton Vetoes Hit Home," *Congressional Quarterly Weekly Report* 55:40 (October 11, 1997), 2459–66.

12

Budget Policy Transformations

Lance T. LeLoup

Presidential budgeting has been transformed during the twentieth century. From the adoption of the Budget and Accounting Act of 1921 under President Harding to the balanced budget agreement reached between President Clinton and the Republican Congress in 1997, both the federal budget and the way it is used by the American presidency have changed profoundly. At the end of the century, presidential budgeting changed public policy by shifts in the composition of federal revenues and outlays, and the expansion of the budget as a policy instrument. The institutions and processes of presidential budgeting have changed in terms of the power and capability of Congress, modes of interaction between executive and legislative institutions, and the shift to a more public, politicized process subject to the influence of external audiences and stakeholders. Presidents face more constraints than ever in budgeting. Yet despite all these changes, budgeting has become more important, not less important, to presidents. Budgeting has always provided both dangers and opportunities to presidents. In the last generation, however, the presidential stakes in budgeting have skyrocketed.

In the second half of the twentieth century, presidential budgeting has been transformed in the following ways:

- As a result of greater congressional capability in budgeting, the president's budget has evolved from a definitive policy statement to an opening bid in ongoing negotiations with Congress.
- Presidential budgeting has shifted from a more closed process domi-

nated by insiders to a more politicized and tactical process, based on building public images and support.

- The president's budget office has evolved from a source of "neutral competence" in budgeting to a political arm of the White House oriented to honing the administration's budget strategies and tactics.
- Presidential budgeting has moved from a process distinct from other policymaking processes to become the central governing process for the nation, encompassing a vast range of issues.
- Where the president's budget once stabilized the economy, the economy now destabilizes the budget, leading to highly uncertain budget forecasts, and vulnerability of programs to economic changes.
- With the increased prevalence of divided government and the growing influence of Congress, accountability in presidential budgeting has grown increasingly diffuse.
- As entitlements, mandatory spending, and deficit reduction came to dominate federal budgeting and reduce presidential discretion, presidents increasingly focused on multiyear, macrobudgetary goals as opposed to annual adjustments in agency budgets and gimmicky budget reforms.

The transition from microbudgeting to macrobudgeting has been the central feature of the transformation of presidential budgeting, even though for fifty years, only the president's budget looked at taxing and spending as a whole. *Macrobudgeting*—high-level decisions on broad spending, revenue, deficit or surplus totals, and budget shares, often made from the top down—has become increasingly prevalent for presidents. *Microbudgeting*—decisions on agencies, programs, and line-items, usually made from the bottom up—remains an important but less urgent aspect of presidential budgeting. Table 12.1 compares macrobudgeting and microbudgeting in the presidency. While both levels of budgeting involve the president, key actors, the policy focus, the nature of the budget process, and relevant reforms all are quite different.

The Evolution and Development of Presidential Budgeting, 1921–1970

The Budget and Accounting Act of 1921 created a real national budget for the first time. Prior to this time, agencies submitted requests directly to Congress and funding was recommended by various committees and approved by the House and Senate. By the beginning of the twentieth century, the United States had outgrown that fragmented system; the lack of some form of centralized control led to confusion and inefficiency. One of the reforms of the Progressive era was the movement to create a national budget. These efforts came to fruition in 1921. The Budget and Accounting

Table 12.1

Characteristics of Microbudgeting and Macrobudgeting in the Presidency

	Microbudgeting	Macrobudgeting
Key actors	Agencies, MB budget examiners	President, White House staff, OMB director
Policy focus	Agency budgets, programs, annual marginal changes	Deficit or multiyear trends, surplus, budget shares, percent of GDP, economic assumptions
Budget process	Fragmented, bottom up	More centralized, top down
Reforms	Program budgeting, PPBS, MBO, ZBB	Implementing top-down budgeting, CBMS

Act created a national budget *to be formulated and submitted to Congress by the president.*[1] It also created the Bureau of the Budget (BOB), housed in the Treasury Department, to help the president assemble the requests from agencies. The Budget and Accounting Act was reform oriented to saving money by increasing control of expenditures and making an executive accountable for that control. Congress intended to reform its budgetary procedures as well after 1921, but the fragmented spending process was too entrenched. Congress did succeed in clarifying authorizations from appropriations, and prohibiting standing committees from directly approving spending, but did little to make the budget process more centralized.[2]

In the 1930s, the administration of Franklin D. Roosevelt substantially increased the size and scope of government. Not only were new agencies and programs created, some to directly employ people, but the first entitlements were created by the Social Security Act of 1935. As the government became more complex, the institutionalized presidency began to grow as well. In 1939, BOB was moved from the Treasury to the newly created Executive Office of the President (EOP), where it became even more closely tied to the presidency and management of the executive branch. During World War II, the budget process became part of the most centralized allocation and management of national resources in the nation's history. The Employment Act of 1946, a posthumous embodiment of the theories of John Maynard Keynes and the policies of Roosevelt, tied the federal budget to fiscal policy. It required the president to create a balance of taxes and spending that would promote full employment as much as practicable.

After the war, Congress made serious attempts to catch up to the executive branch by centralizing its budget process and allowing members to vote on the budget as a whole. Republicans took control of Congress and, after a prolonged period of deficits, were determined to reassert their power of the purse while balancing the budget. The Legislative Reorganization Act of 1946 enacted a congressional budget.[3] After three years of failed attempts, however, Congress abandoned the idea. It simply proved too difficult to match the budget totals to the actions of the appropriations committees. In 1950, in what would be the last attempt at a congressional budget in a quarter century, an attempt was made to simply lump all the spending bills together in an omnibus appropriations bill. Because so many supplemental appropriations were needed afterward, the practice was abandoned.

The president's annual budget became a definitive policy statement for government. Any mistakes could generally be left to the professionals in the executive branch without damaging the president. Over its first forty years, the BOB had developed a reputation for integrity, and a significant degree of "neutral competence."[4] Although the spending committees may have resented the influence of BOB, Congress largely accepted the information it provided and used the president's requests as the basis for authorization and appropriation. That is not to say that there were not bitter fights, partisan disputes, or that Congress was not influential in making decisions on agencies and programs.[5] Congressional action was crucial to agency and program funding, and it was often an equal partner with the president in policy development and expanding government commitments. Congress scrutinized the president's budget carefully, including taxes and deficits or surpluses, but had no way to comprehensively restructure the president's budget.

The budget process in the executive and legislative branches was marked by routines and stability, characteristics that dominated descriptions and theories of budgeting by Aaron Wildavsky and others of that era.[6] It was a bottom-up process that focused on microlevel decisions on programs and agencies. Presidents had influence by instructing the BOB about what direction various spending categories should be going in. More than half of the budget went to defense, and the rest generally went to agencies that spent the money to conduct their operations. Social Security was funded through payroll taxes paid into a trust fund, and the current financing basis of the program was sound.

The nature of presidential budgeting was reflected in the kind of budget reforms that were proposed. Planning Program Budgeting Systems (PPBS) was implemented in the Defense Department in 1961 and applied to the entire executive branch by President Lyndon Johnson in 1965. It was a reform designed to make budget choices more rational, clarify objectives, compare alternative means, and increase the use of analysis. Management by Objective

(MBO) was favored by President Nixon after PPBS was abandoned in 1971 and it was largely a less structured attempt to do the same thing. Zero-based budgeting (ZBB), implemented by President Carter in the 1970s, was also part of this "rational" budget reform tradition. All of these reforms focused on agencies or smaller organizational units and programs, tried to separate means from ends, and to use the budget process for better policymaking. While these reforms may have called attention to presidential management and efficiency concerns, none of them had much impact on budget totals or trends.

By 1970, the era of economic and budgetary stability was coming to an end, making these reforms increasingly irrelevant. In the early 1960s, the Kennedy–Johnson tax cut helped stimulate demand and boost the economy. The budget seemed to be an effective tool for fine-tuning the economy, but the costs of fighting both the War on Poverty and the war in Vietnam proved too great. Budget deficits worsened, and 1969 would be the last year the budget was balanced for nearly three decades. The economic growth that had allowed the president to develop new programs and for existing programs to expand no longer seemed assured. In the next decade, the transformation of presidential budgeting, as it had developed since 1921, would begin in earnest.

Fifty years after the passage of the Budget and Accounting Act, presidents had become more powerful and presidential budgeting a more important governing process. But it remained only one of many sets of policy processes for the president to work through. Allen Schick even argued in 1970 that budgeting was becoming less useful to presidents:

> [T]he budget process tends to operate as a constraint on presidential power rather than as an opportunity for the development and assertion of presidential policies and priorities. Accordingly, contemporary presidents may find it to their advantage to spend comparatively little time on budget matters and to insulate themselves from the process.[7]

The constraints would grow even greater in the ensuing decades, but rather than insulate themselves from the process, presidents would find budgeting increasingly more compelling and critical to their success in office.

Congressional Budget Reform and Entitlement Growth in the 1970s

Nixon and Congress

Although fragmented and decentralized, the old authorization–appropriations process generally succeeded in maintaining fiscal discipline. That capability began to erode in the late 1960s and early 1970s, precipitating growing antagonism between the president and Congress over budgeting. Interbranch friction was exacerbated by President Richard Nixon, who attacked Congress as profligate and incapable of keeping the budget in balance. Between 1967 and 1970, Congress tried to limit spending by setting caps through a continuing resolution, a tax bill, and supplemental appropriations.[8] Spending exceeded the caps in all cases. The growing confrontation between the president and Congress over impoundment and budgetary power would eventually result in the passage of the Budget and Impoundment Control Act of 1974.

President Nixon also wanted to make changes in the BOB, changes that would eventually lead it away from the tradition of neutral competence toward becoming a more politicized, partisan arm of the presidency. His initial thrust, however, was simply to weaken the budget office and transfer power to the White House staff. Nixon distrusted the BOB and found it too powerful, suspecting it was populated with disloyal Democrat bureaucrats who were undermining the presidency. His reform of the BOB into the Office of Management and Budget (OMB) was ostensibly intended to increase the emphasis on management in the budget office, as reflected in the name. It was also an attempt to reduce the influence of the budget office on policy. Nixon failed to weaken the influence of OMB, but he made the agency more political. For example, Congress passed legislation requiring confirmation of the OMB director and deputy director, without trying to remove the sitting OMB director. The episode reflected the deteriorating relationship between branches and the politicization of the budget office.[9]

Nixon continued to assert the authority to impose economies on the federal government with or without the permission of Congress. The practice of impoundment had been derived from the Anti-Deficiency Act of the early twentieth century and had developed so that the president would not have to spend funds that were no longer necessary. Presidents including Truman, Eisenhower, and Johnson had all impounded funds without much problem. But Nixon clearly went beyond what Congress viewed as acceptable, using impoundment to impose his policy preferences over those of Congress. By 1973, he had impounded an estimated $18 billion, far more than any other president.

Bipartisan majorities in Congress moved to reform their budget processes and stand up to the president. In July of 1974, just weeks before Nixon would resign from the presidency, Congress passed the Budget and Impound Control Act, often called the Congressional Budget Act (CBA). The CBA made a number of important changes in the congressional budget process and presidential budgeting as well. The direct consequences for presidential budgeting seemed obvious at the time, but the degree to which a more powerful, capable Congress would challenge and revise the macrobudgetary priorities of the president would not be fully recognized for years. Nixon's main legacy in budgeting was to spur Congress to adopt meaningful budget reform for the first time during the century, reorganize and politicize OMB, and remove impoundment from the presidency. The new restrictions on impoundment eliminated a presidential prerogative that had been used prudently since early in the century.

The Growth of Entitlements

The Nixon era and the decade of the 1970s left another important legacy that would alter the future of budgeting as well. Entitlement spending mushroomed from $65 billion in 1970 to $267 billion in 1980, an increase of over 400 percent.[10] As a share of the budget, entitlements increased from 33 percent to 47 percent during the decade. Part of the growth was due to inflation, but much of the increase was due to the liberalization of benefits and expansion of programs. Large increases in Social Security were approved, food stamps increased 1,000 percent during the 1970s, Supplemental Security Income (SSI) was consolidated and benefits expanded for persons not eligible for Social Security, and Social Security benefits were "indexed" to inflation. As double-digit inflation became a reality in the second half of the decade, indexing drove entitlements up at record rates as well.

Presidents Ford and Carter were the first two presidents to face Congress under the new Congressional Budget Act. The difficulties that Ford confronted after succeeding Nixon and pardoning him carried over to the budgetary arena as well. Nonetheless, he was given good marks for his mastery of the budget. A reporter described his effectiveness at a press conference: "Ford conducted the performance like a virtuoso, with impressive familiarity with the intricacies of the budget, rattling off figures and elaborating with detailed analysis. Physical grace may have been missing on the Vail ski slopes, but not here. . . ."[11] The problem was that such familiarity with the details was becoming less important for presidential success in budgeting. The Democratic Congress took pleasure in passing the first congressional budget and adding substantially to Ford's proposals.

Jimmy Carter started out in a stronger political position than Ford, but suffered many of the same problems. Congressional Democrats, anxious to accommodate the new president, passed a revised budget resolution in 1977 to encompass his new proposals. Carter angered congressional leaders, however, when he withdrew without notice his proposal for a $50 tax rebate. The miffed chair of the House Budget Committee chastised the president that he was no longer dealing with the Georgia legislature. As many first-year presidents do,

Carter immersed himself in the preparation of his first budget, reviewing dozens of detailed briefing books, and personally holding meetings with agency officials. Activity at that level proved unproductive, and one observer noted that as his term progressed Carter was "getting over his penchant for trying to decide every aspect of every program."[12] Carter's first budget director, Bert Lance, became a major embarrassment to the president and was forced to resign, leaving OMB with continuing problems.

Both Ford and Carter were frustrated with budgeting. Fiscal policy seemed increasingly paralyzed by increasingly inflexible mandatory spending and stubborn economic problems. CBO challenged OMB as an objective source of budget information. Political activities by OMB officials increased during the Ford–Carter years in terms of the monitoring of Congress, more frequent contact with interest groups, and in the degree that political concerns were included in budget analysis.[13] Deficit and budget projections were less accurate, and inflation drove up outlays rapidly without any action by the president. In 1979, Carter's appointment of Paul Volcker as chairman of the Federal Reserve marked not only a switch to tighter monetary policy, but a decline in the importance of discretionary fiscal policy as reflected in the national budget. Budgeting was changing, but presidents still approached it as their predecessors had for decades.

Emphasis on Macrobudgeting: Reagan and the Deficits in the 1980s

The elections of 1980 laid the groundwork for a watershed year in the history of presidential budgeting. The surprisingly large margin of victory for Ronald Reagan, the Republican capture of the U.S. Senate for the first time in twenty-four years, and the reduction of the size of the Democratic majority in the House would create an environment favorable to the president. Reagan's 1981 economic and budget plan would have a lasting legacy. It represented an unprecedented exercise in top-down budgeting in the executive branch. It showed for the first time the potency of the congressional budget process for a president who commanded majorities or for a congressional majority. It would contain an historic defense buildup and huge tax cut, creating a decade of chronic deficits that would in themselves contribute to the transformation of budgeting. Emphasis on deficit reduction in ensuing years would cement the emphasis on macrobudgeting in both branches.

During the transition in 1980, Reagan named David Stockman, Republican member of Congress from Michigan, as his budget director. Stockman would play a critical role in formulating the administration's economic and budget policy as well as its strategy for getting it adopted. With the president-elect's approval, Stockman had already made elaborate plans to slash the federal budget by the time Reagan was inaugurated. Many of these plans had been formulated while he was in Congress. Stockman understood the big picture as well as the arcane technical detail of budgeting better than perhaps any previous budget director and better than anyone in the Reagan White House.

Although President Reagan did not understand or care to understand any of the detail and budget minutiae, he understood clearly that what Stockman wanted to do fit nicely with his big picture. Only weeks into his term, Reagan submitted the outlines of an alternative to Carter's last budget, which would be the essence of the so-called "Reagan Revolution." The administration and its allies chose the strategy of using the reconciliation process to lump its taxing and spending priorities in a single bill. Moribund during the 1970s, the reconciliation process was originally designed to come at the end of the congressional budget process to reconcile the actions of the appropriations committees with the budget resolution.

The role of OMB in budgeting changed more completely in the early Reagan years from an inward orientation toward the executive branch to an external orientation toward Congress. To institutionalize this orientation to Congress, Budget Director Stockman instituted a computerized tracking system—the Central Budget Management System (CBMS)—to monitor the president's requests at all stages of the congressional budget process. He helped facilitate the growing emphasis on macrobudgeting over micro-budgeting during his tenure in office. Stockman changed the way the administration presented a budget to Congress, changed the language from programs and line-items to aggregates, multiyear trends, and budget shares. He changed the paradigm of presidential-congressional negotiations over the budget.

Reagan had prevailed in 1981, but the Achilles' heel of the economic and budget plan was the faulty, cooked numbers that the budget projections were based on. Even by late 1981, it was clear that the deficits were on a dangerous upward spiral. The deficit topped $200 billion in FY 1983, some 6.2 percent of GDP, and chronic deficits would continue. The deficits not only shaped changes in presidential budgeting but increased the conflict and instability of congressional budgeting. In the decade-long confrontation between Democratic congresses and Republican presidents over how to deal with deficits, Congress would embark on a number of experiments and innovations in its own budget procedures in an attempt to reduce the deficits and strengthen their hand against the president. Some of them, like the Balanced Budget and Emergency Deficit Reduction Act of 1985, commonly known as Gramm-Rudman-Hollings, have been judged a colossal failure. What critics often overlook, however, is that in reforming and centralizing its budget procedures, Congress greatly enhanced its ability to effectively challenge the president's priorities. This increased capacity has exacerbated the shift of the president's budget from definitive policy statement to the starting point for negotiations.

During the 1980s, despite the defense buildup, the share of entitlements and mandatory outlays continued to grow as the proportion of discretionary expenditures fell, especially domestic discretionary spending. As the content of the budget changed, so did the institutions and processes of presidential-congressional bargaining over the budget change. Increasingly, arrangements outside normal legislative channels were used in an attempt to resolve budget deadlock. In 1983, a bipartisan commission was used to break the impasse over how to save Social Security from insolvency. Commissions were later adopted to tackle tough military base-closing decisions. Legislative-executive "summits" became more prevalent. In five of the years between 1982 and 1990, some form of summit was convened. The president had become no more than a coequal with the Congress in attempting to reduce deficits and shape long-term taxing and spending trends.

During the 1980s, the deficits and budgeting came to dominate national politics. Budgetary politics encompassed an ever-growing number of issues, becoming the centralized governing process of the nation, rather than a distinct and separate process. It is perhaps ironic that these changes in presidential budgeting occurred under the watch of a president who had less hands-on involvement with the budget process than any recent president. Ronald Reagan was able to effectively communicate major themes and directions and used television and the print media to take his budget proposals to the people. On the other hand, Reagan detached himself from daily budget matters, leaving responsibilities for things like agency appeals and actual congressional negotiations with others. In the new world of presidential budgeting, influence depended more on controlling the agenda for negotiation and the direction of long-term trends than on familiarity with details or personal involvement.

By the end of the 1980s, presidential budgeting was largely transformed. With deficits still too high, the emphasis remained on macrobudgeting over microbudgeting. With its orientation toward Congress, the highly political Office of Management and Budget had adopted an entirely new role in addition to its traditional budget preparation and monitoring role. Although top-down budgeting to the degree practiced in the executive branch in 1982 and 1983 was not repeated, executive budgeting remained more top-down than it had in the previous forty years. While Congress struggled under procedural instability and change in an environment of greater conflict with the presidency, it emerged with more centralized processes capable of challenging the president and imposing its own budget priorities. Leaving office in 1989, Reagan left his successor, George Bush, a legacy of conflict with Congress that Bush hoped to reverse.

Bush and Clinton: Presidential Budgeting in the 1990s

The difficult challenges and pitfalls presented by the transformed world of presidential budgeting hit the Bush presidency particularly hard. Perhaps bowing to the inevitability of negotiations with Congress, Bush's very first budget in 1989 left $10 billion in cuts unspecified, to be filled in later. In 1990, his budget message consisted of only a few paragraphs, followed by a long introduction to the budget by his budget director, Richard Darman. In 1990, when Bush had to retract his main campaign pledge and after the summit package he endorsed was defeated, he virtually abdicated budgetmaking to the Congress. He took refuge in foreign policy and international affairs, largely avoiding budgeting as much as possible. After his defeat in the 1992 presidential election, he became the first president to not even submit a real budget to Congress. Instead, he opted to simply provide current policy projections and allow his successor, Bill Clinton, to formulate his own budget. It had started out much more positively for George Bush four years earlier.

Three months after his inauguration, in April 1989, President Bush and congressional leaders announced a budget agreement for the FY 1990 budget, seemingly ushering in a new era of cooperation despite a continuation of divided government. However, the agreement was more a bipartisan political statement than a policy compromise, papering over major differences. In addition, the agreement was rife with budget gimmicks. By the fall of 1989, both sides were squabbling again. As the discussion of the 1990 budget agreement in the introduction suggested, Bush had even greater problems that year. In his budget message, Darman used analogies from childrens' games, books, and TV programs to demonstrate problems inherent in the federal budget: the Budget as Cookie Monster gobbling up money; its future threatened by Pacmen, unfunded federal obligations; a journey through wonderland, the strange world of budget gimmicks.[14] His unusual budget message was prophetic of what would befall the president and his budget that year, particularly the costs of the savings and loan bailout.

Between the bailout, a faltering economy sapping revenues, and technical errors in estimating both revenues and entitlements, the deficit projections exploded by unprecedented amounts. While Bush's abandonment of his no new taxes pledge was alternately seen as an act of betrayal and an act of political courage, it was at least an act of political realism. But his popularity and professional reputation sagged because of his handling of the budget in 1990. What emerged from Congress—the Omnibus Budget Reconciliation Act of 1990 (OBRA 1990) including the Budget Enforcement Act—made a major contribution to deficit reduction and a more sensible congressional approach to deficit reduction. Congress abandoned the Gramm-Rudman-Hollings mandatory deficit reduction approach in favor of expenditure caps and a pay-as-you-go system (PAYGO). The president would no longer have to submit a budget that met the deficit target, but would be under new constraints to restrict new spending programs, tax cuts, or expanded entitlements. Instead of responding to things beyond its control, such as the vulnerability of the budget to the economy, Congress would keep discretionary spending in check and make sure that new programs were deficit-neutral.

Bush made budget history during the Gulf War in 1991. Faced with such huge deficits, the administration demanded payments from those Persian Gulf states who had the most to gain from the liberation of Kuwait, particularly Saudi Arabia. The United States collected some $50 billion in total to defray the additional costs of Operation Desert Shield and Operation Desert Storm.[15] While some found it demeaning for the Secretaries of State and Defense to travel the globe with hat in hand taking up a collection, others argued that the budgetary situation in the United States made it essential and just. It was one more reflection of how deficits permeated virtually every aspect of national policymaking.

Economic and budget problems were one of the main factors behind George Bush's defeat in the presidential election of 1992. Perhaps the most dramatic indicator of the transformation of presidential budgeting during the Bush years was the ability of Congress to reshape federal priorities in 1990, largely without the participation of the administration. Fifteen years after the enactment of the CBA, and after eight years of honing their budgeting skills in combat with the Reagan administration, Congress had proved itself capable of establishing a multiyear budget for the nation that established new revenue trends, altered entitlements, slashed defense, and capped domestic discretionary spending.

Clinton's relentless focus on the economy during the campaign paid off, but soon after the election, his attention shifted to the budget deficits. Less than three years after OBRA 1990, Clinton and his advisers were shocked to find that without some kind of major deficit reduction package, the deficits would surpass half a trillion dollars by the end of the decade.[16] Deficit hawks within the administration's transition team convinced the president that another five-year deficit reduction plan in the range of $500 billion was needed; a modest stimulus package could be included, but tax cuts promised during the campaign would have to be postponed. On February 17, 1993, President Clinton proposed a five-year deficit reduction plan of $493 billion in addition to a modest stimulus and investment package. The administration claimed that the package was equally balanced between tax increases and spending cuts, although Republicans disputed the classification of certain items. They noted that Clinton was proposing the largest tax increase in history.

For the first time in twelve years, the presidency and Congress were under unified party control. That did not mean easy sailing for the president's program, however, since the Congress had proven its abilities and independence. Because of the size of the tax increase, the package was a hard sell for many Democrats. A Senate filibuster knocked the stimulus plan out of the package, and the other major change concerned the administration's proposed energy tax. Clinton had asked for a controversial BTU (British Thermal Unit) energy tax. The Senate replaced it with a smaller gasoline tax and made up the difference with further entitlement cuts.[17] The president pulled out all the stops in lobbying for the passage of his budget plan in what would become the last gasp of party government for the rest of the decade. Not a single Republican in Congress cast a vote for the program.

The budget vote was shaping up as the defining moment of Clinton's young presidency. Like Ronald Reagan twelve years earlier, Clinton appealed to the public on television while twisting arms on Capitol Hill. His budget passed by a razor thin margin in the Senate, 51–50, with Vice-President Gore breaking a tie. The Omnibus Budget and Reconciliation Act of 1993 (OBRA 1993) passed the House on August 5 by a vote of 218–216 only after a freshman Democrat switched her vote. This "near death" experience provided the president with an important victory both substantively and symbolically. Unlike OBRA 1990, which could only fend off ballooning deficits because of the economic slowdown, OBRA 1993, with the help of a robust economy, put the deficits on a rapidly declining path that would lead to budget surpluses by the end of the decade.

Success on his main legislative priority in 1993 was followed by a devastating defeat of Clinton's top domestic priority in 1994: health care. The complex plan ran into sweeping opposition from interest groups and stakeholders and was never even brought up for a vote. Republicans seized on the health-care debacle to nationalize the 1994 midterm elections and run an anti-government campaign based on their "Contract with America." The results were stunning, with Democrats losing control of both houses of Congress for the first time in forty years and leaving Clinton to face the most aggressive, disciplined, and focused Congress of the century. As the new Republican Congress, led by House Speaker Newt Gingrich (R-GA), detailed the agenda of the 104th Congress, Clinton was relegated to holding a press conference to announce that he was not irrelevant. That would prove true as the political fortunes of both branches took surprising twists and turns in 1995 and 1996.

President Clinton's FY 1996 budget was unveiled on February 6, 1995. It provided modest tax cuts and spending cuts that would result in net savings of $81 billion over five years, far below the nearly $800 billion in cuts that euphoric congressional leaders would need to finance their tax cuts and balance the budget. The president's budget was less than an opening bid; it was tacit acknowledgment that Congress would write the budget in 1995. Even his OMB director, Alice Rivlin, said, "We will see as time unfolds what they [Republicans] intend to do to bring the deficit down."[18] But it was not a complete abdication either, rather a dramatic change of tactics in the radically changed political environment. The president would shape the budget through negotiation and the threat and use of his veto powers. In the end, the president would at least fight the Republicans to a standoff.

The first 100 days of the 104th Congress were a flurry of activity, even if the bulk of the items of the Contract were not enacted. Republicans suffered a major defeat when the balanced budget amendment, heavily lobbied against by the president, was defeated by a single vote in the Senate. The centerpiece of the Republicans' agenda was a multiyear plan to balance the budget while allowing large tax cuts for Americans. Medicare, the most rapidly expanding entitlement, was targeted for major reductions. As budget negotiations wore on through 1995, the Democrats began a campaign against the Republicans, accusing them of trying to destroy Medicare. Although many neutral observers considered this tactic demagoguery, it began to work. The president's approval ratings began to climb while those of the Congress declined. Negotiations between the White House and Congress over a five-year plan to balance the budget continued to deadlock.

Congressional Republicans decided to play political hardball with the president and force him to accept their numbers or veto spending bills that would shut down the government. Clinton called their bluff and vetoed the legislation on two separate occasions. Both times, nonessential government workers were sent home. Public opinion went strongly against the Republican Congress. They entered 1996 battered and discouraged. Only a year after the Republicans' triumphant victory, seizing the agenda of government from the presidency, it was President Clinton who had gained politically. Republicans abandoned their quest for a balanced budget agreement and finally approved a budget for the remainder of FY 1996. Despite his recovery from the 1994 elections, many Republicans did not expect Clinton to be in office long, and in any case wanted to wait until after the 1996 elections to pursue the balanced budget agreement.

The 1996 elections returned Republicans to power in Congress, although by reduced majorities, and President Clinton was reelected by a substantial margin although he did not reach his goal of 50 percent of the popular vote. The result was a political environment very different from 1995. Each side realized that it would be forced to deal with the other if a balanced budget plan was to be adopted. The economy was driving up tax revenues, making the job of balancing the budget easier. The political battles of 1995–96 provided important lessons, particularly for congressional Republicans who had miscalculated badly. Speaker Newt Gingrich had his own ethical problems that threatened his tenure as Speaker and seemed to dampen his confrontational style.

This altered political and economic environment changed President Clinton's budget strategy as well. Claiming credit for the drop in the deficits, his requests to Congress included modest tax cuts and spending cuts, as well as new initiatives in children's health, restoring welfare benefits to legal aliens, and major education programs. Unlike some years, the president's budget was not pronounced "dead on arrival," and served as the basis for congressional deliberations.[19] One of the reasons for this is that Clinton had moved toward Republican positions in a number of important areas: a balanced budget, Medicare cuts, and an acceptance of tax cuts including in capital gains, something Democrats had fervently opposed for decades. White House and congressional negotiators were helped at the last minute by a new set of deficit projections that reduced the amount that they would have to cut. On May 2, 1997, effusive Republican leaders announced the balanced budget agreement with the president that they had sought for so long.

Implementing the agreement into first a budget resolution, and then two reconciliation bills, one for spending and one for taxes, continued the pattern of constant posturing and maneuvering for advantages in negotiation. This was presidential budgeting under divided government in the 1990s. Clinton effectively used the veto and veto threat. Both sides claimed victory. Clinton kept Medicare cuts to what he proposed, won major tax preferences for education, increased discretionary spending, child health benefits, and restoration of certain welfare benefits. Republicans won the cherished balanced budget, and enacted significantly greater tax cuts than the president had requested, including capital gains. The Balanced Budget Act of 1997 and the Taxpayer Relief Act of 1997 represented a significant milestone and a seeming end to the deficit wars that had begun in 1981 under Reagan. By 1998, economic growth allowed President Clinton to propose a balanced budget immediately and the budget debate shifted to how to deal with budget surpluses.

Clinton used the line-item veto in 1997 on a number of occasions during the completion of appropriations bills. The administration argued that the main purpose of using the veto was not so much the actual savings, but by encouraging fiscal discipline. "For the line item veto to have its power as a deterrent effect on unnecessary spending . . . the President has to be willing and is willing to use it when necessary."[20] The president first used the item-veto in eliminating three provisions of the Taxpayer Relief Act estimated to save some $500 million. He line-item vetoed seventy-seven provisions from the appropriations bills totaling $491 million, for a total amount of nearly $1 billion. Table 12.2 shows the various appropriations bills in 1997, the number and amount of line-item vetoes, and their percentage of the total bill. Clearly, the savings as a share of the total budget is minuscule. Only for the military construction bill, where 3 percent was cut, could the amount be considered substantial. Clinton did much less than he could have, sparing questionable spending items in the district of Newt Gingrich and the state of Senate Majority Leader Trent Lott. The line-item veto was important, however, in a symbolic way and as a bargaining tool in microbudgeting. Its brief history suggested that while presidential budgeting has moved to a focus on microbudgeting, presidents are still interested in districts and deals.

Conclusions: Presidential Incapacity or New Opportunities for Leadership

Presidential budgeting has clearly been transformed. The complex series of negotiating strategies and media tactics involved in the Clinton administration's reaching a balanced budget agreement with Congress in 1997 seems light years from the experiences of Eisenhower or Johnson. The experiences of Bush and Clinton in the 1990s reveal how powerful Congress has become in macrobudgeting, capable of formulating its own comprehensive budget, with the expertise and staff support needed to shape the federal budget. Presidential budgeting has come a long way from the era when executive branch budgeting was largely a closed, self-contained process. It has become the central policymaking process of government, folding in a vast array of issues. As such it is the centerpiece of political conflict, subject to exhaustive public debate, interest-group lobbying, and media scrutiny. In this transformation, accountability has become increasingly diffuse. Just as both sides shared the blame for big deficits in the 1980s, both Congress and the president claimed credit for balancing the budget in the 1990s.

Allen Schick, an astute observer of the budget process for many years,

Table 12.2

Line-Item Vetoes in FY 1998 Appropriations Bills

Appropriations bill	Total appropriated in final bill	Mandatory budget authority	Discretionary budget authority	Number of line-items vetoed	Number of line-items vetoed (thousands)	% of total appropriated vetoed	% of eligible (discretionary) funds vetoed
Agriculture, rural development, and related agencies	$49,749,679	$35,048,000	$14,701,679	5	$1,940	0.0039	0.0132
Commerce, Justice, State, and Judiciary	31,816,907	522,000	31,294,907	1	5,000	0.0157	0.0160
Defense	247,708,522	197,000	247,511,522	13	144,000	0.0581	0.0582
District of Columbia	4,972,567	0	4,972,567	0	0	0.0000	0.0000
Energy and water	21,152,202	0	21,152,202	8	19,300	0.0912	0.0912
Foreign operations	13,190,968	44,000	13,146,968	0	0	0.0000	0.0000
Interior and related agencies	13,789,438	55,000	13,734,438	2	6,200	0.0450	0.0451
Labor, Health and Human Services, and Education	268,013,775	206,611,000	61,402,775	0	0	0.0000	0.0000
Legislative branch	2,248,700	92,000	2,156,700	0	0	0.0000	0.0000
Military construction	9,183,248	0	9,183,248	38	287,000	3.1253	3.1253
Transportation and related agencies	13,062,718	689,000	12,364,718	3	6,230	0.0477	0.0504
Treasury, Postal Service, and independent agencies	25,587,079	12,713,000	12,874,079	1*	8,000	0.0313	0.0621
Veterans Affairs, HUD, and independent agencies	90,735,430	21,332,000	69,403,430	7	14,015	0.0154	0.0202
Total	791,211,233	277,312,000	513,899,233	77	491,685	0.0621	0.0957

Sources: OMB, House and Senate Appropriations Committees, *Congressional Quarterly Weekly Reports,* 1997, and author's calculations.
*Policy rider vetoed—the $8 million saved here is technically not appropriated money.

has argued since the early 1970s that these changes are destroying important institutional routines in the executive branch and largely incapacitating
presidential budgeting.[21] The experience of the 1980s resulted in "im-
provisational budgeting," which, he argues, led to "tearing down of executive institutions rather than building them up."[22] His concerns include the
demise of the president's budget as definitive policy statement, the decline
of careful analysis by OMB in budget preparation, and the decline of presidential influence in budgeting. Has the transformation of presidential budgeting in fact incapacitated the presidency or simply changed the nature and
rules of the game for effective leadership?

Perhaps the greatest change in the institutional environment of federal
budgeting has been the increase in the capacity of Congress to challenge the
president. Much of that capacity has been subject to intense criticism because of the messy, chaotic, and inconsistent processes that have emerged.
But budgetary capacity is not a zero-sum game; a stronger Congress does
not necessarily mean a weaker president. During the most recent era, both
Reagan and Clinton were able to substantially change public policy by
gaining narrow majorities in Congress. Even when facing a determined,
coequal Congress, both Reagan and Clinton were able to significantly shape
policy outcomes. Only Bush, of recent presidents, seemed more incapacitated than empowered in the transformed budget world.

The transformation of the budget into a centralized governing process
does not incapacitate the president, but it increases the risks. The transformation in recent decades fundamentally changes the role of the president in
an effective budgeting system. It increases the importance of clarifying
broad budget priorities, raises the stakes for budget battles, and places a
premium on being able to define the budget debate and gain public support
for the president's position. The shift in emphasis from microbudgeting to
macrobudgeting makes it more necessary for the budget to serve as a comprehensive policy document. This trend toward macrobudgeting has taken
place around the world, including Europe in the 1980s, and emerging democracies in Central and Eastern Europe during the 1990s.[23] Across the
globe, the emphasis on broad budget aggregates for multiyear periods is
essential for fighting deficits, preventing major crises in pension and health-
care programs, and in helping assure international economic stability.

Certainly there have been costs associated with the transformation of
presidential budgeting. Objective analysis within the executive branch has
diminished. With so much time at OMB fighting budget skirmishes on
Capitol Hill, there is simply less time to do other things. The old annual
budget preparation process still goes on, but is less relevant than before.
Despite these changes, misty-eyed nostalgia for the good old days at the

Budget Bureau when examiners were careful and PPBS seemed relevant, is pointless. The forces that have transformed presidential budgeting—the growth of entitlements, powerful Congress, economic instability—are simply the new reality. Presidential budgeting would be truly incapacitated had it not been transformed. True, budget procedures and tactics have been highly variable from year to year. Improvisation can be destabilizing, but it can also be innovative, discovering through trial-and-error processes that are more appropriate and effective in dealing with seemingly intractable budget crises and more capable and aggressive political opposition.

Now that the budget is in balance and surpluses are projected for the future, will presidential budgeting revert to the way it was? No. Will presidents shift their focus to microbudgeting, confronting Congress over program details and agency budgets? Only slightly. Eliminating chronic deficits will change the nature of the budget debate between parties and the relationships between the presidency and Congress. Rather than the deficit issues of spending cuts versus tax increases, the debate over surpluses will surround paying off debt, tax cuts, and new spending initiatives. Nonetheless, presidential budgeting will remain transformed and will not return to the days when budgeting was a more orderly and closed process. The budget remains highly vulnerable to economic downturn: what looked like a surplus could easily become a deficit. Entitlement growth and the impact of the baby boomers on Social Security and Medicare will require an emphasis on macrobudgetary management for decades to come. In the twenty-first century, budget surpluses may allow a more even balance between estimating multiyear budget totals and fighting over specific program issues in a given year. But presidential budgeting is permanently transformed, central to both the president's policymaking role and political leadership.

Notes

1. See Larry Berman, *The Office of Management and Budget and the Presidency: 1921–1979* (Princeton, NJ: Princeton University Press, 1979).

2. Robert A. Wallace, *Congressional Control of Federal Spending* (Detroit: Wayne State University Press, 1960), 10.

3. Jesse Burkhead, "Federal Budgetary Developments: 1947–48," *Public Administration Review* 8 (Autumn 1948): 267–74.

4. Hugh Heclo, "OMB and the Presidency—The Problem of 'Neutral Competence,'" *Public Interest* 23 (Winter 1975): 28–30.

5. Richard C. Fenno, *The Power of the Purse* (Boston: Little, Brown, 1965).

6. Aaron Wildavsky, *The Politics of the Budgetary Process* (Boston: Little, Brown, 1964).

7. Allen Schick, "The Budget Bureau that Was: Thoughts on the Rise, Decline, and Future of a Presidential Agency," *Law and Contemporary Problems* (Summer 1970),

reprinted in Aaron Wildavsky, *Perspectives on the Presidency* (Boston: Little, Brown, 1975), 362.

8. Lance T. LeLoup, *The Fiscal Congress: Legislative Control of the Budget* (Westport, CT: Greenwood Press, 1980), 8–9.

9. Ibid., 24–26.

10. Congressional Budget Office, *The Economic and Budget Outlook FY 1986–90* (February 1985), 199.

11. Dom Bonafede, "From Bungler to Budget Juggler," *National Journal* 8 (January 31, 1976), 152.

12. *Time,* January 30, 1978, 21.

13. Shelly Lynn Tompkin, "Playing Politics in OMB: Civil Servants Join the Game," *Presidential Studies Quarterly* 15, 1 (Winter 1985): 158–70.

14. Office of Management and Budget, *Budget of the United States Fiscal Year 1991* (Washington, DC), January 29, 1990.

15. CBO—1991 estimate of foreign contributions.

16. Congressional Budget Office, *The Economic and Budget Outlook FY 1994–98* (January 1993), 38.

17. Lance T. LeLoup and Patrick Taylor, "The Policy Constraints of Deficit Reduction: President Clinton's 1995 Budget," *Public Budgeting and Finance* 14 (Summer 1994): 3–25.

18. George Hager, "Clinton's Message to Congress: Seek No Cover Here," *Congressional Quarterly Weekly Report* (February 11, 1995): 404.

19. Lance T. LeLoup, Carolyn Long, and James Giordano, "President Clinton's Fiscal 1998 Budget: Political and Constitutional Paths to Balance," *Public Budgeting and Finance* 18 (Spring 1998: 3–32).

20. Gene Sperling, Chair of President's National Economic Council, White House Office of the Press Secretary, "Press Briefing" October 6, 1997, 2.

21. Allen Schick, "The Budget as an Instrument of Presidential Policy," in Lester M. Salamon and Michael S. Lund, eds., *The Reagan Presidency and the Governing of America* (Washington, DC: Urban Institute Press, 1984), 91–125.

22. Allen Schick, *The Capacity to Budget* (Washington, DC: Urban Institute, 1990), 168.

23. Lance T. LeLoup et al., "Budgeting in Hungary During the Democratic Transition," *Journal of Public Budgeting, Accounting, and Financial Management* 10 (Spring 1998: 89–120).

13

Economic Policy: Comparative Advisory Arrangements

James E. Anderson

The Employment Act of 1946 formally assigned the president the responsibility for maintaining a healthy national economy, that is, an economy featuring "maximum employment, production, and purchasing power." Public expectations have strongly reinforced this statutory mandate. Successfully managing the economy has proved a daunting task for presidents because, to paraphrase an old public administration adage, their authority is not commensurate with their responsibility. Much of the authority to take actions affecting the macroeconomy resides with Congress and the Federal Reserve Board. Nevertheless, presidents who do not successfully stabilize the economy may experience hardship at the polls, as did Jimmy Carter and George Bush in their quests for reelection.

To satisfactorily carry out the responsibility of stabilizing the economy, the president needs help in appraising the state of the economy; in developing appropriate policies to control inflation, reduce unemployment, stimulate economic growth; and in securing the adoption and implementation of his preferred policies. Myriad agencies and officials in the executive branch, as well as players in the private sector, stand ready to assist the president in his/her role as economic manager. In this chapter, which looks mostly at the 1946–80 period, my concern is with the advisers and advisory arrangements used by presidents to secure needed economic information, advice, and policy proposals. Then, I examine some of the administrative arrangements or structures used by various presidents to coordinate the economic policymaking process. Some conclusions on the economic advisory process complete the chapter. Throughout, the emphasis is on macroeconomics policy.

I have chosen to concentrate on the 1946–80 period because the large budget deficits that occurred since the early 1980s left little scope for budgetary manipulation for fiscal policy purposes. As Herbert Stein argues, "Fiscal policy . . . determines an appropriate size of the deficit or surplus to which decisions about expenditures and revenues are then adapted. Of course, any budgetary process will finally lead to a total of expenditures, revenues, and by subtraction, a deficit or surplus. The distinctive feature of fiscal policy is that there is a rule or principle which determines the size of the deficit or surplus first and which requires the expenditures and revenues to conform to that."[1]

Instead, since the early 1980s the attention of policymakers has focused on reducing the budget deficit and trying to balance the budget. Consequently, the major burden for economic stabilization has rested on monetary policy, primarily the domain of the Federal Reserve Board. Should budget deficits be brought under control, as seemed likely in the late 1990s, fiscal policy could again become an important executive function.

The Economic Subpresidency

Presidents in need of help and advice on macroeconomic issues can draw upon many government agencies, officials, private citizens, and organizations. The set of advisers that a particular president depends upon, whether continually or occasionally, can be designated as the economic subpresidency.[2] (Professor Thomas Cronin says that subpresidencies exist for foreign and national security affairs, aggregate economics, and domestic policy.)[3] As a part of the presidency and under control by the president, the economic presidency shares neither authority nor responsibility with the president. Rather it serves to assist the president, at his level, by helping him to define policy problems and alternatives, to make and communicate decisions, and to secure their acceptance and compliance.

The economic subpresidency comprises all who perform such activities with respect to macroeconomic matters, whether they act individually or as members of an agency or organization. Persons are included in the economic subpresidency when, and to the extent that, they aid the president in the macroeconomic policy area. Some participants, such as the secretary of the Treasury and the Council of Economic Advisers (CEA), likely will be deeply and continuously involved; others, such as the secretaries of state and labor, will only sometimes be involved. Inclusion in the economic subpresidency depends upon what one does rather than where one sits; the concept is functional rather than structural in origin.

Persons are included in the economic subpresidency both when they personally interact with the president and when their relationships with one another pertain to the exercise of presidential authority. The economic advisory relationship between the director of the Office of Management and Budget and the president illustrates subpresidency status; so does cooperation between the Council of Economic Advisers, the Treasury secretary, and other officials in developing a policy proposal requested by the president. On the other hand, when the Treasury secretary is concerned with routine departmental administration, he would not be acting as part of the economic subpresidency.

Most of the people who make up the economic subpresidency are occupants of established positions who expect to be involved in economic policy and who are expected by others, including the president, to be involved. The president has discretion in deciding whom to appoint to various economic positions, in determining how much or little they will be drawn upon, and in deciding how their advisory actions will be structured or coordinated. To some extent, then, the president is constrained by organizational or institutional considerations; however, he also has leeway in putting his personal imprimatur on his economic subpresidency. As we will see, the composition of the economic subpresidency does not differ greatly among presidencies. There have, however, been significant variations in coordinative arrangements and operating styles, depending upon presidential preferences.

The White House Office

Of the hundreds of people employed in the White House, only a small fraction can accurately be described as staff aides to the president, and of these only a handful at best are likely to be involved in macroeconomic policy. Presidents Eisenhower, Nixon, and Ford all had special assistants for economic affairs in the White House, but the duties of these assistants varied considerably.

Neither the Kennedy nor the Carter administrations had an economist in the White House. CEA chairman Walter Heller requested early in the Kennedy administration that an economist not be appointed to the White House staff. Charles Schultze reputedly made this a condition of his acceptance of the CEA chairmanship in the Carter administration. During the Johnson administration the CEA sought to prevent such an appointment by performing a variety of "chores," such as speechwriting, for the White House. "One of the things we were interested in was making it unnecessary for Califano to want to have his own economist," CEA member Arthur Okun stated. "We would do anything that he needed to be done. He didn't need an economics staff of his own. We managed to convince him several times when that issue came up."[4] CEA officials obviously thought such a White House official would become a major competitor.

White House officials sometimes serve as policy coordinators. A good example is Joseph Califano in the Johnson administration. All memoranda on macroeconomics policy flowed through Califano's office on their way to the president, but he appears to have done little screening of them. Some, though, were rewritten because of their long and tedious original style.[5] Califano spent much time arranging and participating in meetings, advising the president about what was happening in policy deliberations, and conveying presidential requests and instructions to other officials. Usually, however, he was not a major contributor of substantive information and ideas to the decision-making process.[6]

In the Carter administration, Stuart Eizenstadt, head of the Domestic Policy Staff, sometimes coordinated the handling of economic issues because no one else was willing or available to take on this responsibility. Under Carter, economist Henry Owen, who was formally assigned to the NSC staff, directed planning for the annual economic summit conferences and handled some other foreign economic policy issues.

Generally, what one finds is that presidents have not drawn heavily upon White House personnel for assistance in the macroeconomic area. When they have, it has been more for coordination of the economic subpresidency than the provision of substantive advice and information. Several presidents have used White House or other executive office personnel to handle foreign economic policy issues.

The Council of Economic Advisers

Established by the Employment Act of 1946, the Council of Economic Advisers has always been a small agency. Currently it comprises the three council members, fifteen to twenty professional staff members (mostly senior economists who serve for a year or two), and a couple dozen support personnel. It draws mostly on academia for council and professional members, and is characterized by a high rate of staff turnover. On the one hand, this provides the agency with highly qualified personnel who bring new ideas and enthusiasm to it. On the other hand, it means that the CEA has limited organizational memory and an infirm institutional status. Charles Schultze, who chaired the CEA during the Carter years, approved of staff rotation because in his view it helped prevent "the development of institutional perspectives" that might bias the actions of the CEA.[7]

The CEA has a number of tasks. Its sole formal responsibility involves preparation of the annual economic report for the president. Beyond that, the council serves "as an intelligence agency to the President, providing him with a continuous flow of information about the state of the economy and its problems."[8] Also, the CEA helps prepare economic forecasts in cooperation with the other Troika agencies (see further on) and serves on a variety of interagency committees. The sole client for its services is the president; its influence depends upon the working relationship that it establishes with the president.

Although it has sought to avoid programmatic or operating responsibilities, the CEA has not always been successful in this respect. It was deeply enmeshed in the effort to secure compliance with the Johnson administration's wage–price guidelines, in part because of the disinclination of the executive departments to become much involved. In the Carter administration the CEA played a leading role in both the design and the implementation of the Regulatory Analysis Program, which entailed executive office supervision of regulatory agency rule-making intended to hold down the financial costs imposed on the economy. Actions of this sort distract from the council's advisory functions and also likely reduce its reputation for impartiality or freedom from policy biases.

The influence of the CEA has fluctuated among presidential administrations. The 1960s, which an exuberant Walter Heller proclaimed the "age of the economists," were its peak years of influence. For a time during the Johnson years it was even thought that the council had the ability to "fine tune" the economy and maintain a desirable balance between inflation and unemployment. Several factors then contributed to its influence.[9] First, it demonstrated competence and alacrity in providing information and advice on macroeconomic issues. Second, it generally lacked policy biases emanating from program responsibilities, clientele pressures, or organizational commitments, while it shared the president's interest in high employment and low inflation. Third, the CEA was able to communicate ideas and information to the chief executive in a succinct, well-organized, and readable manner. Fourth, the council was willing to get involved in presidential policymaking and politics rather than act simply as a detached provider of expert advice. Council members viewed themselves as political economists and in their policy recommendations took into consideration presidential needs and circumstances. Fifth, under the leadership of Walter Heller and Gardner Ackley the council actively strove to expand and protect its position and influence. As earlier noted, it made itself useful to the White House, and sought to participate in a wide range of matters. Sixth, other agencies in the executive branch lacked the economic support personnel necessary for effective participation in economic policy formation. The increased attention devoted to microeconomic issues by the CEA has also contributed to its lessened influence in the macroeconomic area. Schultze estimated that he spent 70 percent of his time on microeconomic matters.[10]

Twice during its existence the CEA has faced a strong threat of extinction. The CEA got off to a slow and rocky beginning in the Truman administration. Among other problems, there was conflict between Edwin Nourse, the chairman, and the other two members, Leon Keyserling and John Clark, over whether the CEA should testify before congressional committees. Also, some differences between Truman and Keyserling emerged on economic growth or expansion.

Disenchanted with Keyserling and the CEA, congressional conservatives were able to impose a 25 percent reduction on the council's 1953 fiscal year budget. Some other agencies received similar cutbacks. Supporters of the CEA in the Senate were able to secure authorization for the council to spend those remaining funds in the first nine months of the fiscal year. This carried the CEA through the remainder of the Truman administration at full budget level. This ploy left to the Eisenhower administration the decision of whether to extend the life of the CEA.

President Eisenhower's basic preference was for the continuation of the CEA as a collective body.[11] In March 1953 he appointed Arthur Burns as an economic adviser and directed him to study and report on the economic advisory situation. Burns recommended that a multiple-member council would serve the president's interests better than a single adviser. The approval of Congress for a revamped council via a reorganization plan was readily obtained. In the autumn of 1953 the CEA was rescued from limbo and began again to operate with Arthur Burns as its new chairman.[12] Regular funding for the CEA was restored in the 1954 budget.

The second dust-up over the CEA occurred in the middle of the Reagan administration. CEA chairman Martin Feldstein irritated administration officials by publicly expressing concern about the huge budget deficits generated by Reagan's economic policies and calling for tax increases and spending reductions to lower the deficits. When Feldstein departed from the council in July 1984 the administration delayed replacing him and did not designate one of the remaining council members as acting chairman. President Reagan, who had expressed doubt about needing a council of economic advisers following his election, considered abolishing the CEA. Eventually, the president relented and in May 1985 appointed Beryl Sprinkel, who had served as undersecretary of the Treasury for monetary affairs, to chair the CEA. It was subsequently reported that, while the council was "alive and thriving again," it would keep any dissent within the walls of the White House.[13]

The CEA is usually depicted as representing the views of the economic profession in policy deliberations. More accurately, because economists are not like peas in a pod, the council espouses the policy perspectives and theories of economists who share the president's perspective or who are comfortable in his ideological camp. This especially holds true for macro-economic matters. Thus, Democratic presidents have usually selected economists with a liberal perspective and a bent for Keynesian economics. Republican presidents, in contrast, typically appoint members to the council with conservative and/or monetarist orientations. This practice helps ensure that advice flowing from the council will be congenial to the president, but that, in itself, does not guarantee it will have an impact. As Charles Schultze, chairman of the CEA during the Carter administration, has said: the council can be "valuable—if the President wants to use it."[14]

The Office of Management and Budget

The OMB is the oldest and largest agency in the Executive Office of the President. Although it is directed by presidential appointees, most of its several hundred members are civil servants. For several decades, OMB (before 1970, the Bureau of the Budget) had a reputation for neutral competence and saw its prime responsibility as serving the long-term interests of the presidency rather than the short-term interests of a particular president. This began to change in the 1960s as the agency was increasingly pulled into the immediacy of presidential politics and became politicized.

OMB's role in macroeconomic policy formation stems from its responsibility for preparing the president's annual budget and from the fiscal effects of the budget. The budget, or, more precisely, the budget surpluses and deficits produced by deliberate variations in taxing and spending, can be an important means for economic stabilization. Consequently, the OMB director will be an important presidential adviser on fiscal policy, particularly when variations in expenditures are at issue. Budget directors customarily serve on committees or councils set up to handle macroeconomic issues.

Economists Kermit Gordon and Charles Schultze, the first two budget directors in the Johnson administration, were influential participants in the development of fiscal policy proposals. In comparison, James McIntyre was one of the most conservative top-level officials in the Carter administration. Though as OMB director he was an important provider of information, he was a less influential policy adviser than were some of the more liberal and assertive members of the Carter economic subpresidency. Position alone is not a guarantee of influence.

The Department of the Treasury

The Treasury Department has a substantial power base because of its responsibilities for tax collection, currency control, international monetary policy, and national debt management. Within the government, it has the best sources of information on tax revenues, the tax structure, and financial markets. Typically, the Treasury Department is the lead agency in the development of tax policy and its presentation to Congress. This was true for both the 1964 Kennedy–Johnson tax cuts and the Tax Reform Act of 1986.

In the area of foreign economic policy, the Treasury Department has generally dominated the CEA and other players because its large staff gives it an informational edge. Ackley states that in the Johnson administration, the Treasury was able to dominate the Cabinet Committee on Balance of Payments because its staff work was performed by Treasury officials and reflected Treasury policy positions.[15] In 1978 the Treasury Department took the lead in fashioning the Carter administration's program to support the value of the dollar in international financial markets.[16]

Because of his organizational position, the secretary of the Treasury will probably be less activist and expansionist oriented than other economic advisers. Concern about the soundness of the dollar, the balance-of-payments situation, and revenue adequacy will shape his thinking. Also, the Treasury is an important link between an administration and Wall Street and the financial community. Although it is often said that the Treasury does not have a clientele like the Departments of Labor or Commerce, this is not really accurate. Kermit Gordon declined appointment as secretary of the Treasury during the Johnson administration because he lacked the support of the banking and financial community, and did not want to try to secure it. Nicholas Brady and Robert Rubin, Treasury secretaries during the Bush and Clinton administrations, respectively, benefited from their Wall Street backgrounds.

As with other advisers, the influence of the Treasury secretary fluctuates. When contests develop within an administration over who is going to be its economic spokesman, the Treasury secretary is likely to win, as did William Simon in the Ford administration and Michael Blumenthal in the Carter administration. Blumenthal, however, won the mantle of economic spokesman only a few months before he was cashiered by the president in the summer of 1979. In the Johnson administration there was no contest because the president himself handled the spokesman role.

Other Departments

In the 1960s the other cabinet departments were generally denied a significant place in deliberations on macroeconomic policy issues. Sometimes departments such as Commerce and Labor were consulted after proposals had been developed and reactions were being solicited from the business and labor communities and others. They did not find this very satisfying. Additionally, such departments as Commerce and Labor were seen as claimant or clientele departments whose responses on policy issues predictably would coincide with the interests of the groups that they represented.

Robert McNamara, the secretary of Defense, was often involved in deliberations on economic policy in the Johnson administration. This, however, was more a consequence of his background (former president of the Ford Motor Company) and ability than his bureaucratic habitat. Johnson respected his ability and judgment and thus drew him into the economic policy arena. George Shultz, a professional economist who served as secretary of Labor, director of OMB, and secretary of the Treasury in the Nixon administration, and who was secretary of State for five-and-a-half years in the Reagan administration, never took on a leading economic role in the latter administration. Shultz did act to improve the quality of economic analysis within the State Department.[17]

In the 1970s and 1980s, more departments were accorded places on advisory or coordinating bodies dealing with economic policy (which usually included both micro and macro issues). The broader jurisdiction of these units helps account for the broader membership, but the department's strengthened capacities for economic analyses were also undoubtedly a factor. Thus in the Carter administration, the Departments of Labor, Commerce, and Housing and Urban Development were accorded membership in the Economic Policy Group. The most active role was taken by Secretary of Labor Ray Marshall, a former professor of economics, who secured the inclusion of a public service employment program in the 1977 economic stimulus package and was a leader in the development of the voluntary wage–price guidelines instituted the next year. In the Reagan administration, the Cabinet Council on Economic Affairs included representatives from the Departments of Agriculture, Commerce, Energy, and Labor.

When international economic policies are involved, the Department of State is an important player. Often the department is represented by the undersecretary for economic affairs rather than the secretary. The department is frequently charged with being too responsive to the interests of foreign governments, which may lessen its influence.

The Federal Reserve Board

The Federal Reserve Board's responsibility for regulating the money supply and interest rate makes it the primary developer of monetary policy. Although the president appoints the members and chair of the FRB, with the consent of the Senate, beyond that the board is nominally independent of the executive. Neither the president nor Congress can direct the FRB in how to make monetary policy, for example, whether to expand or tighten the money supply in particular instances. There is, however, much communication between the president and such agencies as the CEA, the Treasury, and the FRB. Some of this involves the exchange of information and data that the various agencies need and find useful in carrying out their duties. And some of it involves "pressure"—efforts by the executive to influence the FRB in conducting monetary policy and attempts by the FRB to influence the formation of fiscal policy. Reduction of the budget deficit has been an oft-expressed concern of FRB chairman Alan Greenspan in recent years.

The chair of the FRB, who speaks for and customarily dominates the board, may actively try to influence presidential action. For example, Arthur Burns, who chaired the FRB from 1970 to 1978, was a leading advocate of wage–price controls and participated in the deliberations leading to President Nixon's decision in August 1971 to impose controls. In time, however, Burns overplayed his hand and lost his welcome at the White House.[18] With the inception of the Ford administration in August 1974 Burns was restored to grace and remained an influential participant in economic policy matters throughout the Ford term.

When the Carter administration took office in 1977, Burns's relationship within the executive began to decline. There were policy differences between Burns and administration officials, who also found him inscrutable in private meetings and unpredictable.[19] When Burns's term as chair expired in early 1978, the president decided to replace him with G. William Miller. Although his term as an FRB member had six years to run, Burns chose to leave the FRB. This tale points up the conditionality of influence.

In practice, the FRB is frequently described as "independent in but not of the government." It cannot be controlled by the executive but it is responsive to the executive. Although the president cannot compel the FRB to follow his preference, the monetary policy that emanates from the board's actions is usually acceptable to the president, even if it is not all what he might prefer.[20]

Other Participants

A president is free to seek advice from wherever he chooses. And some presidents choose to seek advice from the private sector. Lyndon Johnson drew on such Washington notables as Clark Clifford, David Ginsburg, and Abe Fortas for advice on many important matters. They also served on ad hoc committees that made recommendations to the president on fiscal policy. He obviously viewed them as broad-gauged, wise, and experienced persons who could provide useful judgments on the wisdom and feasibility of economic proposals. He also often consulted business and labor leaders before he made decisions. Former officials, such as Walter Heller and Kermit Gordon, were drawn upon after they left government service.

Advisory boards also may be created to advise the president. As an example, the President's Economic Policy Advisory Board (PEPAB), which existed during the Reagan administration, consisted of "a dozen or so distinguished Republican businessmen and economists." It met a couple of times a year and offered advice on such topics as the budget deficit and import restraints. William Niskanen reports that "it is difficult to identify a single issue in which this group's generally sound advice contributed to a change in policy."[21] President Reagan seemed resistant to advice coming from economists, and more so if it was critical in tone.

Vice-President Walter Mondale was a major political and policy adviser to President Jimmy Carter. Mondale regularly met alone with the president, participated in many policy meetings, and received copies of all policy memoranda sent to the president.[22] He probably provided more advice on the political than the substantive or technical aspects of policy matters, as he had far more political experience than most members of the Carter White House.

Coordinative Arrangements

In this section some of the arrangements or structures used by four presidents—Johnson, Nixon, Ford, and Carter—to coordinate the advisory process and to better mobilize it for their purposes will be examined. In the absence of effective coordinative devices the president is likely to be bombarded by divergent and conflicting advice from various officials, or, significant information or perspective may be absent from the advice that he does receive.

The Johnson Administration: The Heyday of the Troika

"Troika" is the term first used by Walter Heller to designate the cooperative relationship of the Council of Economic Advisers, the Bureau of the Budget (BOB), and the Treasury Department in providing President Johnson with economic information, advice, and policy proposals, mostly in the macroeconomic area.[23] These functions included preparing periodic economic forecasts. The Departments of Agriculture, Commerce, and Labor, which previously had important roles in forecasting, were now excluded, except as suppliers of economic data. The allocation of responsibilities among the Troika agencies accorded primary responsibility to the Treasury Department for revenue estimates, the Bureau of the Budget for expenditure estimates, and the Council of Economic Advisers for overall economic forecasting. This was not a rigid division, however, and the agencies sometimes challenged one another's estimates or assumptions.

The agencies also carried some policy biases into the Troika operation. Because of its responsibilities for debt management and the balance of payments, and its ties to the financial community, the Treasury Department was an advocate of price-level stability. It also tended to support more fiscal restraint. BOB, in turn, displayed little enthusiasm for expenditure reductions because the burden of action here would fall on it, and expenditure reductions were not easily achieved. The CEA was an avid advocate of economic expansion. In practice, these biases were moderated as the Troika agencies and principals sought agreement on their policy recommendations. In addition, strong pressure was exerted by LBJ for consensus recommendations from the Troika.

For the Troika principals, policy considerations were more important than technical forecasting, although one or more of them might have been involved in earlier stages of the forecasting process. There was no rigid separation of functions among the three levels; cooperation and frequent interaction prevailed. The principals might send the option framers' report to the president with a covering memorandum. A meeting to discuss it with the president might be requested, if that seemed necessary. Or, the Troika might make a policy recommendation to the president, and perhaps include some additional analysis of the economic situation.

As the primary mechanism for the development of policy proposals, the Troika really did not continue beyond the Johnson administration. The lower levels of the Troika operation have been employed since then, as best I can determine, for making economic forecasts. Early in the Reagan years there were newspaper reports about conflict over supply-side theory, monetarism, and loyalty to the president's economic program.[24] During the Clinton administration, the Troika operation annually produced a couple of major economic forecasts. The Troika officials as a unit, however, have given way to other arrangements for policy development.

The Troika's area of dominance was *domestic* policy. Foreign economic policy was handled primarily by other means. Balance-of-payments problems were the concern of the Cabinet Committee on Balance of Payments. Chaired by the secretary of the Treasury, its members included the secretaries of Defense and Commerce, the undersecretary of State, the Agency for International Development (AID) administrator, the special trade representative, the director of BOB, the CEA chair, and a White House representative. The Cabinet Committee met approximately quarterly to review the balance-of-payments situation and also held some meetings with the president. Various policy recommendations, including that for the 1968 balance-of-payments program, came from this group. A number of other officials were drawn into the formulation process for that program.

In summary, macroeconomic policy formation in the Johnson administration was handled through the use of a variety of committees or groups, mostly of an informal nature. Some were temporary, perhaps meeting only once; others, such as those presented here, lasted though much or all of the administration. There was an ad hoc quality to all of this, but also an element of stability. Perhaps it can be called "regularized ad hocracy," if one can tolerate some contradiction in a characterization.

The Nixon Administration: The Time of the Czars

One of Richard Nixon's first presidential actions was the establishment by executive order of the Cabinet Committee on Economic Policy. Chaired by the president himself, its members comprised the vice-president, the secretaries of Agriculture, Commerce, Housing and Urban Development, Labor, and Treasury, two counselors to the president, the director of BOB, the chairman of CEA, and the undersecretary of State for economic affairs. The committee was assigned the task of assisting the president "in the development and coordination of national economic programs and policies," and "in the formulation of the basic goals and objectives of national economic policy."[25] The cabinet committee was a means for both demonstrating concern and for enabling other sorts of anti-inflationary policies to be considered.[26]

The Cabinet Committee on Economic Policy was not an effective body because it was too large in size and unwieldy in operation. The president, who never had an intense interest in economic policy (except, perhaps, for its consequences for his electoral prospects) became disinterested in the committee and ceased to meet with it. By September, if not earlier, the administration economic policymaking process was in disarray. A *Wall Street Journal* article bore the headline, "A Bewildering Array of Experts Help Shape Nixon Economic Policy." The first sentence of the article queried: "Who's in charge of economic policy here?" Answers ranged from everybody to nobody.[27] Obviously the president's attempt to provide formal structure for the economic policy process was in trouble. For a time the CEA became the primary force shaping the administration's economic policies.

In December 1970, President Nixon made a dramatic change when he appointed John Connally, former Democratic governor of Texas, to be secretary of the Treasury. Connally was a self-made millionaire, articulate, flamboyant, forceful, and possessed of a reputation for being a wheeler-dealer yet having very little knowledge of economics or interest and experience in economic policy.[28] The president accorded Connally much leeway in the economic area; while drawing on various officials and groups for advice and assistance, Connally closely held his authority. He usually met alone, and frequently so, with the president.[29]

The president's decision in August 1971 to impose wage–price controls, beginning with a ninety-day freeze, to combat inflation was widely seen as a triumph for Connally. Shultz and the CEA, dedicated to free market principles, had stoutly opposed the use of controls. The pragmatic Connally became an advocate of controls as a dramatic and effective way to chill inflationary pressures. FRB chairman Burns was also an influential supporter of controls.

Connally left the Treasury Department in May 1971 and was succeeded as secretary by Shultz. In January 1973 Shultz was also appointed assistant to the president for economic affairs and chairman of the newly created Council on Economic Policy (CEP). Comprising the secretaries of Agriculture, Commerce, Labor, Transportation, and State, the director of OMB, the chairman of CEA, the director of the Cost of Living Council, and the executive director of the Council on International Economic Policy (CIEP), in addition to Shultz, CEP was supposed to coordinate all economic policy. In actuality it rarely met, but it did give Shultz a means for dealing with top economic policymakers. Shultz also became the chairman of CIEP. This concentration of power in Shultz's hands reflected Nixon's trust and confidence in him as a coordinator of economic policy.

As it evolved, the heart of the coordination process was a daily early-morning meeting of the executive office and Treasury members of CEP. "These meetings were informal," Shultz has recorded, "but they were successful in permitting those who attended to grasp the interconnections between various economic issues and to form a common view on how to approach those issues." Most of the work of the CEP was done through a series of working groups, in which Shultz was the common denominator, that were formed from concerned departments and agencies to handle particular issues—international monetary affairs, trade legislation, wage–price controls, and so on. Information and advice were obtained from a variety of officials who were not members of the CEP.

As economic czar, Shultz operated in a more collegial fashion than Connally. As Stein recalls: "Under Shultz we operated in this committee format. The options we developed would be presented to the President and if they were important issues, then a group would meet with the President."[30]

Shultz, however, was always at the center of the process. When it became known in the spring of 1974 that Shultz was planning to leave the administration, a struggle to take his place as economic coordinator ensued until Kenneth Rush succeeded Shultz. However, in an administration racked and divided by the Watergate controversy, the struggle for dominance in the economic area continued. As one observer put it, Ash, Simon, and Rush "have quickly learned how to pull separately, even as they try to pull together. . . ."[31] At the end of the administration, Rush was still trying to consolidate his power.

The Ford Administration: An Adventure in Multiple Advocacy

On August 8, 1974, Richard Nixon resigned from the presidency and Gerald Ford began the nation's thirty-eighth presidency. Unlike the Johnson administration, which retained the economic policy mechanisms of the Kennedy administration, it was decided in the early weeks of the Ford administration to use a different organizational structure to tackle economic policy. What emerged was the Economic Policy Board (EPB), created by Executive Order No. 11808 on September 30, 1974.[32]

The membership of EPB included the secretaries of Agriculture; Commerce; Health, Education, and Welfare; Housing and Urban Development; Interior; Labor; State; and Treasury; the OMB director; the CEA chairman; the CIEP executive director; and the special assistant to the president for economic affairs. Treasury Secretary William Simon was designated as its chair and also as the administration's "principal spokesman . . . on matters of economic policy." William Seidman, the special assistant for economic affairs, was named as executive director. The broad membership reflected the president's desire that the cabinet officers be given a more prominent role in economic policy coordination. Initially, it was Ford's notion that Simon should have responsibility for policy development and Seidman should take charge of the coordination of economic affairs. However, Simon's role was mostly ceremonial, whereas Seidman became EPB's operative head, setting agendas, running meetings, and managing task forces created to study issues.

Approximately once a week the EPB executive committee met with President Ford, who liked to hear debate on policy proposals before he made decisions. Roger Porter, who served as the executive secretary of EPB, states that the central purpose of these meetings "was to provide the President with an oral exchange of views on important policy decisions to supplement the written options papers. From the discussions he could gauge the intensity of his advisers' feelings about issues, clarify his own thinking, and ask questions about matters raised in the written memorandum."[33] Seidman, as executive director, sought to ensure that there were fair and balanced presentations on issues and that all important viewpoints were presented; that is, he acted as an "honest broker." [34] According to Porter's analysis, 15 percent of the issues (174 of 1,151) dealt with by EPB over its 27–month existence involved macroeconomic policy.

Departments and agencies occasionally bypassed EPB, taking some issues directly to the president. Alan Greenspan, chairman of CEA, expressed the view that EPB "was a very efficient mechanism for surfacing and resolving minor administrative economic problems. On major macro policy questions it was not an efficient mechanism, and therefore we really worked around it in the key decision making processes. I know I did."[35] Porter indicates that in 1975 the administration's $28 billion tax reduction proposal was put together by an ad hoc group that worked confidentially apart from EPB, although EPB did get involved in refining its details.[36] Such actions were done with the acquiescence of the president, of course. Also, economic advice was provided directly to the president by various officials, such as Greenspan and FRB chairman Burns.

Though not without its limitations, EPB appears on balance to have been a successful policy development and coordination entity, at least from an administrative perspective. A report prepared for the Clinton administration by two Washington research organizations concluded that the Ford administration was "the best organized of all recent administrations in its ability to lay all the resources of the government before the President and ensure that his decisions were carried out." Another of the report's conclusions was that "good organization does not always yield good policy."[37]

The Carter Administration: The EPB as "Floating Crap Game"

One of the early decisions of the Carter administration was to abolish the EPB and to put in its stead the Economic Policy Group (EPG). Carter administration officials believed that the Economic Policy Board was too formalized and rigid in its operations. By mid-February 1977 their deliberations had crystallized on an alternative. A joint memorandum from Treasury Secretary Michael Blumenthal and CEA chair Charles Schultze to the president, in which several other administration officials concurred, recommended the creation of an Economic Policy Group.[38] They proposed that this new cabinet-level committee should help formulate and coordinate both domestic and foreign economic policy. The full membership of EPG would include all cabinet members, plus the director of OMB, the CEA chair, and the national security adviser. The vice-president, the assistant to the president for domestic affairs, and the secretary to the cabinet would be ex-officio members. A small staff drawn from member agencies would help manage and coordinate EPG activities; policy analysis would be handled by ad hoc groups. Final policy proposals would be formulated by the EPG itself. President Carter approved all of the Blumenthal–Schultze recommendations and the new entity was launched.

In March 1977 Schultze submitted his resignation as EPG co-chair on the ground that this position, which put him in the role of interagency coordinator, was incompatible with his role as personal economic adviser to the president, a position that he held along with the CEA chairmanship. In a memorandum announcing that decision, President Carter indicated that he concurred. Blumenthal thus became the sole chairman of EPG. The president also stated in his memorandum that EPG "is the body to which I shall look for coordinating government-wide economic plans and policies and bringing me recommendations for action."[39] Carter's pledge to rely upon the EPG was congruent with his early emphasis on cabinet government.

The first few months of EPG's operations were fraught with problems. An early examination of EPG's activities by the president's Reorganization Project concluded that it was not an "especially effective or efficient policy making vehicle." Some of the papers prepared for EPG discussions did not focus sharply on policy options. The large size of meetings—eleven principals plus aides—tended to reduce "the frankness of discussions and enlarge the likelihood of leaks." Option papers prepared by EPG for presidential decision making were sometimes covered by option papers prepared by presidential aides such as Stuart Eizenstadt, the special assistant for domestic affairs, and Zbigniew Brzezinski, the special assistant for national security affairs. The study noted that the president apparently preferred working from papers produced by Eizenstadt and Brzezinski.[40] These were officials in whom he clearly had confidence.

Discussions within the administration during the summer of 1977 led to some alterations in EPG. It was decided that regular meetings of the executive committee should be discontinued. Henceforth it would deal only with "very substantial matters—those genuinely needing a structured review at Cabinet level—and on regular reviews of macroeconomic prospects and plans." To provide continuity, to monitor the flow of domestic and international economic activity, and to check on the progress of EPG projects, a new Steering Committee was created. The principal members were the secretaries of State and Treasury, the CEA chair, and the OMB director. Eizenstadt and Vice-President Walter Mondale were made ex officio members. The EPG would continue in the future to work through cabinet-level committees, relying upon them for leadership and staff work on particular issues.[41]

Yet more tinkerings with EPG were announced by President Carter in May 1979. Henceforth, he decreed, the EPG would "normally operate" through its Steering Committee, which now comprised the secretary of Treasury, the CEA chairman, the OMB director, and the adviser to the president on inflation (Alfred Kahn). Ex officio members were the vice-president, the director of the Domestic Policy Staff (Eizenstadt), and an NSC representative. Participation of other cabinet-level officials would be invited as appropriate for the issues under review. Secretary of the Treasury Blumenthal was designated by the president as the administration's "chief economic spokesman."[42]

There was a strong tendency for the EPG meetings to expand in size despite efforts to cut back on the formal membership. This led Schultze in retrospect to characterize it as a "floating crap game" in discussing an incident in the planning of the 1978 anti-inflation program. Involved was a proposal for a tax-based wage insurance program (TIP) that would award tax credits to workers who complied with anti-inflationary wage standards. An EPG working group considered TIP and was generally unfavorably disposed toward it. TIP was included in the president's anti-inflation program and sunk like a lead balloon on Capitol Hill.

Jimmy Carter apparently felt that he was not well served by the EPG. There was constant friction among some of the EPG members (Eizenstadt and Blumenthal, for instance) and the president did not like playing the role of referee. He wanted policy options to reach him in an orderly and harmonious manner.[43] Instead, he was bombarded by advice and policy recommendations from a variety of sources. Conflicting viewpoints abounded. In 1979 he was urged to appoint "an effective and powerful coordinator of economic policy," but he chose not to do so.[44] Nor did he ever have an effective chief of staff to coordinate economic matters. As a consequence, he had to muddle through as best he could.

Concluding Comments

The economic advisory process has evolved through a number of phases.[45] The 1946–60 period was characterized by a lack of structural arrangements. The Truman administration relied mostly on a few cabinet officers and White House aides in an unstructured way. The Eisenhower administration did create the Advisory Board on Economic Growth and Stability, chaired by Arthur Burns. It consisted of several undersecretary-level officials and sought to coordinate agency and administration policies. It was not a major provider of advice to the president.

After 1960 the economic advisory process became more structured, although many of the structural arrangements established survived only for a single administration, if that long. During the 1960s, when the Troika was dominant, it was possible to draw a fairly bright line between macroeconomic and microeconomic policies. Subsequently, however, it became more difficult to distinguish macro from micro policy. Moreover, the line between domestic and international economic policies blurred. Agencies developed greater capabilities to handle economic analysis. As these developments occurred, there emerged both pressure and the need for expanded participation in economic advisory bodies.

The 1970s saw more inclusive, and more formal, economic advisory arrangements. Expanded participation increased the range of perspectives and information available to the president. It may also have enhanced the legitimacy of decisions as more officials had their views and interests taken into account and had less cause to feel left out or ignored. On the down side, expanded participation made agreement or consensus more difficult to achieve.

Presidents drew their advisers from the occupants of the same general set of departmental and executive office positions. This reflected a combination of presidential preferences and organizational constraints. Those appointed to particular positions—for example, secretary of the Treasury, OMB director—expect, and were expected, to become major participants in the development of macroeconomic policies. Usually, this is what happened. During the Johnson administration, however, John Connor's expectation that as secretary of Commerce he would be a major economic policy player was not met. This was a major cause of the friction that existed between Connor and Johnson.

There was substantial variation in the economic advisory and coordinative arrangements that presidents utilized. The standard explanation is that these structures will reflect the president's interests, management preferences, and decision-making style. Thus, President Nixon, apparently not liking the give-and-take of committee deliberations, preferred to assign economic policy responsibility to a dominant official (or czar). In comparison, the EPB, with its multiple-advocacy format, was preferred by President Ford, who liked to hear the opposing arguments or viewpoints of his advisers. Also, it appears that each president had an urge to handle economic policy differently than his immediate predecessor, especially when the latter was of a different political party. Thus, the Carter administration replaced Ford's EPB with its Economic Policy Group. Initially, the formal structure of EPG did not differ greatly from that of EPB. The same cannot be said for its operating style.

Presidents were not captives of their economic advisory systems, although sometimes they did tolerate arrangements that were not satisfactory.

President Carter and the EPG are a case in point. Presidents sometimes rejected the advice they were given because they disagreed with its substance or because they considered it politically infeasible. Thus, the Troika recommended a major tax increase early in 1966 to restrain the economy. President Johnson did not dispute the economic correctness of that advice but declined to move because of political factors, including a notable lack of support in Congress for increasing taxes.[46] In August 1967 Johnson did call for an income tax increase, which was enacted ten months later along with an expenditure cutback insisted on by Congress. Johnson has often been criticized for not calling for a tax increase in 1966.

Advisory arrangements cannot guarantee that presidents will make good or wise decisions, but they should be designed to ensure that presidents will make informed decisions. How can it be ensured that the president will get good advice—information, alternatives, judgments—on economic issues? What is the best way to organize the economic advisory process? There are no simple or easy answers to these questions, but the 1946–80 period provides a rich legacy of presidential experience on which one can draw.

Notes

An earlier version of this paper was presented at a meeting of the Midwest Political Science Association. I wish to thank Shirley Anne Warshaw for her helpful comments.

1. Herbert Stein, *Presidential Economics,* 2nd ed. (Washington, DC: American Enterprise Institute, 1988), 290–91.

2. This discussion draws on James E. Anderson and Jared E. Hazleton, *Managing Macroeconomic Policy: The Johnson Presidency* (Austin: University of Texas Press, 1986), ch. 2

3. Thomas E. Cronin, *The State of the Presidency,* 2nd ed. (Boston: Little, Brown, 1980).

4. Arthur Okun Oral History Interview in Erwin C. Hargrove and Samuel A. Morley, eds., *The President and the Council of Economic Advisers* (Boulder, CO: Westview Press, 1984), 280.

5. Interview with Joseph Califano, May 17, 1980.

6. Quoted in Lawrence C. Pierce, *The Politics of Fiscal Polly Formation* (Pacific Palisades, CA: Goodyear, 1971), 99.

7. Comments made at a panel on "Economic Policy Making in the White House," annual meeting of the American Political Science Association, Washington, DC, August 1984.

8. Memo, CEA to the President's Task Force on Government Reorganization, "Economic Policy Formation" folder, Files of James Gaither, LBJ Library.

9. Anderson and Hazleton, *Managing Macroeconomic Policy,* 20–25.

10. Hugh S. Norton, *The Quest for Economic Stability: Roosevelt to Reagan* (Columbia: University of South Carolina Press, 1985), 210.

11. Raymond J. Saulnier, *Constructive Years: The U.S. Economy Under Eisenhower* (Lanham, MD: University Press of America, 1991), 29–30.

12. Edward A. Flash, Jr., *Economic Advice and Presidential Leadership* (New

York: Columbia University Press, 1965), 100–10; John W. Sloan, *Eisenhower and the Management of Prosperity* (Lawrence: University Press of Kansas, 1991), 43–44.

13. *New York Times,* August 8, 1985, 8.

14. Dick Kirschten, "Academic Question," *National Journal,* vol. 16 (September 8, 1984), 1675.

15. Interview with Gardner Ackley, August 15, 1979.

16. *New York Times,* November 13, 1978, D3; *Washington Post,* November 2, 1978, 6.

17. William A. Niskanen, *Reaganomics* (New York: Oxford University Press, 1988), 299.

18. *National Journal,* vol. 7 (August 31, 1974), 1321.

19. Executive Order 11808. *Weekly Compilation of Presidential Documents,* vol. 10 (1974), 1216–17.

20. Cf. John T. Woolley, *Monetary Politics: The Federal Reserve and the Politics of Monetary Policy* (New York: Cambridge University Press, 1984).

21. Niskanen, *Reagonomics,* 308–9.

22. Paul C. Light, *Vice-Presidential Power* (Baltimore: Johns Hopkins University Press, 1984), 201–20.

23. This discussion of the Troika and its activities draws on Anderson and Hazleton, *Managing Macroeconomic Policy,* ch. 3; and Pierce, *The Politics of Fiscal Policy Formation,* chs. 3 and 6.

24. *New York Times,* September 28, 1981, 31.

25. *Weekly Compilation of Presidential Documents,* vol. 5 (1969), 163.

26. Herbert Stein, Oral History Interview, in Hargrove and Morley, *The President and the Council of Economic Advisers,* 368.

27. *Wall Street Journal,* September 19, 1969, 1.

28. See, generally, Richard J. Whalen, "The Nixon–Connally Arrangement," *Harper's,* vol. 243 (August 1971), 29–42.

29. Frank V. Fowlker, "Economic Report/Connally Revitalizes Treasury, Assumes Stewardship of Nixon's New Economic Policy," *National Journal,* vol. 3, (October 2, 1971), 1988–97.

30. Herbert Stein, Oral History Interview, in Hargrove and Morley, *The President and the Council of Economic Advisers,* 372.

31. Daniel J. Balz, "Economic Report/Jockeying for Top Position Complicates Economic Policy-Making," *National Journal,* vol. 6 (July 13, 1974), 1027–37.

32. My discussion of the Economic Policy Board relies heavily on Roger B. Porter, *Presidential Decision-Making: The Economic Policy Board* (New York: Cambridge University Press, 1980).

33. Ibid., 67.

34. L. William Seidman, *Full Faith and Credit* (New York: Times Books, 1993), 24–32.

35. Alan Greenspan, Oral History Interview, in Hargrove and Morley, *The President and the Council of Economic Advisers,* 430.

36. Porter, *Presidential Decision-Making,* 205–6.

37. Seidman, *Full Faith and Credit,* 27. See also Daniel J. Balz, "Juice and Coffee and the GNP: The Men Who Meet in the Morning," *National Journal,* vol. 8 (April 3, 1976), 426–33.

38. Memo, W. Michael Blumenthal and Charlie Schultze for the President, February 12, 1977, WHCF, FG6–18, Jimmy Carter Library.

39. Memo, Jimmy Carter for Members of the Economic Policy Group, March 5, 1977, WHCF, FG6–4, Jimmy Carter Library.

40. President's Reorganization Project, Draft Paper on the Economic Policy Group, April 30, 1977. Copy in the author's possession.

41. Memo, W. Michael Blumenthal for the Economic Policy Group, August 2, 1977, WHCF, FG66–18, Jimmy Carter Library.

42. Memo, Jimmy Carter for the Heads of Executive Departments and Agencies and the White House Staff, May 30, 1979, WHCFR, FG6–18, Jimmy Carter Library.

43. Erwin C. Hargrove, *Jimmy Carter as President: Leadership and the Politics of the Public Good* (Baton Rouge: Louisiana State University Press, 1988), 75.

44. Memo, Henry Owen for the President, July 20, 1979, Eizenstadt Papers, Box 143, Jimmy Carter Library.

45. Erwin C. Hargrove and Michael Nelson, *Presidents, Politics, and Policy* (New York: Knopf, 1984), 185–89; George C. Edwards III and Stephen J. Wayne, *Presidential Leadership,* 3rd ed. (New York: St. Martin's, 1994), 414–16.

46. Interview with Gardner Ackley, August 15, 1979. See also M. Stephen Weatherford and Thomas B. Mayhew, "Tax Policy and Presidential Leadership: Ideas, Interests, and the Quality of Advice," *Studies in American Political Development,* vol. 9 (Fall 1995): 308–14.

14

Foreign and Defense Policy

Louis Fisher

Especially in the period after World War II, presidential policymaking has been fundamentally altered in foreign affairs and national defense. The first 160 years of the republic, up to 1950, generally witnessed a substantial amount of shared power between Congress and the president, as one would expect from the explicit text of the Constitution and the values of the framers. But beginning with President Harry Truman's commitment of troops to Korea in June 1950, presidential actions have been characterized more by unilateral decisions than by collective judgment. The implications for constitutional government and democratic control are profound.

Constitutional Principles

It is well settled that domestic powers for the federal government are either enumerated in the Constitution or implied in the enumeration. Thus, Congress not only has the express power to legislate but the implied powers to carry out legislation effectively, including the powers to investigate, to issue subpoenas, and to hold executive officials in contempt. Similarly, the president has the implied power to remove certain executive officers to permit him to remain accountable for discharging his express duty to see that the laws are faithfully executed.

Is the realm of foreign affairs different? Norman Thomas and Joseph Pika point out that the powers of the United States in international affairs "are not granted expressly by the Constitution; rather they derive from the nation's existence as a sovereign entity in the international community. To say that the national power over international affairs is inherent means that it does not depend on an affirmative grant of power in the Constitution. The exclusive and plenary character of that power means that it cannot be exercised by the states or anyone else and that its exercise is not limited by the reserved powers of the states."[1]

This definition of foreign affairs gives wide scope to presidential power. Authority over international affairs is not expressly granted, it derives from the notion of sovereignty; being inherent, no affirmative grant of constitutional power is needed; the power over international affairs is exclusive and plenary and cannot be exercised by the states or "anyone else." Does "anyone else" include Congress? How much independent power does the president have in foreign affairs and defense? Is he subject to the system of checks and balances?

When Thomas and Pika speak of inherent powers in international affairs, they mean something that goes beyond the exercise of such actions as recognizing foreign governments. They derive that function from the president's express power to "receive Ambassadors and other public Ministers."[2] In this sense, the power to recognize other governments is implied in an enumerated power. What presidential powers can be derived more generally from inherent and extraconstitutional sources, such as sovereignty? To what degree can the president discharge the duties of international affairs without the check of Congress or the courts? Are those duties truly "exclusive and plenary," or subject to constraints by other branches?

These issues recall Justice Sutherland's broad definition of presidential power in his famous decision in 1936, *United States v. Curtiss-Wright Corp.* Congress had authorized the president to declare an arms embargo in South America whenever he found that it "may contribute to the reestablishment of peace" between belligerents. The issue before the Court was a simple one: had Congress delegated too broadly? The previous year, in two cases, the Court had struck down a delegation of *domestic* power to the president.[3] Would this delegation also fall or could it be distinguished?

Sutherland could have argued that when Congress delegates in the international realm, it has more latitude than when delegating over domestic affairs. Conditions in foreign affairs are so subject to change that Congress might find it necessary and proper to grant the president greater discretion. Sutherland could have kept the focus on Congress: how much could it yield of *its* powers? Instead, he used the occasion to define presidential power broadly, reaching beyond the bounds of the case to discover extraconstitutional powers for the president.

Sutherland argued that foreign and domestic affairs are different "both in respect of their origin and their nature" because the powers of external sovereignty "passed from the Crown not to colonies severally, but to the colonies in their collective and corporate capacity as the United States of America."[4] The problem with this analysis is that external sovereignty did not skirt the colonies and the states and pass directly to an independent president. In 1776, there was no president. There was not even an executive branch. Only one branch of government operated at the federal level: the Continental Congress, which carried out all functions of government, executive and judicial as well as legislative. Several studies make it clear that the states in 1776 functioned as sovereign entities and independently entered into treaties, borrowed money, solicited arms, laid embargoes, collected tariff duties, and conducted separate military campaigns.[5]

What was the distribution of power after ratification of the Constitution? To what degree was presidential power enhanced by the status of the United States as a sovereign entity? Did the full scope of international affairs fall to the president? That would be a difficult argument to make. The Constitution clearly allocates foreign affairs and defense to Congress as well as to the president. The president makes treaties jointly with the Senate. Congress was given the express power over foreign commerce, duties, and tariffs, and to declare war. In 1787, when the Constitution was being drafted, it would not be too much to say that the power over foreign commerce was the power over foreign affairs. It was through commercial policy with other nations that Congress established the core relations that helped establish peace or led to war.

Sutherland's line of argument comes close to reviving the theory of William Blackstone, the eighteenth-century jurist. He defined the king's prerogative as the power to make war or peace, to make treaties, issue letters of marque and reprisal (authorizing private citizens to undertake military operations), and the power to raise and regulate fleets and navies.[6] Whatever concerned foreign affairs or external relations belonged to the executive. The framers of the American Constitution clearly broke with that concept of government. They gave Congress the power over war and peace; the president retained limited defensive powers to "repel sudden attacks."[7] The president shared the treaty power with the Senate. Congress alone was given the power to issue letters of marque and reprisal and to raise and regulate the military.

The president's independent role in foreign affairs is reflected in Sutherland's treatment of the power to negotiate agreements with other countries: "He *makes* treaties with the advice and consent of the Senate; but he alone negotiates. Into the field of negotiation the Senate cannot intrude; and Congress itself is powerless to invade it."[8]

This vastly overstates the president's power to negotiate treaties. Although Thomas and Pika say that negotiations and communications with other governments "have been from the early years of the Republic a presidential monopoly,"[9] for both practical and constitutional reasons, treaty negotiation has often been shared with Congress. President George Washington and other chief executives frequently reached out to members of Congress in negotiating treaties, seeking their advice on how best to negotiate a treaty and including them in delegations that negotiated treaties. Because treaties generally require appropriations from Congress, these delegations include not only Senators but also members of the House.[10]

The "fast-track" process for trade legislation gives Congress an even more central role in the negotiation process. The implementing bill for trade agreements, such as NAFTA, is part of a quid pro quo between the branches. In return for an expedited procedure for implementing bills (no amendments allowed in committee or on the floor, and a deadline fixed to vote on the bill) the president assures members of Congress that they will be closely involved in the negotiations that produce the bill. In 1991, President George Bush gave Congress "his personal commitment to close bipartisan cooperation in the negotiations and beyond."[11] Members of Congress cannot be expected to vote up or down on an implementing bill unless they have been actively involved in the negotiations of the various draft stages.

Sutherland claimed that the president's power did not depend solely on statutory grants from Congress. Because of what he called the "very delicate, plenary and exclusive power of the president as the sole organ of the federal government in the field of international relations,"[12] the president had to be free to invoke inherent and extraconstitutional powers. Sutherland's influence has been profound. As Thomas and Pika note: "Long-standing usages and the practical aspects of the conduct of foreign relations have combined to make the president the sole organ of the United States in the conduct of its external affairs."[13]

What is meant by the president's authority to act as "sole organ" in the field of international relations? What are the boundaries of "conduct"? Can the other branches restrict presidential actions done in the name of conduct, including the initiation of military force? Do such formulations imply that the president makes foreign policy singlehandedly?

Sutherland borrowed the term "sole organ" from John Marshall, who used it during his service in the House of Representatives in 1800. The fact that Marshall a year later would become chief justice of the Supreme Court gives the citation added luster. Yet Marshall never argued, in the 1800 debate or elsewhere, that the president could act unilaterally in foreign policy and was not subject to legislative checks. Instead, the record is clear that Marshall understood that foreign policy was made jointly by the legislative and executive branches. "Sole organ" had nothing to do with plenary or exclusive powers, much less extraconstitutional sources derived from the notion of sovereignty.

This interpretation is evident from the debate in 1800. Opponents of President John Adams were arguing that he should be impeached because he had sent back to England someone who had been charged with murder in the American courts. The basis for impeachment was that the president had usurped judicial power and had thus violated the doctrine of separated powers. At that point Marshall took the floor to deny that there were any grounds for impeachment. By returning the person to England, Adams was merely carrying out an extradition treaty between the two countries. Far from acting singlehandedly, he was implementing a policy that had been made jointly by the president and the Senate (for treaties). Only after U.S. policy had been decided by both branches, either by treaty or by statute, did the president become the "sole organ" for *implementing* national policy. It was here that Marshall said that the president "is the sole organ of the nation in its external relations and its sole representative with foreign nations."[14] In this sense, the president merely *announced* national policy. He did not *make* it.

Marshall's rejection of the president as a unilateral policymaker in foreign and defense policy is reflected in his opinions while on the Court. During the Quasi-War with France from 1798 to 1800, President Adams issued a proclamation directing American ships to capture vessels sailing *to or from* French ports. This exceeded the scope of authority delegated by Congress, which had only authorized the president to seize vessels sailing *to* French ports. Marshall, speaking for the Court, held that Adams exercised power that he did not have.[15] Once Congress set the boundaries, by statute, the president could not go beyond them.

The limited context of Marshall's statement has been recognized by the courts. Justice Robert Jackson said that the most that can be drawn from *Curtiss-Wright* is the intimation that the president "might act in external affairs without congressional authority, but not that he might act contrary to an act of Congress." He further noted that "much of the [Sutherland] opinion is dictum" (that is, remarks extraneous to the issue before the Court).[16] In 1981, a federal appellate court dismissed "certain dicta" in Sutherland's opinion: "To the extent that denominating the President as the 'sole organ' of the United States in international affairs constitutes a blanket endorsement of plenary Presidential power over any matter extending beyond the borders of this country, we reject that characterization."[17]

The Use of Military Force

Although the Constitution grants explicit and broad authority to Congress over military affairs, Thomas and Pika are no doubt accurate in stating that historical practice "has resulted in a vast expansion of presidential authority to use force at the expense of the powers of Congress. The dominance of the president in this regard has been almost total in wartime; in times of peace Congress has partially reclaimed the ground it lost. Nonetheless, the result has been the continual aggrandizement of presidential power."[18]

Part of the growth of presidential power comes from a standing army and navy. When President John Adams decided that it might be necessary to take military action against France, he lacked not only the constitutional authority to act on his own but also the military capacity. After he asked Congress to prepare the nation for war, a number of statutes were passed to grant supplemental funds for a naval armament, increase the number of ships, reinforce the defense of ports and harbors, and take other measures. Congress had to act first to create the capability of action. Similarly, President James Madison appealed to Congress in 1811 to pass legislation to put the country on a war footing for hostilities against England. Thus prepared, Congress declared war the following year.

A different scenario developed in 1846. President James Polk had reasons to encourage military action against Mexico as a way of gaining additional territory, particularly upper California and New Mexico. He ordered General Zachary Taylor to occupy disputed territory along the Texas–Mexico border. After a clash between American and Mexican forces, he notified Congress that "war exists." Within a few days Congress declared war, but the policy initiative clearly came from Polk.

President Abraham Lincoln's actions during the Civil War also established important precedents for the use of executive power, especially in times of emergency. In acting to suppress the rebellion, he called up the state militias, spent funds for unauthorized purposes, suspended the writ of habeas corpus, and imposed a naval blockade of Confederate ports.[19] Yet it would be too much to say that Lincoln acted as a "dictator" or refused to recognize the constitutional authority of Congress. In fact, he had genuine doubts about the constitutionality of some of his actions, especially the suspension of the writ of habeas corpus, and asked Congress to ratify and make legitimate what he had done, "whether strictly legal or not." He did not claim powers that existed outside the Constitution. The superior lawmaking body remained Congress, and it was to legislators that Lincoln made his appeal. Congress eventually passed legislation "approving, legalizing, and making valid all the acts, proclamations, and orders of the President, etc., as if they had been issued and done under the previous express authority and direction of the Congress of the United States."[20]

The most dangerous precedent for unilateral executive power was established by President Truman when he ordered, purely on his own authority, American troops to Korea in 1950. At no time did he come to Congress for legal sanction, either before or after. In an effort to suggest some legal footing, he cited two resolutions passed by the United Nations Security Council. In fact, he dispatched U.S. forces before the Security Council adopted the second resolution, which was the one that called for military action.

The impact of Truman's action on the UN machinery was extremely damaging. Under Article 43 of the UN Charter, member states would make available to the Security Council—in accordance with "special agreements"—armed forces and other assistance. These agreements would spell out the numbers and types of forces, their degree of readiness and general location, and the nature of the facilities and assistance to be provided. Each nation would then ratify those agreements "in accordance with their respective constitutional processes."

Section 6 of the UN Participation Act, passed in 1945, defined the meaning of "constitutional processes" for the United States. The statute requires that the agreements "shall be subject to the approval of the Congress by appropriate Act or joint resolution."[21] There was no ambiguity at all about the source of legal authority for committing troops. The president would have to come to Congress first and obtain its approval before entering into military action with the United Nations. The Senate approved the UN Charter only after Truman wired this message from Potsdam: "When any such agreement or agreements are negotiated it will be my purpose to ask Congress for appropriate legislation to approve them."[22]

With these presidential assurances and statutory safeguards, how did Truman act singlehandedly in ordering troops to Korea? Supposedly he acted "under the aegis of the United Nations."[23] Several times Truman claimed that the military operation was "a police action under the United Nations."[24] Yet he never came to Congress for authority. How could this happen? How did he evade the procedures of the UN Participation Act?

The answer is that Truman never negotiated a special agreement, nor is there any likelihood that such special agreements will ever be negotiated. The very procedure adopted to guarantee Congress control up front has been made a nullity.[25] Truman's reliance on Security Council resolutions for legal authority set an important precedent. It was later used by President Bush to justify a unilateral decision to order offensive forces against Iraq in 1991. Only at the eleventh hour did he come to Congress, which authorized the action. President Bill Clinton relied on Security

Council resolutions for legal authority to invade Haiti and to send ground forces into Bosnia. At no time did Clinton acknowledge the need to obtain any authority from Congress.[26]

How can presidents rely on the United Nations for legal authority instead of having to seek approval from Congress? Their conduct violates both the text and the legislative history of the UN Charter and the UN Participation Act. There is nothing in the language of the Charter or the statute, nor is there anything in the hearings, committee reports, or floor debate, to indicate that Congress has ever consented to transferring its authority to the United Nations. Nor could it do so. The Senate, in ratifying the UN Charter, had no authority to abdicate its prerogatives and those of the House of Representatives.

The War Powers Resolution

From 1950 to the early 1970s, Congress largely took a backseat in decisions to commit U.S. forces abroad. President Truman offered U.S. aid to the French in Indochina; President Dwight D. Eisenhower made the first commitment of American soldiers to that region; and President John F. Kennedy substantially increased the number of American military advisers from 700 to 16,000. The next step in military involvement came in August 1964, when President Lyndon B. Johnson reported two attacks against U.S. vessels in the Gulf of Tonkin. With little debate or independent investigation, Congress passed the Tonkin Gulf Resolution, supporting the determination of the president to take "all necessary measures to repel any armed attack against the forces of the United States and to prevent further aggression."[27]

The Tonkin Gulf Resolution marked a careless abdication of congressional power. There is substantial doubt as to whether the second attack even took place.[28] A few years later, in reporting the National Commitments Resolution of 1969, the Senate Foreign Relations Committee apologized for it subservient performance. It explained that if blame were to be apportioned for the expansion of presidential power, "a fair share belongs to the Congress" because of its record of acquiescence and passivity.[29]

In what some studies interpret as a reassertion of legislative authority, Congress in 1973 passed the War Powers Resolution. The rhetoric accompanying this statute far exceeds its language or its effectiveness. Although Congress claimed in Section 2(a) that the purpose of the War Powers Resolution was "to fulfill the intent of the framers" and to ensure that the "collective judgment" of both the Congress and the president will apply to the introduction of U.S. troops into combat, other sections undermine and contradict those worthy objectives.

The framers of the Constitution gave the president limited powers to repel sudden attacks. Offensive actions were left to Congress. Yet the War Powers Resolution grants to the president, for a period of sixty to ninety days, the authority to conduct military operations on his own initiative. He need not come to Congress for authority. Nothing in that grant of power assures "collective judgment." As it turns out, the president may use military force for periods in excess of sixty to ninety days because the resolution is written in such a way that the time limit applies only if the president reports under a very specific section: not Section 4, not Section 4(a), but only under Section 4(a)(1). Otherwise, the clock for sixty-to-ninety days fails to tick.

Not surprisingly, presidents do not report under Section 4(a)(1). They report, for the most part, "consistent with the War Powers Resolution." The only president to report under Section 4(a)(1) was Gerald Ford, in the *Mayagüez* capture, and his report had no substantive importance because it was released after the operation was over. As Thomas and Pika note, presidents "have been able to circumvent the intent of the resolution by not activating the sixty-day clock."[30] The War Powers Resolution allows presidents to unilaterally use military force against other countries for as long as they like, until Congress gets around to adopting some kind of statutory constraint. These after-the-fact legislative restrictions are subject to a presidential veto and require a two-thirds majority in each House for an override. Nothing in the language or operation of the War Powers Resolution justifies the claim in Section 2(a) that the intent of the framers was fulfilled. That intent was violated systematically and fundamentally.

Why is the resolution not repealed? Thomas and Pika point out the advantages available to legislators. If a military operation goes sour, Congress can condemn the president for failing to comply with the procedural requirements of the resolution. If the operation is successful, legislators can pat themselves on the back because they never interfered. "Either way, Congress cannot lose."[31] Perhaps Congress does not lose politically, although passivity and hiding behind procedures are not attractive qualities. On institutional and constitutional grounds, however, Congress comes out a loser. Presidents take the initiative; Congress plays catch-up.

Rather than debating the merits of military action and legislating support or restrictions, members of Congress often go to court where they claim that the president violated particular sections of the War Powers Resolution. Federal judges routinely turn aside these cases, telling members that if they do not like what a president does they should use the many institutional weapons available to them. Congress should not expect courts to defend legislative prerogatives. The doctrine of separation of powers assumes that each branch will protect itself.

Nothing in the text of the War Powers Resolution or practice under it supports Congress as a coequal branch. The statute placed Congress in a subordinate role and the scope of independent presidential power has expanded since 1973. This is not a healthy situation, either for Congress or for the country. Thomas and Pika identify the important factors: "Congress has a vital role to play in refining, legitimating, and reviewing all policies."[32] That is, Congress should behave like a legislative branch and not shrink from opportunities to take responsibility and be held accountable. There is little reason to think that the president will exercise much in the way of self-restraint in foreign affairs and military action, or that the courts will intervene in military disputes to limit the president. The only effective check is Congress.

Covert Operations

Just as Congress has suffered institutionally by deferring regularly to the president in foreign affairs and national security, so was President Ronald Reagan seriously damaged by the Iran-Contra affair. Either he was aware of the operations and therefore violated statutory restrictions (the Boland Amendments) and his own administration policies (to remain neutral in the war between Iran and Iraq), or he was in the dark. To remain in the dark about some technical issues in the Food and Drug Administration is permissible for a president. To not know what is going on in national security is intolerable. Either way Reagan stands condemned. Thomas and Pika rightly call Iran-Contra a "major blunder."[33]

Of all the revelations coming out of the Iran-Contra affair, the most startling constitutional claim was the assertion by some administration officials that whenever Congress uses the power of the purse to restrict the president in foreign affairs, the president may pursue his goals by soliciting funds from private citizens and foreign governments. Colonel Oliver North testified that the president could authorize and conduct covert operations with nonappropriated funds.[34] Admiral John Poindexter, who had served as national security adviser under President Reagan, told Congress that the administration could withhold information from legislators because the Contras were being assisted with nonappropriated funds: "We weren't using appropriated funds. They were private, third-party funds."[35]

These arguments, particularly from a national security adviser, display a remarkable ignorance of American values and history. The framers were well aware of English kings who, denied funds by Parliament, turned for revenue from private citizens and foreign governments. For such attempts Charles I lost both his office and his head.[36] That lesson was incorporated into the political principles of the framers. George Mason advised his colleagues at the Philadelphia convention that the "purse & the sword ought never to get into the same hands whether Legislative or Executive."[37] Thomas Jefferson praised the transfer of the war power "from the executive to the Legislative body, from those who are to spend to those who are to pay."[38]

If there had been evidence that President Reagan used the National Security Council as a means of circumventing the Boland Amendments, and that he intended to use private and foreign funds as a substitute for public funds, he would have committed an impeachable offense. Such actions destroy constitutional and democratic government. Reagan would have failed in his constitutional duty to see that the laws are faithfully executed and he would have precipitated a major crisis by merging the power of the sword with the power of the purse.

Aside from constitutional deficiencies, there are severe practical and political weaknesses to the North–Poindexter theory. Soliciting funds from foreign governments to carry out U.S. foreign policy exposes government officials to widespread compromise and corruption. Accepting funds from other nations creates an implicit quid pro quo, requiring the United States to reciprocate by giving donor countries special consideration in such tangible forms as foreign assistance, military assistance, arms sales, and trade concessions.[39] Instead of developing foreign policy in the open, through executive declarations and congressional statutes, foreign policy emerges from deals worked out in private.

At the time of the Iran-Contra affair, Congress had already passed legislation to prohibit quid pro quos. The Pell Amendment in 1985 outlawed the use of any U.S. funds to provide "assistance of any kind, directly or indirectly, to any person or group engaging in an insurgency or other act of rebellion against the Government of Nicaragua."[40] The clear purpose was to prevent recipients of U.S. funds and material from giving assistance to the Contras as a condition, or quid pro quo, for obtaining aid. In 1989, President George Bush signed additional legislation to restrict quid pro quos. The new law states that appropriated funds for foreign assistance may not be provided to "any foreign government (including any instrumentality or agency thereof), foreign person, or United States person in exchange for that foreign government or person undertaking any action which is, if carried out by the United States Government, a United States official or employee, expressly prohibited by a provision of United States law."[41]

Legislation was also enacted to tighten the Intelligence Oversight Act of 1980, which had required presidents to make a "Finding" on the necessity of a covert operation. During the Iran-Contra affair, President Reagan issued an "oral" finding and also tried, through another finding, to retroactively authorize what the Central Intelligence Agency had done. He subsequently established the Tower Commission to study the Iran-Contra affair and make recommendations to prevent future mishaps. After receiving the Commission's report, Reagan issued National Security Decision Direction (NSDD) 266, which prohibited the staff of the National Security Council from undertaking covert operations. Later he issued NSDD 286, requiring written findings (although permitting oral authorizations for short emergencies) and prohibiting retroactive findings.

Both houses of Congress investigated the Iran-Contra affair. In a joint report, Congress supported written findings and the prohibition on retroactive findings. It also objected to vague phrases in the Intelligence Oversight Act, such as one about the president giving the Intelligence Committees "timely notice" of covert actions. The joint report recommended that Congress be notified prior to the commencement of a covert action "except in certain rare instances and in no event later than 48 hours after a Finding is approved."[42]

When President Bush took office in 1989, he proposed an informal accommodation as a substitute for statutory restrictions. In a letter to Senator George L. Boren, on October 30, 1989, Bush agreed that in "almost all instances" he would give the intelligence committees prior notice of a covert action. In "rare instances" he would provide notice "within a few days." Any failure to inform Congress within those periods would be based not on statutory interpretations of the oversight act but on "my assertion of the authorities granted this office by the Constitution."

Congress was not satisfied with this informal understanding. It wanted restrictions placed in law. In 1990, the intelligence authorization bill established new statutory procedures for reporting covert actions. Bush vetoed the bill, in part because of language in the conference report that accompanied the bill. He claimed that the report language undermined the understanding set forth in his letter to Senator Boren. He also noted that prior notice could be withheld only in "exigent circumstances" and that notice "in a timely fashion" should now be interpreted to mean "within a few days" without exception. He argued that such interpretations would unconstitutionally infringe on presidential power.[43]

The two branches continued to pursue the issue, eventually reaching a settlement the next year. The intelligence authorization bill in 1991 revised the Intelligence Oversight Act of 1980 by requiring a number of significant reforms for presidential findings: they must be in writing, they cannot have retroactive effect, they may not authorize any action that violates federal law or the Constitution, and they must identify any third party (foreign nation) that is involved in the covert action.[44]

The Value of Collective Judgment

The damage done by individual presidents who act unilaterally in foreign affairs and national security, often at substantial cost to themselves and their administrations, is a conspicuous lesson of the years since 1950. Truman's involvement in Korea so wounded him and his party that the Republicans had an easy winner with Dwight D. Eisenhower. Johnson's entanglement in Vietnam set the stage for Nixon's victory in 1968. The Iran-Contra fiasco discredited Reagan. Even Bush's military initiatives in Panama and Iraq yielded no political benefit for his reelection effort in 1992.

To be effective and sustainable, national policy needs to be developed by both branches over time. Secretary of State Henry Kissinger announced in 1975:

> "Comity between the executive and legislative branches is the only possible basis for national action. The decade-long struggle in this country over executive dominance in foreign affairs is over. The recognition that the Congress is a coequal branch of government is the dominant fact of national politics today. The executive accepts that the Congress must have both the sense and the reality of participation: foreign policy must be a shared enterprise."[45]

A good sentiment, but the pattern since 1975 simply underscores that Congress will not be included by the executive branch unless it insists on a role. Legislative passivity tosses the ball to the president, inviting unilateral actions that will probably be harmful to the president and the country.

During the 1980s, Secretary of Defense Caspar Weinberger announced important guidelines on the use of military force. He said that American combat troops should not be sent abroad unless there is congressional and public support. Of six tests to apply in cases of military force, one cautioned:

> "Before the U.S. commits combat forces abroad, there must be some reasonable assurance we will have the support of the American people and their elected Representatives in Congress. This support cannot be achieved unless we are candid in making clear the threats we face; the support cannot be sustained without continuing and close consultation. We cannot fight a battle with the Congress at home while asking our troops to win a war overseas."[46]

These are also important principles, but too often the need is couched only in obtaining the "support" of Congress rather than its authority. Our constitutional and legal system is subverted when presidents believe that some vague measure of congressional support is sufficient.

It is often argued that the need for advance congressional authority places unhealthy constraints on a president who has to act quickly and decisively for the national interest. There is little in American history to support that theory and much to contradict it. When the president acts with congressional support, with full statutory authority, he acts with strength. Independent executive actions lead to isolation and weakness.

Thomas and Pika put it right:

> "Perhaps the most important lesson . . . is that since 1945 most of the nation's successful foreign policies—the Truman Doctrine, the Marshall Plan, NATO, the Panama Canal treaty, arms control, and the Persian Gulf War—'have been adopted by Congress and the people after meaningful debate.' For the most part, the major failures—FDR's Yalta agreements with Stalin, the Bay of Pigs invasion, the Vietnam War, and the Iran-contra affair—have been initiated and implemented unilaterally by presidents."[47]

If we took that lesson to heart, our political and constitutional system would be on firm ground and all three branches would prosper.

Notes

1. Norman C. Thomas and Joseph A. Pika, *The Politics of the Presidency,* rev. 4th ed. (Washington, DC: Congressional Quarterly Press, 1997), 414.

2. Ibid., 415.

3. *Panama Refining Co. v. Ryan,* 293 U.S. 388 (1935); *Schechter Corp. v. United States,* 295 U.S. 495 (1935).

4. 299 U.S. 304, 315–16 (1936).

5. Charles Lofgren, *"United States* v. *Curtiss-Wright Export Corporation*: An Historical Reassessment," *Yale Law Journal* 83, 1 (1973); David M. Levitan, "The Foreign Relations Power: An Analysis of Mr. Justice Sutherland's Theory," *Yale Law Journal* 55, 467 (1946); Claude H. Van Tyne, "Sovereignty in the American Revolution: A Historical Study," *American History Review* 12, 529 (1907). The Supreme Court has recognized that the American colonies, after breaking with England, exercised certain elements of sovereignty. *United States v. California,* 332 U.S. 19, 31 (1947); *Texas v. White,* 74 U.S. 700, 725 (1869).

6. William Blackstone, *Commentaries on the Laws of England*, vol. 2, 238–62 (1803).

7. Max Farrand, ed., *The Records of the Federal Convention of 1787,* 2 vols. (New Haven, CT: Yale University Press, 1937), vol. 2, 318–19.

8. 299 U.S. at 319 (emphasis in original).

9. Thomas and Pika, *The Politics of the Presidency,* 414.

10. Louis Fisher, "Congressional Participation in the Treaty Process," *University of Pennsylvania Law Review* 137, 1511 (1989).

11. *Public Papers of the Presidents*, 1991, I, 450.

12. 299 U.S. at 320.

13. Thomas and Pika, *The Politics of the Presidency,* 414.

14. Annals of Congress, 6th Cong., 613 (1800).

15. *Little v. Barreme,* 6 U.S. (2 Cr.) 169 (1804).

16. *Youngstown Co. v. Sawyer,* 343 U.S. 579, 636 n. 2 (1952).

17. *American Intern. Group v. Islamic Republic of Iran,* 657 F.2d 430, 438 n. 6 (D.C. Cir. 1981).

18. Thomas and Pika, *The Politics of the Presidency,* 423.

19. Ibid.
20. 12 Stat. 326 (1861). See Louis Fisher, *Presidential War Power* (Lawrence: University Press of Kansas, 1995), 38–41.
21. 59 Stat. 621, sec. 6 (1945).
22. 91 Cong. Rec. 8185 (1945).
23. *Department of State Bulletin*, vol. 23, 43 (1950).
24. *Public Papers of the Presidents*, 1951, 504, 522.
25. Fisher, *Presidential War Power*, 84–87.
26. Louis Fisher, "Sidestepping Congress: Presidents Relying on the UN and NATO," *Case Western Reserve Law Review* 47 (1997), 1237.
27. 78 Stat. 384 (1964).
28. Fisher, *Presidential War Power*, 117.
29. S. Rept. No. 129, 91st Cong., 1st Sess. (1969), 8.
30. Thomas and Pika, *The Politics of the Presidency,* 427.
31. Ibid., 429.
32. Ibid., 430.
33. Ibid., 435.
34. "Iran-Contra Investigation," Joint Hearings Before the Senate Select Committee on Secret Military Assistance to Iran and the Nicaraguan Opposition and the House Select Committee to Investigate Covert Arms Transactions with Iran, 100th Cong., 1st Sess., vol. 100–7 (Part 2), 37 (1987).
35. Ibid., vol. 100–8, 158.
36. Paul Einzig, *The Control of the Purse* (London: Secker and Warburg, 1959), 57–62, 100.
37. Farrand, *Records of the Federal Convention,* vol. 1, 139–40.
38. *The Writings of Thomas Jefferson,* Paul Leicester Ford, ed. 1892–99, vol. 5 (New York: G.P. Putnam's Sons [part of 10–volume set]), 123.
39. Alex Whiting, "Controlling Tip Cup Diplomacy," *Yale Law Journal* 99 (1990), 2043.
40. 99 Stat. 254, sec. 722(d) (1985).
41. 103 Stat. 1251, sec. 582 (1989).
42. H. Rept. No. 100–433, and S. Rept. No. 100–216 (November 1987), 423.
43. *Public Papers of the Presidents*, 1990, vol. 2, 1729–30.
44. 105 Stat. 441–45 (1991).
45. *Department of State Bulletin*, vol. 72, 562 (1975).
46. Statement by Caspar Weinberger, Secretary of Defense, news release, Office of the Assistant Secretary of Defense (Public Affairs), November 28, 1984.
47. Thomas and Pika, *The Politics of the Presidency,* 436.

Part V

Conclusion

15

Power, Policy, and Accountability

Mary E. Stuckey

*Although Americans are attracted to the idea of a political
leader dedicated to the public interest who seeks comprehensive
policies and rejects politics as usual, their political institutions
and processes are most suitable to leaders who strike bargains
between group interests and are content with incremental policies. Leaders who call attention to problems and deficiencies in
our society and propose measures, often painful, to deal with
them quickly fall out of favor with a public whose members prefer leaders who make no demands on them, assure them of their
essential goodness, and pamper them with platitudes.*[1]

—Norman C. Thomas

Ever since James Madison penned his insightful analysis of the nascent
American political structures in *Federalist #10,* discussions of accountability in the American context have been dominated by a search for institutional structures that will promote strong individual leadership while
minimizing the possibilities of such leadership becoming "irresponsible."
Such discussions are as perennial in the United States as are similar debates
over federalism in Canada; they tend to increase proportionally in times of
crisis concerning such leadership.[2] The tension between the perceived need
for strong leadership and the fear of what a strong leader may do has never
been adequately resolved, either in theory or in practice.[3] Discussions of
responsible leadership therefore tend to focus on the need to limit the
amount of power available to the president, but as Theodore Sorenson noted

in 1974, "the cardinal problem is not the amount of power but the control and accountability of power."[4] That is, no matter how much—or how little—power a president may have, that power is always available for abuse. The problem is how to control the use of power, not how to limit its extent.

In many ways, then, the problem of presidential policymaking has been the problem of devising structures that allow for leadership without raising the specter of abuse.[5] Because our system drives us to look for structural answers to political questions, the effort has been to devise institutions that will allow a president enough latitude to design and implement "good" policy, while denying him the space to forge policies that are inimical to a never-precisely-defined "public good." Policymaking thus cannot be separated from the structures, arrangements, and processes of accountability. As Steven A. Shull points out in the introductory chapter, incorporating these elements is what makes a policy approach to studying the presidency so compelling and daunting.

Indeed, in an important sense, accountability *is* policymaking: "in its simplest form, accountability refers to an authoritative relationship in which one person is formally entitled to demand that another answer for—that is, to provide an account of—his or her actions; rewards or punishments may be meted out to the latter depending on whether those actions conform to the former's wishes."[6] That is, governments and the individuals who operate them are held accountable for what they do, which is to produce policy. But policy is not produced in a vacuum. Indeed, in a democracy, policymaking in theory is directly connected to the will of the public (see Cohen and Collier chapter herein).[7] But in practice, of course, this connection is neither simple nor is it completely linear, as demonstrated by Ragsdale and Rusk's chapter.[8]

Presidents are often held individually accountable for systemic actions; demarcating the difference between the individual temporarily "in charge" of a large set of bureaucratic and separate institutions and those who actually perform the tasks required by those institutions is no easy task, as revealed by James E. Anderson's chapter. But such demarcation is necessary if controls are to be placed on either the individuals or the institutions themselves. This dilemma is at the heart of the problem of accountability.

The Problem of Accountability

Charles O. Jones has written a compelling account of an idea widely shared by political scientists: "Though a government of separated institutions sharing or competing for power has many virtues, *focused responsibility is not one of them.* Accountability is highly diffused by dint of the dispersal that is characteristic of separatism. . . . A system like ours has substantial *individual accountability* but limited *collective accountability*."[9] Political accountability is thus understood as primarily focused on the person of the president.[10] Yet it is also true that by focusing on the president, the issues surrounding organizational involvement in all phases of the policy process are ignored.[11] As Theodore Lowi first pointed out some twenty years ago, it is important to note how the entire system functions—or fails to function—accountably.[12] If a policy is favored by "the government," removing a president will have little effect on that policy. Institutions tend to be stronger than individuals, and presidents often find themselves acting as presidents rather than as individuals who exercise the power of the presidency. Their own choices, decisions, and actions may well be more reflective of institutional interests than of individual preferences.

Consequently, a number of scholars have pointed to an important distinction between political and institutional accountability: "political and institutional means of achieving accountability often work at cross purposes. . . . If presidents are to be held responsible to the electorate, which judges them on the basis of performance, they need ample power and resources to meet the voters' expectations."[13] Thus, presidents can be held accountable for what they do or fail to do, but the institutions that comprise our governing systems must also be subjected to control and evaluation. Ever since the founding, we have been searching for appropriate and effective structures that will permit and facilitate such control and evaluation.

The creation and maintenance of these structures are especially problematic in the contemporary context, where "the hallmark of modern U.S. government is presidential leadership,"[14] which can only be exercised given certain institutional arrangements.

> Throughout this century, presidents have struggled to provide themselves with a structural capacity for leadership by building institutions of their own. For many reasons—political opposition, the pressure of events, the scarcity of resources, and imperfect knowledge about what works—this has not been a simple, linear process of development. But the trajectory is clear, and the motivating force behind it is the president's drive for leadership in a system largely beyond his control.[15]

To be successful, presidents must at least appear to "lead," to dominate and control the mechanisms of government. Just as those seeking to contain the presidency look to structural impediments on the exercise of presidential power, presidents themselves look for institutional arrangements that will facilitate the exercise of presidential power.

As James P. Pfiffner's chapter in this volume reminds us, however, political structures are embedded in political contexts. It is at least possible that as presidential terms vary over time, specifically among the first, last, and reelection years, that differing sorts of structures of accountability may be relevant. Or, to use Pfiffner's division of presidential tasks, it is possible that these structures may need to vary across the domains of presidential activity; that differing notions of what constitutes accountability and differing structures designed to promote those notions·may apply to the tasks of organizing a new administration, selecting appointees, and pursuing a policy agenda. The contributions provided by Paul J. Quirk and Bruce Nesmith and Richard W. Waterman also point to the importance of context, this time regarding domestic policy issues. Jeffrey Segal and Robert Howard's chapter on the courts indicates how important context is with regard to other institutions in the federal government as well. Thus, from the evidence presented throughout this volume, it appears clear that political structures designed without due regard to context and activity are not likely to prove viable.

As early as Richard Neustadt, in fact, political scientists have noticed that different presidents have been able to devise different uses for similar structures in their ongoing search for political resources.[16] Individual style and ability matter, although it is difficult to know exactly how. The problem of accountability is thus also a problem of personality. Individual presidents are held accountable to the public interest, but the standard of judgment is unclear; they are held responsible for things over which they have, at best, limited control,[17] and they try, with uneven success, to influence the standards by which they will be judged.

Consequently, just as the study of the presidency in general can be divided into "president-centered" and "presidency-centered" studies,[18] the specific topic of accountability can be broken into both political accountability, which relates primarily to the person of the president, and institutional accountability, which relates primarily to the structures of the presidency.

Political Accountability

Analysts generally consider political accountability to mean elections,[19] but elections are at best an imprecise means of enforcing accountability, as both the chapter by Lyn Ragsdale and Jerrald Rusk and the debates over retrospective voting indicate.[20] We also know that the president's ability to influence policy is related to popularity,[21] and that the public evaluation of the president is linked to perceptions of his policy positions,[22] making it clear that there is a reciprocal, if potentially marginal, relationship between popularity and policy choices.[23]

The search for accountability has always involved the link between the president and the people, although in the absence of "an organized, focused opposition with leadership centered in one person who will be continuously visible and vocal as the alternative to the president," this link is an insufficient guarantee of accountability.[24] Thus, even political constraints need to be buttressed by institutional arrangements, bringing up the question of whether organizations are better served through internal or external systems of control.[25]

While some scholars find at least a modicum of comfort in the heightened ties between presidents and the people that have become known as the "rhetorical presidency," most find this relationship a cause for concern, as it seems to afford the president more opportunities to avoid responsibility than it offers the people to enforce accountability.[26] As Sorenson noted in the aftermath of the Watergate scandal, "A presidency that is viewed by both the public and its occupant as larger than life can soon tempt that occupant to feel larger than the law."[27] Certainly, there have been few problems of accountability raised by presidents who saw themselves as subordinate to the law, but these presidents rarely earn for themselves reputations for greatness, either.

Presidents, however, generally see themselves as thoroughly constrained—by the other branches of government, especially Congress, by the law, by the media, and by the public. Richard W. Waterman's chapter provides evidence that at least some of those involved in the policy process agree with this assessment. The rhetorical presidency has created—or at the very least, has coincided with—a dramatic increase in public expectations. As Peri Arnold has shown, a gap between expectation and resources has long been a problem for presidents, who are consequently always on the hunt for new resources. Yet no matter how great those resources, they are never enough.[28] More resources mean heightened expectations, which require presidents to find more resources, which in turn raise expectations. The cycle is endlessly self-perpetuating, and is potentially dangerous for both presidents and for the system in which they are embedded, as ever-escalating expectations and constant searches for resources strain a set of institutions designed for minimalist governance.

As Shirley A. Warshaw's chapter shows, the institutionalized presidency has grown along with public expectations. The sort of strong but flexible advisory structure that she advocates has the potential to serve as an informal check on presidents, as it would give them both the advice they want and the protection (sometimes from themselves) that they need. But like all purely political means of encouraging responsible leadership, in practice its viability is uncertain at best. Anderson reveals how presidential advisory structures in economic policymaking must be compatible with presidents' managerial styles.

The rhetorical presidency stresses the ongoing and constant nature of the president's relationship to the public. This phenomenon might appear to render elections, the primary form of political accountability, markedly less useful. As elections become ever more mediated, and as the distinction between campaigning and governing becomes ever more blurred, it becomes more and more difficult for elections to function as a mechanism of accountability. Presidents constantly campaign and their political rhetoric is therefore constantly devalued as "political" by an increasingly cynical media and an increasingly inattentive public. The "meaning" of elections in such a political environment is, at best, difficult to gauge with any accuracy, but Ragsdale and Rusk make a heroic effort to relate elections to subsequent decisions.

Further, as the chapter in this volume by Jeffery E. Cohen and Ken Collier indicates, the nature and extent of the media's influence over policy and public opinion remains unclear, and close attention to the specific presidential task, whether promoting issues, building influence in Congress, or appealing to selected constituencies, is needed if the extent and limits of that influence is to be understood. This idea is generally supported by Joseph A. Pika's contribution as well. It does appear, however, that purely political mechanisms of accountability are, like those that are purely institutional, unreliable at best.

Despite such nostrums, the situation is not entirely bleak. The system as a whole, moreover, has never depended overmuch on elections, which are something of a "final solution" as far as individual political actors are concerned. In order to promote responsible leadership on a day-to-day basis, we have long relied upon institutionalized means of accountability. Toward this end, the chapters by George C. Edwards, Lance T. LeLoup, and Louis Fisher all reveal the crucial oversight role played by Congress.

Institutional Accountability

Institutional accountability is most often discussed in conjunction with separation of powers and checks and balances, the theory being that the responsibility of any one governmental institution can best be ensured by the strength of the others. In this context, political parties and Congress are most often looked to as agents of accountability, although there has been some discussion of looking to the executive branch itself.

Responsible parties are most often seen as the best guarantors of accountability, promising as they do to promote clear policy platforms and thus transforming both the electoral and governing processes.[29] Yet the political parties and the systems in which they are embedded stubbornly resist such strengthening; the system seems to facilitate if not to demand weak party structures. Sidney M. Milkis's chapter indicates that strong presidents are also strong party leaders, which would in turn indicate the possibility of parties serving as institutionalized and politically sensitive mechanisms for providing accountability. The notion that divided government may be one form of such a mechanism is an intriguing one, well worth pursuing. At the very least, there seems to be no immediate cause to believe that strengthened parties, however desirable, will be a part of our national politics any time soon.

The media and interest groups, which seem to have acquired many of the parties' traditional duties as purveyors of political information and its interpretation, are not well suited to replace the parties as mechanisms of policymaking and enforcers of accountability. The media are not primarily political institutions, nor are they motivated by democratic—or even political—concerns. They may be the "watchdogs" of democracy, but that is not their main function, nor is it one that they seem to handle particularly well.[30] Interest groups have the potential to fragment even further as their numbers continue to increase.

As Fisher's chapter indicates, wise presidents treat Congress as a partner if not an ally in the policy process. And, indeed, Congress is a more promising site than either parties or the media for institutional accountability, as it already possesses the constitutional and statutory wherewithal to protect itself and challenge the executive, if it would but exercise its power.[31] Yet as a means of holding executives accountable, Congress seems to have fallen into a morass of persistent scandalmongering and investigative escapades that appear to be doing more to disenchant the electorate with governance in general than to promise much in the way of institutional accountability. That this phenomenon is related to the practices of the media and the preferences of the public seems likely. That it is going to have consequences other than enforcing accountability seems certain.

Partly because of such investigations, however, reforms of the executive itself are also occasionally suggested as a means of providing some institutional responsibility within the presidency. Such reforms tend to follow in the wake of a serious scandal such as Watergate or Iran-Contra, and are complicated by the factors of individual styles of decision making, staffing preferences, and procedural choices of particular presidents.[32] Because of the personalized nature of the office, institutional arrangements that constrain one president may fail to affect or may cripple another. And any grant of power is open to abuse, institutional arrangements notwithstanding.

Further, promoting accountability through institutionalized measures and barriers to executive action is not so easily accomplished. The policymaking environment is both complicated and complex, involving many stages, and any attempts to control that environment must take this complexity into account.[33] In addition, institutional accountability may operate indirectly, and controlling one aspect of the system is likely to have unanticipated, and perhaps undesirable, consequences for other aspects.[34]

As the chapters by Waterman, Edwards, LeLoup, and Anderson all reveal, part of the problem of institutional accountability is that presidents have incomplete control over the participants or processes of policymaking. While they can and do exercise considerable indirect influence through appointees, the White House staff, and the other "insiders" involved, policymaking remains a permeable collection of processes, and holding individual presidents singularly responsible for its outcomes is clearly unwise.

In short, as Colin Campbell and Bert A. Rockman show, the presidency involves a balancing act between what are at least the potentially incompatible if not completely inconsistent goals of both providing representation and securing the polity's long-term interests. The delicate system designed by the framers appears to demand careful balance between energy and safety in the executive. Presidential leadership increasingly requires the negotiation of the tensions caused by these two factors within an environment of both political and institutional accountability. Yet in the prevailing political climate, the stress is increasingly on the side of "energy," and neither set of safeguards seems to promise much in the way of reassurance that either the system or those who operate within it can be made to act responsibly. We demand an energetic executive who sits amidst a very energetic system, and safety, to the extent that it is a concern at all, is something that appears to operate only after the fact of serious abuse of power.

Policy, Power, and Accountability

The responsibilities belonging to a superpower, and perhaps especially to "the last of the superpowers," are immense. National leadership appears to demand a commensurate amount of presidential leadership. Yet, just as smaller countries are perennially afraid (with justification) that the United States will abuse its power, there is a similar fear (with similar justification) that empowering the president will lead to inevitable abuses of power as well. Since our nation's founding, the tendency has been to devise institutional and procedural brakes on power, especially on presidential power. But the problem is that abuses of power have never been legitimated; strengthening formal limits will do little to stop such abuses. In discussing the Nixon presidency, Sorenson made a point that is equally relevant today:

> [T]he Nixon presidency is not, in my opinion, convincing evidence of the need to reduce or restructure the Office of the President. The Nixon White House may have authorized, condoned, or engaged in burglaries, perjury, illegal surveillance, the abuse of Internal Revenue files, and other activities cited by the House Judiciary Committee; but Nixon did not actually possess the power—the *legal right*—to do so . . . they were not instances of powers that must now be withdrawn from the President, because he did not possess them then and does not possess them now. Additional legal curbs would not have prevented Watergate.[35]

Nor, it may be added, would additional legal curbs have prevented Iran-Contra, or the scandals associated with either the Bush or Clinton administrations. In focusing so persistently on institutional cures for what we perceive as institutional problems, we may be contributing to the problem of accountability; we certainly are not contributing to its solution, as presidents may perceive themselves as so hemmed in by structural impediments that they may consider themselves to have no choice but to violate the law in order to "serve the public interest." It may be appropriate to look elsewhere for solutions to the dilemmas of accountability.

Political debate, for instance, is increasingly seen as an impediment to the policy process rather than as an integral part of that process. Pundits—and consequently the public—worry about "deadlock," divided government, and political stalemate; they become frustrated with elected officials who engage in "politics," apparently preferring to see evidence of cooperation and compromise. This trend creates potential problems for both political and institutional accountability. For a responsible party model to work, for instance, focused and explicitly partisan public debate must be viewed not only as a legitimate part of the governing process, but as integral to that process. Even without formal reforms or a clearly strengthened party system, such debate can be a tool for providing accountability. Of course, for this to be the case, the debate must be focused on the substance of policy rather than the politics of personality (when the Speaker of the House refers to the president as a "spoiled brat," for example, it is difficult to see this as contributing to either democratic debate or democratic accountability). In an ever more mass-mediated environment, such debate is clearly technologically possible. Whether it is particularly likely is considerably more questionable. In fact, such debate, or indeed any changes at all, depends almost entirely on the public's willingness to demand, or at least to accede to, changes in our communal national life.

As Harmon notes, "whatever benefits it might offer, the rational reform of government institutions is no substitute for, and in fact may well prevent, strengthening the communal bonds that form the substance of the institutions themselves."[36] In other words, no manner of administrative tinkering can replace the sense of personal responsibility to an important and attentive community. Absent that community, no administrative reforms are likely to prove effective. In a strong political community, accountability may well arise naturally, regardless of institutional arrangements. Without it, questions of accountability, like those of policymaking generally, may be the least of political problems.

Notes

1. Norman C. Thomas, "Jimmy Carter, Public Policy and the Public Interest," *Journal of Policy History* 4(4) (1992): 453–66; at 465.

2. Charles Hardin, *Presidential Power and Accountability: Toward a New Constitution* (Chicago: University of Chicago Press, 1974); Anne Phillips, *The Politics of Presence* (New York: Oxford University Press, 1995); Barbara S. Romzek and Melvin J. Dubnik, "Accountability in the Public Sector: Lessons from the Challenger Tragedy," *Public Administration Review* 47(3) (1987): 227–38; Theodore Sorenson, *Watchmen in the Night: Presidential Accountability After Watergate* (Cambridge, MA: MIT Press, 1975); Norman C. Thomas, "Presidential Power and Accountability After Reagan," in Ryan Barilleaux and Mary E. Stuckey, eds., *Leadership and the Bush Presidency: Prudence or Drift in an Era of Change?* (New York: Praeger, 1992).

3. Hardin, *Presidential Power and Accountability*.

4. Sorenson, *Watchmen in the Night*.

5. Thomas, "Presidential Power and Accountability After Reagan."

6. Michael M. Harmon, *Responsibility as Paradox: A Critique of Rational Discourse on Government* (Thousand Oaks, CA: Sage, 1995).

7. Romzek and Dubnik, *Accountability in the Public Sector,* 228.

8. See also, Dennis M. Simon, "Presidents, Governors, and Electoral Accountability," *Journal of Politics* 51(2) (1989): 286–304.

9. Charles O. Jones, "The Separated System," *Society* 33(6) (1996): 18–23, at 18.

10. Theodore Lowi, *The Personal President: Power Invested, Promise Unfulfilled* (Ithaca, NY: Cornell University Press, 1985).

11. Barbara Ferman and Martin A. Levin, "Dilemmas of Innovation and Accountability: Entrepreneurs and Chief Executives," *Policy Studies Review* 7(1) (1987): 187–99; Donald F. Kettl, "Performance and Accountability: The Challenge of Government by Proxy for Public Administration," *American Review of Public Administration* 18(1) (1988): 9–28.

12. Theodore Lowi, *The End of Liberalism: The Second Republic of the United States,* 2nd ed. (New York: W.W. Norton, 1979).

13. Thomas, "Presidential Power and Accountability After Reagan," 194. See also Bert Rockman, *The Leadership Question: The Presidency and the American System* (New York: Praeger, 1986); Norman C. Thomas, "Aiming at a Moving Target: Critical Perspectives on the U.S. Presidency," *Governance* 1(3) (1988): 288–311.

14. Terry Moe and Scott A. Wilson, "Presidents and the Politics of Structure," *Law and Contemporary Problems* 57(2) (1994): 1–44, at 1.

15. Ibid., 15; see also Ragsdale and Rusk in this volume.

16. Richard Neustadt, *Presidential Power: The Politics of Leadership* (New York: Free Press, 1960).

17. Jones, *The Separated System*; C. Stevenson, "The Evolving Clinton Doctrine on the Use of Force," *Armed Forces and Society* 22(4) (1996): 511–35.

18. Gregory L. Hager and Terry Sullivan, "President-Centered and Presidency-Centered Explanations of Presidential Activity," *American Journal of Political Science* 38(4) (1994): 1079–1103.

19. Thomas, "Presidential Power and Accountability After Reagan"; Thomas, "Jimmy Carter, Public Policy and the Public Interest."

20. Henry W. Chappell and William R. Keech. 1985. "A New View of Political Accountability for Economic Performance," *American Political Science Review* 79(1): 10–27.

21. Paul Brace and Barbara Hinckley, *Follow the Leader: Opinion Polls and the Modern Presidents* (New York: Basic Books, 1992); G. Edwards, *Presidential Influence in Congress* (San Francisco: W.H. Freeman, 1980); G. Edwards, *The Public Presidency: The Pursuit of Popular Support* (New York: St. Martin's Press, 1983); G. Edwards, *At the Margins: Presidential Leadership of Congress* (New Haven: Yale University Press, 1989); Charles Ostrom and Dennis Simon, "Managing Popular Support: A Strategic Perspective," in *The Presidency and Presidential Policy Making,* eds. George C. Edwards III, Steven A. Shull, and Norman C. Thomas (Pittsburgh: University Press, 1985); Benjamin Page and Robert Shapiro, "Presidents as Opinion Leaders: Some New Evidence," in Edwards, Shull, and Thomas, *The Presidency and Presidential Policy Making*; Douglas Rivers and Nancy L. Rose, "Passing the President's Program: Public Opinion and Presidential Influence on Congress," *American Journal of Political Science* 29(2) (1985): 183–96; David W. Rohde and Dennis M. Simon, "Presidential Vetoes and Congressional Response: A Study of Institutional Conflict," *American Journal of Political Science* 29(3) (1985): 397–427.

22. Marilyn Roberts and Maxwell McCombs, "Agenda Setting and Political Advertising: Origins of the News Agenda," *Political Communication* 11(3) (1994): 249–62; Dan Thomas and Lester Sigelman, "Presidential Identification and Policy Leadership: Experimental Evidence on the Reagan Case," in *The Presidency and Presidential Policy Making.*

23. Jon Bond, Richard Fleisher, and M. Northrup, "Public Opinion and Presidential Support," *Annals of the American Academy of Political and Social Science* 499 (September 1988): 47–63; Ostrom and Simon, "Managing Popular Support."

24. Hardin, *Presidential Power and Accountability,* 3.

25. Frank Sorauf, "Who's in Charge? Accountability in Political Action Committees," *Political Science Quarterly* 99(4) (1984–85): 591–614.

26. Those who see this as a potentially positive development include Marc Bodnick, " 'Going Public' Reconsidered: Reagan's 1981 Tax and Budget Cuts and Revisionist Theories of Presidential Power," *Congress and the Presidency* 17(1) (1990): 13–28; Kenneth Collier, "The President, the Public, and Congress," paper presented to the Annual Meeting of the Midwest Political Science Association, Chicago, IL, 1995; and Rockman, *The Leadership Question.* Among those who are less optimistic are James W. Ceaser, Glenn E. Thurow, Jeffery Tulis, and Joseph M. Bessett, "The Rise of the Rhetorical Presidency," *Presidential Studies Quarterly* 11(2) (1991): 158–71; Kathleen Hall Jamieson, *Eloquence in an Electronic Age: The Transformation of American Speechmaking* (New York: Oxford University Press, 1988); Samuel Kernell, *Going Public: New Strategies of Presidential Leadership,* 2nd ed. (Washington, DC: CQ Press, 1993); Lowi, *The Personal President*; Mary E. Stuckey, *The President as Interpreter-in-Chief* (Chatham, NJ: Chatham House, 1991); and Jeffrey Tulis, *The Rhetorical Presidency* (Princeton, NJ: Princeton University Press, 1987).

27. Sorenson, *Watchmen in the Night,* 141.

28. Peri Arnold, "Strategic Resources and Policy Leadership in the Pre-Modern Presidency: The Case of Theodore Roosevelt's Naval Policy" (Typescript, 1995); Mary E. Stuckey, "The Traps of Power: The President, Foreign Policy, and the American Public," *The Brown Journal of World Affairs* 3(1) (1996): 291–198.

29. Hardin, *Presidential Power and Accountability*; Thomas, "Aiming at a Moving Target."

30. T. Patterson, *Out of Order* (New York: Knopf, 1993).

31. Sorenson, *Watchmen in the Night*; Thomas, "Presidential Power and Accountability After Reagan."

32. For a discussion of Watergate, see Hardin, *Presidential Power and Accountability*; Sorenson, *Watchmen in the Night*. For a discussion of Iran-Contra, see Thomas, "Presidential Power and Accountability After Reagan."

33. Ferman and Levin, "Dilemmas of Innovation and Accountability;" Steven A. Shull, *A Kinder, Gentler Racism?* (Armonk, NY: M.E. Sharpe, 1993).

34. Dennis M. Simon, "Presidents, Governors, and Electoral Accountability," *Journal of Politics* 51(2) (1989): 286–304.

35. Sorenson, *Watchmen in the Night*, 52.

36. Harmon, *Responsibility as Paradox.*

16

Comparing Policy Leadership

Colin Campbell and Bert A. Rockman

Syndromes and Eras of Policymaking

In the largely three and half decades between the 1960s and late 1990s spanned by Norman Thomas's career, there have been several distinctive sets of values emphasized in the policymaking literature. The first of these focused on inputs and legitimation of process. To put a slightly different tag on it, a truly pluralized policy process required legitimately diverse representation, especially of relatively marginalized groups who were themselves the direct clients of programs. While this is a perennial issue of democratic theory and of theories of representation, it bubbled up particularly during the 1960s and even early 1970s, inspiring efforts during the Johnson administration to bring the "outs" inside. Programs designed to open up the system and to monitor the workings of the bureaucracy were much in vogue in an effort to extend the compass of pluralism. Whether or not such efforts merely sowed the seeds for confusion and a lack of accountability or, in fact, genuinely extended the range of democracy remains today a hotly contested matter. The emphasis on representation in policymaking, however, arose from a political conception of the marketplace. To be in the money economy, one needed to have currency. To be in its political equivalent, one needed to have stakes. The political reforms of the 1960s often were about creating these stakes for those not otherwise in possession of them.

Yet another reform movement influencing the policymaking process also became prominent in the 1960s, and, while changing forms over time, focused on the role of "rationalism" in policymaking. The role of policy analysis wedded to synoptic modes of policy evaluation began to flower in the 1960s. It sprang from a tradition in American government as deeply rooted as the emphasis on pluralism, namely the Progressive tradition, which emphasized knowledge and managerial rationality. It was in that tradition that Lyndon Johnson proclaimed that PPBS (Program Planning Budgeting Systems) should be adopted by all agencies of the federal government, an edict that certainly resulted in the bemusement of many agencies' officials who were unable to figure out exactly what their program goals were. Moreover, as the Progressives earlier sought to insulate administration from the hurly-burly of politics, many features of the movement toward rationalism were also strikingly apolitical. Critics, such as Aaron Wildavsky,[1] wondered how agencies could conceivably ignore their own pasts, dependent as they were on interest groups and key actors in Congress who would insist that the agencies pay attention to their political roots.

Over the next decade and a half, management techniques came and went. All offered hopes that the disruptive world of politics would recede before the preachments of management technicians and policy analysts. All were offered in the spirit that systems overruled interests or instincts, and that administration in the public domain could be reduced merely to a management problem. But the trend toward systematization techniques such as management by objectives (MBO) and Zero-Based Budgeting (ZBB) were fundamentally at odds with the realities of fragmented power. The allure of management and evaluative techniques in the absence of sufficient authority proved illusory.

Rationalism returned, then, to an old American problem (from the perspective of the rationalists), namely how to build coherent and integrative (read executive) power. These issues especially came to the fore during the later period of the Carter presidency, whose authority seemed too fragile to cope with severe policy challenges resulting from stagnant economic growth and inflation (a phenomenon referred to as stagflation). Richard Rose wondered whether the U.S. system actually could produce government rather than merely a proliferation of subgovernments.[2] Of course, what was frequently meant by the conception of coherent authority was a planner's dream, namely, a cohesive pro-active government able to coordinate effective responses to complex problems. It was all the more astonishing then that the 1980s produced for a time a perversely cohesive program (from the standpoint of traditional proponents of pro-active government) for draining government of its energies while empowering the invisible hand of the private sector. The eras of Reagan in the United States and Thatcher in the United Kingdom bore testimony to the power of ideas, will, and leadership, though Thatcher's circumstances allowed more of her goals to be met. This infusion of authority by strong-willed leaders in circumstances congenial to the exertion of their will created at least temporary cohesion, albeit not the stuff from which rationalists' dreams of pro-active government were made. Contrary to the rationalists' pleas to do more, government was now being set to do less.

A more recent set of reforms, more developed so far outside of the United States than in, also bears the stamp of the rationalist tradition but in a very different way. Its logic is manifested in the "National Performance Review" chaired by Vice-President Al Gore.[3] The NPR emphasizes the strides made elsewhere in making governmental practices increasingly conform to those of the private sector, in treating citizens as customers, and organizing government to the demands of the information age of the present and future rather than the industrial age of the past. Flexibility and adaptability are the watchwords of the reinventing government syndrome or what is known elsewhere as the *new public management*. Government, accordingly, would need to act as though it were in a marketplace satisfying the short-term demands of its "consumers." Service provision, it follows, would need often to be privatized or out-sourced or, at the very least, decentralized. Such a design, if that is the appropriate language, itself creates complex issues of authority, as most managerial reformist schemes do. New public management reforms assume, among other things, that management flows undisturbed from a single source of authority in the executive, a matter that raises special, though not exclusive, complications for the U.S. system of divided authority.

Throughout his career as a scholar, Norman Thomas's work was often devoted to the potentially opposed problems of making government more legitimate and broadly accessible, especially to those with fewer resources, while also constructing sufficient authority by which to allow governmental policymaking to become more rational and comprehensive (especially in a pro-active way). It is always a difficult matter to characterize the shadings of another's thoughts and beliefs, but Thomas's assumptions about government seemed to suggest that while government had problems, government itself was *not* the problem, despite that being the fashion of the Reaganites and even, if differently, of the reinventors of Gore's NPR. Presumably, government could be the solution if it were able to reconcile the need to articulate diverse interests with the capacity to aggregate them in order to produce public goods and constrain private desires to gain rents.

In this chapter, consequently, we look first at the seemingly competing concerns of representative government and rational government that animated much of Thomas's writings. The second part of the chapter focuses especially on the new wave of policy management reforms and their implications for government, policy direction and coordination, and accountability. The case of New Zealand, however geographically far from America, is close to the hearts of government reinventors precisely because it has done the most to reinvent government in accordance with the new rationalist modality. Thus, we examine some of the causes and key features of government reinvention in New Zealand and speak about some of its implications. Finally, we end by discussing some of the implications of the New Zealand experience and its relative, the NPR, in regard to the U.S. case. Most especially, we ask how this latest version of rationalism fits with two traditional concerns—on the one hand, the role of representativeness and legitimacy in decision making and, on the other, the concern for the integration of governmental authority.

A Representational Rationalist?

As noted, these dual and even dueling values dominated Thomas's writings. In his early years during the 1960s, he revealed a strong commitment to democratic legitimacy. This took the form of linking marginalized groups with policies that most directly affected their lives, for example, educational and housing opportunities for African Americans. A then fashionable approach to policymaking in the 1960s and even the early 1970s was pluralism. But there were two contending approaches to pluralism. One, identified especially with Robert Dahl[4] and Nelson Polsby,[5] essentially argued that pluralism was already the basic pattern of governing and policymaking in America. Others, notably Jack Walker,[6] argued that the extant pluralistic pattern was one still laden with powerful exclusionary biases. More inclusiveness, in this view, would help produce a genuinely democratic distribution of power resources. Thomas was firmly in this latter camp, believing that there were still significant imperfections in the representative nature of American politics. Much of his written work probes the outer bounds of the pluralist idea as to how American politics and government actually work.

In time, edging toward the 1980s, Thomas became increasingly absorbed by the issue of policy coherence. For a pluralist, this seemed to cut across the grain. Policy rationality was the mantra, paradoxically, of party government proponents and of public administration aficionados who seemed unable to exorcise the spirit of Progressivism from their souls. Of course, the two otherwise meant different things by policy rationality. Yet, the one thing they had in common was that coherent policy seemed to require cohesion of authority—precisely what the American system seemed incapable of attaining. Pluralists, however, believed that incrementalism fit the American democracy just fine. In the pluralist conception, no political system should strive for a degree of policy coherence beyond what it was capable of achieving without deeply antagonizing intense minorities in a relatively heterogeneous society. Had Thomas strayed beyond pluralism by embracing rationalism? With the emphasis on coherence was he seeking a degree of tidiness that would impinge most immediately and emphatically on those outside the mainstream? Or, was Thomas simply closing the circle—that is, exploring the role of legitimacy based on representation for attaining rationality? Was he a hybrid—a kind of representational rationalist?

Thomas's interest in the mechanics for advancing representativeness is evident in several of his works. In "Urban and Rural Representation and State Legislative Apportionment," he and his co-author, John P. White, claim that political science had been insufficiently attentive to the effects of malapportionment on democracy at the state level.[7] Indeed, Thomas suggested that the representational issues surrounding the divide between cities and rural areas were exacerbated by the uneven distribution of political party strength and organization within the most highly urbanized states. Differential party strength, in turn, could result from variability in the ballot form. In a 1968 article, "Voting Machines and Voter Participation in Four Michigan Constitutional Revision Referenda," Thomas found evidence suggesting that voting machines exacerbated the urban–rural divide.[8] Rural areas had proven slow to convert from paper ballots, and the paper ballots seemed to induce less "roll off" (ballot fatigue) as voters worked their way through referenda. Consequently, for offices not at the top of the ballot, there was a rural skew in voting participation. Expressing his concern for representational equity, Thomas observes that the differential use of machines and ballots "enhances the interests of some individuals and groups at the expense of others and is, in the context of my own normative criteria of a democratic society, undesirable."[9]

Equality of access issues carried over to Thomas's work even a decade later. "Public Subventions to Nonpublic Education: Values, the Courts and Educational Policy" sympathetically treated appeals for greater state support of parochial schools, citing pluralism and distributive justice among possible rationales.[10] "Equalizing Educational Opportunity Through School Finance Reform: A Review Assessment" analyzed the impact of the U.S. Supreme Court's 1973 *Rodriguez* decision, which served to dampen efforts to equalize the resources available to public schools within the same jurisdiction. Thomas questioned the strictness of the Court's test for a failure of equal protection.[11] However, he pointed out that despite these restrictions state courts and legislatures still were able to discover some latitude for advancing equalization.[12]

Other salient features of Thomas's representational rationalism were his absorption with the extent to which the diversity of American society was reflected in the composition of the elite, in how they made policy, and in the resulting coherence of their policy outputs. In an article with Allan Kornberg, Thomas compared the socioeconomic backgrounds of U.S. senators and Canadian Members of Parliament and found that the U.S. senators are more "elite" in their backgrounds than the Canadian MPs.[13] However, the authors note that background need not predict behavior. Consequently, there may not be a failure of representative democracy since senators from very wealthy and socially prominent families have also strongly advocated social welfare programs.[14] Following upon this, Thomas published an article with M. Kent Jennings which explored differences in the social roles and political resources of men and women among party elites.[15] The authors noted a considerable gap in political resources between men and women, which they associated with the relatively limited exposure of female political activists to the work force. Behaviorally, this gap extended also to males feeling more comfortable with the Burkean trustee (or discretionary) view of representation while females disproportionately favored the narrower representational compass of being the (directed) delegate of a constituency. While Jennings and Thomas press the case for greater inclusion of women in occupational roles from which they had been excluded, these two works present a nuanced, even paradoxical, view of representation through which legislatures can be representative in behavior even if their membership falls short of representativeness. Representation itself involves an aptitude for independent judgment and self-reliance more than merely a sociological reflection of constituencies.[16]

Shortly after the publication of these pieces, Thomas began to turn his attention directly to the policy process in an effort to ascertain the relative influence of various groups and institutions. "The Presidency and Policy Formulation: The Task Force Device" (with Harold L. Wolman) examined the effectiveness with which Lyndon Johnson used task forces.[17] The authors noted that the more public the proceeding, the more likely that the technique simply serves public relations and symbolic roles. Insofar as such task forces proved effective in identifying distinctive solutions, however, the more they tended to engender the hostility of the bureaucracy. An article titled "Bureaucratic-Congressional Interaction and the Politics of Education"(1970) extensively describes the policy complex surrounding education in the federal government.[18] In fact, this article emphasizes the central pro-active role of bureaucratic actors. Not long after the time of this article's publication, a rational choice model of budget-maximizing bureaucrats seeking their personal utility was beginning to gain currency.[19] Contrary, however, to the self-aggrandizing model of personal gain put forth in Niskanen's rational choice model, Thomas discovered that permanent officials, especially those in the Department of Health, Education and Welfare's Office of Education, facilitated linkage with other less directly connected actors in the policy process.[20] Far from being personal income seekers, bureaucrats were discovered to be facilitating the representation of marginal groups in the policy process.

In another article with Wolman, attention turned once again to the issue of equity—this time with reference to African-American participation in the housing and education policy processes.[21] The authors found here evidence of the deficiencies of the "pluralistic description of the American political system" in that African Americans exerted little influence in these two policy areas of crucial importance to them.[22] Thomas and Wolman argued that this condition constitutes an instance in which pluralism, if at all attainable, must receive a jump start in the form of initiatives through which African Americans might be better able to overcome their "lack of leadership, disorganization, and resultant frustration."[23] In this perspective—one which fit with the participation revolution of the times—government was not supposed to be merely a neutral arbiter or referee among the players already in the game. Its role also could be conceived as that of stimulating participation and leveling the playing field.

As problems arose, however, with the new modalities of participation that were especially spawned by a number of Great Society programs, and as fiscal slack turned into stagflation, the problems of achieving policy rationality and coherence seemed increasingly imperative. Moreover, a string of presidencies perceived to have failed—Nixon, Ford, and Carter—highlighted problems of policymaking. The policymaking paradigm was shifting from inputs and processes to outcomes and substance. By the mid-1970s, consequently, Norman Thomas began to focus increasingly on matters of policy rationality. He saw a rich field of inquiry in macroeconomic policymaking, the study of which U.S. political scientists had given relatively limited attention, notwithstanding its mounting importance during the 1970s.[24] Of course, as the U.S. economy experienced greater stresses in the 1970s, an extensive literature on the politics of macroeconomic conditions shortly followed. This focus, Thomas believed, dovetailed with his interest in the presidency. Arguably, macroeconomic policy served as one policy field in which the president enjoyed special prerogatives and therefore could advance rationality: "Of all the participants in the policy arena he alone is potentially able to provide cohesion and purpose."[25] But Thomas sought to emphasize greater rationality in accordance with difficult representational dilemmas. In "The Politics of Intergovernmental Fiscal Assis-

tance and Controls," his articulation of the possible contradictions of representativeness and policy rationality reached full height in his assertion that
achieving rationality in education policy inevitably involves dialectics between competing world views:

> This is not a neat, orderly, or ideal pattern, and few, if any, persons or groups
> involved in or concerned with education can expect to achieve more than a
> portion of their goals. But the tension between the centrifugal forces of local-
> ism and the centripetal forces of interdependence imparts a creative dynamic
> that has so far prevented development of a static equilibrium that stifles adap-
> tation and change.[26]

New Paradigms of Policymaking and Traditional Structures of Governance

In the more than twenty years that have elapsed since Thomas fully articu-
lated the complexity of attaining policy rationality as an objective within the
context of American pluralism, there has been a significant shift in the
prevalent view of accountability in advanced democracies. These changes
have altered thinking about how rationality and equity are to be reconciled,
indeed, even the extent to which rationality (in the form of integrated direction) and equity (in the form of representational due process) are to be
valued at all.[27] This shift is known as the new public management and in
the United States as "reinventing government."

The economic crises of the 1970s fueled the emergence of new para-
digms for governance not just in the United States but in other advanced
democracies, especially Anglo-American systems. In the early 1980s, Norman Thomas launched a comparative study of the American, British, and
Canadian responses to economic stress and decline.[28] He became concerned
with the risks of fragmented pluralism in these systems and the ways in
which this fragmentation blocked the possibilities of coherent and planned
policy responses—at least until the highly ideological approaches of Ronald
Reagan and Margaret Thatcher took hold in their respective countries.[29]
Thomas had ascertained that the paradigm for governance was dramatically
transforming itself and that this transformation was affecting traditional
pluralistic politics.

Institutional structure has usually been connected to thinking about the
prospects for policy cohesion as well as for representation. Despite sharing
a common language, the American system of separated powers could not be
more different than the classic Westminster system prevalent in the other
Anglo democracies, and most especially in the United Kingdom itself.
Whereas the loosely jointed separation of powers system might have some

advantages in promoting the accessibility of various interests, the classic Westminster paradigm may be thought to have some advantages with respect to the cohesion it can potentially generate through party government.[30] The Westminster model was especially admired by American political scientists in the middle part of this century for its ability to produce responsible party government. Because of the first-past-the-post electoral system, parliamentary elections in the classic Westminster model usually result in majority party government. The government, under the leadership of the prime minister, assumes collective responsibility—most immediately to Parliament, but ultimately back to the public, which might not renew its mandate in the next general election. In addition, each minister is individually responsible to Parliament—the theory being that parliamentary displeasure with certain policies or actions might force the minister to resign. Most ministerial portfolios involve oversight of a government department. In the Westminster system, career public servants overwhelmingly staff these organizations through which strict hierarchical accountability functions as a glue. In exchange for their loyalty (and in instances of policy or managerial failure, their silence) ministers delegate to career civil servants a high degree of control over management of their departments and grant, in turn, security of tenure.

Of course, practice never correlated perfectly with theory. The rise of strong party discipline in the latter part of the nineteenth century meant that backbenchers exerted only limited control over cabinets. The process by which parties garner electoral support through the appeal of their leaders has often given prime ministers sufficient leverage to run command-oriented regimes rather than consultative cabinet governments. Such a command orientation also tends to be consistent with notions of strong presidential government in the United States. Career officials under the Westminster system make up a cadre that traces its ancestry to the royal household. But like bureaucrats most anywhere, they have their own interests and agendas to pursue, however diverse these may be. Despite the inevitable diversity of perspectives generated within any civil service engaged in undertaking different tasks, the normative glue (or at least rationale) of career officialdom under the Westminster system traditionally has been a caste of mind that emphasizes the long-term public interest. Such a caste of mind, of course, is often overtaken by immediate pressures exerted by political or policy exigencies. There have been, as well, failures even of the contractual core of the Westminster system—namely, ministers who have refused to take blame and officials who have refused to be silenced. In any case, Whitehall accountability is in reality multifaceted. Officials have to mediate responsibility to and between such varied constituencies, principals, or even ideas as their ministers, their departmental superiors, the prime minister, Parliament, clients, and the national interest. Thus, the concatenated chain of accountability postulated by the Whitehall model rarely pertains in reality. In fact, laments of its passing might well amount to nostalgia for something that never actually existed. Despite the realities that attenuate the distinctiveness of the Westminster model, it is still less pluralized and fragmented than the American system. If the role of the civil service under the Westminster system seems not what it is in theory supposed to be, it is in reality as well as theory different from what it has been in the United States. Everything is relative.

The separation of powers system in the United States could not contrast more sharply—at least in concept—with the Westminster system. The founding fathers largely construed the arrogance of the mother country toward the thirteen colonies as resulting from the autocracy of the executive as embodied in the crown. For the most part, therefore, the founders of the American state embraced the concept of separation of powers as protection against autocratic rule. Both the executive and legislative branches, consequently, found themselves with independent mandates. This places the career bureaucracy in the position of serving two masters—the president and Congress. This dual, really multiple, principals problem makes cabinet government extremely difficult as career bureaucrats, ever mindful of likely congressional responses, often divert cabinet secretaries from an administration's agenda to one emanating from policy alliances between officials, legislators and their staffs, and relevant interest groups. This phenomenon was especially apt to occur when Republicans presided over the White House while Democrats controlled the Congress. Congressional Democrats typically had developed a stake in many programs that Republican presidents sought to cut back or eliminate.

If the Westminster tradition has erred on the side of career officials who develop and ply their own views of the national interest, the U.S. tradition has displayed a weakness for short-term, politics-driven policymaking. Reformers in the United States have struggled with what exactly the definition and character of the public service ought to be. Early in the century the dominant model, stemming from the notion of management as a machine, was that of the competent management of complex organizations. This view espoused a dichotomy between policy, which was supposedly the sole domain of politicians, and administration, which was supposedly the province of civil servants. But the immense national mobilization associated with the New Deal made this simple view no longer viable, assuming it ever had been. Thus, although the notion emerged that career officials were inevitably involved in policy, they nonetheless contributed neutral competence to the process of policymaking. This meant that they were expected to bring their subject-matter expertise and practical experience to bear on resolving the challenges of the time. Ironically, the theory of neutral competence set career public servants up as potential scapegoats as the policy agenda itself became increasingly controversial. The Left often became frustrated with the difficulty of expanding the frontiers of the welfare state and increasing popular participation. They began to see neutral competence as the cult of "Can't Do" rather than "Can Do." The Right alternatively saw bureaucrats as empire builders parlaying their expertise and experience into ventures designed to maximize their personal utility and that of their allies. With the dominance of the Right toward the end of the 1970s and throughout most of the subsequent period, the legitimacy of the bureaucracy came under attack, challenged especially by a confluence of inflammatory public rhetoric and anti-bureaucratic, essentially anti–public sector, ideas.

The two energy shocks of the 1970s along with increased vulnerability to Asian competition created pressures on the U.S. economy and the economies of other Anglo countries (Britain, Canada, Australia, New Zealand). The popular pendulum consequently swung against further expansion of the role of the state, especially as the juggernaut of entitlement expenditures became increasingly uncontrollable. Demography here seemingly had become destiny. More older people meant more pensions and also more health-care expenditures. Indeed, arguments in favor of shrinking government were poised to win the day.[31] Public choice theory increasingly provided the theoretical foundation for those wanting to arrest the growth of government and, indeed, shrink it. The work of Buchanan and Tullock and Niskanen, for example, focused on the bureaucracy as a self-interested stimulant to overspending through the exploitation of career bureaucrats' expertise and positional advantage in catering to the needs of legislators and interest groups in order to maximize their own budgets.[32] Accordingly, government oversupplies goods because a multiplicity of subgovernments skews demand from what a hypothetical representative demand structure would produce.

The objective, therefore, of budget constraint advocates was to remove politics from the appropriations and budget processes, and produce (or at least talk about) automated mechanisms for reining in government expenditure. In this view, politicians can best assert control through the automatization of budgeting, requiring, first, much tighter coordination between Congress and the executive branch on target outlays, second, a requirement that dollar-for-dollar personal (unhidden) income tax increases cover spending beyond the agreed levels, and, third, more centralized White House control of the Office of Management and Budget to enforce the political priorities of the president.[33] In practice, the separation of powers has made automatization of budgeting in the United States as elusive as comprehensive rationality proved to be in the 1960s.

However, budget constraint and public choice have generally been in a symbiotic relationship. Reformers in other Anglo-American countries have attempted to adapt public choice theory to their own circumstances. One of the earliest and most significant of these efforts occurred when a disenchanted group of Conservatives invited William Niskanen to the United Kingdom to offer a series of lectures on public choice.[34] Once again, Niskanen advocated automatization of budgeting. But his recipe, as was the case in the United States, reflected a limited understanding of politics. Niskanen, as with some of his other neoclassical economist colleagues, was concerned to reinvent institutions whose incentive structures would be more compatible with the goal of budget constraint no matter what the magnitude of the transaction costs. Thus, he urged prime ministers to appoint ministers without consideration of representational issues such as their personal or regional backgrounds.[35] He also recommended that ministers be shuffled randomly through the course of a government to assure that they not align themselves too strongly with their departments. Niskanen had a very large influence on Margaret Thatcher. One could certainly detect strong elements of the central control prescription in such early Thatcher moves as imposing budget discipline with a "Star Chamber" of senior ministers and abolishing the Policy Analysis and Review system of interdepartmental studies of programs which, as often as not, failed to recommend the tough options necessary to cut back spending.

New Paradigms of Policy Management: The Case of New Zealand

Although the appeal of public choice theories as explanations for the growth of government became increasingly attractive to conservatives beyond the United States, public choice prescriptions still spoke very much with an American accent, reflecting the American experience. This experience, moreover, contrasts quite sharply with that of the Westminster systems for two main reasons. First, permanent officials in the United States tend to focus their careers much more narrowly than do their opposite numbers in the parliamentary systems.[36] This makes them more prone to defend relatively narrow bureaucratic interests. Second, and more fundamental, the parliamentary systems do not have truly transformative legislatures. That is, rank-and-file legislators in these systems lack the capacity to mold and reshape laws and budgets independently of the guidance provided by the political executive as embodied in the leadership of the governing party or coalition.[37]

This means that American prescriptions for limiting budget-maximizing tendencies in Westminster systems might amount to overdosing. The presence of long tenure in specific agencies of U.S. bureaucrats and the presence in America of a transformative (policymaking) legislature with functional specialization and organizational complexity induces the development of strong client–patron relationships which, in turn, tend to sustain sub-governments. These traditionally have been especially important in the United States and often have been dominated by key interests imbedded in legislative subunits.[38] Such patron–client relations tend to be more inhibited in parliamentary systems, especially those of the Westminster type.

Here the experience of New Zealand with public choice bears special attention. In the late 1970s, the nation was buffeted especially severely by the energy shocks and the dissolution of preferential trade agreements with the United Kingdom. The latter had previously ensured markets for the agricultural products that still serve as the nation's core source of foreign exchange. Structurally, New Zealand bore many of the marks of post-colonialism. A lack of both internal capital and foreign investment drove a strong tendency to accept the provision of essential goods and services as being the responsibility of the public sector. The nation indulged itself with the luxury of upward of forty departments that tended to function as fiefdoms narrowly focused on specialized policy domains. New Zealand's unicameral parliament was certainly the weakest of any of the Anglo-American legislatures. Prime ministers typically guided cabinet monocratically rather than consultatively. Often key senior officials exerted as much influence on the overall direction of the government as did ministers. Prime ministers frequently tapped the Treasury as if it were their own department. All of this hampered considerably the capacity of other actors in the New Zealand system and, thus, limited their incorporation into the policy management process.

Management reforms in New Zealand emphasized organizational flexibility and adaptiveness and a personnel system operating on contracts based upon performance. The reforms were explicitly market-oriented, and emerged from an intense review of the role of the state conducted within the Treasury before the Labour government, which had come to power in 1984, renewed its mandate in 1987. The review provided an intellectual justification for the reforms, and its documents copiously cited American agency literature, especially that centering on aspects of the behavior of the firm.[39] The review documents asserted that the proposed reforms would establish an iterative process inferred in classic views of democratic accountability such that bureaucrats would become the agents of politicians who, in turn, would serve as the agents of the populace.[40] They distinguished here between strategies for improving performance and those attempting to enhance accountability. Performance improvement focuses on whether officials actually produce the outputs required by the politicians, whereas accountability enhancement focuses on whether the goods and services which politicians purchase from bureaucrats align with their asserted goals.

The classic iterative views of accountability, noted above, which especially assign "administration" to civil servants and "policy" to politicians, usually defy valid operationalization and, in any event, often prove naive. This naiveté was revealed in the New Zealand formulation in at least two major ways.

First, the New Zealand reforms alleged that special interests, because of the transaction costs connected to gathering information and influencing policymakers, can twist public policies in their favor.[41] The fragmented nature of the system in the United States traditionally works to the advantage of such interests. However, the status quo within New Zealand, which the reformers worked so assiduously at changing, bore little of the socioeconomic heterogeneity of the United States. By contrast with the United States, as well, New Zealand remained relatively closed politically in regard to accessing decision makers. Furthermore, political contestation followed the set piece format of parliamentary adversarial politics rather than the sometimes amorphous public free-for-all found in the United States. Under these circumstances, the transaction calculus for influencing policy in New Zealand generally has lacked both the elements of complexity and intensity that Robert Dahl speaks of in regard to polyarchical systems.[42] In the United States money counts for more (as does specialized knowledge) to gain a market share in a more convoluted yet more open political marketplace.

Second, the New Zealand reformers also imported from American institutional economics the notion of agency problems in aligning the incentives that prevail in public sector delivery systems with the policy objectives of legislatures and authorized governing bodies.[43] Strictly speaking, accountability demands that agencies follow the expressed preferences of their principals. Because of legislative autonomy in the United States and also judicial review, the methods by which agencies are purported to circumvent or shirk accountability or be accountable to one rather than another principal provides for a rich lode mine of research and theory—mostly, in fact, theoretical speculation. Agency problems exist in Westminster systems, but not nearly to the same degree of complication. In fact, New Zealand in the mid-1980s was even less complicated than other Westminster systems, especially Canada and Australia. New Zealand cabinets were relatively weak and, subsequently therefore, so were ministries' capabilities to spin policies as they saw fit. The prime minister and the Treasury exerted powerful influence, if not even monocratic guidance on the government. Yet there persists a monocratic tradition governing bureaucratic guidance in New

Zealand. This tradition now must accommodate to an environment requiring more consensual practices and informed consideration of how to cope with the realities of coalition government.

The New Zealand governmental reforms were very far reaching and have been commented upon widely as a beacon for those seeking to create a highly flexible, adaptive government forever on its toes. The American National Performance Review, among others, noted approvingly the adaptive system produced by the reforms in New Zealand. Far from traditional theories of accountability, the New Zealand government developed a purchaser/provider orientation, emphasizing competition, markets, contracting out, flexible personnel systems, and performance accounting. Meanwhile, the agency responsible for reviewing departmental performance sought especially to widen the frame of reference, altering therefore, to some degree, the new conception of accountability based on contract, to an older one based on a trustee relationship.[44]

The American political scientist Allen Schick gives due credit to the New Zealand reforms for breaking down some of the command-and-control orientation of departments and introducing greater incentives for managerial initiative.[45] However, he also identified several shortcomings in the reconstituted system. These included considerable unevenness in departments' sense of mission and performance, the straitjacket effect of the "sinking lid on operating budgets," the failure to incorporate cost and performance data in budget decision making, and, most importantly, the tendency for narrow concerns to crowd out collective ones and for the short-term to obscure the long-term.[46] Schick makes his clearest contribution by underscoring the need for shifting the focus of ministers' relations with their departments from purchaser/provider to more that of owner. This would enshrine their responsibility for achieving overarching social and economic objectives beyond the parameters of departmental outputs.[47]

Strategic guidance and collective enterprise are fundamental ideas crucial to governance that are lacking in the purchaser/provider model of government. An adjustment of rhetoric has already occurred in New Zealand signaling an attempt to broaden the focus of chief executives so that the outputs they proffer relate to the government's core goals. Here, group dynamics, such as the weekly meeting of permanent secretaries in the U.K. or the Canadian practice of giving key guidance roles to committees of deputy ministers during times of crisis, enable top officials to wrench themselves away from the quotidian issues of their home departments. Of course, these possibilities are more evident in Westminster style systems than in most others and probably least apparent in the U.S. case where the term "cabinet" is used merely to describe the president's appointed heads of departments.

Still, the primary point is that public management, as Mark Moore points out, is multi-dimensional and not just focused on an efficiency criterion determined exclusively by a price system.[48] Officials have to devise strategies that look outward toward external constituencies, upward toward superior hierarchical authority, and downward toward primary work and production. The private sector metaphors dominating the New Zealand reforms and those that have followed its lead, including the National Performance Review in the United States, are one-dimensional. Ultimately, the issue is whether flexible practices of policy management can fit into an authoritative system of governance in which futurity concerns, institution-building, and legal authority are constituent features or whether government as we have known it must become a subordinate element of market-driven practices with their short-term foci.

Looking to the Future

The traditional governance model of large bureaucratic organization has become irrelevant to the present according to the reinventors of government. It is slow, cumbersome, filled with wastelands of red tape and superfluous overhead functions. If government acted like the private sector, it would operate more efficiently, please the customers, save money, do things cheaper, better, faster, and so on. As with most nostrums, this one too is oversold.

Exactly why reinventing government has become a pandemic urge has no easy answer,[49] though in the era of the global economy, public penny-pinching is helpful to attract investment and keep currency exchange rates strong. Privatizing and contracting out and making personnel systems more flexible (hence less expensive because people can be let go when their contracts run their course) help keep the costs of government down where they can be kept down beyond the big entitlement programs. Trying to look relevant to the information age and proficient and business-like is also important in a world made of appearances.

Yet reinvention obviously has appeal because much of what it describes about government is true. Government is slow, ponderous, and thick with the overlay of rules from purposes of the past. A sleek new adaptive machine responsive to the customers and with little purpose of its own seems to be much in vogue if not necessarily much in demand. Two decades ago, of course, Herbert Kaufman told us that the price of accountability and also the production of public goods might be the production of red tape.[50] The other side of the coin, however, is that a government without the means of accountability could result in chaos. Programs of the Great Society era designed to help the poor in the United States, such as Community Action, often resulted in putative advocates for the poor lining their pockets at the expense of both the poor and the taxpayers. Why? Essentially, because there were few rules and little accountability and few specified standards regarding procedures in regard to these programs. Today, the problem is little different, except perhaps that those in a position to reap advantages are deemed to be more socially acceptable. The absence of procedure or of institutionalization threatens equity, a matter that is not the inherent strength of market devices.[51]

In this regard, we find ourselves returning to Norman Thomas's quest, namely how to reconcile representation and legitimacy in policymaking with the desire to find the authority to integrate choices so as to achieve policy rationality. Representation and legitimacy depend upon rules and accountability and fundamental fairness of procedures. Much of the effort to create this also creates the complications and cumbersomeness that the reinventors would like to cut through. An even greater conflict is manifested between the principle of integrating authority and the disaggregation of government manifested in purchaser/provider market-based models of governance. A new rationality based on the optimization of wants has emerged to replace a putatively outdated concept of rationality based on the principle of trusteeship. These are all very much opposing ideas of how government should operate and, even more, what the role of government should be. Yet each addresses deficiencies in the other. The question that remains unanswered for now is whether these very diverse conceptions of how government should work can be effectively reconciled by finding the proper spheres within which each may work best. Trying to find those answers should occupy us for some time.

Notes

The authors wish to thank Francis Creighton of the Graduate Program in Public Policy, Georgetown University and Andrew Konitzer of the Department of Political Science, University of Pittsburgh, for their invaluable assistance.

1. Aaron Wildavsky, "The Political Economy of Efficiency: Cost Benefit Analysis, Systems Analysis, and Program Budgeting," *Public Administration Review* 26 (1966): 292–310.

2. Richard Rose, "Government Against Subgovernments: A European's Perspective on Washington," in Richard Rose and Ezra Suleiman, eds., *Presidents and Prime Ministers* (Washington, DC: The American Enterprise Institute, 1980).

3. Report of the National Performance Review, *A Government That Works Better and Costs Less* (Washington, DC: Government Printing Office, 1993).

4. Robert A. Dahl, *Who Governs? Democracy and Power in an American City* (New Haven, CT: Yale University Press, 1961).

5. Nelson W. Polsby, *Community Power and Political Theory* (New Haven, CT: Yale University Press, 1963).

6. Jack L. Walker, "A Critique of the Elitist Theory of Democracy," *American Political Science Review* 60 (1966): 285–95.

7. John P. White and Norman C. Thomas, "Urban and Rural Representation and State Legislative Apportionment," *Western Political Quarterly* 17 (1964): 724–41, at 741.

8. Norman C. Thomas, "Voting Machines and Voter Participation in Four Michigan Constitutional Revision Referenda," *Western Political Quarterly* 21 (1968): 409–19.

9. Ibid., 419.

10. Norman C. Thomas, "Public Subventions to Nonpublic Education: Value, the Courts and Education Policy," *Detroit College of Law Review* (1976): 199–233, at 206.

11. Norman C. Thomas, "Equalizing Educational Opportunity Through School Finance Reform: A Review Assessment," *University of Cincinnati Law Review* 48 (1979): 255–320, at 286–87.

12. Ibid., 318.

13. Allan Kornberg and Norman C. Thomas, "Representative Democracy and Political Elites in Canada and the United States," *Parliamentary Affairs* 19 (1965–66): 91–102.

14. Ibid., 102.

15. M. Kent Jennings and Norman C. Thomas, "Men and Women in Party Elites: Social Roles and Political Resources," *Midwest Journal of Political Science* 12 (1968): 469–92.

16. Ibid., 487.

17. Norman C. Thomas and Harold L. Wolman, "The Presidency and Policy Formation," *Public Administration Review* 29: (1969): 459–70.

18. Norman C. Thomas, "Bureaucratic-Congressional Interaction and the Politics of Education," *Journal of Comparative Administration* 2 (1970): 52–80.

19. William A. Niskanen, *Bureaucracy and Representative Government* (New York: Aldine-Atherton, 1971).

20. Thomas, "Bureaucratic-Congressional Interaction," 64.

21. Harold L. Wolman and Norman C. Thomas, "Black Interests, Black Groups and Black Influence in the Federal Policy Process: The Cases of Housing and Education" *Journal of Politics* 32 (1970): 875–97.

22. Ibid., 894.

23. Ibid., 897.

24. Norman C. Thomas, "Political Science and the Study of Macro-Economic Policy Making," *Policy Studies Journal* 4 (1975): 7–15, at 9.

25. Ibid., 11.

26. Norman C. Thomas, "The Politics of Intergovernmental Fiscal Assistance and Controls," in Edith K. Mosher and Jennings L. Wagoner, Jr., eds., *The Changing Politics of Education: Prospects for the 1980's* (Berkeley, CA: McCutchan, 1978), 89–99, at 98.

27. See, inter alia, Colin Campbell, "Public Service and Democratic Accountability," in Richard A. Chapman, ed., *Ethics in Public Service* (Edinburgh, UK: Edinburgh University Press, 1992), 110–33; Colin Campbell and John Halligan, *Political Leadership in an Age of Constraint: Bureaucratic Politics Under Hawke and Keating* (Sydney: Allen & Unwin, 1992), 193–218; also published as *Political Leadership in an Age of Constraint: The Australian Experience* (Pittsburgh: University of Pittsburgh Press, 1992); and Colin Campbell and Graham Wilson, *The End of Whitehall: Death of a Paradigm?* (Oxford, UK: Blackwell, 1995), 249–88.

28. Norman C. Thomas, "Policy Responses to Economic Stress and Decline in Anglo-Atlantic Democracies," in Colin Campbell and B. Guy Peters, eds., *Organizing*

Governance: Governing Organizations (Pittsburgh: University of Pittsburgh Press, 1988), 129–63.

29. Ibid., 130.

30. R. Kent Weaver and Bert A. Rockman, eds., *Do Institutions Matter? Government Capabilities in the United States and Abroad* (Washington, DC: Brookings Institution, 1993), 445–61.

31. Richard Rose and B. Guy Peters, *Can Government Go Bankrupt?* (New York: Basic Books, 1978).

32. James M. Buchanan and Gordon Tullock, *The Calculus of Consent: Logical Foundations of Constitutional Democracy* (Ann Arbor: University of Michigan Press, 1962); and Niskanen, *Bureaucracy and Representative Government.*

33. William A. Niskanen, *Structural Reform of the Federal Budget Process* (Washington, DC: American Enterprise Institute, 1973), esp. 17–19; 55–57.

34. William A. Niskanen, *Bureaucracy: Servant or Master? Lessons from America* (London: Institute of Economic Affairs, 1973).

35. Ibid., 60.

36. Hugh Heclo, *A Government of Strangers: Executive Politics in Washington* (Washington, DC: Brookings Institution, 1977), 116–20.

37. Nelson W. Polsby, "Legislatures," in Fred I. Greenstein and Nelson W. Polsby, eds., *Government Institutions and Processes,* vol. 5, *Handbook of Political Science* (Reading, MA: Addison-Wesley, 1975), 257–301, at 277.

38. Morris Fiorina, *Congress: The Keystone of the Washington Establishment* (New Haven, CT: Yale University Press, 1977).

39. A frequent exemplar of such literature, for example, is A.A. Alchian and S. Woodward, "Reflections on the Theory of the Firm," *Journal of Institutional and Theoretical Economics* 143 (1987): 110–36.

40. Graham Scott and Peter Gorringe, "Reform of the Core Civil Service: The New Zealand Experience," *Australian Journal of Public Administration* 48 (1989): 81–91.

41. Graham Scott, Ian Ball, and Tony Dale, "New Zealand's Public Sector Management Reform: Implications for the United States," *Journal of Policy Analysis and Management* 16: (1997): 357–81, at 360.

42. Robert A. Dahl, *Polyarchy: Participation and Opposition* (New Haven, CT: Yale University Press, 1971), esp. 8 and 76–80.

43. Scott, Ball, and Dale, "New Zealand's Public Sector Management Reform," 360.

44. Ibid., 389.

45. Allen Schick, *The Spirit of Reform: Managing the New Zealand State Sector in a Time of Change.* A report prepared for the State Services Commission and the Treasury, New Zealand, 1996.

46. Ibid., 3–7.

47. Ibid., 44.

48. Mark Moore, *Creating Public Values: Strategic Management in Government* (Cambridge, MA: Harvard University Press, 1995).

49. Christopher Hood, "De–Sir Humphreyfying the Westminster Model of Bureaucracy: A New Style of Governance," *Governance* 3 (1990): 205–14.

50. Herbert Kaufman, *Red Tape: Its Origins, Uses, and Abuses* (Washington, DC: The Brookings Institution, 1977).

51. Steven E. Rhoads, *The Economist's View of the World: Government, Markets, and Public Policy* (Cambridge, UK: Cambridge University Press, 1985), esp. 82–112.

Index